Strategic Project Organizing

T0320891

# Strategic Project Organizing

FIRST EDITION

Graham Winch

Eunice Maytorena-Sanchez

Natalya Sergeeva

OXFORD
UNIVERSITY PRESS

Great Clarendon Street, Oxford, OX2 6DP,
United Kingdom

Oxford University Press is a department of the University of Oxford.
It furthers the University's objective of excellence in research, scholarship,
and education by publishing worldwide. Oxford is a registered trade mark of
Oxford University Press in the UK and in certain other countries

Public sector information reproduced under Open Government Licence v3.0
(http://www.nationalarchives.gov.uk/doc/open-government-licence/open-government-licence.htm)

Published in the United States of America by Oxford University Press
198 Madison Avenue, New York, NY 10016, United States of America

British Library Cataloguing in Publication Data
Data available

Library of Congress Control Number: 2021947533

ISBN 978-0-19-886199-7

Printed in Great Britain by
Bell & Bain Ltd., Glasgow

# Brief Contents

# Detailed Contents

# List of Vignettes

# List of Cases

# Preface

*Strategic Project Organizing* has been long in gestation, very much enabled by the UK's West Coast Main Line. Our two institutions—the Bartlett School of Sustainable Construction at University College London, and Alliance Manchester Business School at University of Manchester—have their offices within walking distance of the two principal termini on that line: Manchester Piccadilly and London Euston. All three authors have worked at both institutions, and the ideas presented here were developed with successive generations of MSc students at both institutions, MBA students at AMBS, and executive education delegates at AMBS. In particular, delegates on project leadership programmes for both BP and BAE Systems gave us much insight into the realities of project organizing and helped us to formulate more clearly the ideas in this book.

Over the years, we have interacted with many colleagues and friends while developing the ideas we present here. Alan Johnston, Tom McNatt and Jim Moore were subject-matter experts from BP, and we all worked with them between 2009 and 2016. Dr Cliff Mitchell, the AMBS Deputy Programme Manager for the BP Managing Projects programme, also made significant contributions to our thinking, particularly for Chapter 8. We are particularly grateful to Viktoriya Pisotska for preparing Case 8. We also worked closely with Prof Nuno Gil and Prof David Lowe in developing the concepts that underpin Chapter 9 for teaching on the BP programme. More generally, our learning about strategic project organizing from an owner perspective working with BP underpins Chapter 5. Indeed, this learning was the original motivation for the development of the three domains perspective as well as the Project Leadership Model.

Prof Stuart Forsyth was our principal subject-matter expert from BAE Systems with whom Eunice and Graham worked from 2016 on. Stuart taught us much about strategic project organizing from a supplier perspective. This thinking, together with research that Graham conducted with Eric Schneider, underpins much of Chapter 6. Dr Carl Gavin, AMBS Programme Director for BAE Systems' Leading Complex Projects, Programmes and Portfolios, was also a continual source of insight. Working with both BP and BAE Systems taught us the importance of consummate project delivery, but only in the context of equally consummate project shaping.

The intellectual foundations of our perspective on strategic project organizing lie principally in the Carnegie School's insight that organizations are fundamentally information processing systems. However, as you will see, we have much elaborated this profound insight. Amongst more recent contributions, the work of Prof Deborah Ancona and her colleagues on the incomplete leader and Prof Amy Edmondson on teaming and psychological safety has been particularly influential. Our understanding of the importance of managerial cognition has been deepened through collaboration with Prof Fran Ackermann, and on narratives and storytelling by research discussions with Profs David Boje, Barbara Czarniawska, Tor Hernes, and Eero Vaara. These influences are particularly important for Chapters 2 to 4.

Within the research literature on projects, we have multiple influences who are too numerous to mention here, but can be identified from the references to the chapters. However, our principal intellectual debt is to Peter Morris whose 1994 book, *The Management of Projects*, showed the way to what was possible by moving beyond project management as a sub-discipline of operations management towards a whole lifecycle perspective on how we change our world. Peter sadly passed away after a long illness as this book was going to press, so we humbly dedicate it to him.

Graham Winch
Eunice Maytorena-Sanchez
Natalya Sergeeva
Manchester and London, September 2021.

# About the Authors

Graham Winch is Professor of Project Management at Alliance Manchester Business School. Currently an Associate Editor of the *International Journal of Project Management*, Graham has run construction projects and researched project organizing across a wide variety of engineering sectors. He was also Programme Director for BP's Managing Projects executive education programme, and Academic Sponsor for BAE Systems' Leading Complex Projects, Programmes and Portfolios (LCP3) executive education programme.

Dr Eunice Maytorena-Sanchez is a Senior Lecturer in Project Management at Alliance Manchester Business School. Following qualification as an architect in Mexico and postgraduate studies at University College London, Eunice has developed expertise in assisting project organizations to develop a clearer understanding of their organizational challenges by helping them develop their capabilities in stakeholder management, strategic project management and risk, uncertainty and complexity management. She has worked with many organizations in the public, private and non-for-profit sectors in the UK and abroad. Her teaching focuses on leadership and management of projects at undergraduate, post-graduate (MSc, MBA) and executive programmes. She was programme director of GROW—an engineering leadership development programme—and Deputy Director of the Leading Complex Projects, Programmes and Portfolios (LCP3) executive education programme.

Natalya Sergeeva is Associate Professor in Project Management at the Bartlett School of Sustainable Construction, University College London. She is a leader of Construction Economics and Management MSc Programme. Natalya is a consultant in the area of project and innovation leadership and narratives. She has worked with private and private organizations worldwide in providing her advice. Natalya's current research grant projects include "Narratives of Innovation: The Case of UK Infrastructure" sponsored by ESRC, "Innovation Champions in UK Infrastructure Megaprojects" sponsored by the PMI research programme, and "Storytelling by Sustainability Managers" sponsored by APM.

# How to Use this Book

**Introduction**
Projecting the modern world

**1.1  Introduction: projecting and the modern world**

Strategic project organizing is about how organizations change their world and thereby change ours. Initiating and executing such change is an uncertain adven-

## Introduction to the chapter

This chapter-opening feature outlines the main concepts and themes to be covered within the chapter. The succinct overview will help you review your learning and effectively plan revision, ensuring that you have considered all key areas.

---

**Vignette 1.1  The Great Green Wall**

The Great Green Wall (GGW) project launched in 2005 to restore and sustainably manage land in the Sahel region of Africa to address land degradation and poverty. Originally conceived as a 7,000 km vegetation barrier roughly 15 km wide to stop the Sahara expanding, it has evolved into an integrated ecosystem landscape approach. The project involves 11 national governments and international development agencies under the auspices of the African Union aligned with UN SDG 15, Life on Land.

Significant progress has been made to date, with 17.8 m hectares (ha) in restoration by 2020 against a target of 100 m ha by 2030, over 5.7 m trees planted, and 10.2 m direct beneficiaries. However, the restoration rate needs to accelerate from 1.9 m ha/year to 8.2 m ha/year to meet the 2030 target. A major barrier to acceleration is 'the lack of proper project and GGW program management structures at all levels', including:

## Vignettes

Learn from real-life situations with these short illustrations covering a range of businesses and project management events.

---

think that someone else can do the creating, and they will stick with the projecting, but no projection can become reality unless someone works out how to deliver it. So, we give it particular emphasis in Chapter 4.

**Exercise 3.1**

Think about a respected leader that you know or have worked with. Which dimension of the PLM are they stronger in? How do they compensate for their weaknesses in relation to the model?

**3.3  Judging**

The incomplete leader model focuses on the four dimensions of what project leaders

## Application exercises

Apply the key concepts and theories from the chapter to a variety of business situations by completing the exercises available throughout the chapter.

---

**4.11  Further reading**

Brown, K. A., Ettenson, R., and Hyer, N. L. 2011. 'Why every project needs a brand (and how to create one)'. *MIT Sloan Management Review*, 52(4): 61–68.
Discusses the importance of the project 'brand' as a narrative to mobilize resources for a project.

Davies, A., Dodgson, M., Gann, D. M., and MacAulay, S. C. 2017. 'Five rules for managing large, complex projects'. *MIT Sloan Management Review*, 59(1): 73–78.
Incisive overview of the challenges of innovating on megaprojects.

Sergeeva, N. and Winch, G. M. 2021. 'Project narratives that potentially perform and change the future'. *Project Management Journal*, 52(3): 264–277.
Differentiates between different project narratives in relation to a project life cycle and demonstrates them in three case studies.

## Further reading

Seminal books and journal articles that have contributed to the field of project management are provided in an annotated list at the end of chapters, offering you the opportunity to broaden your understanding. Key research references are indicated by * in the endnotes to each chapter.

### 4.12 Summary review questions

1. What is the connection between projecting and creating in the SPO PLM?
2. To what extent is innovating important in SPO?
3. What is the difference between narrating and storytelling in SPO?
4. How do project narratives change over the project life cycle?
5. What is the role of leading in crafting project narratives?

 *Visit the Oxford Learning Link site for this text to find answer guidance to the questions and exercises in this chapter.*

## Summary review questions

Reinforce your learning and test your understanding through these end-of-chapter review and in-chapter discussion questions which cover the main themes and issues raised in the chapter.

---

**Case 4**    Crafting the project identity narrative and innovating on Tideway

Tideway is a major player in the overall upgrade of the London's Victorian sanitation systems. It is building the 25 km Tideway tunnel under London's River Thames that aims to prevent the tens of millions of tonnes of untreated waste that currently pollute the river each year due to storm water overflow. The scheme is the biggest investment in London's sewage system since 1875 and the largest water infrastructure project in United Kingdom. Thames Water, London's water utility, created a new independently regulated company, Bazalgette Tunnel Ltd, to be owner and operator of Tideway, financed largely by pension funds because the project was too big for its own balance sheet. Construction started in 2016 and is expected to complete in 2025. There are 24 construction sites in London, spanning from Acton in west London to Beckton in the east. Tideway is Bazalgette's brand for the megaproject and does not include 'tunnel' in order to highlight the project mission and its outcome, which is to address the environmental problem of discharging waste

## End-of-chapter cases

At the end of each chapter except the first, an extended case study with accompanying discussion questions provides an excellent opportunity for you to further understand the material covered in the chapter by critically analysing a real-life situation.

---

## Glossary

**Adoptive innovation** Where a technology already used and proven by other organizations externally is adopted by a member—or usually collaborating members—of the project coalition to meet the owner's requirements.

**Agile project delivery** Project delivery through time-boxed iterative cycles in which scope is flexed rather than schedule or budget.

**Ambiguity** The condition where the required information is potentially available but cannot be adequately processed by the decision-maker.

**Bottleneck** Failure in supply of resources for a package within a project.

**Bridging window** Part of the innovation framework of a project, used during project shaping, when innovative ideas are generated, and learning and practice from other projects are used.

**Budget** Provides a cost model of the project broken down by task to give how much the work breakdown structure will cost to deliver.

**Capture management** The management of the first two phases of the supplier's project life cycle

## Glossary

A comprehensive glossary is provided at the end of the book to check your understanding of key terms.

# How to Use the Online Resources

This book is accompanied by a bespoke package of online resources that are carefully integrated with the text to assist the learning and teaching of the subject.

## Students can benefit from:

- web links to relevant videos;
- web links to resources on group work;
- answers to the end-of-chapter review questions in the book.

## Lecturers are supported by:

- a question test bank;
- teaching notes on each of the end-of-chapter cases;
- guides to each of the in-chapter discussion questions to support classroom discussion;
- a major teaching case on Food Corp with accompanying teaching notes;
- PowerPoint lecture slides;
- additional PowerPoint slides for a three-day teaching block using the Food Corp case.

Visit https://learninglink.oup.com/access/winch1e to find out more.

# Introduction
## Projecting the modern world

## 1.1 Introduction: projecting and the modern world

Strategic project organizing is about how organizations change their world and thereby change ours. Initiating and executing such change is an uncertain adventure, an adventure we call strategic project organizing (SPO). According to Daniel Defoe, 'about the year 1680 began the art and mystery of projecting to creep into the world'[1] in what came to be called the 'age of projectors'.[2] Defoe might be accused of forgetting the achievements of the pyramid and cathedral builders, but he is most interested in projects as investments for private advantage and public benefit rather than glorifications of deities. With Defoe, we see projecting as about how we transform the world we live in today and create new opportunities for the future. SPO is about mastering the art of projecting.

This transformation is most obvious with transportation. Starting with turnpikes and canals, and then railways, project forms of organizing developed and matured as investors transformed the natural landscape and integrated economic activity, thereby creating larger and larger markets for manufactured goods.[3] This transformation continues in the twenty-first century with transportation megaprojects as the global economy switches to services and enhanced connectivity becomes vital. One example is the construction of the Chinese high-speed rail network—35,000 km in the 15 years to 2019, thereby transforming national connectivity. Another is Grand Paris Express—extending the famous Paris Métro by 200 km of lines and fully automating the whole system, thereby transforming working patterns in the city. Cities are a fundamental feature of the modern world and its twenty-first-century knowledge economy, and their development also relies on projecting; water, energy, and sanitation networks[4] were vital to their expansion over the past 400 years, and remain so today.

The world presently faces a broader set of challenges. The United Nations Sustainable Development Goals (UN SDGs) require radical transformations in how the global society and economy works—see Vignette 1.1 on one green major project. This is clearest in the transformation to a carbon-free economy that depends on new ways of generating and transmitting energy and the development of new modes of transportation, but for many even access to clean water and effective sanitation remains a profound challenge. Pandemics are becoming more frequent, and here too, much of society's proactive response takes the form of projecting, such as new vaccines, emergency hospital facilities, or developing contact-tracing apps—see Vignettes 1.2 and 7.2, and Case 9. In areas such as science, the age of projecting also saw major advances,[5] which continue to this day with projects such as the Large Hadron Collider[6] and Square Kilometre Array.[7]

Information technology is profoundly changing our world and has stimulated the invention of new ways of projecting. The telegraph played a vital role in projecting during the nineteenth century and access to telecommunications networks is becoming essential for full participation in twenty-first-century society. Within organizations, information systems are enabling new ways of working and transforming the delivery of services to customers in both the public and private

## Vignette 1.1   The Great Green Wall

The Great Green Wall (GGW) project launched in 2005 to restore and sustainably manage land in the Sahel region of Africa to address land degradation and poverty. Originally conceived as a 7,000 km vegetation barrier roughly 15 km wide to stop the Sahara expanding, it has evolved into an integrated ecosystem landscape approach. The project involves 11 national governments and international development agencies under the auspices of the African Union aligned with UN SDG 15, Life on Land.

Significant progress has been made to date, with 17.8 m hectares (ha) in restoration by 2020 against a target of 100 m ha by 2030, over 5.7 m trees planted, and 10.2 m direct beneficiaries. However, the restoration rate needs to accelerate from 1.9 m ha/year to 8.2 m ha/year to meet the 2030 target. A major barrier to acceleration is 'the lack of proper project and GGW program management structures at all levels', including:

- governance: the lack of political will of national governments and their reluctance to establish appropriate national agencies to deliver GGW on their behalf;
- monitoring and evaluation: the ability to know whether project objectives are actually being met so as to ensure that international financing bodies are achieving their objectives for carbon sequestration and the like;
- finance: uneven commitment of national funds and the lack of market-based returns for international financing agencies, given the prevalence of smallholder farming in the Sahel;
- technical: the appropriate choice of plantings and ensuring that they survive long enough to deliver benefits such as forest products and carbon sequestration.

In order to address these challenges, it is recommended to strengthen the Pan-African Agency of the GGW to establish a GGW Trust Fund to finance the portfolio of projects; establish rigorous measurement systems; provide technical expertise; enhance knowledge-sharing; and overall programme and portfolio management.

*Source*: Climatekos (2020).

sectors. It is difficult to imagine what 'lockdowns' might have been like during the COVID-19 pandemic without online communications, which relied on both high-capacity broadband networks and a host of hardware and software innovations. Information systems have challenged established approaches to projecting in two different ways. First, they have made it very clear that simply producing a new system is pointless unless people know how to use it and adapt to the opportunities it offers—benefits realization is to the fore with information systems. Second, the rapid pace of innovation means that speed in development is crucial, which has stimulated innovation towards agile forms of project organizing through iterative cycles.

Like Defoe, we will focus on the projects as beneficial investments for both private advantage and public benefit through SPO. Before we do that, we need to define what SPO is. Fundamentally, it is the practice of the *art of projecting* in Defoe's sense; that is, it is how an organization achieves strategic change through projects. By organization, we mean an entity in the public, private or third sectors; by strategic change, we mean an investment initiated with deliberate intent; and by project, we mean 'a temporary endeavor undertaken to create a unique product, service or result'.[8] Clearly, not all change in economy and society is as the result of SPO (the recent COVID-19 crisis is testament to that), but our responses to that externally initiated change typically involve projecting, as we will see. Broadly, we can group strategic change into three broad categories of project:

- infrastructure projects enable other things to happen, particularly the provision of goods and services—examples include fibre broadband networks, urban transit systems, and satellite systems for geo-positioning;
- new product development (NPD) projects create new goods and services in response to market opportunities—examples here include anti-viral vaccines, ever-smarter phones, and TV blockbuster series;
- transformation projects create new organizational forms in response to opportunities derived principally from information systems—examples here include online retailing systems, collaborative working environments such as MS Teams, and the transformation of public services such as benefits payment systems.

These categories are, of course, mutually supportive. The transformation of collaborative working with MS Teams requires both a variety of innovative new hardware and software NPD projects and investment in broadband infrastructure. These transformations are also becoming increasingly complex as technologies advance with growing rapidity and society becomes more vocal on whether and how such transformations should take place.

These challenges place the art of projecting at the centre of social and economic life in the twenty-first century, yet it is typically taught and practised as a set of tools and techniques promoted by professional associations rather than a way of organizing to transform our future.[9] Our focus in this book is rather different. It is on how we proactively transform our future by organizing and on the central relevance of projecting to the challenges of the twenty-first century. In the rest of this chapter, we explain why a new approach to the art of projecting is required before providing an overview of the contents of the book. However, before we do that, we will look more closely at the so-called fourth Industrial Revolution.

---

### Exercise 1.1

What is the most exciting project you can think of? Why do you think it is exciting, and what are its principal benefits for economy and/or society?

---

## 1.2  The fourth Industrial Revolution

As Daniel Defoe sensed, projecting underpinned the first Industrial Revolution as he analysed the infrastructure investments that enabled the transformation that started around 1750 into a sustained economic growth unprecedented in

### Vignette 1.2    Working like crazy

'It was crazy . . . we worked as a team, 24/7 . . . on Friday March 13 we had nothing, and on Friday March 20 we had the app delivered.' Nicolás Jodal is Chief Executive Officer (CEO) of GeneXus, one of the leading firms in Montevideo's thriving tech cluster. At the time, Uruguay had four confirmed cases of COVID-19, but he instantly realized how an app could support the national response to the pandemic, so he mobilized a team of 150 people from 12 firms with the support from the Agency for Electronic Government and Information and Knowledge Society to develop the CoronavirusUY app. All work was voluntary, free, and seen as a civic duty. The app concept built on ideas from China and South Korea adapted to the needs of Uruguay. The initial aim was to connect the worried well to health-care providers to prevent the health system being overwhelmed. Next came contact tracing; because it already had the app, Uruguay was chosen by Google and Apple as one of four countries to pilot their Exposure Notifications application programming interface (API).

At the start, the team did not know whether the project would be a success: it was formed by people who had never worked together; there was no development process; no formal communication channels across the team; and there were no written functional requirements; and yet they did it! They embraced redundancy by using a number of teams working towards the same goal until a winning approach emerged based on 'whichever was first and met quality standards'. The app is credited with helping Uruguay's successful strategy of containment without resorting to mandatory lockdowns and very low infection rates.

*Sources: Financial Times*, 13 December 2020; 25 December 2020; http://www.genexus.com (accessed 25 January 2021); BBC News Mundo, 25 May 2020; Fondo Monetario Internacional (FMI), 'El secreto del éxito de Uruguay contra el COVID-19' (accessed 25 January 2021).

human history. The first Industrial Revolution was associated with a new source of energy—steam—and a new form of transportation infrastructure, the railway. In combination and independently, these two innovations transformed economy and society—first in the United Kingdom, and then around the world. Towards the latter half of the nineteenth century, a second Industrial Revolution took place, again associated with a new form of energy—electricity—and new forms of transportation driven by the internal combustion engine on land, sea, and air. The crucial social changes during these two revolutions were the rapid growth of cities, which demanded new infrastructures to protect public health and to enable urban transit, and the enabled rise of the consumer society, and hence the NPD project.

The third Industrial Revolution started during the 1940s, associated with the development of the computer and a new form of energy—nuclear power. While the promise of nuclear power has not (yet?) been fully realized, the computer has transformed our lives in extraordinary ways. Starting with large, cumbersome, mainframe computers, a remarkable cluster of innovations put a computer on every desk from the 1980s onwards and in every pocket from the 2000s on. These innovations led to the rise of the organizational transformation project to enable organizations make the most of these new opportunities. Also during this period, health care was transformed as pharmaceutical companies turned into innovation factories through intensive research and development projects.

The pace of technological change has been accelerating relentlessly since the first Industrial Revolution in the hills around the city of Manchester, where this chapter is being written. Talk is now of a fourth Industrial Revolution,[10] built around the digital technologies of the Internet of Things (sensor networks); big data (the automated collection of data from sensors), and machine learning (the ability to automate the analysis of that data). These digital technologies build on the third Industrial Revolution which gave us the Internet, high-performance computers, and their combination in distributed, and often mobile, networks. Just as projecting underpinned the first and second Industrial Revolutions by providing the transportation networks that made manufacturing possible and the utility networks that made cities possible, projecting will underpin the fourth Industrial Revolution by delivering the cyber-physical systems of the twenty-first century, presented in Vignette 1.3, which combine all three types of projects identified in section 1.1. Also part of this revolution are new sources of energy from renewables (principally wind and solar) as well as batteries for the storage of energy to enable the electrification of mobility. In health care, biotechnologies and neurotechnologies are opening up wide new opportunities.

With the benefit of hindsight, we can see that these revolutions are cumulative, each building on the transformations of the one before in the manner shown in Figure 1.1. We can also see how the fourth Industrial Revolution is having to address the problems created by the first two due to their reliance on fossils fuels to generate electricity and provide mobility. We can also see how

## Vignette 1.3    Cyber-physical systems

Cyber-physical systems are defined as systems where physical and computational elements are deeply intertwined to create self-managing systems for various purposes. They combine the principles of automation technologies from the third Industrial Revolution with the digital technologies of the fourth Industrial Revolution, combining sensors, networks, and machine learning to create a new generation of systems that can interact with humans through many new modalities. Cyber-physical systems are increasingly paired with digital twins which provide parallel models to enable simulation of the behaviour of the physical system under various conditions, including stress scenarios. Major applications include:

- Industry 4.0, taking factory automation and the associated supply chains to new levels to achieve responsive 'mass customization' in manufacturing and localized production through 3-D printing, integrating new materials such as graphene;

- smart cities, treated as systems of systems where high monitoring allows responses to be rapidly made to stress points, and digital twins enable managing assets through their life cycles and analysing the complex trade-offs required between sectors to achieve net-zero targets.

- mobile telephony linking personal hand-held devices through global 5G networks, which can also be used to track $CO_2$ emissions, detect traffic accidents, provide situational awareness to first responders, and monitor cardiac patients;

- autonomous vehicles are perhaps the ultimate cyber-physical system, combining sensors such as radar, lidar, and sonar with positioning technologies such as the global positioning system (GPS), odometry, and inertial measurement managed by advanced control systems to identify appropriate navigation paths and avoid obstacles;

- smart grids for energy distribution, which provide resilience through self-healing properties, allow the connection of localized generation units such as rooftop solar panels, remote metering of usage, and the management of peak charging loads generated by electric vehicles.

*Sources*: CDBB (2020); Lee et al. (2015); Tao et al. (2019); Wikipedia (accessed 28 October 2020).

each introduced a distinctive type of project, as defined in section 1.1. The first Industrial Revolution relied upon infrastructure projects; the second Industrial Revolution emphasized the NPD project; and the third introduced the organizational transformation project.

## Exercise 1.2

Do you think that the fourth Industrial Revolution will give rise to a fourth distinctive type of project or render the distinction between the three types of project used here meaningless?

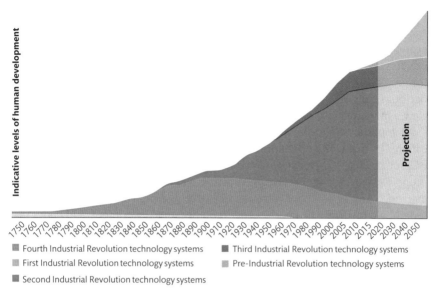

Figure 1.1 The four Industrial Revolutions.

*Source*: Schwab (2018: figure 2). Used with the kind permission of the World Economic Forum.

## 1.3 Projects and society

This book is about SPO—how organizations individually and collectively within the project coalition go about achieving desired outputs and outcomes from their investment projects. However, as much of the discussion in this introductory chapter indicates, projecting has enormous social and economic implications because it is about how we consciously create our future. In this section, therefore, we briefly indicate how our perspective on strategic organizing contributes to these wider debates across two broad themes. One is about the contribution of projects—particularly infrastructure projects—to economic development. The second is about the implications for work and society of the increased **projectification** of organizations.

Economic investment is a fundamental—probably the fundamental—contributor to economic growth, but that investment must produce net economic benefits for that growth to happen. If investment projects do not realize net economic benefits, then economic decline ensues. An important critique of transportation infrastructure investment[11] argues that often such investment is wasted because of distortions in the investment appraisal process due either to optimism bias or strategic misrepresentation. The former is the result of delusion and the latter of deception[12] in investment decision-making, and the solution is held to be much greater rigour in investment appraisal and greater professionalism in cost–benefit analysis. An alternative view is that the inherent uncertainties of investment appraisal mean that the 'animal spirits'[13] of investors are required rather than improved better practice, and that many such investment projects will fail[14] but the overall net effect to the economy will be beneficial, thanks to the 'hiding hand' of economic development projects.[15] This debate continues,[16] and in Chapter 5 we show how difficult it is for the project owner—which is the organization principally responsible for investment decisions—to weigh up the relative costs and benefits of investment projects. In our view, a more nuanced debate and further research are required.

An important trend over the past 30 years or so has been the growing 'projectification'[17] of many organizations, which has led to the development of the concept of 'project society' as a society in which project forms of organization dominate economic activity.[18] At one level this is a truism because any economy that is growing and changing will have relatively high levels of capital investment,[19] and the faster the growth, the higher the proportion of capital investment, and hence projects in society to deliver that investment. As we have already seen, each Industrial Revolution generates its distinctive types of project and so any society transitioning these revolutions will be a project society. However, this macro-level analysis hides an important organizational-level trend, which is the growing adoption of the routines—particularly discussed in Chapters 7 and 11—associated with the type of project management that evolved on US defence acquisition projects.[20] Although many of these routines have a much longer history,[21] and there are strong arguments for alternatives models of project organizing,[22] it is this more technocratic perspective that has become dominant. It is noticeable how this projectification process accelerated during the 1990s, particularly for new product development projects in the private sector such as cars,[23] in complement to the development of lean manufacturing in operations management, in pharmaceuticals,[24] and, more broadly, throughout manufacturing.[25] In an important sense, SPO is an overview of the current state of the art of projectification in organizations.

Presently, projectification is spreading to the public sector, where, it is argued, the major challenges of delivering on new policy initiatives—often through spectacular failures in organizational transformation projects[26]—can be addressed through a much more project-orientated approach.[27] Indeed, the argument has been taken further and it is suggested[28] that the economy as a whole should become mission-orientated in order to address the societal grand challenges captured in the SDGs discussed in section 1.1. The argument draws on the Apollo programme to put a man on the moon—perhaps *the* iconic project of the third Industrial Revolution—as an example of what can be achieved by projecting. The public sector as a project owner faces considerable challenges with projectification,[29] but the ideas presented in this book are equally applicable to the public and private sectors.

---

### Exercise 1.3

Is the Apollo mission the most appropriate example for a mission-orientated fourth Industrial Revolution? What other examples of projecting might be more appropriate?

## 1.4 Strategic project organizing: why we need a new approach

As the art of projecting addressed the creation of increasingly complex systems, it became formalized into a distinctive set of managerial practices. Although the foundations of these distinctive practices were laid throughout the nineteenth century,[30] their formalization started to crystallize in the 1950s. This formalization was particularly associated with the US experience of creating complex weapons systems.[31] From this experience emerged the systems paradigm of project organizing, captured by Cleland and King in their seminal *Systems Analysis and Project Management*.[32] They laid the foundations for virtually all subsequent research and teaching on project organizing by introducing some of the key concepts still in use today, including:

- the mutually reinforcing relationship between strategic planning and project implementation;
- projects as organizational systems addressing complex challenges;
- projects as purposive and future-orientated;
- the importance of stakeholders in the strategic planning of projects;
- projects as temporary, matrix organizations;
- the project life cycle;
- project planning and control and the supporting tools and techniques.

Over the following decades many others built upon this paradigm in developing their textbooks.[33] These textbooks share both the strengths and weaknesses of Cleland and King. We have identified the strengths above, but the weaknesses include:

- lack of attention to commercial issues in project organizing, despite the widespread appreciation of the importance of these issues at the time in defence programmes;[34]
- reliance upon a linear, planning approach to strategic management long after it fell out of favour in mainstream management research and teaching;[35]
- a growing disconnection from developments in mainstream management research and teaching across a wide variety of areas;
- reliance upon management science approaches to risk management, leading to the 'ludic fallacy'[36] in project organizing;
- the loss of the mutual interconnection between strategic intent and strategy implementation, as many of the textbooks and professional accreditations within the systems paradigm focused on implementation alone.[37]

Those concerned with the disconnection from developments in mainstream management research and teaching began to theorize the temporary organization as a distinctive form of organizing[38] alongside many other organizational forms.

This perspective has the benefit of reintegrating project organizing into mainstream management research and teaching, and reinforces the life-cycle perspective. However, it further reinforces the disconnection between the strategic decision-making around investment projects by the owner and the temporary organization that delivers the investment by focusing entirely on the temporary organization. It also immediately raises the question of the interface between the temporary organization and the permanent organizations which resource it.[39]

Those concerned with the reliance on a linear, planning approach began to draw on a wide variety of theoretical traditions to address the issues.[40] These concerns coalesced around the Rethinking Project Management initiative,[41] which placed the emphasis upon project organizing as an emergent phenomenon, and stressed the lived experience of being a project manager. This perspective on project organizing generated many important insights from its rich intellectual heritages,[42] but shared with the temporary organizing perspective the disconnection between the strategic and implementation aspects of SPO by focusing on the latter alone. It also lost the essentially purposive character of project organizing because of an overemphasis upon emergence.

Over the years, much of the advanced thinking on project organizing has developed in the pages of a series of handbooks by various editors.[43] These handbooks provide much insight to support the development of teaching, but their format inevitably means that they do not offer a coherent perspective and so are not well suited for supporting university teaching as student texts. The leading research journals in the area, the *International Journal of Project Management* and *Project Management Journal*, have also done much to reshape perspectives on project organizing through an increasing engagement with important developments in mainstream business and management research. We will draw on all these resources and influences as we set out our SPO perspective. This perspective will develop the crucial insights of the systems paradigm, defining projects as purposive, future-orientated, temporary organizations moving through a distinctive life cycle. At the same time, we draw heavily on the research over the past 20 years which has challenged that paradigm to present a fresh and distinctive perspective which we call SPO. We do not align with any particular PM body of knowledge because these are regionally specific and are limited by their focus managing rather than leading.

## 1.5 Plan of the book

The book is divided into four parts, each covering a different aspect of SPO. Part A introduces the core concepts of SPO. In Chapter 2, we introduce the structuring model for the whole book—the Three Domains Model. This model addresses a fundamental paradox in project organizing, which is that while the focus of attention is on temporary organizations, the vast majority of project managers work for permanent organizations. We therefore need to think of the temporary organization and its interfaces with two types of permanent organization. One is the owner organization, which provides the finance for the investment and will (usually) operate the outputs delivered by the project to realize its promised outcomes. The other is the supplier organization, which provides the human and material resources that allow that output to be delivered. We also take the opportunity here to define some core terms that we will use throughout the book, including uncertainty, complexity, project classification, and the project life cycle. The chapter concludes with an inspiring case example—the Eden Project—which shows how all these domains can work together to create something extraordinary.

The Three Domains Model has leading in its core because leading is what binds the parts together into a whole. We therefore focus on leading in Chapter 3 and present our Project Leadership Model (PLM) that we developed from the incomplete leader concept in collaboration with BP and BAE Systems. The emphasis of the incomplete leader concept is on what leaders do, rather than who they are, through sense-making, relating, projecting, and creating. It is called the incomplete leader concept because no one person can be effective at all four activities, so a leader can only become 'complete' by working with a team. However, who leaders are remains important, which we capture in the judging required for effectively leading, which we place at the centre of the PLM. The relationships of leaders with their teams to create complete leaders are then explored in the dynamics of teaming on projects. The chapter concludes with a project director—Patrick Crotty—talking about leading in his own words in Case 3.

Projecting and creating are dimensions of the PLM, yet because they are so pervasive in project organizing it is easy for their importance to be occluded. We therefore dedicate Chapter 4 to projecting and creating in order to emphasize their importance. When discussing projecting, we stress the importance of project narratives as the principal means by which we convince ourselves, our teams, and our stakeholders about the viability of imagined futures. Turning to creating, we emphasize the central role of innovating in SPO, leaving designing to Chapter 7. Our case study explores the development of project narratives and the championing of innovation on the Thames Tideway project in Case 4.

Part B explores the three domains of the model presented in Chapter 2. Chapter 5 focuses on the owner domain, which is usually populated by a single organization from the public or private sectors. The fundamental role of the owner in SPO is to *own* the project mission. Ownership means first raising the finance for the investment from whichever sources are appropriate against a business case in an iterative process of project shaping to envision a project mission. Ownership then means ensuring that the temporary organization delivers the outputs specified in the project mission by both governing the delivery domain and negotiating commercial relations with the supplier domain, while carefully managing external stakeholders. Finally, ownership means moving those outputs into beneficial use in order to realise the benefits that are the reason for doing the project. Our Case 5, a case study of an owner organization, presents the salutary tale of the Berlin-Brandenburg airport.

Chapter 6 focuses on the supplier domain, which is responsible for the resources required for the delivery of the outputs specified in the project mission—attempts to make them also responsible for outcomes have not usually been successful. Therefore, their area of responsibility on the project is narrower but deeper than the responsibilities of the owner, which cover the full project life cycle. A distinctive type of firm, the project-based firm (PBF), populates this domain. Suppliers enable delivery by mobilizing the human and material resources required to deliver the project outputs. As might be expected, they have a very different business model from owners, and therefore need to be managed in very different ways. Case 6, our case study of a supplier organization, highlights BAE Systems, a global supplier of defence materiel to governments.

Turning to the delivery domain, Chapter 7 focuses on the temporary organization that delivers the outputs as a project or a programme. This domain is the sole focus of the systems paradigm and many of the perspectives that have developed since. However, it interfaces with the two other domains in SPO because it is not an autonomous organization but entirely dependent upon the two permanent domains for the resources it requires to deliver the project outputs. We explore the challenges of managing in the delivery domain from the perspective of a project leader. These include the importance of understanding the dynamics of the project life cycle, the development of the project execution plan, team dynamics, and of managing threats to the delivery of outputs within that cycle. We will also emphasize the importance of retaining the insights into systems thinking from the systems paradigm for project resilience and the phenomenon of project escalation. Those who are unfamiliar with the technical competencies of project organizing are recommended to read this chapter in conjunction with Chapter 11, which covers them in more detail. Case 7, our case study here, is project delivery by Stage One, a global supplier of event facilities.

Part C turns to the three interfaces in the Three Domains Model presented in Chapter 2. The governance interface between the owner organization and the temporary organization delivering the outputs required by the project mission is the subject of Chapter 8. This has arguably been the area of the most significant development of best practice over the past 20 years or so, yet was hardly addressed by the systems paradigm or its critics. The chapter discusses the various structures and processes that make up contemporary project governance. These include the stage-gate process for governing delivery through the life cycle; assurance in the 'three lines of defence', by which the owner is confident that the information it is receiving about progress from the project controls system is reliable; and the portfolio management process, by which resources are allocated to different projects by the owner. All of these activities are usually supported by a project management office as controller, supporter, and developer of project governance. Within the owner organization, all these elements are brought together by the project sponsor, as the accountable individual for the project through its life cycle. Case 8, our case study of the governance interface, highlights the relationship between the Biennale Foundation and its 2019 Venice International Film Festival.

The commercial interface in Chapter 9 is between the owner organization and the PBFs in the supplier domain, or rather the tier-one suppliers in the project supply chain. For reasons that are unclear, this interface has been largely ignored by the systems paradigm and its critics, despite its manifest importance on most projects and it being the area of some of the earliest developments in SPO during the nineteenth century. We will explore this interface from the perspectives of both sets of parties on the owner and supplier sides of the interface through contracting strategy and capture management, respectively. We then explore how these perspectives can be combined in various forms of collaborative working. In Case 9, we show how important innovations in the commercial interface have been for the remarkable success of the development of COVID-19 vaccines.

We explore the resource interface in Chapter 10. This addresses how the supplier organizations provide the human and material resources to the delivery domain that the temporary organization needs to deliver on its outputs. This chapter addresses the fundamentally matrix nature of project organizing, where 'pools' of human resources are held by supplier organizations and allocated across a portfolio of projects for different owners by those suppliers. Some of these pools are not held permanently in supplier organizations; rather, they are held in project ecologies within large, urban agglomerations. Knowledge is an important element of human resources, so knowledge integration and learning are discussed. While human resources are the principal element in the resource interface, technological resources—embodied knowledge—are also important, so we discuss the principles behind technology readiness levels (TRLs). Our Case 10 explores the resource challenges of delivering the Manchester 2038 net zero mission.

Part D turns from the organizational level to the individual level to focus on **professional competencies** for project organizing. The overall emphasis of this book is on SPO (treating projects as an organizational phenomenon), but individuals make organizations work. In this final section, therefore, we focus on individual competencies rather than organizational capabilities. Chapter 11 reviews the **technical competencies** that project professionals need to participate in SPO. These are typically laid down in detail in the project management bodies of knowledge developed by the various professional bodies around the world; we here cover them in a generic manner. We discuss the technical competencies for scheduling and budgeting; managing threats to the delivery of the project mission; and managing quality, safety, and environmental issues during delivery. We also explore how the fourth Industrial Revolution is starting to change project organizing itself in Case 11 on the development of project data analytics.

The final chapter, Chapter 12, turns to **social competencies** for SPO and associated career development which are symbiotic with the technical competencies. We examine the development of the professionalization of project managers over the last 30 years or so, and on that basis, the difference between project managing and project leading. Leaders in SPO—whether they are from owner organizations or supplier organizations, or switch between the two—need to move well beyond the technical competencies of project organizing to lead the transformations owners expect from their projects and programmes. We also explore issues of equality and diversity in project organizing and executive programmes for developing project managers into authentic project leaders. The project manager role as the 'person in the middle' is a particularly stressful one, which raises the importance of well-being in project organizing. Case 12 explores future careers in SPO by presenting the Association for Project Management's Future of the Profession thought exercise.

## 1.6 The voyage of life

We emphasize the importance of the project life cycle in SPO. Yet those with a critical eye might suggest that by structuring the book around the Three Domains Model we lose this life-cycle perspective. We do show how the Three Domains Model is dynamic through time in Chapter 2, but we need to emphasize the importance of the project life cycle more structurally in the book. We do this by deploying the paintings from Thomas Cole's[44] 'Voyage of Life' as the epigraphs to each of our four parts, but with new titles. For Part A, we portray 'Awakening'. Projects start as ideas but many—if not most—of these ideas are quickly forgotten. However, some do capture the imagination and become advocated by those with faith in the idea. We can see in Cole's painting the baby starting its voyage of life overseen by a guardian angel, just as ideas for projects need to be nurtured by the faithful. Next, we portray 'Aspiration' and we see our hopeful project leader setting out with a clearly formed image of where the project is heading, but at this stage it is little more than a castle in air. Nevertheless, our project manager sets out with great anticipation towards that vision, with the guardian angel in support. As the project gets into the delivery phase, things get a lot tougher, leading to 'Anguish' as the project manager floats towards the rapids with little but prayers to help. The guardian angel has disappeared behind dark clouds, while sharp rocks and turbulent waters threaten to sink the project. However, still waters are reached in the end in 'Achievement'. The project has arrived in calmer waters—it is battered, with elements of the original mission missing, but it is still afloat and our project leader is older and wiser. Rays of light break through the dark clouds, and the guardian angel has returned.

## 1.7 Summary

In this introductory chapter, we have hopefully excited your imagination in the world of projecting and SPO as the principal way in which organizations and society deliberately transform their futures. We explained why we believe a new approach is required, indicating the limitation of both the systems paradigm and its critiques to the value creation process that is a project. We then laid out the plan of the book's four parts and 12 chapters. Finally, we explained how we are using the images from

Cole's 'Voyage of Life' to show that, fundamentally, SPO is a voyage through the life cycle that is projecting. We now turn to introducing some of the core concepts of SPO as the art of projecting.

## 1.8  Summary review questions

1. What is the meaning of projecting in the modern world?
2. What are the three broad categories of projects?
3. What are the limitations of the existing texts on project organizing?
4. How is the fourth Industrial Revolution different from the other three?
5. How can projecting contribute to the grand challenges of twenty-first-century economy and society?

 *Visit the Oxford Learning Link site for this text to find answer guidance to the questions and exercises in this chapter.*

 *Take your learning further by viewing videos relevant to this chapter on the Oxford Learning Link site.*

## Notes

1. Defoe (1697: 25). Defoe does acknowledge the Roman infrastructure legacy.
2. See Keller (1966) for the seventeenth century; Linder (1994) for the nineteenth century.
3. For examples, see Middlemas (1963).
4. For the case of London, see Tomory (2015) on water, Tomory (2011) on gas, and Hughes (2013) on sanitation.
5. See Brockhoff (2020) on the transit of Venus project in the 1760s.
6. Engelen (2012).
7. Taylor (2012).
8. *Project Management Institute Body of Knowledge*, 6th edition.
9. Morris (2013) makes this point well.
10. Schwab (2018).
11. Flyvbjerg et al. (2003).
12. Flyvbjerg et al. (2009).
13. Keynes (1961: 161); to put Keynes' point in Flyvbjerg's terms, optimism bias is essential for any investment project to be initiated.
14. Sawyer (1952).
15. Hirschman (1967); the analogy is with Smith's 'hidden hand' (1776), which imperceptibly stabilizes economic activity more generally through the interaction of supply and demand.

16. See, variously, Flyvbjerg (2016); Kreiner (2020); Ika et al. (2020).

17. Midler (1995).

18. Lundin et al. (2015).

19. The technical term is 'gross fixed capital formation'. In terms of economic statistics, this comes down to the relative size of the construction sector, which is the most 'projectified' sector, complemented by corporate services which is the next most projectified—see Henning and Wald (2019). This latter sector also includes many construction firms providing architectural, engineering, and project management services—see Winch (2003).

20. Morris (1994).

21. Pinney (2001). For instance, the emblematic Gantt chart dates from before 1914.

22. Lenfle and Loch (2010).

23. Clark and Fujimoto (1991); Cusumano and Nobeoka (1998).

24. Pisano (1997).

25. Bowen et al. (1994a); Giard and Midler (1993); Wheelwright and Clark (1992); Whittington et al. (1999); Winch (1994).

26. King and Crewe (2013).

27. Eggers and O'Leary (2009).

28. Mazzucato (2021).

29. Winch and Cha (2020).

30. See Pinney (2001) for US science and engineering.

31. Morris (1994); Johnson (1997; 2013).

32. 1968 *et seq.*; this is not just our assessment—see Morris (2012).

33. For instance, Kerzner (2017) dominates the market for those taking professional qualifications in project management, while Meredith et al. (2017) is probably the leading undergraduate text.

34. See, for instance, Peck and Scherer (1962) on US weapons acquisition.

35. See Mintzberg (1994) for the standard critique here.

36. The phrase is Taleb's (2007), and identifies that the expected utility framework for decision-making under uncertainty is derived from games of chance.

37. Morris (2013).

38. Early contributions include Bryman et al. (1987); Lundin and Söderholm (1995). See Bakker (2010); Burke and Morley (2016) for reviews.

39. See Bakker et al. (2016).

40. Hodgson and Cicmil (2006) provide an excellent introduction.

41. See Winter et al. (2006) for the original statement; Svejvig and Andersen (2015) for a review.

42. This is well summarized in Clegg et al. (2020).

43. See, for instance, Cleland and King (1983); Turner (1993); Turner (2014); Pinto (1998); Morris and Pinto (2004); Morris et al. (2011); Flyvbjerg (2017); and Sankaran et al. (2017).

44. Thomas Cole (1801–1848) was born near Manchester but emigrated to the United States and became one of the foremost members of the Hudson River School of romantic landscape painters. The version of his allegorical series, The 'Voyage of Life', depicted here hangs on opposing walls of an octagonal room devoted to the work in the National Gallery, Washington, DC.

# Part A

···········································································

# The Core Concepts of Strategic Project Organizing

···········································································

**Figure A** 'Awakening' (Cole's childhood)
*Source*: National Gallery of Art.

In our first part, the project is little more than an 'Awakening' idea of future opportunities as it starts its journey towards realization. It is here that we lay out the *core concepts of strategic project organizing* (SPO) from which we will craft our argument. In Chapter 2, we define our approach to the basic characteristics of project organizing in general and SPO in particular, including:

- the rationale for and overview of the Three Domains Model;
- the definitions of uncertainty and complexity that we will be using throughout our argument;
- a contingency framework for distinguishing between different types of projects;
- the concept of the project life cycle, which we also present allegorically through Cole's 'Voyage of Life'.

Chapters 3 and 4 are best read together because in them we present our framework for understanding leading in SPO as the binder of common interest to common purpose across all the different dimensions of projecting. This is the SPO Project Leadership Model, which is a functional model that captures what leaders do on projects. It has five dimensions:

- *Projecting*, through narrating and storytelling;
- *Relating*, with both the internal project team and external stakeholders;
- *Sense-making*, as coping with uncertainty and complexity;
- *Judging*, as decision-making competency drawing on psychology and experience;
- *Creating*, through innovating and designing the project delivery organization and its interfaces.

To support the understanding of these concepts, we present three case studies. The inspiring Case 2 on Eden explores many different aspects of our approach to SPO in an introductory way to support learning in Chapter 2. Case 3 presents the story of Patrick Crotty in his own words on how he went about leading the Waterloo International project in Chapter 3. Finally, to support learning in Chapter 4, we present innovating and narrating on the Tideway project in Case 4. Having understood these core concepts and worked through these case studies, you are well placed to explore the three domains and three interfaces of SPO in Parts B and C.

# 2 The three domains of project organizing

## 2.1 Introduction: uncertainty at the heart of projecting

Projecting transforms our world but it is not an easy mission. In practice, projects are the principal means by which organizations—both public and private—undertake strategic change by creating something new that did not exist before. Of course, much change in organizations is reactive to unfolding events; projecting, in contrast, is an inherently proactive response to threats and opportunities. As such, there is inevitably a zone of uncertainty that generates the 'mystery of projecting', where the ways in which to combine desired ends with available means are not fully known. Managing through this uncertainty has been called a 'business of smoke and mirrors . . . a business that appeals to us for emotion'[1] in car new product development (NPD) projects.

Initially, the idea for the project is shaped[2] through an iterative process between the owner and its multiple stakeholders to develop the project mission—the strategic reason *why* we are doing the project. The project mission then has to be sustained through the life cycle to *deliver* the required output, but delivery of this output does not achieve the project mission. For that, the output has to be moved into beneficial use to achieve the outcomes[3] originally desired in the project mission. Only when the idea behind the project mission becomes a reality can a project be described as a success. This success may only be achieved many years after the output has been delivered. For some projects, successfully delivered outputs may never achieve their desired outcomes.[4] Outcomes may be in the form of social, economic, or environmental benefits such as increased revenue streams from customers, improved services for the public, or reduced costs—often they are a combination of all three. What is conventionally known as project management within the systems paradigm is an important part, but only part, of strategic project organizing (SPO). Here, we take a broader, more holistic perspective on strategic change.

We structure this perspective, and hence this book, around the three domains of project organizing. The original motivation for the development of this perspective is a paradox. If project organizing is about what temporary organizations do, why are the majority of people working in project organizing permanently employed[5] with, at times, 30-year careers in a single organization? From our reflections on this paradox emerged the Three Domains Model of project organizing, which we have successfully used on MSc, MBA, and executive education programmes.

## 2.2 The three domains of project organizing

We can identify three domains, as shown in Figure 2.1, each populated by a distinctive type of organization:[6]

- The **owner domain** is populated by owner organizations that shape project missions to further their longer-term strategies. Owners expect the beneficial use of the outputs delivered by the project to realize the outcomes anticipated in that project mission. The owner typically provides the financial resources required for the investment. We discuss this domain in Chapter 5.

- The **supplier domain** is populated by a diverse range of different types of project-based firm (PBF). They share a common business model in which they supply the human and material resources required by owners to deliver the outputs, but they are not in a position to achieve outcomes. We discuss this domain in Chapter 6.

- The **delivery domain** is populated by temporary organizations that draw on the financial resources from the owner domain and the human and material resources from the supplier domain to deliver the outputs to the owner. We discuss this domain in Chapter 7.

Each domain must perform both its shared and separate roles on the project efficiently and effectively if output delivery is to be a success. Thus, outputs are delivered by a project coalition[7]—often a shifting coalition—of organizations with different individual performance incentives, which must negotiate the shared performance incentives that underpin successful output delivery. The delivery organization is often characterized as a temporary organization. That means that it is determinate because there is always a termination date for the project organization agreed between the owner and supplier organizations at some point in the future. While this date, of course, may be overrun, the principle still holds. The owner and PBF supplier organizations, on the other hand, are permanent in that they do not have an agreed date for their termination, although they are, of course, always at risk of ceasing to be organizations due to bankruptcy or closure.

As shown in Figure 2.1, these three domains generate a set of organizational interfaces, and their effective management is crucial for effective project organizing:

- The **governance interface** between the owner organization and the temporary organization charged with delivering the outputs is about ensuring that the delivery organization remains in line with the project mission. We discuss this interface in Chapter 8.

- The commercial interface between the owner organization and its suppliers; its effective management ensures that the owner and supplier organizations are aligned in their incentives for the successful delivery of the outputs. We discuss this interface in Chapter 9.

- The resource interface between the temporary organization and the supplier organizations ensures that the suppliers are providing the right human and material resources at the right time to meet the requirements of delivery. We discuss this interface in Chapter 10.

At the centre of the model is leading. We cover this in Chapters 3 and 4; suffice to say here that it is leading which pulls the three domains together and mobilizes them jointly to deliver the new output, be it a bridge, a 'blockbuster' product, or a transformed public service. On some projects, the three domain roles are mainly internal to a single organization. However, they are carried out by different functions, typically with 'internal contracts' between them.[8] For instance, the marketing function may take the role of 'owner', and the research and development (R&D) or

Figure 2.1  The three domains of strategic project organizing.

*Source*: developed from Winch (2014: figure 1).

engineering function the role of 'supplier', and the delivery organization draws on a multidisciplinary team, including manufacturing. While the detailed implementation may be a little different in such cases, the principles of SPO introduced in this book remain applicable.

The model in Figure 2.1 is static, showing the relationships between the three domains and their distinctive populations of organizations that make up the project coalition, but not how they interact through time. Yet projects are fundamentally about time and follow a distinctive project life cycle from inception to completion. Figure 2.2 characterizes the relationships between the three domains through time and indicates typical allocations of responsibilities for shaping the project mission, delivering outputs, and realizing outcomes. We can see that the owner, as an investor, is responsible for shaping the project mission into a coherent value proposition, working with a variety of stakeholders, particularly if the source of finance is not internal to the owner organization. In addition, the owner, as operator, is responsible for transforming the potential benefits of the outputs delivered by the delivery domain into outcomes which achieve the promise of the project mission. This transformation from outputs to outcomes (benefits realization) is typically lagged in time—sometimes for many years. The governance interface connects the project mission and outcomes through the project life cycle and ensures that the project outputs remain aligned with the project mission. If the outputs are misaligned with the mission, then achieving outcomes will be that much more difficult. The governance cycle starts with the development of the value proposition for the project and finishes with benefits realization as the project moves from delivering outputs to achieving outcomes.

Within the delivery domain, the project delivery organization takes the project mission and turns it into an output that can be handed over to the owner organization

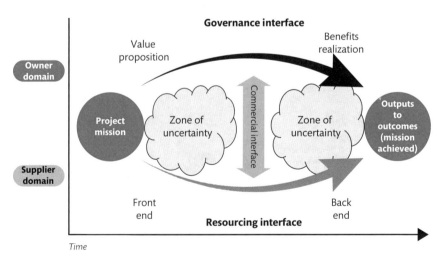

Figure 2.2   A dynamic view of the three domains.

Source: developed from Cha et al. (2018).

and the project closed out. The relationship through the project life cycle between the front end of the delivery process and its back end at close out is challenging and will be explored further in Chapter 7. The commercial interface links the supplier domain that provides the delivery domain with the resources (human and technology) required to deliver the project output to the owner domain that provides the financial resource so that the owner can achieve the project mission. The relationship between these two domains can vary from a purely transactional relationship to a highly collaborative one, as we will see in Chapter 9. The space between the project mission and the intended outcomes in Figure 2.2 is the zone of uncertainty, and so we now turn to conceptualizing this uncertainty.

## 2.3 Conceptualizing the uncertainty between the idea and the reality

The transition through time from the left side to the right side of Figure 2.2 is rarely straightforward, and requires the distinctive approach to projecting that we call SPO. If the characteristics of the output and the way in which it will deliver outcomes for the owner organization were fully known at the start of the project, nothing new would be created. There is, therefore, always a level of uncertainty inherent in the transition through time from the ideas captured in the project mission to outcomes generating real benefits. This point is challenging, but central to the approach to the SPO perspective of this book, so in this section we will define our terms, which will then be used throughout the rest of the book. Our aim here is not to mandate a particular language, but to be clear for the reader how we are using particular terms that are often used ambiguously in academic and professional debates. The fundamental challenge of SPO is uncertainty, where uncertainty is defined as the lack of information required to make a decision,[9] as shown in Figure 2.3. The difference between points $\alpha$ and $\beta$ is the total amount of information required for a decision; while some of this information is typically available on a project at the time of decision, as indicated by point $\gamma$, some is not because it remains to be learned in the future.[10] Making matters more difficult is that the precise positions of $\gamma$ and $\alpha$ are themselves unknown—we might need more information than we presently think we need!

If we then think of what this uncertainty looks like through time, we can generate Figure 2.4. This shows that at the decision point where we develop the value proposition we actually have relatively little certain information—most of what we need to know remains to be learned in the future. Of course, we can be confident that some things will not change over the life of the project, such as the engineering properties of materials. However, it does not necessarily follow that the technology as a whole is mature—we discuss the issue of technology readiness in Chapter 10. We also know with a relatively high degree of certainty the *current* ($t_o$) status of the owner organization and the socio-economic environment in which it makes its living. At some point

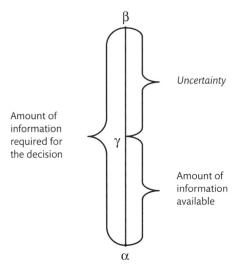

**Figure 2.3** The definition of uncertainty.

*Source*: developed from Winch (2010: figure 1.2).

in the future, the delivery organization will have delivered an output which provides the basis for the owner organization to achieve the outcomes which the project mission expects. By this time, nearly all the information required to underpin the project mission will have been learned, although the operating environment for the output over time remains uncertain because that future is inherently unknowable.[11] Thus the project life cycle is a *dynamic process of uncertainty reduction through time*.

Figure 2.4 distinguishes mission complexity from dynamic uncertainty. Mission complexity refers to the perceived complexity of the outputs defined in the project

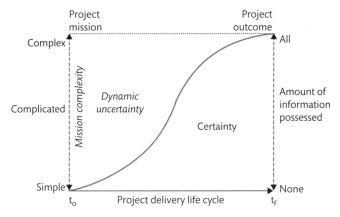

**Figure 2.4** The dynamic reduction of uncertainty through the project life cycle.

*Source*: developed from Winch (2010: figure 1.3).

mission at $t_o$ on a scale from simple to complex. Dynamic uncertainty captures the learning through the project life cycle as more information becomes available closer to the final delivery of the intended outcome at $t_f$. In order to interpret the figure correctly, it should be appreciated that both the left-hand and right-hand axes apply throughout the life cycle of the project from $t_0$ to $t_f$ as the balance between the information required and the information possessed (i.e. certainty) changes. In summary, Figure 2.4 shows that each project has both a starting level of complexity, which is a function of the project mission, and a falling level of dynamic uncertainty from that starting point as it moves through the life cycle. The curve for the transformation of dynamic uncertainty to output certainty is shown as S-shaped because in practice most curves (e.g. cash flow) in project management are S-shaped. Once the output has been delivered, uncertainties still remain around its transition to outcomes for reasons ranging from social complexity to market acceptance.

Readers will note that we are using the terms 'uncertainty' and 'complexity' in particular ways here. There are some important epistemological reasons for placing uncertainty at the heart of projecting because the future is inherently uncertain—it can be neither true nor false simply because it has not happened yet.[12] In other words, we simply do not and cannot know the future—hence, the claim that 'there are no facts about the future'.[13] At best, we can extrapolate from the present through prediction of the future state, but we need to be sure that our understanding of the present is not subject to change. This requirement introduces another concept that we need to understand—complexity.[14] Projecting involves social and technical systems composed of interdependent elements, such as people in social systems, components in technical systems, and sophisticated combinations of the two in *socio-technical systems*. Large numbers of elements in the system generate an exponentially large number of interdependencies between those elements and we can describe the system as *complicated*, as opposed to simple. However, if we do not fully understand the nature of those interdependencies, we cannot fully predict the future state and we have a condition of emergence; that is, the system is characterized by the potential for unpredictable change, and we call it *complex*. It follows that the definitions of simple, complicated, and complex turn on the amount of information we have regarding the interdependencies within the system, that is, on the uncertainty regarding those interdependencies.[15]

## 2.4 Defining uncertainty and complexity

As we have suggested, there is considerable terminological confusion around the concepts of 'risk', 'uncertainty', and 'complexity', and many researchers and practitioners use them—often interchangeably—without conceptual clarity.[16] In order to shine a strong light into the uncertainty between the idea and the reality, we will adopt the following definitions for the purposes of this book. We would also urge you to consider adopting them in your own practice of project organizing.

We will not use the concept of 'risk' at all in our argument because it is so widely used in so many different ways that, like 'quality', it has lost the ability to communicate clearly without significant elaboration. We will, therefore, adopt the following definitions:

1. For a given project:
   (a) a **threat** is a possible future event that could reduce the ability to achieve the project mission;
   (b) an **opportunity** is a possible future event that could improve the ability to achieve the project mission.
2. Uncertainty is the difference between the information required by a decision-maker for a decision and the information available to the decision-maker for that decision, as defined in Figure 2.2.
3. **Ambiguity** is the condition where the required information is potentially available but cannot be adequately processed by the decision-maker.
4. Differences in levels of uncertainty in decision situations are a function of exogenous factors which may be unknown, but also of endogenous factors, which are a function of the relationships between the elements of the socio-technical system:[17]

   (a) **simple** is the condition characterized by clear cause-and-effect relationships with predictable patterns of activity and analytically linear interdependencies;
   (b) **complicated** is the condition characterized by cause-and-effect relationships that require intensive analysis, but are in principle knowable. For instance, chess is a complicated game, not a complex one, because it is entirely rule-bound.
   (c) **Complex** is the condition where the interrelationships between the elements of the system are not fully known to the decision-maker and therefore are emergent, thereby generating uncertainty.

---

**Exercise 2.1**

Think about how you actually use the concepts 'uncertainty', 'complexity', and 'risk' in your daily life. Are you consistent in how you use these concepts?

---

## 2.5 Understanding threat and opportunity: a cognitive approach

A common feature of much of the research on uncertainty and complexity is that it is essentially realist because it conceives possible future events (threats or opportunities) as states of nature rather than states of mind.[18] Indeed, one could suggest that it is epistemologically naïve because it does not distinguish between states of nature and states of mind; that is, between what is and what we can know about it. The cognitive approach that forms a core concept of SPO considers possible future states as states of mind rather than states of nature.[19] Therefore, the framework represents the beliefs about future states as perceived by the decision-maker. These future states are possible future events perceived as threats and opportunities that lie in a continuum (y axis) between certainty and impossibility.[20] These future states of mind can be characterized thus:

- known knowns (often called 'risk'), is when we can make inferences from historical data using appropriate probabilistic techniques, assuming that there will be no change in the validity of that data in the future. The importance of data to analyse known knowns is demonstrated in Vignette 2.1.

- Known unknowns, is when a possible future threat or opportunity event can be identified but there are no reliable data available from which to make quantitative inferences.

- Unknown knowns, is when threats or opportunities have been identified by someone but have not yet been disclosed to the decision-maker—whether deliberately or not.[21] An example of how devastating this can be for a project is given in Vignette 2.2.

- Unknown unknowns, is when threats or opportunities have not been identified; in other words, the decision maker is in a state of ignorance. An example of how to respond successfully to 'unk-unks'[22] is presented in Vignette 2.3, and advice on how to transform them into known unknowns is available.[23]

As Figure 2.5 illustrates, the more information the decision-maker perceives and internalizes about a threat or opportunity, the closer she is to a cognitive state of known knowns. However, the decision-maker remains in the realm of uncertainty unless objective data are available to shift the decision-maker to the realm of known knowns. When discussing systems where all the properties are known, such as engineered systems, we can meaningfully talk of known knowns in a probabilistic sense, but where we are talking about future states, as we always are in projecting, then the concept of uncertainty is more appropriate. The problem with melding the two by using subjective probabilities is that conditions of uncertainty can take on the appearance of certainty for the unwary project manager. He thereby falls both into the 'ludic fallacy', discussed in section 1.4, of treating the probabilities of threats to the project mission occurring in the same way as the probabilities derived from repeated games of chance.[24]

If the future is inherently unknowable, how is any kind of action—let alone the mobilization of large resources inherent in projecting—possible? Keynes's answer to this question was 'animal spirits' or the entrepreneurial desire to create something new, which was also the focus of Knight's work,[25] to move from the germ of an idea to a changed reality. Much of this book will be a steady unpacking of the answer to

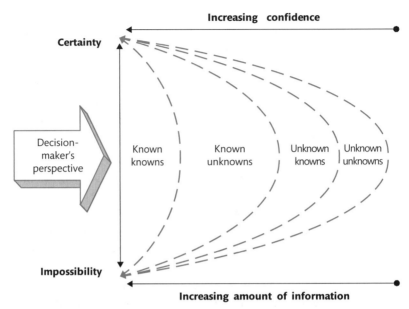

**Figure 2.5** A cognitive perspective on uncertainty and complexity.

*Source*: Winch and Maytorena-Sanchez (2011: figure 14.2).

## Vignette 2.1    Misreading data at NASA

The space shuttle Challenger exploded shortly after launch at dawn on 28 January 1986 due to the failure of O-rings to seal properly in the rocket booster in unprecedented cold launch conditions. Seven crew members lost their lives. There are many important lessons that can be learned from this tragedy, but we will focus on one in particular—the failure to prove the importance of temperature in O-ring performance. Prior to the fatal launch, a pattern of O-ring failure had been identified but its causes were not well understood. Some engineers believed the crucial variable to be temperature, but could not produce objective data to support this contention, so it was cognitively a known unknown. This lack of objective data meant that they were reluctant to speak up in the crucial launch decision meeting the night before because they worked in a strong engineering culture in which opinion had to be fully supported by data. The launch decision meeting was held over a telecon, so the engineers' negative body language could not be communicated to the full meeting.

Subsequent investigation showed that the data did exist at the time of decision; it simply had not been collected and analysed properly. The problem was that the engineers only plotted data from launches which had experienced some failure of O-rings, which were small in number and yielded no obvious pattern. Investigators into the accident plotted O-ring status by temperature data from all launches and found a clear pattern of clustering of O-ring failures at the lower end of the temperature scale. The simple act of plotting the data properly would have shifted the threat of O-ring failure from a known unknown to a known known and probably saved lives.

*Source*: Vaughan (1996).

## Vignette 2.2 Unknown knowns on the Zambesi

In 1973, Mitchell Construction was placed in receivership due to losses on the project to build a new hydroelectric power station on the north bank of the Zambesi River in Zambia, powered by water from the Kariba Dam, to complement one on the south bank in Rhodesia (now Zimbabwe). The nominal owner was Zambian but the Rhodesian CAPCO, which would operate both the new and existing station, held decision-making power as agent. The World Bank provided a large proportion of the capital, with the Zambians providing the balance. At the time, Rhodesia was a pariah state, subject to international sanctions.

Cognitively, this is a case of an unknown known for Mitchell. It became clear that ground conditions were not as described in the tender documents, which 'warranted' that the rock was of good quality on the basis of cores taken in 1961. As Mitchell bled cash, CAPCO refused to sanction additional costs. Later evidence suggests that both Mitchell and the Zambians were caught in a ploy to circumvent the international sanctions imposed on Rhodesia. Zambia was partially dependent for electrical power on Rhodesia, so preferred to exploit the hydroelectric potential of its Kafue Dam. However, the claimed ease of constructing the north bank power station was used to persuade them—and perhaps more importantly, international funding bodies—to back the Kariba project. The ease of the Kariba option turned on the quality of the rock, but later inspection of the cores taken in 1961 showed them to have been deliberately misrepresented in the tender documentation. In order to cover up this misrepresentation, it was necessary to scapegoat Mitchell for the budget escalation because certification for additional budget that took into account the 'unexpected' ground conditions would have exposed the lie.

*Source*: Morrell (1987).

that question, but here we emphasize one important aspect of animal spirits—faith in an imagined future. As the Chair of the UK promotors of the Channel Fixed Link reflected: 'If I was to sum up the overriding ethos which governed the directors . . . it was the unarticulated faith, difficult to define or explain, but an abiding faith that we would get there in the end.'[26] Case 2 on the Eden Project explores faith in projecting.

---

### Exercise 2.2

Why might 'faith' be important for leading projects?

---

## 2.6 What kind of project do we have?

We have already indicated that not all projects are the same with the sectoral categories suggested in section 1.1. Using the concepts of uncertainty and complexity, we can now go further in categorizing types of projects, while indicating how project characteristics can be shared across sectors, but differentiated within sectors. We propose the four-dimensional model shown in Figure 2.6. Our first dimension is perceived **technological complexity**. We can characterize this using the three-part scale from section 2.4 developed earlier, ranging from simple through complicated to

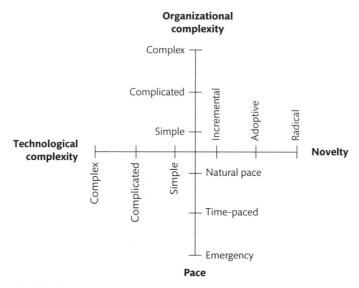

**Figure 2.6** The SPO Diamond Model.

*Source*: developed from Shenhar and Dvir (2007: figure 1.2); their figure conflates technical and organizational complexity which, we suggest, are independent.

complex. A simple project is one where the output defined by the value proposition is largely a repetition of an earlier project, such as building a house. A complicated technology is where all the technological elements are fully understood, but they need to be reconfigured in a different context, such as upgrading to Windows 365. Technologically complex projects (such as a jet fighter) feature some of the most advanced technologies, but technological complexity can also be driven by the need for the output to interface with other systems. The need for new information systems to interface with legacy information systems for integrated functionality is a common example of this. Technological complexity can also be driven by the sheer size of the output system.

The second dimension is organizational complexity, which can also be scaled through simple, complicated, and complex. This dimension is largely independent of the technological complexity dimension. For instance, developing a vaccine is pharmacologically complex, but organizationally simple—it is normally done by a single firm to established protocols. High organizational complexity can be generated by relationships internal to the three domains, such as an unwieldy owner joint venture or myriad layers of subcontracted suppliers. It can also be driven by the complexity of the external environment, such as poorly understood stakeholder relationships, the ambiguity of regulatory oversight, or the rate of change of the socio-economic environment. In particular, these external factors can stimulate attempts to reshape the project mission during the delivery phase. Large infrastructure projects appear to be particularly susceptible to this challenge due to their long life cycles and high stakeholder sensitivity. The sheer size of the delivery organization can also generate organizational complexity.

Novelty is our third dimension, in which we can characterize the level of innovation by the temporary organization to provide the required outputs on a scale of incremental, through adoptive, to radical.[27] An incremental innovation is an application of a technology previously used by a member of the project coalition to the project in hand. Typically, a supplier organization will supply its technology to meet the requirements of the owner's value proposition. An adoptive innovation is one where a technology already used and proven by other organizations externally is adopted by a member—or usually collaborating members—of the project coalition to meet the owner's requirements. A radical innovation is new to the world—an output which offers the potential of radically new outcomes. A radical innovation is not necessarily complex—penicillin was radical, but it was discovered by accident. A major uncertainty with radical innovation is whether the world is ready to turn the radical output into radical outcomes—see Vignette 4.3.

The final dimension is pace. A project may be at natural pace,[28] scheduled from the left of the Gantt chart in a way that is as efficient as possible. Alternatively, it may be time-paced and scheduled from the right of the Gantt chart because the output needs to be ready for beneficial use by a certain date, earlier than would be defined by the natural pace. Olympic Games facilities are a classic example of this type of project pace, but occur in many competitive markets where the first-to-market with a new product reaps outstanding rewards. Finally, there are emergency projects where external events demand action as quickly as possible—disaster recovery projects are a classic example here.[29]

## Vignette 2.3   Unk-unks and opportunity on the Millennium Bridge

The pedestrian Millennium Bridge across London's River Thames opened to the public on Saturday 10 June 2000 and closed two days later when it generated a dangerous-feeling sway due to vibrations set up by pedestrian movement. This was entirely unexpected and prompted unwarranted fears of collapse. How could leading structural engineers such as Arup make such a mistake—surely this was a known known? The problem lay in the combination of the lightness of the structure as a pedestrian bridge and the swaying movement of people as they walk; when the latter meets the resonant frequency of the former, movement starts. This is not the same effect as synchronized movements of marching soldiers; the sway synchronizes the movement, not the other way round. The effect is not linear—for the Millennium Bridge, it starts suddenly at around 166 people.

From a cognitive perspective, this is an unknown unknown. This problem was unreported in the literature that bridge engineers read and not mentioned in the codes they follow. The principal earlier publication on the topic was published in an earthquake engineering journal unlikely to be read by bridge engineers. Other observed cases only emerged in correspondence following the reporting of the Millennium Bridge problems and showed that it was independent of the bridge design—for instance, the Passerelle Léopold Sédar Senghor, which opened across the Seine in Paris in December 1999, suffered similar problems. Arup was able to turn this threat event into an opportunity by taking full responsibility and developing an elegant damper solution which did not compromise the design intent, which then allowed it to market its leading-edge expertise in long-span pedestrian bridges.

Sources: Sudjic (2001); Wikipedia (accessed 27 October 2008).

The SPO Diamond Model allows the project leader to start to strategize the project life cycle. As we will see in many different ways throughout this book, differences in social and technological complexity, and in novelty and pace affect both the shaping of the project and organizing for its delivery. A successful project leader always needs to know the answer to the question 'What kind of project do we have?'

---

### Exercise 2.3

Think about different projects you know about. Assess them against the SPO Diamond. What lessons do you draw from this experience?

---

## 2.7 The project life cycle

Our final core concept is the project life cycle.[30] There are multiple life-cycle models available, each adapted to the requirements of the particular owner organization or project-based sector, but a generic one with clear phase descriptors can be adapted from practice in the oil and gas sectors,[31] as shown in Figure 2.7. We will present elaborated versions of this life-cycle model in Chapters 8 and 9. The model shows four principal phases of projecting with the first two forming shaping and the second two forming delivery:

- Appraise addresses the question of whether we have a viable project for investment to produce the desired returns as captured in the project's value proposition.
- Select addresses the question of how the project is going to be delivered in terms of the selection of the elements of the socio-technical system that forms the output of the project.
- Define covers the detailed specification of the scope of the project to ensure that all the elements are in place to support effective delivery.
- Execute is the phase which typically generates the most attention in project organizing research because it delivers the specified output of the project, but is highly dependent upon the successful management of the prior three phases.

While project shaping often proceeds in fits and starts, as can be seen in Case 2 on the Eden Project, with the project always at risk of postponement or cancellation, project delivery is more focused and cancellation is rare if project shaping has been effective. This shift between these two phases can be called the project peripety,[32] which is well captured in Smit's comment in Case 2 on turning a dream into a reality.

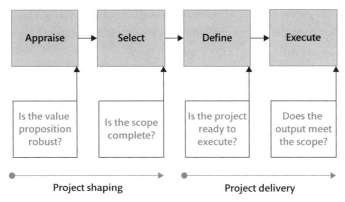

Figure 2.7 The SPO Life-Cycle Model.

*Source*: authors.

## 2.8 Summary

This chapter has introduced the basic concepts of SPO. We presented the three do-mains as a holistic model of organizing for projecting. We then showed how this model changed through the project life cycle as a dynamic reduction of uncertainty through time characterized as a learning process. Perhaps most importantly, we pro-vided definitions of key concepts that underlie SPO before presenting the SPO Dia-mond and the SPO Life-Cycle Model. We now move on to examine in more detail the centre of the Three Domains Model—leading.

## 2.9 Further reading

Kay, J. and King, M. 2020. *Radical Uncertainty: Decision-Making for an Unknowable Future*. London: Bridge Street Press.
  Stimulating restatement of the Knight/Keynes approach to uncertainty and the importance of narratives in addressing that uncertainty.

Browning, T. R. and Ramasesh, R. V. 2015. 'Reducing unwelcome surprises in project management'. *MIT Sloan Management Review,* 56(3): 53–62.
De Meyer, A., Loch, C. H., and Pich, M. T. 2002. 'Managing project uncertainty: from variation to chaos'. *MIT Sloan Management Review*, 43(2): 60–67.
  These two provide differing conceptualizations of uncertainty and complexity from the one presented here, while drawing on similar analytic traditions.

## 2.10 Summary review questions

1. What is the difference between uncertainty and complexity?
2. Why do the owner and supplier domains differ from the delivery domain?

3. Why does dynamic uncertainty reduce through the project life cycle?

4. What is a cognitive view on understanding threat and opportunity?

5. What are the main stages of the project life cycle?

 *Visit the Oxford Learning Link site for this text to find answer guidance to the questions and exercises in this chapter.*

 *Take your learning further by viewing videos relevant to this chapter on the Oxford Learning Link site.*

## Notes

1. Cited in Walton (1997: xvii).

2. We take the concept of project shaping from Miller and Lessard (2000).

3. This important distinction between outputs and outcomes comes from Axelos (2020), which uses the distinction to differentiate projects that deliver outputs from programmes that deliver outcomes. We disagree with this distinction because it is difficult to see what the point of doing a project is if it does not produce a beneficial change.

4. A classic example of this 'white elephant' phenomenon is the Humber Bridge in the United Kingdom, which was authorized in order to win a parliamentary by-election. It opened in 1981 as the longest single-span bridge in the world, but never adequately covered its costs from tolls because inadequate numbers of motorists wish to use it. It was refinanced in 1996 and again in 2015, while half the debt was written off in 2012.

5. Cheung et al. (2020).

6. This section is based on Winch (2014*). The distinction between owner and supplier is essentially the same as that between project-supported and project-based organizations—see Lundin et al. (2015)—but more descriptive of what each type of organization does as a member of the project coalition in contributing to the realization of the project mission.

7. Winch (2010).

8. Nakhla and Soler (1996).

9. Galbraith (1977).

10. These Greek letters are pronounced alpha, beta, and gamma, respectively.

11. Keynes (1937).

12. Aristotle (1974).

13. Goodpasture (2004).

14. Weaver (1948); Simon (1962); De Meyer et al. (2002); Geraldi et al. (2011); Ramasesh and Browning (2014).

15. This relational definition of emergence is a 'weak' definition of emergence—see Elder-Vass (2010); Simon (1996).

16. Chapman and Ward (2011: 3). However, their basic default definition of uncertainty as 'lack of certainty' does not, in our view, move us forward very far.

17. The typology is taken from Snowden and Boone (2007).

18. This section is based on Winch and Maytorena-Sanchez (2011).

19. Savage (1954).

20. These are taken from Keynes (1921).

21. We take this concept from Stephens (2003).

22. *Time*, 9 March 1970, reported that 'aerospace-men have come down with a severe case of what they call the "unk-unks"—the unknown unknowns', http://www.time.com/time/magazine/article/0,9171,878813-1,00.html#ixzz0qHiPgqG6 (accessed 8 June 2010).

23. Klein (2017); Mullins (2007).

24. Taleb (2007).

25. Keynes (1961); Knight (1921).

26. Henderson (1987: 15).

27. The scale of 'new to the application', 'new to the organization', and 'new to the world' is a familiar one in the innovation literature—see Tidd and Bessant (2021).

28. We take the concept of 'natural pace' of a project from BP.

29. Wearne and White-Hunt (2014).

30. Morris (1994); Lundin and Söderholm (1995).

31. Merrow (2011).

32. Engwall and Westling (2004).

 **Case 2**    Telling future truths at Eden

The Eden Project (http://www.edenproject.com) (accessed 16 August 2021) in Cornwall is one of the most successful UK Millennium projects. It opened in March 2001 to provide an outstanding experience for around 1 million visitors per year—double the number originally envisaged in 1997. Constructed in a redundant south-facing china clay pit, a large covered biome provides a humid tropical environment, while a smaller one provides a warm temperate environment, totalling between them 2.1 hectares. The cool temperate environment is in the third, uncovered, outdoor biome. An education centre—The Core—opened in 2005. The driving forces of the early days of the project were Tim Smit, who had rescued and opened to the public the nearby Lost Gardens of Heligan in 1992, and Jonathan Ball, a successful local architect. The project presented an enormous range of challenges and provides a vivid example of the power of what Smit calls 'telling future truths'.

In 1993, the UK Government established the National Lottery to fund, amongst other good causes, the Millennium Commission. Its purpose was to celebrate the forthcoming second millennium with calls for 'a scientific or engineering project that becomes one of the wonders of the third millennium'. Amidst disparaging remarks about Æthelred, the English king at the time of the first millennium, the call was for a future-orientated initiative that would excite and inspire. A number of projects of various kinds were supported by the Millennium Commission with the aim of celebrating the coming of the third millennium and leaving a lasting legacy. The most successful of the 12 larger Landmark projects was the Eden Project.

The idea for Eden was distilled from a conversation over a bottle of whisky in a West Country farmhouse kitchen one night in May 1994. Smit and Ball complemented each other with Smit's horticultural expertise and fluid ability to articulate compelling narratives, and Ball's architectural expertise and extensive networks amongst the higher echelons of both Cornish and London society. These latter connections included official roles for the Royal Institute of British Architects and membership of one of the grander gentlemen's clubs.

The project mission they generated in the autumn of 1994 from the initial whisky-fuelled idea was:

> To create under one roof a range of natural habitats found on planet Earth . . . An international resource designed for research, education, and public enjoyment to herald the new Millennium, bequeathing a gift of incalculable value to those who will follow us . . . our hope for and belief in the future.

Funded by pump-priming money from the local government sources, a mix of Smit, Ball, other local players, and horticulturalists energetically shaped this project mission. The project was possibility and not fantasy, due to the launch of the Millennium Commission in February of that year. They captured early ideas in a variety of architectural sketches in both plan and elevation, sometimes prepared on restaurant menu cards. They resulted in Eden being submitted as the UK entry to the architectural Venice Biennale in 1996.

An outline proposal was submitted in April 1995. The first paragraph of that submission read:

> The concept of the Millennium is rooted in recognition of that significant midnight when we look backward to the past and forward to the future simultaneously. Its social value lies in concentrating our minds on past achievements, present problems and future possibilities. Any project designed to mark this transition should excite interest, understanding and involvement in shaping a desirable future.

This outline proposal was turned down as underdeveloped, but this did not faze Smit. Upon receiving the news, he said to Ball, 'We're going to bluff it out. We're going to tell everyone that we have caught their [the Millennium Commission's] imagination and have been asked to work it up some more. And what's more, we're not going to take no for an answer.'

A significant rethink was required and the team decided to assemble some of the leading players in the UK construction industry to add credibility to their efforts. However, funds were very tight, and so these players were recruited through Ball's personal contacts on the basis that they would not be paid unless the project were successfully funded. Remarkably, they agreed to participate.

The architects, Nicholas Grimshaw and Partners, worked on developing the design concept. They soon realized that their original idea (a reprise of Grimshaw's Waterloo International—see Case 3) would not work propped against the side of the clay pit because the structure was too heavy for the span and the ground too uneven and continually changing due to continued working of the pit for clay. The inspiration for Grimshaw's final design was a soap bubble that can mould itself to whatever surface it alights upon; their technical solution a geodesic dome. The erection of the structure on the 858 m long ground beam required the largest freestanding scaffold in the world, followed by installation of the cladding panels by abseilers. Civil engineering works included moving 800,000m$^3$ of fill by the construction manager McAlpine JV. This consisted of Sir Alfred McAlpine plc and Sir Robert McAlpine Ltd, who came together for the first time since the firm had split in 1940 due to a family dispute because it was 'the ultimate construction project'.

Ball managed to convince all of these firms, together with some of the leading international consultancies such as Ove Arup and Davis Langdon, to work for free to develop the design, while Smit and the team lobbied the Millennium Commission. The Commission did not fund development work prior to full bids, and so it was not obvious anything was amiss and the team struggled on private donations and small grants. By mid-1996, the lobbying achieved results and Eden was back in the competition with a submission due in December for a budget of £74.3 m. The news that Eden had been successful was announced in May 1997, and so the McAlpine JV was notified as preferred bidder for the delivery phase of the project in June 1997. The relationship was reinforced by appointing a Director of Sir Robert McAlpine to the Eden Board in 1998. This relationship would be of enormous benefit during construction, when the project nearly ran out of cash, owing the JV millions and the McAlpine director steadied the boat by saying 'We're still here.'

Funding came from a wide variety of sources—the Millennium Commission provided only 50 per cent of the total financial resource requirement of nearly £80 m. Smit's credibility with the success of Helligan enabled seed corn funds from the county (Cornwall), local charities, and private interests. The ability of Ball to network both locally within Cornwall and nationally to garner enthusiastic commitment was impressive, mobilizing the right people to solve difficult problems—particularly those associated with finding the other half of the funding for the project. These skills encouraged the head of a neighbouring county, Somerset, to back publicly the Cornwall project for European Commission structural funds at his own county's loss. At the formal signing of the legal agreements for the finance, Eden's legal lead noted that 'the most extraordinary thing about it all was that we'd persuaded such a wide group of people, many of whom would have found it easier to walk away, to stay at the table and find a reason for saying yes'.

With the funding announcement, the project reached a turning point and Smit asserted that:

> There comes a time in all great ventures when the talking has to stop. We'd created the constituencies, we'd talked the hind legs off donkeys, we'd been snake-oil salesmen with attitude and a dream to peddle, but turning a dream into a reality needs iron in the soul, money in the bank, and military organization.

Finally, the clay pit was purchased in October 1998, and the construction contract signed in January 1999. By this time, the McAlpine JV had worked for nearly two years without a contract, as had most of the consultants. Intensive construction on site started in February 1999, and the complete facility opened in March 2001 ahead of schedule and to budget. Eden is a remarkably successful project; Smit ascribes this success, fundamentally, to the fact that 'the act of faith that enabled so many people to sign up to Tinker Bell Theory was a testament to the Spirit of Eden taking hold'. In that sense, 'Eden was never about plants and architecture, it was always about harnessing people to a dream and exploring what they are capable of.'

*Sources*: Ball (2013); Smit (2000), (2001).

## Discussion questions

1. What role did Tinker Bell theory play in the shaping of the Eden Project?

2. How was the project peripety characterized by Smit?

3. How does this case illustrate the importance of 'Awakening' and 'Aspiration' in Cole's 'Voyage of Life'?

# 3 Leading

## 3.1 Introduction: leading at the core of strategic project organizing

The challenge of leading derives, in essence, from the problem of uncertainty discussed in Chapter 2. Absent uncertainty and the organization can be programmed to deliver; accept uncertainty and a continual process of interpretation of the organizational context and capabilities is required in a manner that the organization's members and stakeholders find credible. Leading is one of the most energetically discussed topics in management. The range and richness of this debate is almost overwhelming, but most would agree that leading 'is the essential social essence that gives common meaning to common purpose'.[1] A very helpful way of looking at these debates is to identify the 'memes' of leadership:[2]

- **Warrior**: this meme has obvious military connotations, in which the successful leader wins the 'war' against the competition or against adversity. It is very much a model of the 'leader as hero' and is widespread in the more sensational management literature. Traits associated with this meme are courage, honour, and cunning.
- **Problem-solver**: in this meme, the leader is the one who generates wise solutions to difficult problems that others cannot solve. Traits associated with this meme include wisdom, integrity, and tenacity.
- **Politician**: many leaders are seen as great communicators and this meme emphasizes those who can mobilize large groups, particularly through their oratory and example. Traits associated with this meme include charisma, oratory, and diplomacy.
- **Teacher**: this meme is traditionally associated with religious leaders but is now widely associated with the contemporary styles of leadership recommended in many management texts. Traits associate with this meme include humility, authenticity, and empathy.

In strategic project organizing (SPO) we focus on the leader as problem-solver which, we suggest, is the most appropriate meme for leading complex projects. This is supported by the brief from one of our executive education clients to move beyond the warrior meme of 'project leader as hero' who turned around failing projects to leading in a way that prevented projects becoming failures in the first place. Vignette 3.1 indicates the strengths and weaknesses of the 'warrior' meme for an expedition project. We focus on the leader as problem-solver by introducing the SPO Project Leadership Model (PLM) shown in Figure 3.1 that our executive education delegates find compelling. However, leaders only exist in relation to followers, and so we go on to discuss how leaders relate to their teams through teaming. We complete the chapter with a case study of an experienced project leader explaining what he does in his own words.

## 3.2 The incomplete leader

The dominant perspective on leading projects is about who leaders are—their styles, their traits, how they appear to others—and how they should behave.[3] A rather different approach is to focus on what leaders *do* and *how* they do it rather than who they are, and to argue that the single person in a leadership position does not have to do everything. The leader is therefore 'incomplete'[4] in relation to these ideals with the corollary that the leader should be complemented by other members of the senior team as an incomplete leader with a complete team. We therefore align ourselves with perspectives on functional leadership.[5] The PLM shows what leaders do in four dimensions of activity which, of course, overlap, but which can usefully be thought of as distinct. *Relating* and *sense-making* are the 'enabling' dimensions of the PLM because they are how the leader garners the information about what is going on around the project. The project leader then uses this information for *projecting* the project mission and then *creating* how that mission will be delivered. At the heart of the PLM is *judging*, which captures the combination of the decision-making frames, the psychological traits, and consolidated experience that are the foundations of wise judgement. The model is one of the incomplete leader because no one person can be equally good at all four activities, and so the leader will need to work with others in the senior leadership team of the project to ensure that all activities are effectively covered. We discuss each of these dimensions in turn.

### 3.2.1 Sense-making

Managing in an uncertain world is first and foremost a sense-making process,[6] as discussed in section 2.5, where Figure 2.5 summarizes the many varied dimensions of sense-making. Sense-making lies at the heart of leading projecting in an uncertain world, and even when sense appears to have been confidently made with the communication of plans, these are always contingent on the amount of information to hand at the point of the project life cycle when they are made, as shown in Figure 2.4. Sense-making is, therefore, an active process throughout the project life cycle,

Vignette **3.1**    The project leader as hero: Sir Ernest Shackleton

The years leading up to 1914 were the heroic age of Antarctic exploration. In 1914, Shackleton led an expedition to cross the continent but in January 2015, *Endurance*, the expedition's ship, became trapped in the Antarctic pack ice. The ice slowly crushed the ship and the crew abandoned it to live on the ice in October 2015. They slowly made their way across the ice and launched their boats to reach the uninhabited Elephant Island in April 1916. No ships regularly passed the island, so one of the boats was fitted out for a sea voyage and, commanded by Shackleton, sailed 1,200 km across treacherous ocean to South Georgia, the closest inhabited island. Landing on the 'wrong' side of the island, the team had to cross mountains and glaciers to reach the whaling settlement at Stromness in May 1916. The balance of the crew on Elephant Island was not rescued until August. No man was lost from this crew.

This is a remarkable story of leading and teaming under extreme adversity which became mythologized through the publications of Shackleton himself and others, and the basis for leadership development programmes. However, the expedition overall was badly planned and dangerously optimistic in its aspirations. Many of the supplies delivered were inadequate, particularly for the support expedition to the other side of the continent; almost none of the men could ski, despite Amundsen's (the first man to reach the South Pole in 1911) demonstration of its importance; the dog handler was left behind in Buenos Aires. A later Antarctic explorer, Fuchs, argued that 'the loss of the *Endurance* may have saved a worse disaster'. As *warrior leader*, Shackleton was exemplary; as *problem-solving leader* he was less so.

*Sources*: King (1999); Morrell and Capparell (2001); Shackleton (1999).

although the emphasis does shift more towards sense-giving as the project nears delivering the output and realizing the outcomes. We will return to this dimension again and again throughout this book.

### 3.2.2 **Relating**

One of the most important activities of the leader is *relating* both internally with project teams and externally with stakeholders. Relating can be both a formal structured process and an informal one through social networking—the latter is probably more important. A principal aim here is to elicit the unknown knowns identified in Figure 2.5 regarding threats and opportunities to the achievement of the project mission that somebody knows about, but which they are not telling the project leadership team. Internally, leaders need to ensure that different project teams do not play 'project chicken',[7] that is, hold back on reporting bad news on the progress of their particular subproject until another team has already done so. For obvious reasons, this stifles the flow of information on project status upwards in the project information loop shown in Figure 11.3. Again, we will return to this dimension many times throughout the book.

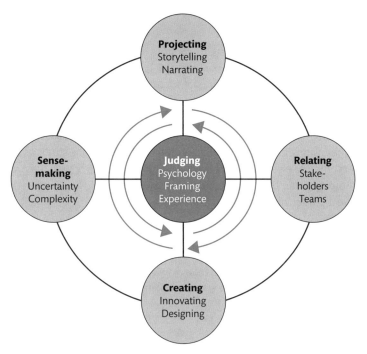

Figure 3.1  The SPO Project Leadership Model.

*Sources*: developed from Forsyth and Gavin (2017) and Winch (2010: figure 16.4).

### 3.2.3  Projecting

Sense-making and relating provide the information from which the emblematic activity in leading SPO—*projecting*—is done. The information garnered from these sources during project shaping allows the definition of the project mission through future perfect thinking, which is the process by which we organize future-orientated action (as opposed to present-orientated behaviour) by projections of future states in which an 'action always has the nature of a project'.[8] While 'to project' literally means to throw forwards, we always do that with an end in mind—otherwise all future-thinking is mere fantasy. Projecting has two facets. One is the generation of a compelling narrative from that future perfect thinking which convinces stakeholders, mobilizes resources both financial and human, and enthuses the project teams. These together form the project mission into a compelling 'why' statement for the project.[9] The project mission thereby forms a 'reference narrative'[10] which ties the projecting and creating dimensions of the PLM. The second facet of projecting is storytelling, which infuses the narrative with emotion and meaning for project participants. The importance of projecting in SPO means that we will spend more time developing the dimension in Chapter 4.

### 3.2.4 **Creating**

There are two very different facets to *creating* in the PLM. The first is designing how the project mission will be delivered—this is a central theme of Chapters 8–10 of this book. The second facet is innovating in order to deliver better against that project mission. Projects are inherently innovative—some more so than others—and so innovation is central to SPO. This aspect of the PLM can easily be downplayed. In teaching MBA classes, asking the students to score themselves as leaders against the four dimensions, creating typically gets the lowest score. The students appear to think that someone else can do the creating, and they will stick with the projecting, but no projection can become reality unless someone works out how to deliver it. So, we give it particular emphasis in Chapter 4.

---

**Exercise 3.1**

Think about a respected leader that you know or have worked with. Which dimension of the PLM are they stronger in? How do they compensate for their weaknesses in relation to the model?

---

## 3.3 **Judging**

The incomplete leader model focuses on the four dimensions of what project leaders do, but who they are and how they think influences how they do what they do. So, we have reintroduced this dimension with three facets. The first is the decision-making frames that shape judgement—models of what good decision-making looks like. The second is the psychological traits capturing both the leader's psychological profile and the leaders' ability to empathize with others through emotional intelligence. The third captures the leader's experience and ability to draw on that experience to make the most appropriate decisions.

### 3.3.1 **Framing decisions**

An early discussion of the challenges of managing projects distinguishes two decision-making frames for judging called Dr Optimizer and Dr Skeptic.[11] Dr Optimizer sees the project as an exercise in management science and planning as a mechanistic delivery tool. Dr Optimizer does not need to judge because he has data. Dr Skeptic, on the other hand, sees it as a problem of organization and retains an openness and questioning mindset as the project moves through its life cycle, learning as she goes. Dr Skeptic relies on judging, not optimizing tools, while Dr Optimizer forgets that there are no facts about the future. These two archetypes are rooted in very different decision-making frames. It follows that we need to articulate the model of decision-making—the micro-foundations—that underpins our perspective on SPO. We do this in Table 3.1.

The rational optimizer (RO) frame of Dr Optimizer and the boundedly rational satisficer (BRS) frame of Dr Skeptic place rationality at the heart of their decision-making.

The principal difference between the two is that the latter draws upon the behavioural critique[12] of the optimizing assumption in economics because rationality is inevitably bounded in the pervasive absence of complete information. Decision-makers therefore have to make satisfactory (i.e. 'to satisfice') decisions that meet their minimum criteria for benefits rather than optimal decisions that maximize their benefits. However, this model remains inadequate due to its emphasis on rationality in the face of uncertainty. Drawing on jurisprudence, we can propose a frame of 'reasonableness' rather than rationality, where prudent decision-makers make sense of the situation to select appropriate choices in the light of social norms of reasonable behaviour. This notion of reasonableness is well established by precedent in, for instance, cases under the law of tort. Thus, *Blyth v. Birmingham Water Works* held that:

> Negligence is the omission to do something which a reasonable man, guided upon those considerations which ordinarily regulate the conduct of human affairs, would do, or doing something which a prudent and reasonable man would not do.[13]

We therefore suggest that the most appropriate decision-framing for project leaders is the prudentially reasonable sense-maker (PRS). This framing underpins our perspective on SPO under uncertainty throughout this book. The practical differences between the three frames for decision-making is illustrated by the debate on surgical facemask use by the public during the COVID-19 pandemic summarized in Vignette 3.2.

### Vignette 3.2    SPO micro-foundations: facemask behaviour in pandemics

During the COVID-19 pandemic, there was considerable discussion regarding the wearing of facemasks by the public in non-clinical settings in order to reduce transmission of the virus. During the peak of the pandemic, there was no sound evidence of their efficacy in offering protection derived from the gold-standard medical clinical trial methodology, although as understanding grew, the medical arguments for general use in non-clinical settings strengthened and governments mandated their use. From an RO point of view, this lack of certain information meant that there was no benefit to the individual from mask-wearing, yet there are costs associated with wearing them such as discomfort, libertarian principles, and pride in one's appearance. Therefore, an RO would not choose to wear one. However, the inevitable uncertainty around the nature of the evidence combined with the finding that transmission rates might be reduced by mask-wearing has led some to argue for the use of the 'precautionary principle', which offers a satisficing criterion for the BRS. The precautionary principle addresses uncertainty by reversing the decision criterion to place the burden of evidence on not wearing masks.

However, a PRS would go further and argue that wearing a surgical mask clearly signals to others that one is committed to tackling the pandemic by minimizing the spread of the virus and therefore their concern for those around them and society more generally. The World Health Organization argued that mask-wearing could make 'people feel they can play a role in contributing to stopping spread of the virus ... [and] be a form of cultural expression, encouraging public acceptance of protection measures in general'.

*Sources*: Gandhi and Rutherford (2020); Greenhalgh et al. (2020); Jefferson et al. (2011); Peeples (2020); World Health Organization Interim Guidance, 6 April 2020, 5 June 2020.

> ## Exercise 3.2
>
> Review Vignette 3.2. Did you choose to wear any kind of mask in situations where they were not mandated by government? If so, why? If not, why not?

### 3.3.2 **The psychological traits of leading**

A second facet of judging is the psychological disposition of the decision-maker associated with the trait theory of leadership. This has a long history in writing about leadership, and has advanced recently with the consolidation of personality research into the 'big five' traits[14] presented in Table 3.2, which are largely stable through life. Some of these traits are positively associated with leadership. In particular, extraversion is a trait displayed by effective leaders, while openness, low neuroticism, and conscientiousness also feature.[15] Interestingly, agreeableness is not associated. From this evidence, leading is not about being nice to people, but it is about thinking laterally, and exhibiting commitment, emotional stability, assertiveness, and an

Table 3.1  Framing decision-making: the optimizing, satisficing and sense-making frames

|  | Rational optimizer (RO) | Boundedly rational satisficer (BRS) | Prudentially reasonable sense-maker (PRS) |
|---|---|---|---|
| Definition | 'Every agent is actuated only by self-interest'[a] | 'Individually defined pursuit of self and other interests' | 'Collectively defined appropriate behaviour for role and circumstance' |
| Interactions | Opportunistic | Opportunistic | Trustworthy |
| Objectives | Optimal benefit | Best available benefit in light of cognitive constraints | 'Meet collective standard of prudent, reasonable person' |
| Decision process | Do I have all the information required for my decision? | What are the options that meet my criteria? | What sort of situation is this? |
| Decision criteria | Which option is optimal for me? | Which option best meets my criteria? | What is most appropriate for me in this situation? |

*Sources*: developed from Winch (2015: table 1). The quotations in the table are from Van de Ven and Lifschitz (2013), unless indicated.
Note: [a]Edgeworth (1881), cited in Sen (1977: 317).

action orientation. A study of programme directors found that only openness was (weakly) correlated with project output success.[16]

A second approach from a traits perspective is that of emotional intelligence. Intelligence is usually defined as the ability to reason—a cognitive dimension rather than a personality dimension. Emotional intelligence is therefore the ability to reason about emotions and is correlated with agreeableness in the big five.[17] General intelligence (in comparison to the team) is important for an effective leader,[18] but many suggest that emotional intelligence is as important, if not more important.[19] It can also be suggested that while general intelligence is more importance for the RO and BRS leaders within the decision-making frames, emotional intelligence is relatively more important for the PRS decision-making frame than general intelligence. We present one model of emotional intelligence in Table 3.3. Recent research[20] has shown that output success by leaders from the owner domain of complex projects is correlated with the self-awareness, empathy, and social skills dimensions of emotional intelligence. These correlations are also stronger on more complex projects compared to less complex ones. We would suggest that as the project reaches the outer dimensions of the SPO Diamond shown in Figure 2.6, then judging becomes more and more important. We should also note that emotional intelligence also has a dark side[21] because the ability to regulate with one's own emotions and to understand others' emotions provide the means to be manipulative in interpersonal relations. Just as with high general intelligence, high emotional intelligence requires ethical integrity for effectiveness—a point to which we return in Chapter 12.

### 3.3.3 The experience of project leaders

While most observers would agree that relevant experience is central to effective leadership, there is relatively little empirical evidence to this effect, presumably due to the challenges in operationalizing such a diverse independent variable.[22] When the dependent variable is narrowed to strategic thinking (arguably an important element in projecting), then general intelligence is the most important contributor, followed by relevant experience.[23] Interestingly, extraversion contributes to the gaining of relevant experience rather than to strategic thinking directly. The implication here is that extraverts are more proactive in seeking out challenging assignments that build up experience. Experience appears to contribute to effective judging, both directly in terms of having been in a similar situation before and therefore have a better sense of what might work, and through the development of intuition, defined as the ability to recognize patterns in ambiguous data.[24] Experience also enables leaders to identify the presence of absence—something that should be happening but is not, such as the dog that did not bark.[25] We will return to this issue of experience for the development of project leaders in Chapter 12.

Table 3.2  The big five psychological traits

| Personality trait | Description |
| --- | --- |
| Openness to experience | High: intellectually curious, open to emotion, and willing to try new things. Low: perseveres, pragmatic; data-driven; dogmatic and closed-minded. |
| Conscientiousness | High: focused; prefers planned rather than spontaneous behaviour. Low: flexible and spontaneous; sloppy and unreliable. |
| Extraversion | High: enjoys interacting with people, full of energy; enthusiastic and action-orientated; creative; assertive. Low: quiet energy levels, low-key, deliberate, less involved in the social world. |
| Agreeableness | High: values getting along with others, generally considerate, kind, generous, trusting, and trustworthy, helpful; willing to compromise interests with others. Low: places self-interest above getting along with others; generally unconcerned with others' well-being; often competitive or challenging. |
| Neuroticism | High: tendency to experience negative emotions, such as anger, anxiety, or depression; emotionally reactive and vulnerable to stress; moody. Low: less easily upset and less emotionally reactive; calm, emotionally stable, and free from persistent negative feelings. |

*Sources*: developed from Goldberg (1990) and Judge et al. (2002).

## 3.4 Teaming

So far with the PLM, we have focused on what leaders do and who they are. However leading is a fundamentally relational activity and in a distributed context is only meaningful in relation to a team. This team may be a senior leadership team or a delivery team for a particular task in the work breakdown structure (WBS). Either way, good teaming is an axiom of successful projecting, where teaming is a verb defining 'a dynamic activity, not a bounded, static entity ... largely determined by the mindset and practices of teamwork'.[26] While a group is a number of people engaged in a common activity, teamwork adds value to the group because it is a team.[27] This relational aspect emphasizes the importance of the relating dimension of the PLM, and emotional intelligence as a trait. It is the focus of leader/member exchange (LMX) theory[28] which stresses the importance of the quality of the relationship between the team leader and her members in terms of the perceived equity and empathy of that relationship, which increases both team performance and commitment. An important aspect of LMX quality is the trust developed through the perceived ability of the team leader to be consistent in communications with the team in terms of applications of standards, treatment of team members, and not ignoring key issues.[29]

Table 3.3 Emotional intelligence

| Component | Definition | Hallmarks |
|---|---|---|
| Self-awareness | The ability to recognize and understand one's moods, emotions, and drives, as well as their effect on others | Self-confidence; realistic self-assessment; self-deprecating sense of humour |
| Self-regulation | The ability to control or redirect disruptive impulses and moods and the propensity to think before acting | Trustworthiness and integrity; comfort with ambiguity; openness to change |
| Motivation | Passion for work for reasons that go beyond money or status and the propensity to pursue goals with energy and persistence | Strong drive to achieve; optimism, even in the face of failure; organizational commitment |
| Empathy | The ability to understand the emotional make-up of other people and skill in treating people according to their emotional reactions | Expertise in building and retaining talent; cross-cultural sensitivity; service to client and customers |
| Social skill | Proficiency in managing relationships and building networks and an ability to find common ground and build rapport | Effectiveness in leading change; persuasiveness; expertise in building and leading teams |

*Source*: Goleman (1998).

Effective teaming has been the subject of a large amount of research providing some clear recommendations:[30]

- There is a finite maximum size for a team—most research places this at between five and seven members for project teams. Beyond this, the quality of interpersonal relationships starts to break down, and the team starts to fragment. Teaming is very dependent on high-quality interpersonal relationships, and this can only be fostered through interpersonal contact. This is why many team-building programmes involve the participants getting cold, wet, and muddy. The sense of struggling through together creates these personal bonds, as well as individual self-awareness.

- The team needs a mix of members with complementary competencies. Obviously, these skills are principally the technical competencies required for task execution discussed in Chapter 11. However, the social competences discussed in Chapter 12 are also required, enhanced by a diversity of experience discussed in section 12.4. The team needs to avoid both too homogenous a perspective on how the task should be tackled—known as groupthink[31]—and unmanageable conflict through having little common ground in approaching the task.

- Teams need clear tasks and appropriate incentives in the context of mutual accountability in order to focus their efforts. Teams are no different from individuals in terms of motivation, except that all the team members need to share the same incentives. In particular, rewards such as bonuses and the like need to be on the basis of group output, not individual contributions, as discussed in section 7.3. The team-building process is very much one of the group mutually identifying and owning common tasks; this will always be threatened if the members have different underlying interests.

- Face-to-face interaction is vital for effective teams working under uncertainty, which is why co-location is so important. Virtual communications through tools such as MS Teams are a poor substitute, while email and phone calls fare even worse.[32]

- Creative and problem-solving teams benefit from interpersonal diversity within the team of experience, competencies, and perspectives that requires rotation of personnel. However, it is less clear that this is required for delivery teams, when greater homogeneity brings higher performance.[33] This implies that during project shaping team diversity is important, but during project delivery it is perhaps less important.

- Teams go through a development cycle as they learn to work as a team, often defined as forming, storming, norming, and performing.[34] An important implication of this cycle is that investing in team-building is a cost—initially performance drops below what could be achieved by the group members individually.

- The third Industrial Revolution discussed in section 1.2 brought new technologies to support teaming, such as virtual teaming supported by chat and videoconferencing, and an emphasis on autonomous teams, which is exemplified by the agile teams discussed in section 7.5. However, the fourth Industrial Revolution opens up the possibility of technological agents becoming team members performing tasks such as scheduling teamwork and analysing data, and the development of 'flash teams' formed from gig economy workers in a project ecology, as discussed in section 10.3. In both cases, team leadership and team process design will likely need to become stronger.[35]

---

### Exercise 3.3

Think about those project teams you have worked in and compare the dynamics when all members were co-located with those when some members were dispersed. How did the experience compare?

---

Teams are the basic unit of project organizing, as they are of all organizing,[36] but the application of the teaming principles in SPO is not straightforward. Project teams are very different from other types of management team because they are temporary. The top management team in an owner or supplier organization does not have a determinate life cycle. Similarly, the crew of a fire engine would expect to work together through a number of emergencies and thereby learn to trust each other with their lives. Project teams are convened quickly and know that they will disband in the near future—this is 'teamwork on the fly'.[37] How can project teams go through the development cycle rapidly enough to be effective? There are various aspects to the answer:

- Prior role definitions[38] allow teaming on the fly because members do not have to negotiate their roles in the team. Team members learn appropriate role definitions, particularly around the sharing of their technical expertise prior to joining the team, and play that role as part of the team.
- Clear task-setting for the project team by the senior leadership team is essential, and this is a topic we will return to in section 7.3.
- Co-location in the same office of the team members helps them to move more rapidly through the team formation life cycle and if delivery will mainly rely on virtual teaming, a face-to-face team kick-off event will pay dividends.
- Psychological safety within the team is essential for effective performance, and we will return to this in section 7.6.
- Team-building events can be used to rapidly improve intra-team dynamics.[39]

Another major issue is that projects that require fewer than 10 people are rare. Many require human resources in four figures rather than single figures. Fundamentally, projects are shaped and delivered by teams of teams, not stand-alone teams, and can be thought of as multi-team organizations and their team leaders forming a social network of distributed leadership.[40] Coordination between these teams remains a senior leader responsibility and cannot be relied upon to happen of its own accord;[41] it requires clearly defined project leader roles.

## 3.5  Project leader roles

In large, complex organizations, leading is an inherently distributed activity[42]—no one person can carry the burden alone. This is the essential insight of the incomplete leader model upon which the SPO PLM is based. Leaders need to work with their leadership teams to ensure that the four dimensions are fully covered as appropriate. Leading is also hierarchical in large, complex organizations, with leaders and their teams responsible for the overall direction of the organization as a whole, for discrete subunits within that organization, and leading the teams that deliver to the organization's customers. Projecting involves multiple organizations distributed across the three domains, and so leading is an even more distributed activity than in organizations more generally.

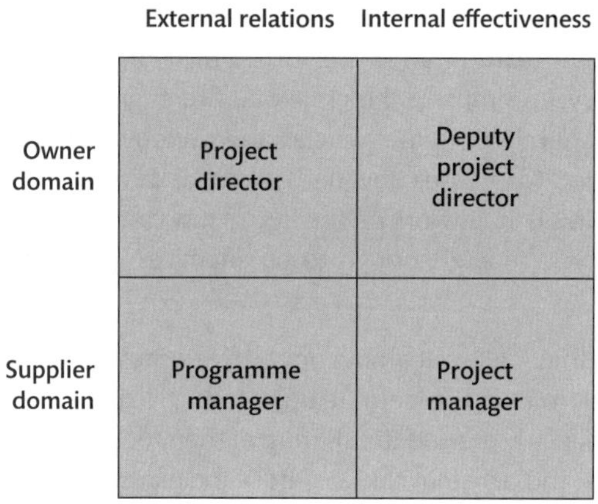

External relations     Internal effectiveness

| | | |
|---|---|---|
| Owner domain | Project director | Deputy project director |
| Supplier domain | Programme manager | Project manager |

Figure 3.2  Distributed leading across the three domains.

*Source*: developed from Winch (2010: figure 15.4); the figure is based on the organization of the Boston Central Artery/Tunnel project.

Hierarchically, we can identify three distinctive levels in project organizing:[43]

- leading the project or programme overall—the project or programme director role;
- leading the principal projects within the programme—the programme manager, senior project manager, or delivery manager role;
- leading the various teams that make up the delivery organization—the project manager role.

Across the three domains there will be many leaders on the project, representing different members of the project coalition. One framework for this distributed leadership is given in Figure 3.2, which shows how those distributed responsibilities are allocated. The two dimensions are the position in the three domains—whether owner or supplier—and the orientation of relating either externally towards stakeholders or internally towards the project delivery organization. Within each member of the project coalition, project leading was split between the more senior manager responsible for external relations and his direct report responsible for internal relations. Vignette 3.3 illustrates another project organization design where, confusingly, three different people had the title of project director.

## 3.6 Summary

Leading is at the heart of the three domains of SPO and therefore guides Cole's hero through the 'Voyage of Life', even if that 'guardian angel' occasionally disappears behind dark clouds. We focused on what leaders do, rather than advocating

## Vignette 3.3   Who was the Tate Modern's project director?

Three different people from three different organizations working on the Tate Modern project had the title of project director and, in effect, shared the project leadership role.

- Project Director 1 was employed by the project owner—the Tate Museum. She was the formal interface between the owner and the supplier domains, who saw her role as being to 'make sure that in 2000 or thereabouts the Tate has a new gallery, a new organisation, and a new institution at Bankside'. Her role was wide-ranging, including fund-raising and relations with the local community, as well as monitoring project progress. She chaired many of the meetings held by the Tate with its principal external advisors.

- Project Director 2 was employed by Stanhope, acting as project management consultants to the owner. He saw his role as 'to help the Tate deliver the project ... a question of managing the design process, and going and buying the construction and making sure the project actually gets built'. The Stanhope role also included advice on property acquisition and the appointment of the design team. He chaired many of the project progress meetings.

- Project Director 3 was employed by Schal, the first-tier supplier for delivery. He argued that 'we like to be involved in the development of the design ... I do think that it is important for us to understand their way of thinking, but equally they need to understand that there is a budget for this job, there is a [schedule] for this job, and there are client brief requirements that have to be maintained, and that's where our role really starts to come into its own'. He chaired many of the meetings with the supply chain.

*Source*: Sabbagh (2000).

a particular style of leadership as defined by one of the memes. *Sense-making* and *relating* provide the information that the leader can use for *projecting* the vision for the project that captures *why* the project is to be done. *Creating* is the process through which *why* is turned into *how*. However, no one person can effectively do all this—the leader is inevitably incomplete and needs to work with a team. All this needs clear judging by the leader, drawing on psychology, framing, and experience. The challenge is multiplied many times as projects grow in size—the kinds of megaprojects which transform our lives typically involve thousands of people. Teaming is therefore the essential complement to leading in SPO. Across the three domains, leading is distributed through networks of leaders horizontally and vertically dispersed. We now turn to focus more closely on the other two dimensions of the PLP—projecting and creating.

# 3.7  Further reading

Klein, G. 1998. *Sources of Power: How People Make Decisions*. Cambridge, MA: MIT Press.
   The seminal review of naturalistic decision-making on how leaders actually make decisions drawing on intuition and experience.

Edmondson, A. C. 2012. *Teaming: How Organizations Learn, Innovate and Compete in the Knowledge Economy.* San Francisco, CA: Jossey-Bass.
Definitive statement of the teaming concept.

Merrow, E. W. and Nandurdikar, N. 2018. *Leading Complex Projects: A Data-Driven Approach to Mastering the Human Side of Project Management.* Hoboken, NJ: Wiley.
Groundbreaking research on leading major projects.

## 3.8  Summary review questions

1. Why do we talk of the 'incomplete leader'?
2. Which are the four dimensions of leading in the SPO PLM?
3. Why is judging at the centre of the SPO PLM?
4. What are the main schools of thought on psychological traits of leading?
5. To what extent is experience important for leading complex projects?

 *Visit the Oxford Learning Link site for this text to find answer guidance to the questions and exercises in this chapter.*

 *Take your learning further by viewing videos relevant to this chapter on the Oxford Learning Link site.*

## Notes

1. Barnard (1968: 283).
2. Zaccaro (2014); a 'meme' is a unit of cultural transmission that replicates and evolves through time (Dawkins, 1976).
3. Müller and Turner (2010).
4. Ancona et al. (2007).
5. Edmondson and Harvey (2017).
6. Weick (1995).
7. Grenny et al. (2007).
8. Schutz (1967: 59).
9. Sergeeva and Winch (2021).
10. Kay and King (2020).
11. Klein and Meckling (1958). They make it clear that they are distinguishing between the application of rationalistic management science tools on projects and their applications in operational situations where much more information is available, and optimization is possible, at least in principle. It

should be noted that Meckling was a strong advocate of the RO model in most business contexts, but not for projects. See his seminal statement of the theory of the firm with an RO micro-foundation in Jensen and Meckling (1976). Please note that we have changed the use of 'Mr' in the original to 'Dr' in support of gender neutrality in the writing.

12. Simon (1955).

13. 11 Ex Ch 781, 1856.

14. Goldberg (1990).

15. *Judge et al. (2002).

16. Merrow and Nandurdikar (2018). While this study has a small sample size, it is important because the dependent variable (leadership effectiveness) is independently verifiable from project outturn data rather than being assessed by others as part of the study.

17. Mayer et al. (2008).

18. Judge et al. (2004).

19. Goleman (2000).

20. Merrow and Nandurdikar (2018). They use a slightly different EI typology from Goleman's.

21. Kilduff et al. (2010).

22. Bettin and Kennedy (1990).

23. Dragoni et al. (2011).

24. Klein (2017).

25. Conan Doyle (1892). In this murder mystery, Sherlock Holmes identified the murderer because the guard dog did not bark at its owner.

26. Edmondson (2012a: 13).

27. Katzenbach and Smith (1993).

28. Gerstner and Day (1997); Martin et al. (2018).

29. Galford and Drapeau (2003).

30. *Stewart (2006).

31. Janis (1972).

32. Pentland (2012).

33. Edmondson and Harvey (2017); Corritore et al. (2020).

34. Tuckman (1965).

35. *Larson and DeChurch (2020).

36. Puranam (2018).

37. Edmondson (2012b).

38. Bechky (2006).

39. Pollack and Matous (2019).

40. Carter and DeChurch (2014).

41. Pentland (2012).

42. House and Aditya (1997).

43. See IPMA certification levels: www.ipma.world/certification/competence/4-l-c-features (accessed 16 August 2021).

44. The Cresta Run is a famous Swiss track dedicated to the Winter Olympic sport of skeleton (i.e. head-first tobogganing at speeds of up to 130 kph.)

## Case 3     Patrick Crotty: Project Director on the Waterloo International Project

'What is distinctive about project management is the time span. It is not unending like normal management. In project work, you bring people together for a specific job and when it is finished they all disband and go elsewhere. Then I move to another project.

When you are working forwards towards the completion of a project, it is like riding on the Cresta Run[44]—it feels as though you are out of control, there is absolutely no way of stopping, and you have got to steer it to stay in that narrow groove all the way to the end. And, almost always, I have done. But it has definitely got no brakes. Nothing stops time.

Another thing that is peculiar to project work is that at different stages of the process, the kinds of problems, the kinds of questions that emerge and that need to be dealt with are different. Yet you need to work with the group of people that you assembled at the start, whose skills may be more suited to one stage than another. You cannot just keep taking people out and putting in more appropriate people because then you lose the benefit of continuity. So I have to be able to judge, more than other types of managers, the significance and the reliability of the advice that I get, depending on who gives it. A lot of that judgement comes down to perception and past experience.

You do have to get up in your helicopter, because it is very easy to get wrapped up in the day-to-day problems. There is so much detail in a vast project like this, you have to come out of that mass of detail occasionally ...

## The project life cycle

Through the life of a project there are a number of quite distinct stages, each with its own challenges and pitfalls, and each requiring different skills from me. To give you an idea of the time frame, I was appointed to the project in the middle of 1989, and I expect to hand over the finished station to the railway operators in May 1993. But within that period there are probably five distinct phases.

## Stage 1

During this stage I was based away from the site, at 100 Piccadilly. There were a number of distinct tasks within this stage. In the first fortnight after being appointed, three of us chopped the job into a series of components, each one of which would become an enquiry, a quotation and an awarded contract. We produced a book called the *Element Scope Definition* which listed each package of tasks which we grouped together to send out, each as one enquiry. We put together some packages, and rapidly awarded them, to do with relocations, and cutting and diverting services and pipes.

A major task in 1990 was building my team. I interviewed everybody who came to work here, even people who already worked for Bovis elsewhere, whereas in the past they would just have arrived and started. I only rejected one or two people, who were inappropriate, but I used the opportunity of the interview to give each person a little inspirational pep-talk.

At that stage of any construction project, you have to make sure your growing team get to know each other and identify whether they can work together. Generally you can make people work together, but inevitably there are stresses and you have to find out what they are, and to make sure everyone is communicating with one another. I had to build my own team, make them pleased to be here and keep them inspired.

You have to make sure that everyone understands the systems that are job-specific. There are lots of systems in big companies like Bovis that are normal and standard, but on every construction project, and probably more on this one than on most, there are job-specific differences. So I had to make that work. We were heavily involved in work with the designers to create enquiries, quotations and the logistics to plan the awards for the main bulk of the project. That was when we concluded the big packages for work to be put out to contract, sent them out as individual enquiries, got back quotes, sifted them, analysed them all and recommended to British Rail with whom they should place their orders for each package.

We were also working quite closely with the people that the project would affect. This is a very big city-centre project with operating railways above, six underground platforms below, which has meant liaising with the London Borough of Lambeth, ambulance, fire and police.

Another key task at this stage was to build up personal credibility with the client and with the designers. Bovis is slightly unusual in not being a builder. Not many people are used to managing contractors, so it was necessary for me to establish credibility and recognition within the design teams ...

In the first stage, we were physically remote from the site and doing lots of work with the designers. It would have looked very small as a project; you would hardly have seen us. There was lots of staff involvement and nothing much to show for it.

## Stage 2

In the first stage I was mostly in an office-type environment; my suit stayed fairly clean. In the second stage we physically moved in and took possession of the footprint of the terminal. The trains stopped running where we were to build and we put hard fences round a much bigger zone of the project. We had progressively to close off some of the routes into the London Underground because we were shifting the underground station to tuck it away under the existing station ...

We did a lot of buying while we had not very serious construction to manage the invitations for contractors to come in, to be interviewed and vetted. In stage two we were doing construction of the shell and we were buying the big mechanical and electrical packages. It is not until you have bought those packages that you can move on from the bidding, competition, handing out of awards and handshaking stage.

Alongside the buying process, the real construction got under way. So my job effectively doubled. I still had the responsibility for what was now a more established team. I got involved in a lot of dialogue with contractors. We started our trade contractors' directors meetings, where I met monthly (now six-weekly) with a main board director for every single contractor—presently this is 30 individuals. Gradually, the physical work on-site gathered momentum, which brought with it the new challenges of safety and operational logistics. When you have a project like that going on in the field, you have contractors with hundreds of men and the surprises and little crises that come along and need handling. We also had to continue our relations with the people who would be affected. We brought in all those other people, like the Highways Authority, the local police and New Scotland

Yard, London Underground, Network SouthEast. We had, for example, to satisfy the Health and Safety Executive that our station roof would be safe. We built a mock-up of it because it was unique and we needed to try out the erection methodology.

## Stage 3

We are now in the third stage where the structure is in place. The big building construction is done and so is the buying. We are now in the business of letting contractors do their designs and then working to co-ordinate one contractor with another. The designer input to the project involves taking the contractor's design and checking it, making sure it complies with specifications. So we are heavily into contractor response and into co-ordination in terms of making things fit—pipes, cables and wires are notoriously designed by different practices to go through spaces that are never big enough or the right shape to take them. So the co-ordination process is heavily reinforced by a Bovis team involved in making sure that pipes are of a certain size. They sometimes have to be made smaller, but with higher pressures and higher volumes that means the pumps have to be higher specification—and you have the problem of the money saved by having smaller pipes being used up on making the pumps a higher capacity. There is also the problem of whose responsibility that is. Did the designer design an impossible system or should the contractor be liable for the cost of the solution? So there is a complex operational and highly technical process going on now.

If you prioritise the process of procurement buying, you buy the structure first and the innards second. It is not until you have bought the innards that you can move on to co-ordination. So typically high-tech co-ordination dominates this third stage. The outcome of this co-ordination process consists of production drawings and the manufacture of things like escalators and life off-site. The high-tech end is not in manufacture yet. So far we have only built one of the fifteen motor control centres. They are the complicated brains of these intelligent building systems. The other fourteen are waiting for the outcome of the co-ordination process which will affect them.

The third stage, then, is all about co-ordination. My role in this third stage is to arrange and chair meetings between the contractors and the consultants. We create the forums for the co-ordination process to happen. It is all very well writing into contracts, "You are responsible for co-ordinating with other contractors", but if you simply beat people over the head as they sit in their separate work-places, that does not get you anywhere. The idea is to make sure that when the contractors go away and draw it and submit it, it all fits together and you can get at it to maintain it. So we have a group of managers whose job it is to facilitate that, and they have to be able to spot the difference between what is technically difficult for a contractor to change and what is simply costly to change. We have to be able to cut across that commercialism.

I have a sort of arbitration role at this stage because it is then that you find out whether the logistics plans are working. Inevitably, you find that some things do not work, some things are missing. There is a lot of potential for quarrels and arguments about what people in other practices and other firms did that was not right. That is normal in the installation phase of construction. There is a tendency for people to blame everyone but themselves and to come back at any criticism with things the other party may have omitted.

One of the things BR have set up is a regular Risk Review, where the leader of each one of the separate practices has a meeting away from the project to "admit things" with no minutes, no notes, no biros or tape recorders. That is helping us a lot. It allows one person to say, "This happened, that happened. I really do not know why." And somebody else will say, "It is because your man did not do that." Some people are responding better and others are not relaxing into it; they are not really participating. We are hoping that the ones who are willing to admit problems in-house without recrimination will encourage others to come out, because we are in that stage where, admit or not, the warts-and-all are going to show.

## Stage 4

During the fourth stage the project will look like a finished building. There will still be contractors doing work in outlying zones, but the big activity will be commissioning, the testing and the setting-to-work of all the electrical and electronic systems. It is all about making intelligent systems talk to each other, proving that they work within their parameters.

In parallel there will be all the things one has not thought of: the mistakes, the defects, remedial work, training the new incoming staff who will operate the terminal. It is rounding out all the accounts. We will be dealing with any financial claims, where contractors think they have done more work than they were contracted to do.

The project can be 99% complete, but in the last three months there is a lot of checking and tying up of loose ends. It is about checking both physically and checking the listings of commissioning schedules. It is about gaining the approval of the Health and Safety Executive, the railway operators, Her Majesty's Customs, the police and fire services. All the incoming occupiers have individually to accept their components: the tram crew, the package handling crew, the Network SouthEast staff. It is all outlined in the Plan for Completion.

## Stage 5

The test of whether you have achieved the fourth stage or not is the architect's Certificate of Practical Completion. That triggers a whole lot of things: for instance, the insurance risk for the project moves; half of the money retained from every payment made to every contractor is released; the station legally begins to be operated by the users; and the one-year defects-liability period begins.

At the end of that one-year period there is a revisiting to inspect and discover whether every defect noticed has been remedied. Generally that period is fairly low-key and would involve only small numbers of Bovis people. My personal input to the defects-liability stage should be quite small, but if the whole thing became fundamentally unworkable or if there were court cases I would be called back. So I do not personally expect to be very heavily involved in that final stage. I would expect to be released from full project duty around June 1993 ...

## Keeping control

We are audited and you must be able to prove to people how you made decisions and why you spent the money. Having said that, when you work for a big organisation, you can go overboard on systems and frameworks. I think you have to be careful of that in project management. You must not let that framework rule everything. You must let the people make the project happen and not have "the system" dominate. There is a job out there that is happening and it is people who are building it.

I have also tried to keep an operational grasp on the project by making myself an essential signatory on the final buying of every single package. I make it my business to be the person who signs for Bovis so I can see who the winning bidder is, and so I know what is going on. That way I am not going to be embarrassed by somebody saying, "I see you have got so-and-so caterers on your project", and for me to say, "Have we?". Also I have some things about which I am a stickler and I sometimes make new members of my team go through hoops before I will sign the buying report—especially if I think they have skipped an important stage in the process that I believe is important.

Increasingly, I am finding that it is more important to keep tabs on people than on systems and programs, which is where I am more naturally drawn. I am changing during this job in a way that I like—if you make a change and it works it reinforces it in you. I hope that I am moving towards being more flexible and having a more humanist approach ...

It is useful for me to keep an image in my mind of how the project is supposed to go and to work hard against any big deflection. It is easy to be too receptive to frightening stories, because lots of people have vested interests in coming to me directly or in a fairly direct route with a smokescreen. People bring you tales of woe. So you have to ask them what makes them think is so different about this project that a particular thing should throw us off track. I will constantly remind people of the program in quite high-powered-level talks. I try to resist alarmism. I am fairly relaxed about relying on my own judgement. When I get disturbing advice, I am not easily thrown off the track.

I am very prepared to set a framework and to make sure that things happen in accordance with it. The framework in this project is primarily guided by safety and time, with cost and quality as controlling influences. Because it is such a highly visible project and because my company knows me, they know that I am prepared to put a lot of pressure on everyone including myself, to stick to that framework. That is both a positive quality and something I have to be careful of: it must not blind me to real issues. But I think that aspect of my contribution is quite important and it is a key to why I finish jobs on time.

I do not leave anything alone. I am always looking into what my people are doing, and not just by meeting them or by reading the correspondence. I go in from different angles. I walk the project, I talk to people, I compare what one person tells me with what I have read in a report. I cross-check all the time and if I find something that does not look quite right, I meddle. I hope I am learning to meddle in a way that supports the people and that does not undermine the lines of authority and their pride in the job ...'

*Source*: Stewart and Barsoux (1994: ch. 4).

## Discussion questions

1. How did Patrick Crotty go about sense-making, relating, and creating on the Waterloo International Project? Why do you think that projecting was less important for him?

2. How did Patrick Crotty build his team?

3. How did he ensure that he stayed in touch with what was happening during delivery?

# 4 Projecting and creating

## 4.1 Introduction: from enabling to acting in leading projects

In Chapter 3, we discussed leading in strategic project organizing (SPO) and introduced the SPO Project Leadership Model (PLM). We now focus in greater detail on the projecting and creating dimensions of that model. The project leader uses *sense-making* and *relating* as the enabling information sources for *projecting* the project mission and then *creating* how that mission will be delivered. Projecting and creating are therefore the action-orientated dimensions of the PLM—'they produce the focus and energy needed to make change happen'.[1] As an important part of *projecting*, we introduce the concept of project narratives, and how they change through the project life cycle. We then distinguish narratives from stories, which are also central to effective project leading. Turning to *creating*, we focus on *innovating* as inherent in project organizing before exploring the role of innovation champions on projects more deeply and we leave *designing* to Chapter 7. We saw in Case 2 how Smit projected by 'telling future truths' and in Case 3 how Crotty carefully designed the processes and procedures that allowed the project to be delivered. In the case for this chapter we show how the Tideway megaproject identity narrative is crafted and their own dynamic interventions to encourage innovating.

## 4.2 Projecting

Projecting in SPO is the process of imagining how a project will be developed and progressed throughout its life cycle, and how private advantage and public benefit will be combined in future value. We distinguish projecting from visioning because the latter is a process within a single organization,[2] whilst projecting mobilizes complex stakeholder networks as well as owner organizations during project shaping. Projects are born through ideas—that 'Awakening' may come in a flash of inspiration or a slow maturation, but in order to transition from 'Awakening' to 'Aspiration' it is shared with others through narratives. Narratives therefore play an enormously important role in projecting by connecting the present with the future,[3] and are the essential means for maintaining and reproducing stability and for promoting or resisting change in and around organizations.[4] The future-orientated nature of project narratives means that they have the potential to change the future,[5] and are performative[6] in the sense that they are words (and other media) that get things done. They are persuasive in nature and are used by project leaders to convince stakeholders to commit financial resources during project shaping and suppliers to mobilize human and technical resources during project delivery.

The project mission is a compelling 'why' statement for the project.[7] In order to develop that mission into a compelling narrative for the project that will motivate staff and suppliers and commit stakeholders, it is usually complemented with other materials that communicate the principles underpinning *how* the project will be done. These include ethical principles, expectations of suppliers, and benefits for stakeholders. For example, the Olympic Delivery Authority published a strategy which outlined the project mission as 'the overarching vision for the London 2012 Olympic Games and Paralympic Games is to host inspirational, safe and inclusive Games and leave a sustainable legacy for London and the UK'.[8] The project narrative therefore ties together the projecting and creating dimensions of the PLM. It can be communicated in spoken (e.g. talks, presentations), written (reports, business cases), and visual (e.g. videos, pictures, PowerPoint packs) forms, as shown in Figure 4.1. It is also iterated and reiterated to many different audiences (internal teams and external stakeholders) and restated in many different ways throughout the project life cycle. For the project narrative to give common meaning to common purpose, project leaders are 'on message' in their conversations with suppliers and stakeholders. Corporate communications tend to be consistent with this message and carefully designed to reach their diverse intended audiences. Visual symbolic narratives are chosen carefully too, such as the tank of fish from Sydney Harbour in the middle of the project office for the Sydney waste water project which symbolized the ambition to remove storm-driven effluent from Sydney Harbour in preparation for the 2000 Olympic Games.[9]

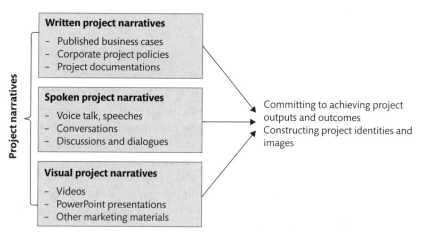

Figure 4.1  Media for project narratives.

*Source*: authors.

## 4.3 Project narratives

In order to communicate the project mission, project leaders craft a narrative that inspires employees, mobilizes stakeholders, excites partners, attracts customers, and engages influencers—one that defines the answer to the question 'why', communicates the strategy, and embodies the project's image and identity.[10] The project narrative is used to explain why the project exists and what makes it unique, and the value and relationships it creates, and communicates these to both internal project team members and external stakeholders. In effect, it creates a 'project DNA' that persists for the life cycle. This in turn helps to create a shared purpose for the team and a projection of its purposeful and successful delivery. In the Eden case in Chapter 2, credibility for the narrative was achieved through both Tim Smit's track record with the Heligan project and Ball's networks amongst the right people in the right places. Novelty was achieved through the scale of the vision generated—Eden was, and remains, unique. It was this novelty combined with credibility which convinced many of the stakeholders to commit to the project and for suppliers to commit resources early without any assurance that they would be recompensed.

The project narrative thereby forms a reference narrative[11] which is central to how leaders project under high levels of uncertainty. The future is inherently unknowable, yet projecting involves trying to shape that unknowable future in alignment with the project mission. Those leaders may be projecting their personal vision in the case of entrepreneurs such as Elon Musk, a corporate vision in the case of corporate leaders, or a vision of a better society in the case of politicians. Musk's passion for cars and space, and passion for innovation, led to the creation of Tesla and SpaceX. The project narrative acts as a reference point against which the resilience of the project mission can be tested. This resilience testing can be done in many ways, such as scenario analysis as 'stories of the future'[12] and evaluation narratives of success and failure on earlier projects. The reference narrative thereby provides the criteria for judging how the responses to threats to the project will be calibrated and opportunities seized.

Project narratives do not emerge into the world fully formed. Just as the process of shaping the project mission can be fraught and iterative over months, or even years, crafting the project narrative that supports that mission can be equally fraught—indeed, the two are symbiotic. Ante-narratives[13] (before-narratives) are narratives that are not yet fully formed as project narratives and are still competing for the attention of stakeholders. Ante-narratives are what come before a coherent and persuasive reference narrative, and, in effect, form alternative future possibilities of our world that can be created by projecting. Ante-narratives are often presented in speeches, or published in newspaper articles and social media blogs, as well as being the stuff of internal strategy debates within the owner organization before the coherent reference narrative is formed about the project and the project mission becomes succinctly stated.

In contrast to the project narratives articulated by those championing the project, counter-narratives can be defined as 'the stories which people tell and live which offer resistance to, either implicitly or explicitly to dominant cultural narratives'.[14] The distinctive characteristics of counter-narratives are oppositional to the project reference narrative. Focusing on counter-narratives enables us to capture some of the political, social, and cultural complexities and tensions in projecting and capture the diversity of stakeholder positions in relation to the project narrative which are explored in section 5.6. The dynamic interaction between ante-narratives, reference narratives, and counter-narratives is part of the power game around project shaping.

There are always counter-narratives to the dominant project narrative and ongoing interactions between them. Archival data such as newspapers and Twitter messages can be used as naturalistic sources[15] to help us learn about counter-narratives articulated by external stakeholders and how project teams deal with these counter-narratives and adapt the reference narrative in response. This dynamic particularly affects megaprojects, due to their significant spatial impact generating conflicting interests between stakeholders. The promoters of a megaproject are interested in supporting its completion, while the protesters are interested in derailing the megaproject. For example, Extinction Rebellion, a global protest movement, is fully opposed nationally and locally to High Speed Two (HS2) in the United Kingdom. Alongside Stop HS2, Extinction Rebellion organized a walk of 200 km along the proposed railway line in June 2020. There is a continuous process of interaction between the promoter and protester narratives as the narrative of the project mission evolves in practice, as can be seen in Vignette 4.1. In sum, there are multiple narratives in project organizing (e.g. reference narratives, ante-narratives, counter-narratives) and these are created, communicated, maintained, and promoted in projects through the life cycle.

Project reference narratives create and project certain futures and not other futures. Such narratives and the process of narrating have important implications for internal and external perceptions of the project. *Project identity* is conveyed internally to the project team and the supply chain, whereas *project image* is projected to external stakeholders such as investors, campaigners, and policymakers.[16] **Project identity narratives** are about what the project managers tell the team in order to achieve shared understanding and vision; they are about a sense of what the delivery organization's purpose is that creates its 'DNA'. Project leaders communicate a narrative about project identity to the project team. This commitment is based on the membership of the group combined with the emotional value that is attributed to this membership.[17]

**Project image narratives** stimulate stakeholders to commit themselves to the project.[18] Constructing a favourable image is of paramount importance as the inability to garner legitimacy and support of external stakeholders can affect the delivery of project outputs. Projects require convincing narratives to build strong brand attributes and brand loyalty, which is why it is important to brand the project with

Vignette **4.1**    Reference narrative and counter-narratives on High Speed 2

HS2 is a £100 bn railway from London to Birmingham and the North of England scheduled to open in phases from 2029 onwards. Trains will travel at up to 360 km/h on 550 km of track. The key benefits proposed by HS2 are: 'HS2 will form the backbone of our rail network'; 'HS2 will directly connect 8 out of 10 of Britain's largest cities'; 'HS2 is an investment in Britain's future'; 'HS2 will create 30,000 jobs'; 'HS2 will be a catalyst for economic growth'.

There are four main themes in the counter-narratives:

**Environmental impact**: 'The proposed route could cause serious and significant impacts on the landscape of the Chilterns' (National Trust Director, 11 March 2011).

**Financial case**: 'The cost is enormous at a time when public finances are under severe strain, and the business plan is based on over-optimistic forecasts of passengers' (academic expert, 14 November 2010).

**Local stakeholder**: 'I'm just gutted, and it will be horrifying if it happens. It would ruin the farm and our land won't be worth anything' (local farmer, 15 March 2010).

**Strategic case**: 'Adding carriages to trains and lengthening platforms would ease overcrowding, and upgrading existing trains and tracks would allow trains to run at speeds up to [290km/h]. Trains at this speed could also run along new tracks which could be built along existing railways or motorways and minimise damage to the environment' (AGHAST: Action Groups against High Speed Rail, 14 November 2010).

Those in favour of the megaproject counter with an appeal to the future, not the past: 'It's not easy, but the idea of not doing it is utter madness. Do we want to live in the 19th century?' (pro HS2 campaigner, 10 January 2012).

*Source*: authors' current research.

a well-crafted external image from the start[19] and hence crafting a project image narrative as part of project shaping is essential for the successful delivery of projects from an external stakeholder management perspective.

**Exercise 4.1**

Think about a project you would like to do in the future. What would the project reference narrative look like?

## 4.4 Project narratives through the project life cycle

We now turn to exploring how narratives change through the project life cycle and how project leaders can adapt to those changes; the relative importance of project image and project identity narratives changes is shown in Figure 4.2. During project shaping, ante-narratives compete for attention and resources and

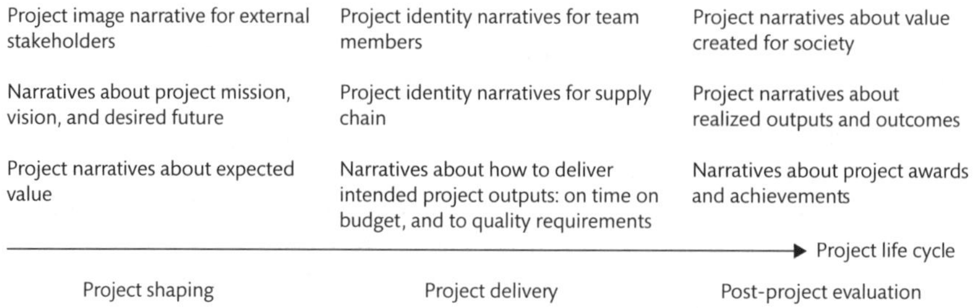

| Project image narrative for external stakeholders | Project identity narratives for team members | Project narratives about value created for society |
| Narratives about project mission, vision, and desired future | Project identity narratives for supply chain | Project narratives about realized outputs and outcomes |
| Project narratives about expected value | Narratives about how to deliver intended project outputs: on time on budget, and to quality requirements | Narratives about project awards and achievements |

➤ Project life cycle

| Project shaping | Project delivery | Post-project evaluation |

Figure 4.2  Project narratives through the life cycle of a project.

*Source*: Sergeeva and Winch (2021: figure 1).

counter-narratives can also start to form. From this dynamic, a clearly dominant project reference narrative may emerge. Our research suggests[20] that narratives which espouse a desired future are more likely to emerge as dominant than ones which are seen as merely solving current problems. Thus, at the project-shaping phase of the life cycle, an image-shaping narrative is articulated with the purpose of projecting the desired future to external stakeholders. This future-orientated narrative about project image and expected value tends to be optimistic. Once the project image narrative has stabilized, the project can move through the project peripety from shaping to delivery, as shown in Figure 2.7; indeed, we suggest that unless the project reference narrative has stabilized from amongst the competing ante-narratives and successfully muted counter-narratives, it is unwise to mobilize the larger resources required for delivery.

During the project delivery phase, the delivery identity narrative becomes more important, articulated by the owner project team and shared with the project-based firms (PBFs) in the supplier domain. In a project coalition, different organizational identities from different organizations coalesce in the temporary delivery organization, and so forming a delivery narrative about the project identity—or project DNA—becomes important for mobilizing effort in one direction. Once the project is completed, narratives about value created for society and narratives about realized outputs and outcomes form the basis for the post-project evaluation **narrative**. These evaluation narratives can be dynamic over time. For example, whilst the Sydney Opera House, completed 10 years late and 14 times over budget, was initially dubbed a 'great planning disaster', it created economic, cultural, and brand value for Australia. The value of Sydney Opera House became established in Australia's sense of national identity, and as a symbol and economic resource.[21] Narratives about project awards and achievements can be shared more widely through social media in the form of learning legacy websites and industry awards ceremonies such as the annual Association for Project Management (APM) Project Management Awards.Project reference narratives are crafted in order to be convincing and appealing to oneself, the project team, and to stakeholders, as well as demonstrating long-term value through project outputs and outcomes. In this sense, they are

**Vignette 4.2**   Image-shaping and evaluation narratives: Sochi 2014 Olympics

In February 2014, the city of Sochi on the Russian Black Sea coast hosted the XXII Winter Olympic Games. At the start of 2013, it was the largest construction site in the world, with almost 96,000 workers and a total cost of £36 bn. When, in July 2007, Russia was awarded the right to host the mega-event, the image narrative for Sochi 2014 was to be hosted in a environmentally sustainable manner with carbon neutrality, zero waste, and extensive environmental impact assessments in place.

One of the most important aspects of the project mission was special attention to the post-Olympic use of the structure. The Fisht Stadium was designed taking into account not only the possibility of holding events related to the 2014 Olympics, but also subsequent opportunities. The stadium was re-opened in 2016 as an open-air football stadium to host matches as part of the 2017 FIFA Confederations Cup and 2018 FIFA World Cup.

In 2009, the Sochi-2014 Environmental Strategy was approved for organizing a 'green' Winter Olympics in the city. The strategy was composed of four themes, each of which was given a symbolic name: 'Games in harmony with nature'; 'Games without climate change'; 'Games without waste'; and 'Enlightenment Games'. However, not all of the goals stated in the strategy led to the expected results. One post-project evaluation report suggests that there was a failure in meeting essential sustainability goals. Extensive construction led to the wholesale destruction of local ecology and hydrology. There was evidence of dumping of construction waste and discharge of toxic fluids, making the water undrinkable for thousands of residents. There was also damage to the Mzymta, a major mountain stream in the Sochi area. The image-shaping and post-project evaluation narratives were not aligned.

*Sources*: authors' current research; Müller (2015).

performative because projecting changes the future. Project success, we suggest, depends, in part, on the development and articulation of a convincing project narrative during both shaping and delivery stages of the project life cycle. As projects are very complex and uncertain temporal endeavours, they entail a continuous process of negotiation between different narratives. These different project narratives (e.g. the image-shaping narrative, identity delivery narrative, project evaluation narrative) all play their roles through the project life cycle and beyond (see Figure 4.2).

## 4.5  Crafting the delivery organization's DNA

The challenge for the project leader is that the owner and each of the supplier organizations making up the project coalition has its own organizational identity. These organizational identities vary systematically between the different types of supplier typically found deployed on a project. In the project coalition that forms the delivery organization, different organizational identities are merging together, and a project leader has to craft the project's delivery identity. Cases 2 and 4 show the ways in which this can be done. Thus, leading projects is multi-identity management in which the project leader tries to develop a distinctive project delivery identity narrative—often called its DNA—in a number of complementary ways:[22]

1. What is noticed and measured—only a limited number of aspects of organizational performance can be actively monitored by the project leadership team. Clear messages by the team regarding those measurements will help project coalition members to identify what is important on this particular project. The categories of performance that stimulate compliments, rather than being taken for granted, help project team members to focus their efforts.

2. The project leader's response to critical incidents helps coalition members to identify what is really driving the leader. If the project leader is passionate about an issue, then failures on that issue will stimulate a stronger reaction against those that fail.

3. Deliberate coaching—again, project leaders cannot provide a role model in all areas of performance. Those in which they choose to be supportive and provide coaching and mentoring will send messages regarding what is important.

4. Explicit and overt criteria for the selection of suppliers—these will send messages regarding what is important. It will also be necessary to remove individuals or suppliers that fail to perform on the most valued criteria.

5. Organizing project review meetings so that open and honest debate are encouraged through psychological safety as discussed in Case 6, rather than finding who is to blame for the latest disruption to schedule. Some project managers have found organizing special off-the-record meetings, where nobody is held to account for what they say, to be an important way of generating a cooperative identity within the project coalition—see Case 3.

6. Engaging in a formal management development programme.[23]

Through crafting a project identity narrative, leaders of projects create the sense of common purpose by which projects successfully deliver outputs and outcomes. On the larger, more complex projects, a DNA of openness and readiness to address issues is vital as threats to the project emerge from complexity as 'unk-unks' (defined in section 2.4) hove into view during delivery. In meeting those challenges, continual reference to the project narrative as the reference narrative for the project is required.

## 4.6 Stories and storytelling

Storytelling has a long history within the study of organizing.[24] The contribution of 'storytelling organization' research is in understanding the sense-making that takes place in pragmatic ways between storytellers and their audiences. Some stories are concerned with specific events or people, while others take the form of biographies.[25] In SPO, we define storytelling as the activity of telling and sharing stories about personal experiences, life-events, and situations. We distinguish between storytelling and narrating, arguing that the first is more personalized, entertaining, and emotional in nature, whereas the latter is directed more towards coherence, stability, and performative intent.[26] Leading a project is a very challenging and exciting experience. Stories and storytelling, and a sense of humour, are important competencies for project leaders. They are therefore 'fragments of organizational discourse that construct identities and interests in time and space'.[27]

Stories are informed by personal experiences, providing the listener with the opportunity to understand the life world of the storyteller. Stories are told from the point of view of the storyteller or another individual or group. They are frequently considered as an integral part of project leading, and the means of connecting past experiences, present issues and future aspirations. Stories imply an ability to make sense of past memories, respond to new experiences in the present, and to use what has been learned in ongoing processes that shape future aspirations and imaginings.

Storytelling provides a means of making sense of shared experiences, and sharing stories is an essential part of project organizing. Storytelling is frequently seen as a useful soft skill that is especially valuable for project leaders. We suggest that storytelling is best understood as a dynamic process that is continuously (re)created through the elaboration, contestation, and exchange of stories. By telling stories, individuals seek to bolster their personal identities, in the eyes of both themselves and others.[28] Stories are inherently social and emotional in the way people seek empathy and understanding from others when they craft personal identities. Self-identity often crucially hinges upon the roles which individuals ascribe to themselves.[29]

Project leaders communicate to the project team and external audiences by sharing stories: personal, professional, funny, and entertaining stories. When project leaders visit project teams, they share stories, and also when they are interviewed and give speeches. Stories help to provide an essential entertaining, social, and emotional engagement with people. As one project leader put it, 'You have to realize early on that your persona, your personality, your DNA will become associated with HS2.'[30] In the vignettes we use in this book, we have various examples of stories shared by project leaders, often captured in direct quotations.

---

### Exercise 4.2

Think about examples of storytelling on projects; how were the stories shared across the project?

---

## 4.7 Creating: designing and innovating through the project life cycle

Creating in the PLM has two distinct elements—*designing* how the project organization will deliver the outputs and outcomes, which will be the focus of Chapters 7-10, and *innovating*, which is our focus here. For SPO, we define innovating along the novelty dimension of the SPO Diamond in Figure 2.6. That could be a product, process, or service new to the specific context, not necessarily to the world, that could have economic, environmental, or societal benefits for the owner and its stakeholders.[31] Innovating is increasingly recognized as an integral part of project organizing. SPO, we suggest, is fundamentally about innovating,[32] because it is about problem-solving, whether by setting out to advance technology or by combining existing technologies in a novel way to deliver the owner's project mission. Innovating can only be achieved collaboratively across organizations by the people within them, and orchestrating such collaboration is one of the great challenges of SPO. Most PBFs have a small team of formal innovation managers and informal innovation champions.

Research on the Heathrow Terminal 5 and Crossrail projects working closely with project leaders has created many insights into project innovating. The conclusion is that 'strong leadership with a coherent vision as well as the use of performance indicators and organizational change programs are essential to support new behaviours required to successful outcomes'.[33] From the Crossrail research,[34] a framework has emerged for innovating on projects structured around four windows of opportunity through the life cycle, which we suggest is widely applicable in project organizing:

1. **Bridging window** during project shaping when innovative ideas are generated, and learning and practices from other projects are used;

2. **Engaging window** when tendering and contractual processes are used by the owner to encourage suppliers to develop innovative ideas;

3. **Leveraging window** when all the parties involved are mobilized during project delivery to develop innovative ideas, new technologies, and improvements;

4. **Exchanging window** during post-project review when innovative ideas can be combined with those of other projects in the innovation ecosystem. Figure 4.3 shows how this works across the project portfolio.

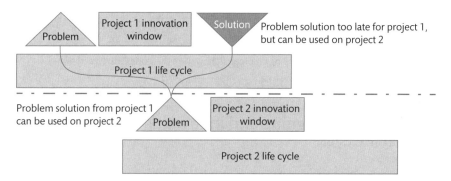

Figure 4.3 The exchanging window in project innovating.

*Source*: developed from DfT (2017: figure 4).

## 4.8 Policy-driven innovating on projects

We will discuss the concept of a project-based sector in Chapter 6. Here, we want to focus in a little more detail on the innovation process on projects, and how innovations are diffused to other projects in the sector and beyond. We argue that innovating on projects is fundamentally about problem-solving in order to deliver on the owner's project mission—the more complex that mission is, the more challenging that will be. There is, however, another driver for innovating in project-based—and indeed all—economic sectors, that is, policy initiatives by government to address particular social issues and the Sustainable Development Goals (SDGs) grand challenges discussed in section 1.1. For instance, concerns for personal privacy and child protection in the online app sector are obliging owners such as Facebook to generate new systems and software for their apps that meet these regulatory requirements or government exhortations.

Similarly, in sectors such as construction, which is responsible for an enormous proportion of carbon generation in its processes and products,[35] strategies for decarbonization of both project delivery and the project outcomes are required. This may happen in two ways, as shown in Figure 4.4. One approach is that owners respond directly to government initiatives and include carbon-related requirements in their project mission during the Appraise phase shown in Figure 2.7 and work with suppliers during the Select phase to choose the most appropriate technologies— hence the dotted line in Figure 4.4. Alternatively, suppliers advise that the project mission can only be achieved within the current regulatory environment by including carbon-reducing technologies. In either case, PBFs implement carbon-reducing technologies on delivery projects and learn from that implementation for their future projects. In this way, PBFs serve as 'middle actors'[36] between government policy initiatives and owners projecting, for instance, a carbon-free future.

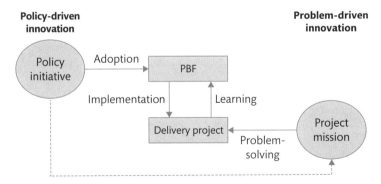

Figure 4.4  Policy-driven and problem-driven innovation on projects.
*Sources*: developed from Winch (1998: figure 1) and Winch (2005: figure 5.2).

## 4.9 Innovation champions

Project leaders play an important role in stimulating innovation and generating an identity of being 'innovative'. Innovation managers can be given responsibility for developing innovation strategies, but it is not sufficient to have a team of innovation managers that lead innovations across the business. Innovation managers encourage everyone in the organization to understand and believe in innovation, to perform and behave consistently, and this is therefore the responsibility of the senior leaders of the owner or supplier organization. Innovative identity is very important for stimulating organizational and technical innovations by PBFs on projects. Similarly, the identity of the innovative owner organization tends to be based on empowering and motivating suppliers and their teams. Owners may employ champions, who have the ability to spend some time working across the owner organization, to identify and bring forward new ideas, engage people, and think about doing things differently.

In this process, innovation champions play a crucial role in stimulating and promoting innovations in projects. In their informal roles, an innovation champion can be anyone in an organization who is 'willing to take risks by enthusiastically promoting the development and/or implementation of an innovation inside a corporation through a resource acquisition process without regard to the resources currently controlled'.[37] Typically, however, they are senior leaders of the organization, as shown in Vignette 4.3, which explores innovation championing in two new products—one that has transformed our world, and one that has not, despite high hopes. Owners and suppliers employ champions who enthusiastically promote innovations, and support and facilitate organizational changes. The role of innovation champions is to contribute to the change process by facilitating, enabling, initiating and advocating change; their role is context dependent.

---

### Exercise 4.3

Have you ever played the role of innovation champion in a business or social context? Do you see yourself or someone in your team as an innovation champion?

---

Vignette **4.3**    Innovation champions in new product development (NPD)

The Sony Walkman launched in 1979 and became so popular that the name became generic for portable media players. It was a wholly new product category and Sony dominated the market for over 20 years—as the Chief Executive Officer (CEO) Morita put it, 'the market research is all in my head; we create markets'. During the transition from the third to the fourth Industrial Revolutions, the Walkman inspired the Apple iPod, which launched in 2001. This rapidly took market share from the Walkman as Sony struggled to move to fully digital portable music players. The iPod's design team went on to design the iPhone, launched in 2007, and the two products have now effectively merged, providing affordances undreamt of in 1979. This series of projects over 50 years, championed by proactive CEOs and backed by creative marketing campaigns, have been outstanding successes and repeatedly transformed successful outputs into triumphant outcomes that have really changed our world.

The Segway launched in 2001 with a strapline that it 'will be to the car what the car was to the horse and buggy', offering a revolution in powered personal transportation that found very limited appeal in reality. It was also championed by an entrepreneurial CEO, backed by creative marketing campaigns, and reconfigured existing technologies to new purposes. It was also a successful output, but lack of market appeal meant that the desired outcomes were not achieved. Segway was sold to a Chinese competitor in 2015, and production ceased in 2020. It remains to be seen whether its successor personal mobility technology—the electric scooter—will share the same fate. Innovation champions were key to both the Walkman/iPhone and Segway developments but were outstandingly successful in the first case and very unsuccessful in the second.

*Sources*: Shenhar and Dvir (2007); Wikipedia (accessed 27 May 2020).

An important innovation incentive is personal recognition. We all like winning awards and getting recognition from peers, in addition to financial rewards. Recognizing contributions to organizational and technical innovations can give its members a sense of wanting to do it again. Internal and external recognition of innovations is really important for sustaining innovation in the longer term.[38] For more radical innovation, there is typically a higher value of reward. Telling stories about successful innovation by the leaders of owner organizations and PBFs, whether innovations were generated by individuals or groups, enhances interest and attention from other firms.[39] Through recognition, owners and PBFs can enhance their reputation and identity as successful innovative organizations.

## 4.10 Summary

In this chapter, we explored the projecting and creating dimensions of the SPO PLM. We first explored projecting and the importance of the project narrative as a reference narrative which binds these two dimensions of the PLM together. We considered the nature and role of project narratives and how project leaders can craft, articulate, and use them when leading complex projects. We also outlined different types of narratives in relation to the project life cycle and the importance of storytelling as the emotional and personal aspect of project narratives. We then turned to the creating dimension and explored the processes of innovating on projects and the particular challenges it brings, as well as the importance of innovation champions.

This chapter concludes the first part of our book. In Chapter 2, we presented the core concepts of SPO—the Three Domains Model, the SPO Diamond Model, and the SPO Life Cycle Model. We also clarified the definitions of uncertainty and complexity that we will use in SPO. In Chapters 3 and 4, we dug deeper into the unifying core of the Three Domains Model—leading—to focus on what leaders do as problem-solvers rather than who they are. We then presented the PLM and its two enabling dimensions of sense-making and relating and its two action dimensions of projecting and creating. In Chapter 5, we turn to the three domains of project organizing, starting with the owner domain.

## 4.11  Further reading

Brown, K. A., Ettenson, R., and Hyer, N. L. 2011. 'Why every project needs a brand (and how to create one)'. *MIT Sloan Management Review*, 52(4): 61–68.
Discusses the importance of the project 'brand' as a narrative to mobilize resources for a project.

Davies, A., Dodgson, M., Gann, D. M., and MacAulay, S. C. 2017. 'Five rules for managing large, complex projects'. *MIT Sloan Management Review*, 59(1): 73–78.
Incisive overview of the challenges of innovating on megaprojects.

Sergeeva, N. and Winch, G. M. 2021. 'Project narratives that potentially perform and change the future'. *Project Management Journal*, 52(3): 264–277.
Differentiates between different project narratives in relation to a project life cycle and demonstrates them in three case studies.

## 4.12  Summary review questions

1. What is the connection between projecting and creating in the SPO PLM?
2. To what extent is innovating important in SPO?
3. What is the difference between narrating and storytelling in SPO?
4. How do project narratives change over the project life cycle?
5. What is the role of leading in crafting project narratives?

 *Visit the Oxford Learning Link site for this text to find answer guidance to the questions and exercises in this chapter.*

 *Take your learning further by viewing videos relevant to this chapter on the Oxford Learning Link site.*

# Notes

1. Ancona et al. (2007: 97).
2. O'Connell et al. (2011); Senge (1990).
3. Emirbayer and Mische (1998).
4. Vaara et al. (2016: 496). There is a considerable literature on narratives and organization, which is well summarized in this text.
5. Sergeeva and Winch (2021).
6. Austin (1962).
7. Winch (2010); Brown et al. (2013).
8. ODA (2007).
9. *Clegg et al. (2002).
10. *Kaplan and Orlikowski (2014).
11. Kay and King (2020).
12. Coyle (2003: 315).
13. Boje (2008).
14. Andrews (2004).
15. Ninan and Sergeeva (2021).
16. Sergeeva and Winch (2021).
17. Veenswijk et al. (2010).
18. Van Marrewijk (2017).
19. Olander and Landin (2008); Brown et al. (2011).
20. Sergeeva and Winch (2021).
21. Hall (1982); Murray (2004).
22. This list is developed from Schein (1992).
23. See Lownds (1998), for example.
24. Boje (2008); Gabriel (2000); Ibarra and Lineback (2005).
25. Drouin et al. (2021).
26. Sergeeva and Green (2019).
27. Vaara and Tienari (2011: 370).
28. Alvesson et al. (2008); Baumeister and Newman (1994); Brown (2015).
29. Lord and Hall (2005); Ashforth (2019); Brown (2015).
30. Cited in Sergeeva and Davies (2021: 54).
31. Damanpour et al. (2009).
32. Davies (2014).
33. Davies et al. (2009: 121).
34. *Davies et al. (2014).
35. Thirty-nine per cent of energy-related carbon emissions when upstream generation is included: UNEP (2020).
36. Janda and Parag (2013).
37. Jenssen and Jørgensen (2004: 65).
38. Cousin (1998).
39. Denning (2005).

**Case 4**   Crafting the project identity narrative and innovating on Tideway

Tideway is a major player in the overall upgrade of the London's Victorian sanitation systems. It is building the 25 km Tideway tunnel under London's River Thames that aims to prevent the tens of millions of tonnes of untreated waste that currently pollute the river each year due to storm water overflow. The scheme is the biggest investment in London's sewage system since 1875 and the largest water infrastructure project in United Kingdom. Thames Water, London's water utility, created a new independently regulated company, Bazalgette Tunnel Ltd, to be owner and operator of Tideway, financed largely by pension funds because the project was too big for its own balance sheet. Construction started in 2016 and is expected to complete in 2025. There are 24 construction sites in London, spanning from Acton in west London to Beckton in the east. Tideway is Bazalgette's brand for the megaproject and does not include 'tunnel' in order to highlight the project mission and its outcome, which is to address the environmental problem of discharging waste matter into the tidal River Thames, rather than the physical output of a tunnel.

The image-shaping narrative of Tideway was always strong as an environmental improvement project to (a) protect the Thames tideway natural ecosystem; (b) reduce pollution from sewage-derived litter; and (c) protect the health of recreational river users. However, the delivery identity narrative was missing. Tideway therefore launched the 'Our Space' initiative and asked employees to reflect on what they were doing on this megaproject in that open meeting space. This included a whiteboard wall map of the River Thames on which to brainstorm ideas. This generated many keywords, and a strong theme emerged as 'reconnecting Londoners with the River Thames'. This identity narrative was captured in a cartoon of all the activities enabled for Londoners on the Thames.

The CEO of Tideway spent 50 per cent of his time on this crafting during the early months of project delivery, playing a crucial role in forming the megaproject's identity narrative. He has also delivered a number of presentations about Tideway and its identity at various external industry and academic events. The CEO is perceived as an inspirational leader, who is reflective and a good storyteller, telling us that:

> I was keen to champion early career professionals to form a collective to consider what they might like to do to further their progress, but also to contribute to the things that we do in the industry. And almost to encourage them to challenge and to question and to really allow them to believe it is OK as a less experienced person to say: 'Why do we do this?' My worries are by the time you get into a position of authority when you can set directions and you can make changes you have forgotten half of the things; you now become blind to some of the things that always were logical. You lose some of that natural inquisitiveness that you have when you are younger. Things that do not make sense and you question it. I was keen to encourage younger people to be confident enough, and to work as a collective to find ways of contributing to changes and how we do things.

The CEO was also keen to encourage early career professionals to be heavily engaged with the innovation programme at Tideway. Tideway is the first megaproject to use the UK industry-wide infrastructure industry innovation Partnership (i3P) platform (http://www.i3p.org.uk, accessed 17 August 2021). The i3P platform builds on the success of

Innovate 18, Crossrail's innovation programme containing more than 400 innovations over a three-year period. I3P's vision is to establish a driver for innovation in the UK infrastructure sector and to provide a mechanism for strategically directing innovation to address the challenges facing the sector. I3P's vision is to create a 'safe space' to identify areas for industry improvement, share innovative ideas, enable members to collaborate on projects that drive value, and establish a collaborative culture of innovation across the owner and supplier domains. Tideway has a team of innovation managers to manage its innovation programme.

The approach to innovating in Tideway is to encourage and stimulate innovating across the supplier domain. The reasons for encouraging innovating in the programme are multiple. First, the research for novel ideas aims to increase project performance in terms of schedule and budget savings. Second, it aims to create beneficial effects for stakeholder communities, making construction works safer, shorter, and less disruptive. Third, innovation is seen as a catalyst to create a world-class workforce which benefits not only Tideway, but also the sector overall. Finally, by proving capability to deliver projects more quickly and effectively through innovation, Tideway aims to attract future investments.

Tideway was granted access to Crossrail's Innovate 18 portal, where it gathers ideas and learns from Crossrail's experiences. A number of best practices were captured from Crossrail (see Vignette 7.3), such as the Central Budget Model to fund ideas and the network of innovation champions. Tideway developed a slightly different innovation process from Crossrail, which consists of a specialist function within Tideway that benefits from a stand-alone budget dedicated to supporting innovating. Not only innovations that can deliver direct benefits to Tideway are selected, but also out-of-scope innovations are considered and shared, if deemed valuable to other organizations within Tideway's network. Compared to Crossrail, another innovative element of Tideway's strategy is the innovation network, where it is developing relationships with organizations outside the construction sector so that Tideway can benefit from the application of existing practices or technologies from other sectors.

In order to align participants' interests across the whole project coalition, support integration, and motivate collaborative behaviours, alliance agreements were developed to enable loss and gain sharing across the commercial interface. These support the innovation journey, and apply to the Optimised Contractor Involvement process, where nominated suppliers are asked to provide inputs to improve the current design with the aim of driving efficiency and innovation into the design and also construction methods. Different forms of incentives and reward schemes are used to motivate innovative ideas from both the suppliers and the owner organization itself. Yet alongside formal incentives, leaders need to create the right culture to support the innovation process, helping people to develop a natural inclination to creative thinking and, at the same time, ensuring tolerance of failure. Leading by example and storytelling were instrumental in achieving these objectives.

To celebrate the spirit of Tideway innovation, it hosted the Tideway Innovation Forum at the original studios where the BBC TV series *Dragons' Den* (http://www.bbc.co.uk/programmes/b006vq92, accessed 17 August 2021) was filmed in June 2017 as they sought to 'Imagine, Innovate and Inspire' a reconnection with the River Thames. They welcomed new ideas seeking £10,000–£20,000 of investment which were likely to improve Tideway delivery, or secure a legacy of innovation, from across their Alliance and stakeholders. The Tideway innovation team assisted innovators to develop their ideas and prepare a business case. With £100,000 available on the day, the best ideas were pitched to the Tideway Dragons: four senior leadership team members. From 30 innovative ideas submitted to the Great Think—an innovation community to discuss, discover, and share ideas hosted by i3P—in the run-up to the event, the innovation team and champions across the Alliance whittled down to the five ideas given the opportunity to pitch to the Den. Each innovation champion had 3 minutes to pitch their idea, and the Dragons just 10 minutes to interrogate them before making a decision. One example of an unsuccessful idea pitched was to develop augmented reality (AR) technology for remote surveys and inspections. Whilst this idea was not successful, the Dragons recognized the future potential and so this idea was passed to i3P for further discussion at a future innovation forum. An example of a successful idea was to develop and trial the 'Rightway Bootcamp', an industry-first, 11-week induction programme covering physical, mental, and financial health supporting Tideway's aim to have everyone leave the project healthier than when they arrived.

Tideway also held engagement campaigns within and outside the company. Colleagues across the Alliance continue to develop novel solutions, implement innovative technologies, and share their knowledge on the i3P platform, with 50 innovations published online, and 80 new ideas submitted to the innovation team. Tideway continues to engage across the industry to support collaboration and innovation. This includes the CEO chairing i3P and hosting its first live funding event, i3P Spark, which had over 30 collaborative submissions from member organizations. The i3P Collaborative Innovation Fund invested £100,000 in three winning pitches from the final in ideas deemed to have the highest potential to benefit the whole UK infrastructure sector.

*Sources*: interviews with CEO and innovation team and desktop research; Stride (2019).

## Discussion questions

1. Why do you think a project internal identity narrative is needed and how was one created on Tideway?

2. To what extent is the innovation programme in Tideway robust, and what else could be done as part of the programme?

3. How and why is the project external image narrative important throughout the project life cycle?

# Part B

# The Three Domains of Strategic Project Organizing

Figure B  'Aspiration' (Cole's youth)
*Source*: National Gallery of Art.

In Part B, the project has a clear 'Aspiration'—a clear mission projected into a desired future towards which our project manager optimistically sets off on the project life cycle with the guardian angel waving off. What could possibly get in the way of achieving this desired future?

We cover in this part the three domains of strategic project organizing (SPO) in turn, with a chapter dedicated to each. In these chapters, we:

- *elaborate* on the project mission as the strategic rationale for the investment project, supported by the project value proposition defined as the relationship between economic case and the financial case for the investment;
- *stress* the importance of the owner's relationship with the stakeholders in the project, including the primordial stakeholder;
- *identify* the different types of project-based firms in SPO: the P-form Corporation, and Contractor, and—often overlooked—the Professional Service Firm, which provides much of the technical expertise and support for the owner and its investment projects;
- *introduce* the SPO Star Model for designing the temporary project organization that delivers the outputs;
- *relate* teaming to the process of future-making as the practice level of strategic project organizing;
- *present* alternative strategies for project delivery, such as agile project management;
- *explore* systems thinking and systems dynamics in project delivery and how they relate to project escalation.

The three domains of SPO are the organizational building blocks of the SPO perspective, so they are treated as distinct organizational forms in Part B. Our case studies to support learning present salutatory lessons from an incapable owner of the Berlin-Brandenburg airport project in Case 5; present how a global P-form corporation manages projects in Case 6; and show how Stage One, an events supplier, delivers its projects in Case 7.

# 5 The owner domain

## 5.1 Introduction: owners as investors and operators

We now turn to the first of the three domains of project organizing, the *owner domain*. This is the domain of the investor and operator organization which is responsible for connecting the left and right sides of Figure 2.2; that is, in both shaping the project mission and realizing benefits by moving from project outputs to project outcomes the owner is the key player. The owner organization makes the investment in acquiring a new infrastructure asset, developing an innovative product, or an organizational transformation in order to improve the performance of its existing operations and market position. All organizations operate by providing goods and/or services to their customers. Whether this provision is incentivized by profit in the private sector, public service in government, or a combination in the 'third sector', all organizations need to operate effectively and efficiently to safeguard shareholders', donors', and taxpayers' funds.

In this chapter, we first discuss which type of organizations project owners are. Next, we introduce the concept of **owner project capability**[1] as a dynamic capability that all organizations require in order to transform their operational capabilities. We then develop the concept of the project mission introduced in section 2.1 by identifying its five principal elements. The discussion will pull out two of these elements, which form the **value proposition** for further discussion of the techniques of investment appraisal and their limitations. Stakeholders are our next topic of interest, before we elaborate further on the capable owner. Finally, we present a cautionary case of an incapable owner on the Berlin-Brandenburg airport project.

## 5.2 Which organizations are project owners?

We have so far taken for granted the organizations which are project owners—this is because all organizations can be, potentially, project owners. Any organization which invests in the development of a new facility such as a factory, in the development of a new product such as an app, or attempts to change the way it works through a formal organizational change process is a project owner. Any organization is potentially a project owner for all three types of project identified in section 1.1, but most specialize in different types of project. For instance, transformation projects with information systems projects at their heart are the most important for the financial services sector. For consumer products companies in the manufacturing sector, on the other hand, new product development (NPD) projects are more important. In the utility and transportation sectors, infrastructure projects are the most important. For all these owners, projects are *not* their core business—meeting their customer needs is their core business. We will discuss the particular group of project-based firms (PBFs) for which projects *are* their core business in Chapter 6.

Different owners have different purposes, and these differences significantly influence the criteria against which they shape their investment projects.[2] A housing provider is likely to be most concerned with projects that deliver affordable, well-built housing as quickly as possible.[3] A high-end fashion house will likely be more concerned with the ability of the latest collection to inspire customers to spend their money. Both will be owners for simple, robust information systems that support their operations. A fintech company, on the other hand, will need to remain at the forefront of innovation in its particular market for digital transformation projects. Some owners are experienced, repeat investors, while others, even for complex projects, are novices. Energy and transportation operators often have a large portfolio of new development, upgrade, and maintenance projects, while opera companies may only commission a new house every 100 years or so. In owners where the supply of all the resource inputs is outsourced, which is typical with infrastructure projects, for instance, then it is clear which the owner organization is. Where a significant proportion of resources may come from internal functions, this can be less clear, as the case of Syngenta in Vignette 5.1 suggests.

## Vignette 5.1    Syngenta GmBH

Syngenta is a global agri-technology corporation focused on crop protection (herbicides, fungicides, and insecticides) and seeds with a particular capability in genetic engineering. For instance, it was the first to sequence the genome of rice and thereby to launch the first genetically modified grain. Its genetically modified corn was the first such food product to receive approval from European Union regulators. Under its new Chinese owner, it is leading the restructuring of the sector by expanding rapidly through the acquisition of agri-technology companies across the globe. It is a high-tech company working in a traditional market dominated by independent farmers. Marketing to farmers and leading-edge research and development (R&D) are, therefore, both central to its continuing success.

In February 2020, Alliance Manchester Business School delivered an executive development programme at Syngenta corporate headquarters in Basel, Switzerland with a particular emphasis upon the project governance interface and the role of the project sponsor, as discussed in Chapter 8. Senior executives from both the Crop Protection and Seeds divisions were in the room. In order to focus the discussions on the governance interface, the Three Domains Model in Figure 2.1 was presented, which provoked a lively discussion between the executives on which function was the project owner in Syngenta.

The marketing executives argued that their function was the project owner because they were the ones that knew what the farmers around the world wanted in terms of new products and so they should own the projects, with functions such as R&D and manufacturing acting as internal suppliers. The R&D executives argued, on the other hand, that they were the project owners because Syngenta was a technology-led corporation and it was the job of the marketing and manufacturing functions to deliver their exciting new products to the market.

Traditionally, the investor in the project has been called the 'client' and this term is still in widespread use. We use the term 'owner' here in deliberate distinction from 'client'[4] because the latter implies that the relationship between client and a supplier is essentially a commercial one with legalistic connotations,[5] while the three domains perspective broadens out the owner's role in project organizing across the owner business model.

---

### Exercise 5.1

Review Vignette 5.1. Do you agree with marketing or R&D on who is the owner in NPD projects?

---

## 5.3 The project owner business model

Business models are summary conceptualizations of how an organization delivers for its customers.[6] From a strategic project organizing (SPO) perspective, we suggest that there is a generic business model for project owners with multiple variations in practice, as presented in Figure 5.1. This shows the owner at the core of the project process, as it makes a strategic investment in order to benefit its customers. The owner needs to raise the finance for the investment. This may come from internal resources such as retained profits or taxes, or it may come from external borrowing from investors of various kinds. Where the finance is secured directly on the output delivered by the project rather than on the assets owned by the organization more generally, this is known as project finance,[7] which is much more common for infrastructure than for other types of project. The owner then needs to operate the output of the project to realize the benefits that provide the funding stream that repays the finance. Funding may be captured directly through tolls and sales or indirectly through reduced costs from greater efficiency and effectiveness. Where public goods are free at the point of use, the funding stream comes from the taxpayers, who are also the customers of the government owner as citizens. In order to move from finance to funding,

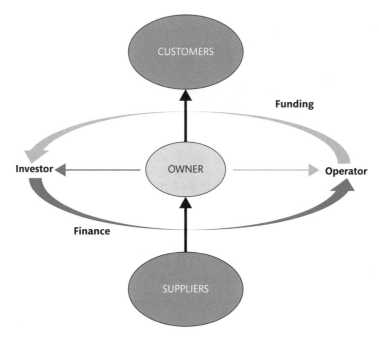

Figure 5.1  The generic project owner business model.

*Source*: Winch and Msulwa (2019a: figure 1).

the owner needs to engage with suppliers to deliver the outputs required by the project mission. The relationship between finance and funding is called the **value proposition**.

## 5.4 **Project capability as a dynamic capability**

The strategy of an organization, be it in the public or private sector, sets the overall direction of the organization—its 'purpose'.[8] The purpose is achieved through operating the resources—human, physical, intangible—available to the organization to meet customer needs and aspirations. This purpose bounds the range of investment projects that the organization will engage in and defines those that it will not—see Vignette 5.2 for the example of BP. Within that range, a project mission has to be developed that aligns each investment with the organization's purpose. The ability to operate resources efficiently and effectively can be defined as the **operational capability** of the organization, through which it matches the resources available to it with the needs of its customers.[9] Successful operations generate additional demands from customers, and so organizations face the challenge of extending and renewing their operational capabilities so that they can meet these additional demands. Successful operations also generate the revenues from which capital investments

## Vignette 5.2   Owner purpose at BP

BP is a leading international oil company (INOC) synonymous with the production, refining, and distribution of hydrocarbons. It made the first commercial oil strike in the Middle East in 1908 and grew to be a major player in the United States, Russia, Europe, and across the globe. In 2017, it stated that 'our strategic priorities help us to deliver heat, light and mobility solutions for a changing world'. This statement clearly bounded the scope of the business to energy exploration, production, and distribution and thereby defined the range of the types of projects that BP as an owner of energy infrastructure would engage in; it therefore also defined those that BP would not engage in. However, this was only the start of the project selection problem. For instance, the statement above raises important questions around:

- the proportion of fossil-based and renewable energy projects within the investment portfolio;

- the proportion of investment in gas and oil projects, and within these categories the exploitation of tight gas and heavy oil;

- the areas of the world where exploration and production will take place, taking into account the engineering challenges of very deep water (e.g. Gulf of Mexico) or arctic conditions (e.g. Siberia) and the commercial challenges of global geopolitics (e.g. Iraq).

By 2020, BP had significantly changed how it answered these questions, stating that 'our purpose is reimagining energy for people and our planet. We want to help the world reach net zero and improve people's lives.' The proportion of renewable energy assets in the portfolio is to increase rapidly and marginal hydrocarbon assets are to be sold. However, BP intends to remain in the heat, light, and mobility business, but as an 'integrated energy company' rather than an INOC.

*Sources*: http://www.BP.com (accessed 2 August 2017, 16 December 2020); BP (2009).

---

can be made and generate the confidence of lenders that the investment is sound because the organization is well run. Organizations also therefore need dynamic capabilities, defined as 'the capacity of an organization to purposefully create, extend, or modify the resource base'.[10]

Project capability[11] is arguably the most important dynamic capability for the endogenous growth of organizations; as ExxonMobil's Chair commented, 'ExxonMobil's results for the third quarter of 2011 reflect a continued commitment to operational integrity, disciplined investing and superior project execution.'[12] Project capability therefore complements dynamic capabilities for the exogenous growth of organizations through mergers and acquisitions. The strategic extension and renewal of operational capabilities is typically organized as an investment project, be it a more sophisticated information system, an upgraded model of car, or a new drug. It follows that the capability to effectively manage an investment project is a vital dynamic capability for any organization which is changing and growing. Project capability is therefore how organizations achieve change in operational capabilities which we capture in the project owner business model in Figure 5.1.

## 5.5  Developing the value proposition

We saw in Chapters 3 and 4 the importance of projecting during project shaping to develop the project mission as a reference narrative for the project. However, a viable project mission needs to be supported by careful analysis; Table 5.1 provides a template consisting of five 'business cases' that define the project mission and provide that support. We discussed the strategic case in Chapters 3 and 4—this answers the crucial question of *why* the project is worth doing.[13] The governance case is the subject of Chapter 8, and the commercial case the subject of Chapter 9. We focus next in this chapter on the value proposition formed by the economic and financial cases.

Value is another word with multiple meanings in business and management generally.[14] For SPO, we define 'value' as the relationship between the finance provided for the investment and the funding stream flowing from that investment, but, as we shall see, even this apparently straightforward 'value-for-money' definition is challenging to operationalize. Moreover, beneficial use of the output involves both users and customers in the co-creation of value to generate the funding stream. For instance, a new customer relationship management (CRM) system needs to be working as intended (the output) but also for both organizations' employees using the system and the customers interacting with the system to engage with its affordances[15] for benefits to be realized. The value proposition therefore captures the specific investment requirements in relation to an identified opportunity to achieve outcomes.

Table 5.1  The project mission in five cases

| | |
| --- | --- |
| 1. Strategic case | Addresses the question *why* the project is being done and the fit of the investment with the purpose of the owner organization. It forms the project mission and is communicated as the project reference narrative. |
| 2. Economic case | Addresses the question *which* options deliver the project mission, while providing acceptable value. No project should go ahead if there is not a supportive economic case, but this is a necessary rather than sufficient condition. This forms part of the *value proposition*. |
| 3. Financial case | Addresses the question *whether* the project is viable by identifying sources of finance and affordable funding streams to repay that finance and to support the asset through life. This forms the other part of the *value proposition*. |
| 4. Commercial case | Addresses the question of whether the project *can* be done in terms of the capabilities of the suppliers to deliver the project mission and whether an equitable commercial deal *can* be struck with those suppliers. |
| 5. Governance case | Addresses the question of *how* the project is to be delivered, including the capabilities of the owner organization for project governance and benefits realization. |

*Source*: developed from HMT (2020; box 5).

A major challenge with developing the value proposition is that estimating both the finance required and the funding stream to repay it are based on projections into an uncertain future. So uncertain is the future that many commentators argue that it is not possible to develop a value proposition 'rationally'. For instance, John Maynard Keynes, one of the twentieth century's leading economists, argued that only 'animal spirits' could inform value proposition development because:

> If we speak frankly, we have to admit that our basis of knowledge for estimating the yield ten years hence of a railway, a copper mine, a textile factory, the goodwill of a patent medicine, an Atlantic liner, a building in the City of London amounts to little and sometimes nothing.[16]

Thus, in the face of the inherent uncertainty of the future, narratives are the only way project leaders can mobilize resources, not through 'rational' calculation.[17]

However, project owners tend to want more assurance—if only for the benefit of their stakeholders—than such narratives alone allow. So since Keynes wrote in the early 1930s, great efforts have been made to develop more analytic techniques for the value proposition. This is done by calculating the expected return on the proposed investment, which provides a basis for comparison between proposed projects and allows the ones with the greatest returns to be selected for investment. The best practice method for calculating the expected return is the net present value (NPV) of the proposed investment. The essence of NPV calculation is that the value of money today is greater than the value of money at a future point in time; therefore benefits accruing in the future need to be discounted to their current value for an appraisal to be made. The rate of discount applied is a function of the opportunity cost of capital, in other words the return on capital that could be obtained if it were invested in the next best type of investment. One benchmark often taken is government bonds. NPV calculation is essentially a cash flow calculation—it compares the outflow of finance required for the investment with the discounted inflow of funding arising from benefits realization, and so it is frequently referred to as a discounted cash flow calculation. So long as the NPV of the funding stream is greater than the financial outflow at the chosen rate of return, then the project is worth pursuing in principle. If financial resources are constrained, then the NPV calculations can be used to prioritize the investment opportunities.

A significant problem with this approach is that market prices may be a poor guide to either or both of the costs of the investment and the quantum of benefits flowing from realization. There are, in essence, two reasons for this:

- market price signals are distorted by various forms of market failure such as monopoly, the tax system, or the availability of otherwise unused resources;
- elements of non-financial costs and benefits are not traded and so are intrinsically difficult to value.

The technique which has been developed to allow such factors to be taken into account in NPV calculations is cost–benefit analysis (CBA), or benefit–cost analysis for those who prefer their glass half full. This involves 'shadow pricing' as a proxy for non-market factors which, once established and agreed, can be fed into the appraisal calculations in very much the same way as market prices. However, because shadow prices—by definition—cannot be directly observed, the methods used to measure them are difficult in practice and frequently contentious.

While CBA does provide important benefits over conventional NPV calculations, it remains restricted to the benefits of the investment for the owner and its customers. However, many investments—particularly those that provide common-use infrastructure—provide much broader socio-economic benefits in terms of general economic growth. For instance, the NPV calculation for the relatively known investment in the facilities for the London 2012 Olympics and for the returns from ticket sales, broadcasting rights, and other income flows needs to be complemented by the stimulating effect on the regeneration of a derelict area of London and to the London economy generally from increased economic activity. Investments by private-sector companies face similar challenges because investments (or failures to invest) may have significant reputational implications, or may be 'loss leaders' to establish positions in particular emerging markets.

## 5.6  Challenges in cost–benefit analysis

CBA is now very sophisticated, yet suffers from a number of weaknesses;[18] in particular, shadow pricing is still much more of an art than a science. This technical challenge is compounded by two further ones. The first is that CBA is inherently performative. That is to say, it does not work as an objective tool for evaluation independent of the investment being appraised; rather, it helps to shape that investment. One example of this is regional economic equality. Investment in economic infrastructure such as transportation provides a stimulus for growth. However, the benefits of such investment are usually measured in terms of time saved for travellers, which in turn is costed by the time value of money for those travellers. The problem is that higher-paid travellers have a higher time value of money than lower-paid ones, so investment will be steered towards more affluent areas. That area will then have a higher rate of growth following the stimulus of that investment, so travellers in the region become even more affluent relatively to those in poorer regions. This creates a virtuous cycle of growth for more affluent regions and a vicious cycle for poorer ones, unless the results of CBA are overridden by other criteria.[19]

A second problem is that CBA is very sensitive to manipulation. The argument is that decision-makers within the owner domain are systematically biased towards overestimation of the benefits of a project and underestimation of the costs in what has been dubbed strategic misrepresentation.[20] Strategic misrepresentation is inherent in the process of project selection because the principal use of the NPV calculation, once it has been shown to be positive, is to rank-order the projects so that the ones showing the highest returns relative to the others are preferred. If all the figures on each side of the equation were known with certainty, then this would not present a problem, but they are not and are therefore about judging, as discussed in section 3.3, not fact. An important consequence of this considerable room for manoeuvre in decision-making is that the persuasiveness of the project promoters becomes a major factor in making a particular NPV calculation stack up better than that of competing claims on the same resources. It should be noted that although the evidence for strategic misrepresentation comes from the public sector due to the greater levels of accountability in that sector, it is no less a problem in the private sector, where 'vanity projects' are rife. It is particularly a problem where business units bid competitively into a corporate centre for investment capital allocations, and so the chief executive officers (CEOs) of those business units can be incentivized to distort their investment appraisals to gain greater investment resources for their business unit from the corporate centre. Where this competition between projects for finance plays out between owners competing for finance from a single pot, as in Vignette 5.3, then projects that destroy value can be authorized.

Recent research in strategy formulation yields some important insights into the dynamics of project selection.[21] This research suggests that in decision-making under uncertainty, the skills with which project promoters play 'framing contests' is important. The skill here is to articulate the case for the project in terms of both the accepted bases of legitimacy for decision-making and the ability to form broader coalitions of support. Arguably, strategic misrepresentation is an adaptive response to decision-making under uncertainty—if you don't know the facts, you might as well give yourself the benefit of the doubt. Because it is pervasive, one could argue that it is not a problem—projects will inevitably overrun, but we simply allow for uplifts in total budget to take this into account. However, the existence of strategic misrepresentation seriously threatens the rationalistic basis of the value proposition, particularly if some project promoters are better at playing the game of strategic misrepresentation than others. Honest project promoters might produce more accurate estimates, but they are also more likely to have funding for their project rejected and so lose the possibility of demonstrating their wisdom.

## Vignette 5.3   When owners compete

As the economy of the western United States grew rapidly, it demanded energy and water—energy for its burgeoning cities and water for its growing population and booming agriculture. The mountains that separated it from the rest of the country supplied a potential solution to both of these problems by damming its powerful rivers. Two US Government agencies fought each other to appropriate federal funds to seize these opportunities, resulting in significant overconstruction of dams on the western rivers with serious outcomes for soil quality, native Americans, and the primordial stakeholder.

The US Army Corps of Engineers, founded in 1802, has long engaged in civil, as well as military, engineering, with a particular emphasis upon flood protection and river navigation. It is currently the largest owner-operator of hydroelectric power generation in the United States. The US Bureau of Reclamation was founded in 1902 to provide irrigation for the western states; it is currently the largest wholesaler of water in the United States and the second largest hydroelectric power producer. Both provide considerable leisure resources as well.

The two began to compete in the 1930s over the Tulare Basin in California, with the Corps favouring the interests of large farmers and the Bureau those of small farmers. Competition continued over the next decades, particularly over the Missouri River basin, and finally in Alaska. Many dams were considered *boondoggles*, defined as 'a project that is considered a waste of both time and money, yet is often continued due to extraneous policy or political motivations' built largely with Federal funds. The intense competition carried on until the later 1970s when the administration of President Carter introduced heightened protection for the remaining western wild rivers.

*Sources*: Reisner (1986); www.usbr.gov; www.usace.army.mil; Wikipedia (all accessed 19 January 2021).

The fundamental problem is that CBA has not really addressed Keynes's point that the future is inherently uncertain; rather, it has shrouded this uncertainty in a specious rationality. This suggests that the project selection process is more a socio-political process than a rational economic calculation. There are also performative biases within CBA which mean that other criteria also need to be used in order to select the most beneficial project. We suggest that the use of formal analysis to define the value proposition is an important source of sense-making material for project leaders and helps to identify vanity projects of various kinds, but in the end it is the strategic case in Table 5.1 which should drive decision-making, not the value proposition. Thus, the project narrative and its resilience are the most appropriate basis for the decision to invest, not the value proposition, for project leaders.

---

### Exercise 5.2

Are you aware of any projects where the challenge of achieving the project mission was seriously underestimated at the outset? Why do you think this happened?

---

## 5.7 The stakeholders' perspective

So far we have been discussing the investment project from the point of view of the owner organization making the investment, but no organization is an island and others usually have an interest in the investment project from their own point of view. These are the project stakeholders, which can be defined as 'any group or individual who can affect or is affected by the achievement of the project mission'.[22] An important subtlety in this definition is that it can be extended to include non-organizational entities which are also *affected by* the achievement of the pro-ject mission. For instance, many investment projects have a significant impact on the natural environment, which we can conceptualize as the 'primordial stakeholder',[23] and we can also extend the concept to heritage assets such as ancient buildings and archaeological remains. Addressing the ethical issues posed by the inherently mute primordial stakeholder is one of the principal challenges in the ethics of SPO, which will be discussed in section 12.5.

We will return repeatedly to the challenges of managing project stakeholders throughout this book. Here we address the principles of identifying and categoriz-ing stakeholders because stakeholders are one of the most significant—if not the most significant—sources of threats to the delivery of the project as they articulate the counter-narratives to the project reference narrative in section 4.3 and un-known knowns discussed in section 2.5. The owner needs to identify all the stake-holders who are affected by the project and then to identify their level of interest in the project mission and their relative power to shape the project mission.[24] The first step is usually achieved through a mapping technique to identify the relationships and the second is usually achieved through placing the stakeholders in a power/interest matrix.[25] In developing this analysis, the key is to look at the project mission from the point of view of the stakeholders concerned. Whether the project team believes that the interests of the stakeholder are legitimate or not, the stakeholder still needs to be included in the analysis. For instance, envi-ronmental activists may not be perceived as a legitimate interest by the owner, but they still have the power to disrupt the delivery of the project mission by lobbying other stakeholders and thereby building a coalition against the project mission, or even through direct action. Primordial stakeholders are inevitably mute in this process, so special regulatory arrangements are typically put in place to protect their interests. For instance, an environmental impact assessment is usually re-quired for major infrastructure projects, while public consultations are often held to allow less powerful stakeholders a voice.

One of the most important sources of legitimacy in decision-making is proce-dural[26]—that is to say that so long as the decision has been reached by agreed pro-cedures that meet norms of rationality and inclusiveness, then the outcome of that process is considered to be legitimate. Thus, the outcome of an electoral process for a government may not be what anyone voted for but it is still legitimate because the process meets accepted procedural norms. Formal processes such as public con-sultations are an important aspect of procedural legitimacy in developing the value proposition for investment projects. The use of best-practice analytic tools also con-fers procedural legitimacy. For instance, CBA was developed by government engi-neers in France and the United States with the ambition of taking the politics out of infrastructure project selection and placing it on a rational, transparent basis.[27] Even if the challenges of uncertainty and complexity discussed in Chapter 1 mean that this ambition cannot be fully realized, the attempt is valuable and its use has undoubtedly improved the legitimacy of project shaping.

> ### Exercise 5.3
>
> Think about projects you are aware of—how have they been affected by the actions of stakeholders?

## 5.8 The capable owner

Many project owner organizations around the world decided to run down their in-house and engineering management capabilities during the recession of the early 1990s, believing that the skills could be provided by their suppliers or hired as needed, rather than embedded in the owner organization. We call this the **Railtrack effect** after the failed UK rail infrastructure company that did not understand that infrastructure operators require in-house project capabilities in order to be effective owners and investors.[28] Perceptions are now changing and many infrastructure owners, including Network Rail, which succeeded Railtrack, are now investing in the project capabilities that allow them to act as a capable owner and to ease the constraints on growth that the absence of capabilities for managing projects entails. The incapability of owners to fully engage with the project process will likely entail disappointment with outputs and failure to realize outcomes,[29] as is well illustrated in Case 5 at the end of the chapter.

We will discuss in more detail the interface capabilities required by owners in Chapters 8 and 9; here, we would like to emphasize one particular issue—connecting the project mission to project outcomes. Figure 2.2 shows how the project mission at the front end of the project life cycle is profoundly connected with the achievement of the outcomes from the project at the back end as the output moves into beneficial use. The organizational challenge is how to connect the value proposition to the achievement of outcomes, or more specifically, how to define outcomes that are achievable. One important connector is to have the 'voice of operations' and the 'voice of the customer' within the team defining the value proposition.[30] The voice of operations is important in order to move from outputs to outcomes by integrating the output into the operational capabilities of the owner organization.

The voice of the customer is important because the operational capabilities that are being changed by the project are inherently orientated towards meeting customer needs, be they patients in hospital, downloaders of an app, passengers on a train, or citizens accessing public services. If the changed operations do not enhance the customer experience, then the investment project cannot be deemed to be a success and funding streams are likely to be meagre or negative. Ensuring that the voices of the customer and operations are part of the development of the value proposition requires specific organizational capabilities. In particular, people with experience in operations and marketing need to be assigned to the team developing the project mission, as well as those responsible for value proposition analysis,[31] and the consideration of the five cases shown in Table 5.1 needs to include these issues.

## 5.9 Summary

We have explored the role of the project owner in shaping the project mission, with a particular focus on the development of value proposition, which underpins the reference narrative for the investment project. We have also stressed the importance of taking a broad view in the development of the value proposition, which includes ensuring that the proposition is deliverable by both the owner team and the supply side, and thinking through how the outputs are going to be turned into outcomes. However, in the face of inevitable uncertainty about costs and benefits, it is the strategic case embodying the reference narrative which weighs most heavily in the project mission. Fundamentally, the question to answer is why we are doing this project and whether it is aligned with our purpose. Value proposition analysis and the commercial and governance cases are all different ways of testing the viability of the project mission, not drivers in shaping the project mission.

Only a capable owner can effectively shape the project mission, see it through delivery of the project outputs, and then realize the benefits desired for the project outcomes. A capable owner has a clear purpose, and has the organizational capability to articulate that purpose in shaping the project mission into the project narrative. That reference narrative also provides the basis for engagement with stakeholders, be they potential investors, regulators, suppliers, or possible opponents of the project. Failure to both develop and adequately deploy owner project capability as a key dynamic capability is the cause of failure of many investment projects to realize the benefits envisaged in the project mission. We now turn to look at the supply of non-financial resources to the project from the supplier domain.

## 5.10 Further reading

Brown, K. A., Hyer, N. L., and Ettenson, R. 2013. 'The question every project team should answer'. *MIT Sloan Management Review*, 55(1): 49.
  Stresses the importance of clarifying and communicating the project mission as an answer to the question why we are doing this project.

Merrow, E. W. 2011. *Industrial Megaprojects: Concepts, Strategies, and Practices for Success*. Hoboken, NJ: Wiley.
  The seminal work providing the project benchmarking data which identifies the crucial importance of owner capability in project delivery.

Thurm, D. 2005. 'Master of the house: why a company should take control of its building projects'. *Harvard Business Review*, 83(10): 120–129.
  A practitioner statement of the importance of owner capability for project success.

## 5.11 Summary review questions

1. Which member of the project coalition is accountable for the value proposition in SPO?
2. What are the differences between the strategic case on the one hand, and the economic and financial cases on the other?
3. How do project capabilities differ from operational capabilities in owner organizations?
4. Why is it important for project owners to manage stakeholders?
5. What is a 'boondoggle'?

 *Visit the Oxford Learning Link site for this text to find answer guidance to the questions and exercises in this chapter.*

 *Take your learning further by viewing videos relevant to this chapter on the Oxford Learning Link site.*

## Notes

1. *Winch and Leiringer (2016).
2. Boyd and Chinyio (2006) provides an extensive analysis of construction owners.
3. Gulino et al. (2020).
4. Aritua et al. (2009).
5. *Oxford English Dictionary*: 'a person using the services of a professional person or organization; a customer of a person or organization offering services'.
6. Massa et al. (2017).
7. Morrison (2012).
8. Mayer (2018).
9. Helfat and Winter (2011).
10. Helfat et al. (2007: 4).
11. Davies and Brady (2016).
12. Fontevecchia (2011).
13. Brown et al. (2013).
14. Ramirez (1999).
15. Volkoff and Strong (2013).
16. Keynes (1961: 149).
17. Kay and King (2020).
18. Volden (2019).
19. Winch and Msulwa (2019a).
20. Flyvbjerg et al. (2003).

21. *Kaplan (2008).

22. Winch (2017: 345).

23. *Driscoll and Starik (2004).

24. Winch (2004).

25. Ackermann et al. (2014).

26. March (1994).

27. Persky (2001).

28. Merrow (2011).

29. Thurm (2005).

30. Winch and Msulwa (2019b).

31. Merrow (2011).

 **Case 5**    Flughafen Berlin-Brandenburg: an incapable owner?

As the Berlin Wall fell in 1989, the divided city of Berlin began to look for new opportunities on the national and international stage. The unified city was served by three airports, two on constrained sites, and so the search began for a site for the new airport. The decision was made quickly in 1996 to redevelop the old East German airport at Schönefeld by building a new terminal building and adding a second runway to be owned and operated by a private consortium. Privatization was abandoned in 2003 in favour of a publicly funded project. As the Berlin mayor put it, 'we now have to tackle it ourselves'. The final go-ahead from the regulators was received in 2006, and construction started on the terminal building in 2008 with a target completion date in 2011. The new airport, coded BER, finally opened in 2020 at the time of the collapse of air travel due to the COVID-19 pandemic, after the project staggered from crisis to mounting crisis. There are many aspects to this case of megaproject failure, but we will here explore the issues around the organization of the owner and operator of the airport Flughafen Berlin-Brandenburg GMbH (FBB). What is included and what is not included in announced budgets is unclear, but best estimates suggest that the total budget escalated from ~€3.1 bn to an outturn cost of ~€6.5 bn—over 100 per cent. While some of this was due to expansion of scope, most was due to extraordinary deficiencies in owner capability by FBB.

The owner organization was established in 1996, but following the failure of the privatization initiative, it became a publicly owned company incorporated under German corporate law with a management board and a supervisory board. FBB had responsibility for running all three of Berlin's existing airports until they closed, as well as the project for the new one. The principal shareholders of FBB are the Länder of Berlin and Brandenburg, and the Federal Government and its loans from the private sector were 100 per cent guaranteed by the Federal Government. The 10 members of the supervisory board are mainly high-profile politicians representing the three shareholders that meet four to five times a year. Chaired jointly by the Mayor of Berlin and the Premier of Brandenburg, it has no project expertise. Operationally, FBB is managed by the management board, and the flavour of the relationship between the two boards is given in the comment by FBB management that 'we solve problems here among professionals. They are politics. We keep them out of it.'

FBB appointed the leader of the consortium that had originally bid for the privatized project as programme director in 2004. He, in turn, appointed Planungsgemeinschaft Berlin-Brandenburg International (PBBI) in 2005. This joint venture between German consultants was to undertake concept design, obtain regulatory permits, and prepare the tender documents for the selection of the tier-one contractor. PBBI was subsequently appointed by FBB in 2007 to oversee detailed design and project execution by that contractor. Thus, the commercial strategy of FBB was a traditional construction one of appointing consultants to undertake concept design work; competitive tendering for a tier-one contractor to undertake detail design and on-site delivery; and oversight of that delivery by the consultants.

However, a single tier-one contractor was not appointed. In late 2007, FBB decided to annul the results of the competitive tender because all four offers submitted exceeded the €630 m budget calculated by PBBI by around €400 m. FBB decided to change contracting strategy and to break the programme into seven packages, while retaining responsibility for detail design. PBBI tendered for and won the contract for detail design in 2008 and preparing the tender documentation for the seven packages. The scope of the overall programme also increased by including the north and south piers as well as the main terminal, whereas only the latter had been the scope of the competitive tender. The FBB programme director moved on during 2008 to Munich Airport. In order to bolster further owner capability, Drees & Sommer (DS) was appointed by FBB as construction manager in 2008. Throughout all this, the opening date of the new terminal building remained posted as 2011.

When the tenders for the seven packages arrived, six of them were between 55 per cent and 175 per cent higher than budgeted. DS conducted a review and found that the tenders were high because the packages were too large to generate strong competition; threats to delivery because PBBI had not completed detail design at the time of tender; and concerns around the management of the interfaces between the packages, which led the suppliers to include large contingencies in their offers. In response, FBB dismissed DS—apparently for saying that the 2011 deadline could not be met. FBB also chose to package further the work into 35 competitively tendered lots. However, it did not change the deadline for the completion of the project, and it still tendered these packages before PBBI had completed detailed design work. FBB 'had bitten off more than it could chew'.

A report in 2012 by Ernst & Young found that FBB had not made the necessary changes to its structure and processes that its much larger responsibilities now required. Since 2005, the scope of the project had increased significantly due to the inclusion of the two piers to the main terminal package and the social complexity of the project had increased from a single tier-one contractor, who would manage the interfaces between the works packages, to 35 works packages with interfaces to be managed by the owner, FBB. Moreover, through a series of separate appointments, PBBI was now in the position of supervising itself to deliver the detailed designs required by the package contractors, which it was failing to do in a timely way. One result of this situation was that FBB issued hundreds of change orders in the design up to 2012 of such substance that regulatory permits had again to be sought.

The first postponement of the completion date came in 2010 when opening was pushed back to 2012, blamed on external factors, including the insolvency of the member of the PBBI Joint Venture responsible for engineering services design and changes in EU regulations. Twenty-seven days before the revised date, opening was delayed again due to failures in acceptance testing of the fire safety installations by the regulatory authorities. The failures were due to inadequate design, compounded by serious installation problems. Completion was put back to 2013, and PBBI and the FBB managing director were dismissed. A review by the new managing director identified the need to further delay completion to the end of 2013 and a requirement of €1.2 bn extra on the budget. In late 2012, the completion date was again postponed—this time indefinitely. Throughout this period, the supervisory board was 'toothless' and no other body was in a position to challenge the decisions of the FBB management board, 'who lost control early on'.

An immediate result of the purge of FBB staff and the dismissal of PBBI was that construction came to a complete stop because owner project capability plummeted from its already low base. In particular, many of those who understood the fire safety system installation were dismissed. Moreover, in a desperate attempt to meet the 2012 deadline, work had been accelerated, leading to hundreds of installation defects, particularly in the cabling systems, compounded by a lack of coordination between the five different installation packages for fire safety. Over 3,600 km of cables had to be re-installed, and the fire safety issue continued to afflict the project. In 2017, it was found that the fire safety sprinkler systems had been installed incorrectly and so 2 km of pipework had to be replaced. Ductwork was not waterproofed and the cabling inside begun to corrode over the years the project was delayed—700 km of cable had to be replaced. The design for smoke extraction was unusual and complex—driven by aesthetic considerations—and the back-up systems for smoke extraction inadequate. One regulatory official stated that 'what the airport ordered was sufficient for a circus tent, but . . . not for the dimensions of the terminal'. It was not until late 2017 that a final, correct opening date was announced, but as late as May 2018, a regulatory inspection identified 863 issues with electrical wiring.

Programme leadership was unstable over time, with sudden departures of programme directors in 2008, 2012, and 2013, and briefly in 2017. That year, the CEO sacked the programme director appointed in 2013; the supervisory board then sacked the CEO and immediately reinstated the programme director, who finally left in 2018. Allegations of corruption circulated round the project for some time, and in 2016, an FBB official admitted taking bribes from one of the installers of the fire safety systems. However, BER is now open and 'it's like I've been able to shake off my old nightmare' said the terminal manager as it opened.

*Sources*: Fiedler and Wendle (2015); Wikipedia (accessed 23 December 2020); *Financial Times*, 6 March 2017, 15 December 2017, 14 April 2018, 30 October 2020.

## Discussion questions

1. What do you think are the principal reasons for the lack of project capability at FBB?

2. Why do you think that FBB as owner attempted to accelerate the completion of the project in 2013?

3. Do you think that the airport will ever achieve the outcomes expected in the initial project mission?

# The supplier domain

## 6.1 Introduction: suppliers as resource bases

In Chapter 5 we explored the owner domain; here, we explore the supplier domain. While project owners are responsible for supplying the financial resources required for projecting, the members of the supplier domain are responsible for providing the human and technological resources that actually deliver the output so that the owner can transform that output into outcomes. In this sense, they can be thought of as the permanent **resource bases** for the temporary delivery organization. Suppliers are typically a distinctive type of firm called the project-based firm (PBF)[1] which is characterized by its core operational capability being project organizing.[2] We will explore various types of PBF in this chapter, but what they all share in common is that they deliver to owners by organizing their operations on a project basis. In this they are distinct from owners, which do not organize their operations on a project basis.

We first explore how PBFs are clustered into distinctive project-based sectors, and the ways in which those suppliers are then tiered in relations of contract and subcontract within the project coalition. We then focus on the project strategies of two distinctive types of PBF which often complement each other within project coalitions—the P-form corporation and the Professional Service Firm. PBFs often work in networks of suppliers, and so we will explore the dynamics of project networks. Finally, we present our case of one leading PBF—BAE Systems.

## 6.2 The project-based sectors

In order to deliver outputs for the owner, suppliers form networks of multiple interfaces with other supplier firms that are usually also project-based, forming complex project networks of many interconnected elements. These networks are themselves sources of complexity in project organizing and form what we call **project-based sectors**.[3] These industrial sectors include those producing complex product systems (COPS)[4] such as aerospace, power-generation equipment, shipbuilding, and the like. There is also a number of project-based sectors which do not produce COPS such as building, management consultancy, and film production. This complex network of PBFs in the supplier domain then engages with project owners across the commercial interface, which we will explore in Chapter 9. Within and between the domains of project organizing, the suppliers which develop many of the innovative products and processes and the owners which adopt these innovations in order to realize their project mission co-create to change our world through projecting.

Project-based sectors form important parts of all developed economies. They are particularly important for the complex projects through which projectors create the complex systems that underpin modern society and economy. The COPS sector alone accounts for around 20 per cent of UK gross domestic product (GDP).[5] The suppliers in the project-based sector engage with owners which are typically from other economic sectors to create outcomes that contribute to these complex systems overall. In this engagement, owners also engage with regulators and governments.[6] Regulators may be economic; this is common in the infrastructure sector because the complex systems operated by infrastructure owners are often, in effect, natural monopolies. They may also be technical, ensuring that, for instance, outcomes comply with accepted environmental and health standards. Regulations may also apply to the delivery process in areas such as safety—we return to this issue in Chapter 11.

Governments are engaged with project-based sectors for two principal reasons. The first relates to the importance of such sectors in the overall economy, particularly as the specialist technology suppliers often operate sophisticated advanced manufacturing facilities. The second is related to government agencies being the owner for many projects—particularly for social and economic infrastructure projects; new product development (NPD) in sectors such as defence materiel and pharmaceuticals; and also for many of the most challenging digital transformation projects. These interorganizational networks of owners, regulators, and suppliers form distinctive institutional fields.[7] For instance, the emerging fintech sector includes fintech owners and operators such as banks and other financial services providers; financial services regulators; app and other software developers; and suppliers of specialist hardware such as card readers. These players are all surrounded by a multitude of consultants and other advisors. Governments retain a policy interest because of the disruptive potential of fintech for financial services, and some governments such as Lithuania have made a 'bet' on the positive future for fintech in their country.[8] The generic structure of such a project-based institutional field is shown in Figure 6.1, with the project-based sector indicated by the dotted line.

PBFs come in many shapes and sizes, but they can be generically grouped into three types. One is the specialist technology supplier, whose contributions are crucial to the creation of complex systems and are often protected by sustained levels of resource-based competitive advantage.[9] These suppliers often have a significant investment in research and development and manufacturing facilities, supplying components such as compressors and process control systems, or complete subsystems such as catalytic crackers. The suppliers of the information systems that

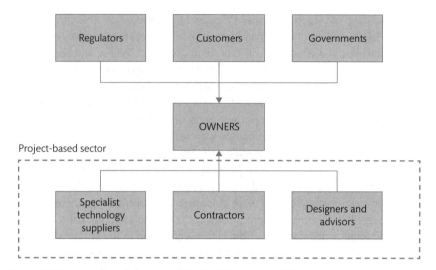

Figure 6.1 The generic structure of a project-based institutional field.
*Source*: developed from Winch (1998: figure 1).

are increasingly embedded in infrastructure outputs, as well as the software and hardware developers that enable digital transformation, also fall into this category. The next type is the **contractors**, which provide more widely available commodity inputs to the delivery domain as well as systems integration in the first tier. Examples here include the more labour-intensive end of project delivery such as site execution in infrastructure and building, but also extras in the film sector and volunteers at Olympic and other major events. It also includes systems integrators[10] such as Bechtel in Vignette 6.1. The final type is the myriad variety of designers and advisors which are often organized in Professional Service Firms (PSFs). These include specialist technology designers such as architects, and more business-orientated advisors such as lawyers. The project-based sector, therefore, is the institutional context in which PBFs engage with owners within a regulatory context set by governments.

## 6.3 Managing the project-based firm

We suggested in Chapter 5 that owner organizations—whether private sector or public sector—require project capabilities as **dynamic capabilities** in order to explore new opportunities and thereby grow and change creating new operational capabilities. PBFs, however, only engage in projects—projects define their operational capabilities rather than their dynamic capabilities. Essentially, the *operational capabilities* of the project-based firm revolve around two bundles of capability.[11] The first is the set of **relational capabilities** required to manage across the commercial interface with the owner that we explore in more detail in Chapter 9. The second

is the set of project delivery capabilities that ensure that the PBF meets its obligations to the owner as part of the project coalition for delivery while also meeting
its obligations to its shareholders as a profitable business. We explore these further
in Chapters 10 and 11. Weaknesses in either of these operational capabilities will
undermine both the profitability of the existing project and business development
for future projects. Growing effectiveness in exploiting these operational capabilities
enables 'market penetration'.[12]

So far as dynamic capabilities are concerned, the PBF need to enter new markets
by winning 'base-shifting projects'[13] through three different potential growth vectors,[14] as shown in Figure 6.2. PBFs tend to expand by exploiting adjacent markets;
their business model is typically based on profits on turnover, which does not re-
lease large amounts of capital for significant research and development (R&D) efforts. Where such efforts are required to meet owner requirements, then the owner
often provides the capital for R&D—this is common in the defence materiel sector,
for instance, but can also be found in sectors such as construction. Market diversification is often through following internationally mobile owners as they enter new
markets, and product development is often by deepening an existing relationship
with an owner to provide it with new services. Diversification is rare for PBFs, which
tend to 'stick to the knitting'[15] like Bechtel in vignette 6.1.

Finally, and perhaps most importantly, PBFs need to learn from their completed
projects, a challenge which is inherently difficult for this type of firm.[16] The one-off
nature of projects, with teams typically disbanded at project termination and then
dispersed between different future projects, makes tacit knowledge diffusion difficult, while the high pace of project delivery can mitigate against explicit knowledge
diffusion through various kinds of lessons-learned activities. These problems are
compounded by the lack of clear accountability for human resource development
within project-based firms,[17] where delivery-orientated project managers focus on
project outputs rather than developing their operational capabilities. Perhaps the

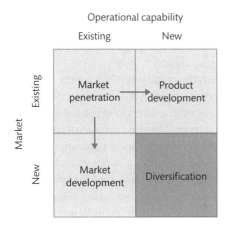

Figure 6.2 Growth vectors for project-based
firms.

*Sources*: developed from Ansoff (1968: table 6.1);
Davies and Hobday (2005: figure 3.4).

principal advantages of the functionally organized firm over the PBF are the greater ease of organizational learning and human resource development. Yet if the PBF is to gain dynamic capabilities, it needs to address these issues.

Supplier configurations on projects are often more complex than in sectors such as manufacturing. This is because—as will be seen in Chapter 9—the owner may contract with a number of different suppliers directly in the first tier of suppliers which are often P-form corporations or multinational PSFs, which form the leading members of the project coalition. First-tier suppliers then subcontract to second-tier and lower-tier suppliers, many of which are either small, regionally based companies or manufacturing-based specialist technology suppliers such as pumps. This tiered structure of contract and subcontract is illustrated in Figure 6.3. It shows what we call the project chain of suppliers with contractually equal status at the first tier, which often need to coordinate their activities iteratively, and the supply chain of sub-suppliers under each first tier supplier with a contractually hierarchical status coordinated by the tier above.

## 6.4 The P-form corporation

Contractors come in all shapes and sizes, from microenterprises[18] through to myriad small and medium-sized enterprises and larger firms. These provide specialist project services of various kinds, both directly to owners and as subcontractors to other PBFs on a make-to-order basis, with little or no involvement in the design processes.[19] Many of these firms make their profits from a rapid turnover of capital on relatively thin trading margins and are vulnerable to downturns in market activity. They survive such downturns because they have few fixed assets and often further subcontract significant parts of their activity. This provides considerable flexibility in operational capabilities, but is not ideal for encouraging innovation to reduce output costs. Industries such as construction dominated by this kind of PBF can become locked into a high-flexibility but low-productivity sectoral business model.[20]

At the same time, growing technological complexity has stimulated the growth of specialist technology suppliers and increasing demands by owners to transfer threats to project delivery to their suppliers are encouraging the development of larger PBFs, which we designate the P-form corporation.[21] Delivering on the project mission can involve very high technologies which are captured in the technological complexity and novelty dimensions of the strategic project organizing (SPO) Diamond in Figure 2.6. Supplying such technologies to owners involves considerable investment in technological capability ready to be deployed on appropriate projects. P-form corporations are increasingly the preferred suppliers of complex capital goods. They differ from other types of PBFs because they also possess substantial production facilities such as shipyards and other kinds of dedicated manufacturing facilities, where small-batch production is the norm, and products are provided either concept-to-order, such as in the defence sector, where the product architecture

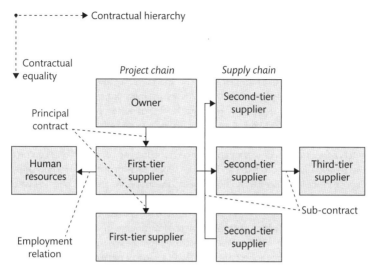

**Figure 6.3** Tiered suppliers in project coalitions.
*Source*: developed from Winch (2010: figure 7.1).

of the output is developed to meet the specific owner's mission, or design-to-order, where an existing product architecture is adapted to the needs of the particular owner's project mission.[22]

There are many ways in which the P-form corporation makes its offer to the project owner. Figure 6.4 shows the ways in which the specialist technology suppliers can create value for owners as their customers. The first dimension is the owner value proposition for the owner in terms of whether the service offer is purely focused on the project output, or whether it also contributes to supporting the owner to achieve project outcomes. The second dimension is the *PBF value proposition* for the PBF itself in terms of the sources of profitable revenue streams in the commercial relationship. Where the relationship is output focused and transactional, we find the traditional 'contractor' relationship that is widespread in many project-based sectors, in which the supplier bids for a particular work package, executes it, and only has further liabilities for the quality of its delivery. This is the usual offer of commodity input suppliers. The suppliers of specialist technology, on the other hand, have been increasingly complementing hardware offers with services in their offers[23] to provide through-life support, ensuring that the output is available to provide outcomes for the owner. This is driven, in particular, by the growing complicatedness of technology subsystems and hence the need for specialist knowledge. Outsourcing of output-focused services is particularly common in the information systems sector, where individual organizations cannot achieve the economies of scale required for the continual upgrading required by information technologies.

## Vignette 6.1    'Building the century': Bechtel Corporation

Bechtel's corporate vision is to 'be the world's premier engineering, construction, and project management organization'. Founded in 1898 to grade rail-track beds, it remains a privately owned family business with a fifth-generation Bechtel currently chief executive officer (CEO). Moving into roads and oil pipelines in the 1920s, its first megaproject was the Hoover Dam in 1931. In the years after 1945, it was a strong advocate of nuclear power and expanded overseas, particularly in the Middle East, building pipelines and refineries as well as hydro and nuclear generation facilities.

Bechtel's core competence was and is engineer, procure, and construct (EPC) contracting— attempts to diversify away from this and confuse supplying with owning were not happy experiences. While it has deep technological expertise in specific areas, its offer to owners is based on its systems integration capabilities to provide a fully functioning output for owners to operate. It developed the turnkey contract, but also seeks to contract on a cost plus basis rather than competitive bidding. It generally avoids investments in significant fixed assets. However, it is not reactive in the market but actively promotes new projects: 'if there's no project, we'll try to find one; if there's no client we'll try to assemble one; if there's no money we'll try to get them some'.

To this end, Bechtel became closely involved with the US Export–Import Bank which provides export credit, and thereby financed many of the owners around the world for whom Bechtel worked. It was also closely involved with the Republican Party—initially in its home state of California, and then in Washington DC—where the 'revolving door' between Bechtel executives and senior government officials became notorious in the 1980s.

*Sources*: http://www.bechtel.com (accessed 28 January 2021); McCartney (1988); Denton (2016).

Increasingly, suppliers are making offers that are both relational and outcome-based in the form of integrated solutions[24] where the project-based firm takes responsibility for the facility through life and the owner contracts for output availability, rather than acquisition of the output itself, and may also provide the finance for the project. For instance, Avanti West Coast does not own the rolling stock it operates on the UK's West Coast Main Line (WCML), but contracts to Alstom for its availability, with Alstom retaining ownership of the trains. Within the public sector, such arrangements are known as public–private partnerships (PPPs) such as the Private Finance Initiative in the United Kingdom, where the public-sector owner and operator such as a hospital pays on the basis of facility availability.[25] It should be noted that such arrangements are only an apparent rupture with the owner business model shown in Figure 5.1 because the owner is still the operator and retains responsibility for generating the funding stream that repays the private finance by turning outputs into outcomes such as passenger transportation services.

### Exercise 6.1

Think how the PBFs differ from corporations in other sectors which are not project-based. What implications might this have for leadership and strategy in a PBF?

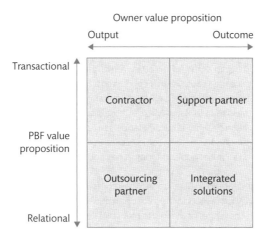

Figure 6.4  The supplier's offer to the owner.

*Source*: developed from Kujala et al. (2010: figure 1).

## 6.5 Professional Service Firms as project-based firms

Another type of project-based firm that is found in many sectors is the Professional Service Firm (PSF) which is both a project-based firm and a professional practice. Indeed, some project-based sectors such as management consulting are dominated by PSFs such as Accenture in Vignette 6.2. Services play a growing role in advanced economies yet, just as there is considerable variety in types of manufacturing, there is similar variety in types of services, and the combination of customization and the relatively high skills required for delivery creates a distinctive niche for the PSF. It is through the deployment of high skills to create customized solutions for owners that the PSF interacts with the labour market governed by a professional institution to provide sophisticated intellectual services to owners.

The underlying business model of the PSF is a very simple one.[26] The profitability of professional practice is the key performance indicator defined as the rate of profit per principal (i.e. partner or director) of the firm. It should be noted that this perspective does not imply a claim that PSF does or should profit maximize; it is merely a statement of the obvious point that unless a PSF makes a surplus in the form of a profit, it cannot survive and grow in the longer term. The greater that profit, the greater is the amount that the principals who jointly own the PSF can choose to invest in developing the firm through base-shifting projects. The PSF business model formula for profit per partner is:[27]

$$\frac{\text{Profits}}{\text{Principals}} = \frac{\text{Profits}}{\text{Fees}} \times \frac{\text{Fees}}{\text{Staff}} \times \frac{\text{Staff}}{\text{Principals}}$$

What are the managerial levers to increase profits per principal? This is the equivalent to return on equity (the capital provided by the shareholders) for a P-form

## Vignette 6.2   Accenture plc

Accenture plc is a global technology consultancy registered in Ireland, and one of the largest global PSFs. It began as the Administrative Services division of the Arthur Andersen accounting firm in the early 1950s, when it conducted a feasibility study for General Electric (GE) which led to GE's installation of a UNIVAC I computer in 1954. It grew rapidly, working in collaboration with the likes of IBM and Microsoft, supporting owners on the implementation of corporate information systems. It became Andersen Consulting in 1988 and split completely from Arthur Andersen to become Accenture in 2001. The partners then voted for incorporation and an initial public offering. It has since grown to an operation of 505 k employees across 51 countries.

Born from the third Industrial Revolution, Accenture's core business is the shaping and delivery of technology for owners in the public and private sectors as they seek to transform digitally to meet the challenges of the fourth Industrial Revolution. It is divided into four main areas of activity:

- *strategy and consulting* draws on Accenture's long-established information systems expertise to advise and implement digital business transformation;

- *experiences* combines technology and marketing expertise to create new offerings for customer-orientated sectors, including app development;

- *technology* is offered through a network of over 100 innovation hubs in areas such as data analytics, cyber-security, and cloud technologies. Under its Industry X brand, Accenture provides information and data analytic services for investment projects in the engineering and construction sectors—see Case 11;

- *operations* provides support in areas such as supply-chain management and customer fulfilment.

Crucial for a leading PSF is thought leadership. To this end, Accenture is a partner in the World Economic Forum, and is one of the leading players in shaping our understanding of the fourth Industrial Revolution.

*Sources*: Jagersma (2020); https://www.accenture.com/gb-en (accessed 20 August 2021); Wikipedia (accessed 26 January 2021).

corporation and is a more appropriate measure because few PSFs are publicly traded. The first lever is **margin**, or the ratio of profits to fee income (profits as a percentage of sales). This in turn is a function of the costs per unit of output and the fee charged per unit of output. All three elements of costs—salaries, other variable costs, fixed costs—can be managed, but only within a limited range. The largest element of costs is salaries, but these are largely set by the labour market and so are difficult to manage. Turning to fixed overheads, PSFs typically have very few capital assets and even if the firm owns the building it works in, it is likely to be owned by the principals' pension fund rather than the PSF itself. Their only assets really are their people. Other fixed costs such as office overheads, and other variable costs such as travel, are hygiene factors[28]—waste should be avoided, but paring them back is unlikely to make much of a difference to performance and if staff are inadequately resourced performance can be undermined. For instance, poor IT systems can reduce staff effectiveness. Clearly, the fee charged per unit of output is crucial to margin.

The second lever is **productivity** which in the PSF is the relationship between staff and fee income. The latter is typically measured in terms of billable hours on a cost-plus contract or earned value on a reimbursable or fixed-price contract—see Figure 9.4. Careful organization of work can get the best out of staff so that they are spending the maximum amount of time on fee-earning work by using appropriate IT tools and by providing back-office support for more mundane tasks. However, there is relatively little opportunity to compete in this area, and pushing up fee-earning hours above the normal working week is rarely sustainable in the longer term. Again, the most effective route to profitability is to increase the fee per unit of output.

The third lever is **leverage** defined as the ratio between the number of salaried staff and the number of principals. The typical organizational structure of a PSF is the triangular one of principals who find the work, associates who oversee the work, and junior professionals who actually do the work—these are colloquially known as the 'finders', 'minders', and 'grinders'. Leverage measures the ratios of staff at each of these three levels. Clearly, for a constant fee level, the greater the ratio of juniors to principals the more profitable the PSF will be for the principals that own it. The problem for PSFs—and it is this that most clearly distinguishes them from P-form corporations—is that there is no systematic difference in educational attainment apart from experience between the juniors and the principals. Juniors join PSFs not just for jobs, but for careers, and also bring in fresh ideas which can enhance the innovativeness of the PSF. Their lack of experience is compensated through the oversight of the associates and principals, who can then charge out the juniors to owners at many multiples of their salary costs.

Managing the trade-offs between margin, productivity, and leverage in the context of the market in which the firm competes is called 'balancing the professional service firm'.[29] Different market positioning through providing different kinds of service can affect the trade-offs between these levers. For instance, more challenging work will tend to reduce leverage because juniors will need greater supervision, but should also allow the attainment of a higher fee level and also provide relatively more senior positions for juniors to be promoted to. Growth is another way of providing promotion opportunities while retaining the leverage ratio, but the growth rates required typically outpace the overall rate of growth in market, and so not all can succeed in this strategy. Some PSFs—particularly in management consulting—have explicit up or out policies so as to control growth while retaining the ability to recruit fresh juniors, and some PSFs will give an associate a job that is too small for the firm to get him or her started on their own. Others take the hint and leave.

---

### Exercise 6.2

What are the key differences between P-form corporations and PSFs from a human resources point of view?

## 6.6 Competitive advantage in PSFs

There is a number of trade-offs to be made in achieving balance, and so we will now analyse the sources of competitive advantage for PSFs and then indicate how they shape these trade-offs. The success of any supplier is a function of its capability to provide some service matched to the need for that service. For a PSF, we can think of operational capability as consisting of its **resources** which consist almost entirely of the competencies of the professionals it employs, and its **routines**—see section 7.4— which are its internal processes for generating appropriate solutions to the owner's problem and the delivery of that solution in the form of task execution for the owner. We can think of dynamic capability as consisting of its sustained ability to win base-shifting projects, which is largely a function of its reputation and its ability to acquire new resources to support that reputation as it grows.

Competitive advantage defined as the balance of the PSFs can be captured in the manner shown in Figure 6.5. The overall market for professional services generates projects to bid for, some of which will be appropriate for the PSF's operational capabilities. The maximum fee level the PSF can charge for the work is a function of the market it is serving; the minimum level is, assuming hygiene factors are under control, a function of the leverage in its organizational structure and its operational

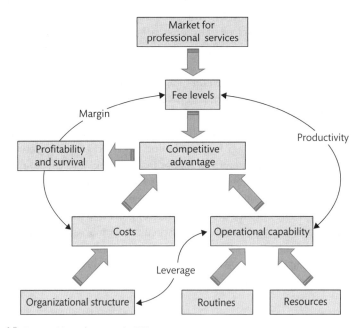

**Figure 6.5** Competitive advantage in PSFs.

*Source*: authors.

capability. Operational capability also determines the types of projects that the practice can bid for, and is a function of the resources available to the PSF in terms of the competencies of the motivated professionals it deploys and the routines it chooses to develop to ensure task execution for the owner. Leverage, as defined in section 6.5 above, captures the cost-base of the PSF. If a PSF becomes under-leveraged in relation to its market, it will be unable to cover its costs with fees; if it becomes over-leveraged, it is likely to suffer deterioration in its operational capabilities and hence fail to deliver to owners, thereby damaging its reputation.

One way of understanding the different configurations of competitive advantage (i.e. balance points between market, operational capability, and organizational structure) is shown in Figure 6.6. It distinguishes two market dimensions—mission complexity and owners' quality preference. *Mission complexity* is defined on the y axis of Figure 2.4. For instance, is the project mission merely a question of adapting known solutions to the particular problem at hand, or are there considerable complexities in terms of stakeholder management, technical requirements, iconic status, or whatever to be addressed? The bulk of PSF work is simple to complicated (as defined in section 2.5) rather than complex, and many of the PSFs tackling less challenging projects are microenterprises working in regional markets. PSFs addressing the more complex missions tend to be larger, and many have multiple offices to attain national or international coverage. The second dimension is *quality preference* in terms of whether the owner wishes to emphasize quality of conception or quality of specification as defined in Figure 7.1. For instance, is an iconic building or a luxury segment consumer product required, or does the owner need to meet a price point

## Vignette 6.3    A tale of two cities

The importance of the owner's project mission underpinning the criteria for the selection of PBFs based on their operational capabilities is well illustrated by the differing approaches to the main stadium for the Beijing and London Olympics. In Beijing, the 2008 Olympics were seen as evincing the arrival of China on the international stage as a mature nation and an opportunity for one-upmanship over Shanghai. Modernizing national elites therefore wanted an iconic, internationally designed stadium that expressed this new status. London was the first city to hold the Olympics for the third time in 2012 and is more confident of its position as a leading global city, with no serious national contender (not even Manchester!). It therefore chose to use the Olympics as part of its urban regeneration strategy and opted for a much more functional design that could be downsized following the games and is presently occupied by West Ham United football club.

The two local organizing committees therefore chose two very different kinds of PSF for their showpiece stadia in order to deliver on their very different project missions. Beijing chose an internationally renowned *strong ideas* PSF—Herzog and de Meuron—as architects for its stadium. Based in Basel, Switzerland, Herzog and de Meuron have designed many public buildings around the world, particularly museums such the Tate Modern in Vignette 3.3, but had not built a stadium before. It has won the top architectural prizes such as the Pritzker Medal. London, in contrast, chose the *strong experience* PSF—Populous—as architects. Based in London, Populous specializes in stadia and other events venues and has designed 12 Olympic venues around the world, including the Fisht Stadium for Sochi 2014 in Vignette 4.2.

*Sources*: Ren (2008); http://www.herzogdemeuron.com (accessed 26 January 2021); http://www.populous. com (accessed 26 January 2021).

for a mass market? Vignette 6.3 provides the example of different Olympic stadium projects showing how these different quality preferences affect the selection of supplier PSF by the owner.

These two dimensions generate four distinctive PSF configurations, as shown in Figure 6.6; all are sustainable market positions with the exception of strong ambition—such firms either evolve into one of the other configurations or they fail. Strong delivery PSFs tend to be highly leveraged because the relative simplicity of their projects means that they can economize on supervision. Strong ideas firms tend to be able to charge a premium in the market, due to their reputation, and so tend to be highly productive. The challenges are greatest in the strong experience firms because the requirement to retain experienced staff tends to weaken margin.

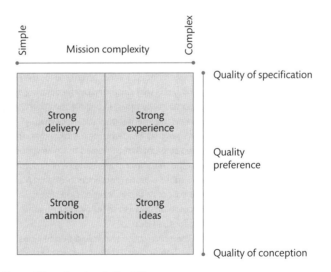

Figure 6.6  Competitive advantage in the PSF.

*Source*: developed from *Winch and Schneider (1993: figure 1).

## 6.7 Project networks

As can be seen from Figure 6.3, PBFs typically work in networks of inter-firm relationships of contract and subcontract, while also forming peer relationships through joint ventures. Forming relationships between firms in such networks is akin to the Jane Austen problem of finding a partner of appropriate wealth, status, and character.[30] The strategic problem for PBFs is a combination of relationship portfolio management and project portfolio management (to be discussed further in Chapter 8), as shown in Figure 6.7. The relationship portfolio defines the set of inter-firm relationships both across the commercial interface with all the owners with which agreements are, or have been, in place, and all the other PBFs with which agreements are in place for current or earlier delivery projects. As shown in Figure 6.3, there may also be other PBFs within the project coalition with which there are no formal agreements. The second dimension is between those projects for which agreements are or have been in place, and those projects which are new opportunities in development. These may be either at bid stage, or may be opportunities in the offing which business development is working on—see Chapter 9 on capture management. Accessing such prospects may involve innovation with an in-house research and development function, or collaborating with other PBFs in the relationship network. Here, project marketing[31] will be trying to understand the owner's project-shaping process and its likely implications for their capabilities, and indeed, potential owners' future investment projects. Capture management teams will be discussing with other PBFs how those capabilities might be enhanced through either formal joint venturing or more informal partnering.

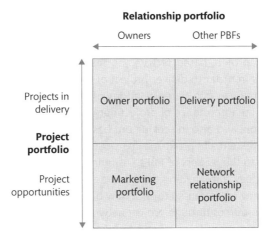

Figure 6.7  Four portfolios for PBFs.

*Source*: developed from Tikkanen et al. (2007).

These dynamic relationships in the supplier domain form **project networks**[32] in which the legacy of the past and shadow of the future weigh heavily.[33] Learning from past collaborations creates a path dependence[34] within the project network as firms favour those PBFs with which they have had positive experiences, and avoid those with which the experiences were negative in their relationship networks. PBFs are also aware that they will need to collaborate with others on future collaborative ventures. Owners will typically evaluate the appropriateness of the proposed collaborative network for their project mission when selecting suppliers, particularly for base-shifting projects. We explore owner contracting strategies and the suppliers' project strategies in response in Chapter 9. In industries such as film and TV production,[35] project networks are often spatially located and meld into the project ecologies to be discussed in Chapter 10.

---

### Exercise 6.3

What is the business development process for PBFs?

---

## 6.8 Summary

In this chapter, we have explored the supplier domain in project organizing. This domain is occupied by a very distinctive type of firm that receives relatively little attention in project organizing—the project-based firm (PBF). A PBF is one that has project delivery capabilities as a core *operational* capability—this is how it meets owner requirements on a day-to-day basis. There are various types of PBF, ranging from P-form corporations through to contractors to PSFs, but they all share this distinctive operational capability at the heart of their business models. These firms form project-based sectors and mobilize on projects in distinctive coalitions of PBFs in order to deliver project outputs for the owner. In that mobilization they organize into tiered relations of contract and sub-contract. We have also shown the importance of project networks of PBFs both in developing market penetration, and also in seeking out base-moving projects to enter new markets. As quintessentially profit-making organizations[36] the PLM dimensions are also relevant to the leaders of PBFs. Visioning is required for the creation of the business strategy and aligning the projects selected to the strategy; sense-making and relating are essential to spot new business opportunities and to develop access to resources through project networks. We now move on to discuss the delivery domain, where owners and suppliers come together temporarily on specific projects.

## 6.9  Further reading

Jagersma, P. K. 2020. *On Becoming Extraordinary: Decoding Accenture and Other Star Professional Service Firms.* Amsterdam: Inspiration Press.
Charts the rise of the super-PSF in management consulting.

Maister, D. 2003. *Managing the Professional Service Firm.* London: Simon & Schuster.
Seminal text on managing PSFs.

Davies, A. and Hobday, M. 2005. *The Business of Projects: Managing Innovation in Complex Products and Systems.* Cambridge: Cambridge University Press.
Detailed analysis of the strategic management of P-form corporations.

## 6.10  Summary review questions

1. How do PBFs differ from project owner organizations?
2. What is distinctive about a project-based sector?
3. What is the difference between a P-form corporation and a PSF?
4. What are the different viable market positionings for PSFs?
5. Why are project networks important for PBFs?

 *Visit the Oxford Learning Link site for this text to find answer guidance to the questions and exercises in this chapter.*

 *Take your learning further by viewing videos relevant to this chapter on the Oxford Learning Link site.*

## Notes

1. *Whitley (2006).
2. Winch (2014); Davies and Brady (2016).
3. Sergeeva and Winch (2020).
4. Hobday (2000).
5. Acha et al. (2004).
6. Gann and Salter (2000); Miller et al. (1995).
7. Zietsma et al. (2017).
8. *Financial Times*, 2 December 2019.
9. Barney (2001).

10. Prencipe et al. (2003).

11. Davies and Hobday (2005); Ethiraj et al. (2005). Turner and Keegan (2001) suggest that these are the responsibility of the 'broker' and the 'steward', respectively.

12. Ansoff (1968).

13. Brady and Davies (2004).

14. Ansoff (1968).

15. Peters and Waterman (1982).

16. Brady and Davies (2004).

17. Huemann et al. (2007).

18. These employ 10 people or fewer (https://stats.oecd.org/glossary, accessed 11 March 2021)—frequently, they are sole traders.

19. Winch (1994).

20. McKinsey (2017).

21. *Söderlund and Tell (2009).

22. Winch (1994).

23. Wikström et al. (2009); Momeni and Martinsuo (2019).

24. Davies and Hobday (2005).

25. Winch and Schmidt (2016).

26. Maister (1993).

27. Fees = average fee income per unit of output; Staff = total payroll cost; Principals = number of partners.

28. Herzberg (1968).

29. Maister (1982).

30. Winch (2010).

31. Cova et al. (2002).

32. DeFillippi and Sydow (2016); Pryke (2012).

33. Ligthart et al. (2016).

34. Manning and Sydow (2011).

35. Sydow and Staber (2002).

36. Few PBFs are found in the public sector, with the notable exception of countries like China and its state-owned enterprises.

 ## Case 6    A 'company of projects': BAE Systems

BAE Systems plc is a global supplier of defence materiel for land, sea, air, and cyber-space operations across four continents with a corporate vision to be 'the premier international defence, aerospace and security company'. It is one of the world's leading P-form corporations, with an internal identity as a 'Company of Projects', acting as both specialist technology supplier and systems integrator across a portfolio of complex projects. It was formed in 1999 from the consolidation of the UK defence project-based sector, and has subsequently made substantial acquisitions in the United States and Australia. It currently employs 85,800 people in over 40 countries. The principal business model is to win projects from defence ministries—usually through competitive bidding—to supply materiel for use by armed forces. In order to do this, it owns and operates arsenals, factories, and shipyards and frequently forms joint ventures with other suppliers of defence materiel to spread liabilities and to satisfy government requirements for local manufacturing. Working at the leading edge of defence technology, it also owns significant intellectual property. The corporation consists of a large number of business units, each specialized in a particular set of technologies and products.

Following a financial crisis in 2002 caused by serious escalation on two major UK projects, BAE resolved to upgrade its project capabilities from the corporate centre down. The result was the formation of the Corporate Project Management Council (CPMC), the strengthening of the Life-Cycle Management (LCM) framework, and the launch of the Project Management Developing You (PMDY) programme. BAE is strongly aligned with the Project Management Institute (PMI), the Association for Project Management (APM), and other associations depending on regional location. The LCM framework was refreshed in 2013 and the supporting resources were further developed. BAE defines project management as 'the capability which integrates the multi-functional activities necessary to execute Projects successfully, maintaining a focus on meeting the needs of our Customers'.

In terms of structure, the Performance Excellence team within the Office of the Chief Executive Officer oversees the LCM and internal governance through the CPMC. Regional PM councils then address local resource and competence development issues. Within business units, projects are structured on either a project matrix or a 'projectized' basis. The Project Management Authority (PMA) is 'the individual appointed by the [Business Unit] Leader to ensure that LCM is appropriately implemented and effectively deployed with the Business'. Capture is the responsibility of the Capture Manager (CM) 'to integrate all the activities necessary to win the opportunity', while delivery is the responsibility of the Project Manager (PM) 'to integrate all the activities required to deliver the output of the Project'. Within the BAE project team, the Control Account Manager has responsibility for particular packages of work against schedule and budget, working with the Project Planning and Control Manager. Where business units organize projects on a matrix basis, Functional PM teams led by the Head of PM 'provide central expert support and develop appropriate local processes. They also manage the local PM resource pool, and associated career development processes.'

In terms of process, the LCM framework is at the heart of managing projects within BAE, forming one of BAE's five Core Business Processes, which sit inside the corporate Operational Framework. LCM is a 13-phase process for the *internal* governance and assurance of BAE Systems' projects and programmes, as shown in Table 6.1. The first five phases cover **project capture**; the next eight phases cover *project delivery*, which is extended in the final two phases to include **in-service support** and final **close-out** of the project. The LCM applies to all projects above £10 m in value and needs to be adapted to the needs of each individual project. Adaptation is the responsibility of the PMA within each business unit working with the Engineering Authority to ensure alignment with engineering design reviews. BAE has been increasingly advocating a 'left shift' in the LCM— that is, investing more in earlier phases of the LCM to enable earlier maturity of the project. Each phase ends with a Phase Review, which acts as a Decision Gate for the project. The roles of the CM and PM overlap during the later phases of Capture because a mature Project Management Plan is a central output of the Bid phase.

Throughout Capture, the project team continually reassesses the answers to the Phase Review questions against three mutually reinforcing criteria:

- Customer Value Proposition, addressing the question, 'Why would the customer buy it?';
- BAE Systems Value Proposition, addressing the question, 'Why would we want to sell it?';
- Delivery Assurance, addressing the question, 'Can we deliver it on time and budget?'

Delivery starts after contract Acceptance with mobilization and flows through to the Delivery and Acceptance of the output by the customer for entry into active service.

Table 6.1  BAE Systems project LCM framework

| Stage | Phase review pass criteria | Phase title |
|---|---|---|
| Capture | Can we win? Do we want to win? | Opportunity and Development |
| | What do we need to do to win? | Opportunity and Qualification |
| | Are we going to bid? | Bid/No bid |
| | Are we ready to bid? | Bid |
| Can we accept the contract? | Pre-Contract Acceptance | Delivery |
| Are the project resources in place? | Project Mobilization | |
| Does the product design meet the requirements? | Preliminary Product | |
| Is the product ready for implementation? | Detailed Product | |
| Is the product ready for testing? | Development and Integration | |
| Is the product ready for delivery? | Product Qualification | |
| Has the product been delivered and accepted? | Delivery and Acceptance | |
| Is the product operating correctly? | Support and Service | Are the closure actions complete? |
| Closure | | |

*Source*: corporate documentation.

Around half of BAE Systems' projects include in-service support and so a Support and Service phase; all projects include a Closure Phase, sometimes up to 40 years after the Capture Phase was initiated.

Each phase is completed with pass or fail answers to the relevant questions at a Phase Review to 'review the suitability and application of the Project plans and processes and the current Design Review status to assess whether the Product is sufficiently mature to move forward to the next phase'. The mandated Phase Review chair for the first three phases is the Business Unit Leader (BUL); subsequently, it is an independent chair appointed by the Project Manager. Both Reviews are supported by Independent Assessors, who provide subject-matter expertise. Above the Phase Reviews, the Bid Status Reviews during Capture and the Contract Reviews during Delivery are both chaired by the BUL, who acts as project sponsor within BAE. Bid Status Reviews are held 'to provide a regular forum for the Business Leadership Team to review Bid progress, address issues, and make decision on how to proceed'. Contract Reviews 'support the Project management process by raising the Project status communication and decision making up the management chain'. A final level of governance is provided at the end of the Bid Phase with the Request for Bid Approval process 'to ensure that all Bids are properly reviewed and approved at the required management level before they are submitted to customers'. Bid Approval provides assurance for senior management that the bid is technically sound and finalizes the pricing. It is chaired by the BUL and may also involve corporate executives for more significant projects.

LCM provides a sophisticated, adaptable, internal project governance framework across all significant projects delivered by BAE Systems, including internal development projects. However, mandating a process and ensuring that it adds value in practice are not quite the same thing. A key issue is *how* reviews at all three levels are conducted. There is continual emphasis in the guidance documents that reviews are meant to be supportive and solution-orientated rather than adversarial and threatening. Effective Decision-Gate Reviews within LCM:

- summarize and synthesize key messages;
- consider progress against the project baseline;
- explore the root causes of issues;
- make clear decisions and allocate responsibility for actions;
- learn from experience, coaching, and team development.

The Phase Review chair is expected to create an environment of 'openness, honesty, trust and engagement . . . [in which participants] actively listen to other points of view and encourage the sharing of information and resources'. It is stressed that 'freedom to admit mistakes and asking for feedback are important elements of creating trust. Any perception of fear can suppress facts and opinions, reduce creativity and be divisive and de-motivating.'

In terms of competencies, different levels of management competency are specified in Table 6.2.

Table 6.2  BAE Systems competencies for leaders

| PM level | Responsibility | Competence |
|---|---|---|
| First Line Manager | Set standards and assign work | Getting things done through others |
| Manager of Managers | Interpret business strategy | Inspiring good people management |
| Senior Leaders | Set the business plan | Creating great workplaces and high-performance cultures |
| Business Unit Leaders | Create the strategy | Engaging employees in delivery of the strategy |

*Sources*: corporate documentation: http://www.baesystems.com (accessed 17 August 2021); corporate documents; interview with Prof. Stuart Forsyth, BAE Systems plc, 2 February 2021.

## Discussion questions

1. Why does BAE Systems have three tiers of governance within LCM?

2. What is the difference in the roles of the Capture Manager, Project Manager, and Project Management Authority in BAE Systems?

3. Why does BAE Systems call its 13 reviews 'phase reviews' rather than 'stage-gate reviews' (see section 8.4.2 for a definition of the latter)?

# 7 The delivery domain

## 7.1 Introduction: temporary project organizing

We have looked at the two domains populated by permanent organizations involved in strategic project organizing (SPO)—the owner domain that shapes the project mission and provides the financial resources required for the project, and the supplier domain that responds to the owner's investment opportunity and provides the human and material resources required for the project. We now turn to the delivery domain and the *temporary* organization that actually delivers the project outputs to the owner, as shown in Figure 2.2. The delivery organization has been at the heart of the traditional approaches to project management but, as Chapters 5 and 6 have shown, it does not tell the whole story of SPO, which is about how permanent organizations come together in a temporary delivery organization to project the outputs from which outcomes can change our world.

We start by looking at the relationship between the *project mission* articulated by the owner as the strategic case for the project, and the **project scope**, which defines in progressive detail what is actually to be delivered to achieve that mission by the delivery organization as defined in the work breakdown structure (WBS). The principal outcome of this definition process from a SPO perspective (as opposed to an engineering design perspective) is the strategic **project delivery plan** (PDP), which provides the overall strategy for the delivery phase of the project, shown in Figure 2.7. One of the principal responsibilities of the project leader within the creating dimension of the Project Leadership Model (PLM) introduced in section 3.2.4 is designing the project delivery organization and we will therefore present the SPO Star Model, which provides a framework for its design as part of the PDP. We then revisit the teaming discussion from section 3.4 to see how teams work together on project delivery through future-making and then turn to the choice of waterfall or agile strategies for project delivery. We complete the chapter by looking at the resilience of the delivery organization using early warning signs, systems thinking concepts, and insights into the process of project escalation. We finish with the case of Stage One, an international events company.

## 7.2 **From project mission to project scope**

Vignette 7.1 presents a summary of BT's Customer Repair and Maintenance Offices (CRMO) project. The vignette identifies the difference between project mission and project scope. The project mission captures *why* the project is being done, as defined in Chapter 5. *Project scope* then identifies *what* needs to be done in order to achieve the project mission, and the 'translation' of the project mission into the scope is the fundamental task of the shaping of the project, shown in Figure 2.7. In Vignette 7.1, the mission identifies why the project has been selected as part of BT's project portfolio, while the scope identifies what has to be done to realize that mission. The scope also includes two elements of safeguarding[1]—the implementation of 'enquiry desks' by integrating the CRMO system with the broader suite of customer relationship management (CRM) systems, and the longer-term option to off-shore the 'back office' elements of the CRMO. In addition to this high-level scope, BT also identified schedule information in terms of an expected end date (nine months hence) and key milestones (five months hence for the opening of the first refurbished office) for the programme. It also developed a budget that provided the basis for the cost–benefit analysis that constituted the value proposition, as defined in section 5.5. Because of the four different types of project in the initiative, BT chose to manage it overall as a programme as defined in section 8.3 to achieve the outcome of improving performance in responding to customers' repair and maintenance needs.

The project-shaping process in Figure 7.1 is the iterative process of generating the project scope from the project mission, defining both the technical specifications for the output and the PDP for its realization. The PDP provides the overall framework for project delivery in a more linear or waterfall fashion. The project scope can be articulated in terms of quality of conception which is the extent to which the output being created subjectively delights the final customers of the owner in line with the requirements of the value proposition and quality of specification which is the technical fitness for purpose of that output.[2] Quality of realization assesses the extent to which a viable PDP has been developed to deliver the project mission in alignment with the value proposition. Consummate project delivery then assesses the extent to which the objectives set in the PDP are successfully realized. This second triangle is the same as the conventional 'iron triangle' of project management (time, cost, quality),[3] while clarifying that 'quality' is quality of conformance to the technical requirements specified in the PDP, including obligations on environmental security, safety, and health[4] which we will revisit in Chapter 11.

The foundation of the PDP is the work breakdown structure (WBS) as shown in Figure 7.2, which captures all *tasks* that need to be completed to deliver the scope.[5] The WBS provides the baseline for managing the project through the Define and Execute stages defined in Figure 2.7. Estimates of schedule and budget are prepared

## Vignette 7.1    BT's Customer Repair and Maintenance Offices programme

BT plc provides advanced communication networks to domestic, government, and commercial customers. With the strategic aim of improving customer service, it chose to invest in its CRMO, which responds to reports from customers of faults in the network. It believed it could do this by implementing new technology recently developed by its own research and development (R&D) department.

The stated *mission* of the project was to improve customer service so that:

- all customers obtain a free line when calling;
- all calls are answered within 10 seconds;
- maximum response time for engineer site visits is 2 hours.

The mission also stated a constraint that:
- the investment costs of the system were to be justified through productivity improvements without generating redundancies.

In order to achieve this mission, the *scope* included:
- reorganizing from 18 area offices to three call receipt offices, two diagnostic offices, and four field offices;
- selecting and implementing CRM technology;
- refurbishing the nine remaining offices to contemporary standards;
- retraining and redeploying staff;
- integrating the CRMOs with the existing customer information system.

Two further development options were to be safeguarded within the scope:
- the early option of integrating the call receipt offices with the rest of the customer service organization through integrated 'enquiry desks';
- the longer-term option of off-shoring call receipt and diagnosis offices.

The scope includes four different types of project, as defined in section 1.1:
- an information systems *infrastructure project* for the CRMO system and its interface with BT's other CRM systems, and associated training;
- a building infrastructure project for refurbishing the new offices;
- a *transformation project* involving decanting people from familiar locations organized geographically and moving them to their new ones organized functionally;
- BT's R&D department had a *new product development* project to develop the CRM technology.

*Source*: Turner (2014).

against the WBS, while the technical aspects of the scope are developed further during engineering development. Clusters of tasks such as major components of the output like the roof of the School of Health shown in Figure 7.2 are often called **deliverables**. Clusters of tasks let to a single supplier such as the 'profile cladding' in

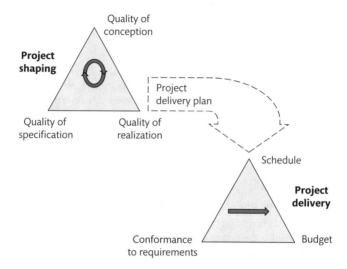

**Figure 7.1** The project delivery plan.

*Source*: developed from Winch (2010: figure 8.3).

Figure 7.2 are usually known as **packages**. The WBS is the basis for the development of three of the principal elements of the PDP, which we will revisit in Chapter 11:

- the **schedule** is a sequential array through time of all the tasks in the WBS and identifies *when* tasks should be executed, and the **critical path** through that array is defined as the longest sequence of tasks with no slack;

- *threats* to the delivery of the scope on schedule and budget analysed both quantitatively (known knowns) and qualitatively (known unknowns) captured in the **threat register** of the project, what might go wrong during delivery;

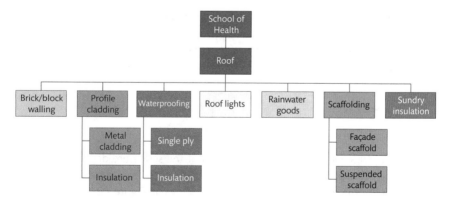

**Figure 7.2** WBS for the School of Health roof.

*Source*: authors.

- the **budget** provides a cost model of the project broken down by task and therefore sums to answer the question *how much* the WBS will cost to deliver.

The other principal elements of the PDP are:

- the contracting strategy for engaging with suppliers for the various WBS packages, which we will discuss in Chapter 9.
- the design of the project delivery organization, which we will discuss next.

## 7.3  Designing the delivery organization

One of the principal elements of creating in the SPO PLM presented in Figure 3.1 is designing the project delivery organization, which is, fundamentally, an organization design problem: 'Designing effective organizations ... is a key task of the leader.'[6] There are many different methodologies for organization design, but the one we have found most suitable for adaptation to the challenges of designing the temporary project organization is the Star Model[7] presented in Figure 7.3. While the SPO Project Star Model (PSM) also applies to the design of the permanent owner and supplier organizations that come together in the delivery domain, our focus here is on the temporary organization that actually delivers the project.[8] The PSM identifies the key parameters in the design of a project delivery organization as a whole. These are:

- **scope**, which defines all the tasks that need to be executed to deliver the project output and is a function of the project mission, as discussed in section 7.2;
- **structure**, the design of the set of reporting relationships within the project delivery organization across the multiple teams from the different PBFs deployed within the project coalition;
- **processes**, the design of the way information flows *between* the various teams deployed on the projects, and in particular the information loop presented in Figure 11.3;
- **incentives**, the ways in which teams and their members are rewarded for their contribution to the project;
- **competencies**, the skills required of the team members deployed on the project;
- **identity**, which is the alignment with the project delivery narrative in both shaping and delivery, as discussed in section 4.4.

All the elements of the model need to be in alignment and support each other, with the project delivery identity as the binding 'DNA'. For instance, it is easy to end up with structures that are functionally orientated in the interests of incentives and

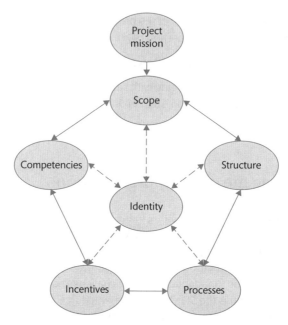

**Figure 7.3** The SPO Project Star Model.

*Source*: developed from Galbraith (1995: figure 2.1).

competencies, but which disrupt the smooth flow of information through the project organization. Similarly, perceived disparities in incentives between the various teams within the structure can generate frictions and disrupt project execution.[9] Alignment of the project delivery organization around the project narrative is the principal challenge for the project leader during delivery. The team is the basic unit of organizing,[10] so the project delivery organization is effectively a social network of teams with team leaders typically acting as the nodes in the network,[11] and the leader's design challenge is to align the processes and incentives of those teams within the project organization structure.

The fundamental elements of process in organizations are the flows of information. However, managing those flows directly is difficult, and we typically shape those flows through designing organization structures. Developing our allegory of Cole's 'Voyage of Life', the analogy of a river is helpful here:

> What is of interest in a river is the flow of water, which irrigates crops, provides a transport route, enables the generation of hydroelectric power and is a source of leisure and repose. Yet it is through altering the banks that we shape the flow—dams and weirs create lakes and power; dykes and canals control direction; docks and locks facilitate transport; bridges and tunnels mitigate the downside of the river as a barrier. At the same time, the action of the water erodes banks, weakens riverine structures, and silts navigation channels. The process—the flow of water—cannot be directly managed, we have to manage the context in which it flows, but those flows also change the ways in which we manage.[12]

Designing the project delivery organization is therefore about designing structures and processes that can shape the information flows on the project in the desired manner—structure and process are a dualism that mutually constitute organization.[13] This design process is particularly important for the smooth flow of the information loop presented in Figure 11.3.

---

### Exercise 7.1

Review Case 3. Which aspects of the Waterloo International Project did Patrick Crotty design as project leader?

---

## 7.4 Teaming as future-making in project delivery

We discussed the principles of teaming on projects in section 3.4. Here, we integrate those principles into the project delivery organization as a dynamic interplay between routines, tasks, and teams in a process of future-making,[14] as shown in Figure 7.4:

- Routines are the learned practices that are carried from project to project and then adapted to meet the needs of particular projects. Routines thereby provide the cognitive resources which teams will use to decide how to complete their allocated tasks.[15] Routines therefore specify *how* tasks are to be executed.
- Teams are the human resources with particular competencies allocated to the delivery organization by the supplier PBFs, identifying *who* will do task

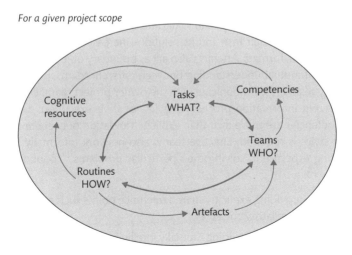

Figure 7.4 Teaming as future-making in project delivery.
*Source*: developed from Winch (2010: figure IV.3).

execution. From a teaming perspective, project teams are inherently learning organizations.[16]

- Tasks specify *what* is to be done in task execution—the set of tasks that has to be completed by the team in order to deliver the project derived from the WBS.

Routines have a number of important features:[17]

- they act as the repository of know-how in the organization;

- they provide the basis for action under uncertainty;

- they provide heuristics which economize on information processing and thereby increase efficiency;

- their use in each project requires improvization, and routines are thereby a source of change as well as stability;

- they provide legitimacy for particular outcomes through perceptions of due process;

- they imply both a procedure and a division of labour, and it is the latter feature which distinguishes them from individuals' habits.

Routines can vary from the formally mandated when they take the form of rules, through management tools and techniques, to informally negotiated and accepted ways of getting along. Although many routines are mandated by the project management office discussed in section 8.4.6, and advocated by the project management professional bodies discussed in section 12.2, they have to be continually adapted to meet the needs of particular projects in interaction with the tasks to be delivered and the competencies of the teams allocated to the project. They are open to formal interventions through improvement programmes and subject to autonomous evolution. Thus, the notion of 'best practice' in project performance is diffused through the adoption and adaptation of recommended routines on particular projects.

Artefacts are generated by teams in visual and textual forms to deepen their mutual understanding of their task and its solution—increasingly, these are in digital rather than physical formats. Artefacts also act as boundary objects[18] that allow the development of mutual understanding between different teams, particularly enabling delivery teams to communicate with the owner project team. Different tasks require different information-processing styles for their execution, and many of these competencies are more tacit than explicit; translation between information-processing styles is required. Effective teams also network informally with other teams seeking expertise in solving their particular problems.[19] Boundary objects take the form of:

- repositories—providing explicitly shared reference points such as international standards and regulatory codes;

- standardized formats—providing mutually intelligible ways of presenting information such as the Standard Method of Measurement for bills of quantities;

- sketches and models—communicating design intent across teams responsible for design tasks, with stakeholders, and through to execution task teams;
- interface maps—providing visualizations of the interfaces between task teams such as responsibility matrices and Gantt charts—see Chapters 10 and 11.

Routines, tasks, and teams are negotiated and renegotiated for a particular project chartered by its project mission. As the project moves through the life cycle, the tasks change, and hence different teams are mobilized which deploy different routines. However, prior choices of routines also shape which teams are selected by which criteria and which tasks are deemed to be in scope to the project. The coordination routines used by team leaders for task execution need to be continually adapted to the needs of the particular project, while retaining enough overt good practice to serve as a legitimation for the actions of the team leader. Thus, teaming on projects is indeed a negotiated order,[20] and future-making through teaming can be thought of as the practice level[21] of SPO.

## 7.5 Strategies for project delivery

The rate of economic and technological change is increasing at pace, rendering the waterfall project strategy embodied in the linear life-cycle model unresponsive to those changes, particularly for new product development (NPD).[22] In response, the past 20 years has seen the rise of 'agile' strategies for project delivery, the most popular of which is Scrum.[23] Agile projects differ in three main ways:[24]

- Schedule is not allowed to slip—each project is delivered through a series of sprints in a process of timeboxing. An important implication of timeboxing is that late-running projects do not hoard human resources such as software engineers.
- Scope is usually allowed to slip—each sprint delivers what it can within the timebox and resources available, rather than delivering to a specified scope, and its relevance to the final user is managed by a product manager.
- Agile teams work autonomously, led by ScrumMasters as team leaders using a well-developed set of routines such as stand-up meetings every morning, which require co-location of the team.
- The agile team engages iteratively with owners and their representatives through 'user stories', which are a form of project narrative.

Agile project delivery works very well for small, stand-alone projects that deliver direct to users who can readily transform the agile outputs into usable outcomes. Once agile teams are included within multi-team delivery organizations, problems start.[25] While timeboxing has many advantages, this is only made possible by flexing scope rather than schedule. Where the scope is delivered to the final user (such as in an app upgrade on a mobile phone), then few problems arise, but once another project team is the 'user' of the outputs from the sprints then problems arise if that output does not allow the second team to do its work as planned. The relative autonomy of Scrum teams, while having important incentive properties, also poses challenges if they choose to work on aspects of scope that are not priorities at the level of the project as a whole. These considerations encourage hybrid approaches,[26] in which agile methods form part of the delivery strategy within an overall linear project life cycle, as shown in Figure 7.5. This shows how outcomes from three-week agile sprints are only released to internal 'customers'; these contribute to upgrades released to customers largely aimed at maintaining the value for the customer (e.g. bug and security fixes). On top of these cycles, new value is generated for customers using a more waterfall product development strategy. Vignette 7.2 gives the example of what might be called an agile strategy in construction.

In summary, agile is a project delivery strategy choice with important implications for project organizing as a whole:

- Agile is a project delivery strategy within the PDP. In effect, it breaks up the Define and Execute stages into iterative cycles of detailed planning

## Vignette 7.2   Agility in construction management

The Nightingale Hospital programme in response to the first wave of the COVID-19 pandemic delivered seven field hospitals to provide surge capacity for the existing NHS England hospitals. They cost £220 m and were delivered in less than three weeks—mainly located in exhibition centres, which were closed due to the pandemic. On the owner side, the programme was initiated from the national centre rather than by NHS authorities. Rapid mobilization was possible because the Department for Health and Social Care used its existing ProCure 22 framework agreement with suppliers. This allowed the establishment of a much more rapid, inclusive, problem-solving orientated leadership of the programme.

For instance, the Instruction to Proceed for the NHS Nightingale North West hospital located in the G-Mex Centre in Manchester was received by the Principal Supply Chain Partner, Integrated Health Projects, on 28 March 2020; site works started on 30 March, and the facility was completed on 12 April—a schedule of 13 days. It opened the next day. The suppliers resourced these efforts by pulling people off other projects and working 24/7 to get the job done. This achievement depended on an innovative project management approach characterized by:

- reverse engineering; not really design and build, but more like build and verify by design;
- live beta testing of a full-scale bed bay mock-up assembled on day 2, confirming the dimensions needed by the nursing team and partition system layout;
- change control through a process of 'see a problem, develop an answer, test it, build it', all captured by an auditable document trail;
- clinical liaison providing the go-between, the translator and fixer joining up the thinking of the clinical teams and the Integrated Health Projects team.

Sources: Bowker (2020); https://procure22.nhs.uk (accessed 20 August 2021).

**Figure 7.5** The hybrid model of software project delivery.

*Source*: authors.

and execution. It does not replace the need for project shaping in terms of appraising why the project is being launched and selecting which technologies are to be used. Agile typically excludes system architecture,[27] which is the Select stage for IT software and hardware.

- Agile can only deliver outputs ('usable software'), not outcomes from the use of that software, so the owner still needs to make the transition from outputs to outcomes.

- Proprietary agile methodologies such as Scrum and XP provide highly standardized routines for teams to deploy on particular tasks, as shown in Figure 7.4, but these can generate resistance from team members.[28]

- Agile is more than just a method, it is a delivery narrative, as defined in section 4.4, advocating a particular delivery identity supported by a 'manifesto', and proselytizers who are true believers in the new method and its innate superiority over waterfall delivery strategies—it is one type of project DNA.

---

### Exercise 7.2

Review Vignette 7.2. How does the delivery strategy for the Nightingale Hospital compare to agile principles?

---

## 7.6 Managing emergent threats to delivery

So far we have focused on the PDP; we now turn to the consideration of the re-silience[29] of that plan in the face of the inherent uncertainty and complexity of projecting. Our first consideration addresses the management of uncertainty. By definition, the threats to the achievement of the project mission due to emergence will manifest themselves slowly and ambiguously, while external threats generated by unk-unks are usually difficult to identify early. For this reason, sensitivity to early warning signs (EWS)[30] of potential threats to delivery is crucial, where EWS are defined as ambiguous weak signals of an impending threat event on a project.[31] So, the project leader needs to use sense-making and relating on the basis of intuition[32] to articulate what is going on. Making a project intervention on the basis of an EWS takes all the elements of judging in the PLM discussed in section 3.3—it also requires courage. To be of any use, an intervention must happen early enough to avoid the potential consequences while the EWS is still ambiguous because waiting for a definitive signal probably means interventions are already too late. At the same time, interventions should not over-respond and thereby make matters worse. The implication is that judging becomes ever more important during delivery as project complexity increases.

There is, of course, no definitive list of EWS as every project is unique. For the project leader, EWS are about noticing early deviations from plan, detecting weak signals, using intuition, managing by walking about[33]—and taking appropriate actions with consummate timing. Spotting emergent trends is an important skill: Goldfinger's decision rule on observing the ubiquity of James Bond that 'Once is happenstance, twice is coincidence, the third time it's enemy action'[34] is not a bad guide here, although Goldfinger's response turned out to be inadequate. Project leaders cannot be omniscient in detecting EWS—those closest to the action in the delivery teams are most likely to detect them. However, such teams are unlikely to be in a position to authorize the changes to plan or mobilize the additional resources to mitigate the perceived threats—only project leaders can do that. In order to encourage delivery teams to 'speak truth to power',[35] psychological safety within the project is paramount. Psychological safety is a feature of the organization, not the individual,[36] and is nurtured by:

- respect for all contributions from team members;
- approachability to leaders by team members;
- a tolerance for failure, but non-acceptance of transgressions from mandated routines (e.g. safety routines);
- clear setting of team tasks in the context of the project mission.

As projects move through the life cycle, support from key stakeholders can waver, and project leaders need to be attentive to this, as well as to EWS. Stakeholder priorities may shift, rumours on project progress may circulate, and project sponsors discussed in section 8.4.3 may change.[37] Project leaders need to include watching for these EWS in particular.

## 7.7 Project delivery dynamics

Project delivery is an inherently dynamic process, full of emergent relationships, so we need tools for understanding how the complicated becomes complex in SPO.

A very important tool for helping us here is systems thinking and its analytic complement, systems dynamics,[38] which views organizations as dynamic systems, rather
than collections of isolated components. A basic principle of SPO is that the project
leader identifies variances from plan and intervenes to correct those variances—see
Chapter 11. However, on complex projects:

- feedback loops can reinforce or balance (i.e. counteract) the consequences of
  interventions;
- unintended consequences (knock-on/ripple effects) may follow from
  interventions;
- time and location may mask the effects, intended or otherwise, of our
  interventions so that unintended consequences are missed.

Projects are rich in emergence—the complexity that arises from the interaction of
multiple feedback loops leading to unexpected effects, often masked by time and
distance between cause and effect. For instance, Brooks' Law states that 'adding
manpower to a late running software project makes it later'.[39] Why? Because exiting
team members have to stop doing productive work to induct the new team members, who also inevitably generate rework until they are fully inducted. What do we
mean by the interaction of multiple feedback loops?

   Consider the issue of schedule pressure on a project which is a function of the
amount of work remaining to be done in the time remaining. A project manager
has a number of options for dealing with this threat—one of which is to introduce
overtime working, as shown in Figure 7.6. Starting at the top, we can see that as time
remaining goes down, schedule pressure goes up. This is indicated by the minus sign
on the connecting arrow, which can also be read as a negative correlation. Similarly,
we can see that when work remaining goes up, schedule pressure goes up, a positive
correlation, indicated by the plus sign on the connecting arrow, which can also be
read as when work remaining goes down, schedule pressure goes down. In order to
deal with schedule pressure, the project manager can make a number of possible
interventions, such as reducing scope (reducing work remaining) or increasing time
remaining. These may not be acceptable options, so the project manager may decide to use overtime to address schedule pressure. As schedule pressure goes up, so
overtime goes up (plus sign on the connecting arrow). With increased overtime, the
work completion rate goes up, and as completion rate goes up, the work remaining
goes down (minus sign on the connecting arrow). This creates a balancing (negative
feedback) loop, which we have called the 'midnight oil' loop, and this does indeed
address the schedule pressure issue. A balancing loop can be identified by having an
odd number of minus signs.

   However, excessive overtime over long periods of time often leads to a reduction
in productivity. This is represented by the positive causal link from overtime to fatigue. The double bar across the connecting arrow indicates a time delay as overtime
increases so fatigue increases after a time delay.

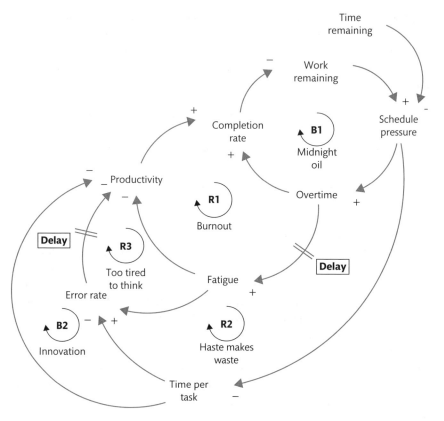

**Figure 7.6** A systems dynamics analysis of project delivery: balancing and reinforcing loops.

*Source*: developed from an original figure by Carl Gavin and Nathan Proudlove.

As fatigue increases, so productivity drops and a drop in productivity leads to a drop in completion rate. This creates a second loop (work remaining, schedule pressure, overtime, fatigue, productivity, completion rate, work remaining) labelled 'burnout'. This is a reinforcing (positive feedback or exponential growth behaviour) loop as it has an even number of negative causal links. Over a period of time the burnout-reinforcing loop will begin to undermine the effects of the midnight oil-balancing loop and schedule pressure will start to rise again. The Elizabeth Line megaproject presented in Vignette 7.3 is an important example of the unintended consequences of accelerating the schedule, which drove complexity into the delivery organization and apparently sent it over its 'tipping point'[40] and out of control.

---

### Exercise 7.3

Trace through the 'haste makes waste' loop and the 'innovation' loop. What effects do they have on schedule pressure? What would happen if additional resources (more people) were added to the project team? Would this increase the completion rate?

### Vignette 7.3    Over the tipping point on the Elizabeth Line

The Elizabeth Line is a complex megaproject with 118 km of track, including 42 km in tunnels, across London. The owner is Transport for London (TfL) and its delivery partner, Crossrail Ltd, a wholly owned subsidiary of TfL. Once the schedule started to slip against the PDP, Crossrail attempted to accelerate in order to maintain the publically agreed end date in 2018. This drove complexity into the schedule, with which Crossrail's reporting systems on progress could not cope. For instance, an attempt to accelerate dynamic testing of the trains meant reducing worksite access for construction (hence slowing that activity down), but because the signalling software was not fully developed, the dynamic testing was not successful. This growing complexity escalated the number of compensation events payable to suppliers by Crossrail because the interfaces between works packages became more difficult to manage.

Reporting from Crossrail to TfL was weak. Briefings typically reported status rather than trends, which made it difficult for TfL to read the true state of progress. KPMG summarize the situation well:

> [Crossrail's] approach was to avoid reporting slippage to the Stage 3 opening date whilst putting plans into place to mitigate the delays ... It seems that over time more and more stretch or optimism became incorporated into the programme through assumptions around shorter activity durations and in some cases parallel running activities to reduce elapsed time but with a consequence that efficiency became more difficult to sustain, float decreased, and time required to complete activities started to exceed the programme time allowed.

The project will likely open four years late in 2022, with an overrun of around £4 bn on a £15 bn budget.

*Sources*: NAO (2019); KPMG (2019); *Financial Times*, 21 August 2020.

## 7.8 Project escalation

Project escalation is the process by which unresolved tensions in project shaping manifest themselves during project delivery in extensions to the schedule and increases in the budget. This is usually due to poor governance (see Chapter 9), where unresolved issues are not flushed out during shaping or projects are allowed to proceed to delivery which should have been stopped. Figure 7.7 offers a model of project escalation. During project shaping, if projecting overrides the value proposition unhampered by the commercial and governance cases shown in Table 5.1, then strategic misrepresentation can drive escalation—this is the 'dark side' of projecting in the PLM. The result is that the PDP is deeply flawed and escalation of schedule and budget during execution becomes inevitable when it is rather too late to revisit the flawed PDP. 'Re-baselining' the project by developing a new PDP is usually the only option in such cases. In order to fend off criticism from stakeholders, the owner typically turns to using the supplier firms as scapegoats, blaming their 'incompetence' for the escalation and thereby obscuring its real drivers. The outcome is yet another

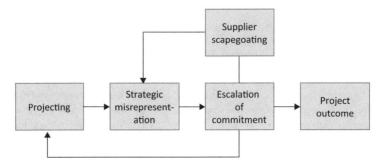

**Figure 7.7** The project escalation process.

*Source*: developed from Winch (2013: figure 1).

project which is late, expensive, and perhaps does not even work properly. While we would not wish to suggest that suppliers always deliver what they say they are going to deliver, we also suggest that the root causes of project escalation more often lie in the owner domain rather than the delivery or supplier domains.

## 7.9 Summary

In this chapter, we have focused on the delivery domain, starting with the translation of the project mission into the project scope during the Select stage. The outputs of the Select stage include the technical specifications defined in the project scope and the PDP which delivers that scope. Project scope is defined by the WBS, which provides the basis for designing the project delivery organization, the structural relationships between the delivery teams, and choosing the delivery strategy. The resilience of the PDP is crucial and needs to be managed through an understanding of EWS, project system dynamics, and project escalation. At the heart of project delivery is teaming, which is where future-making forms the practice level of SPO.

This chapter completes the second section of the book on the three domains of strategic project organizing. We now turn to the third section on the three interfaces of strategic project organizing.

## 7.10 Further reading

Edmondson, A.C. 2019. *The Fearless Organization*. Hoboken, NJ: Wiley.

A major statement of the importance of psychological safety for effective teaming.

Cummings, J. and Pletcher, C. 2011. 'Why project networks beat project teams'. *MIT Sloan Management Review*, 52(3): 75–80.

On the importance of teams maintaining wider informal networks when tackling challenging tasks.

Schoemaker, P. J. H and Day, G. S. 2009. 'How to make sense of weak signals'. *MIT Sloan Management Review*, 50(2): 81–89.
    Thorough review of the challenges of making sense of early warning signs.

## 7.11 Summary review questions

1. What is the principal difference between the delivery domain and the other two domains of SPO?
2. What is the difference between the project mission and the project scope?
3. Why is the PDP so important?
4. What is the WBS?
5. What do you understand by the tipping point in project delivery?

 *Visit the Oxford Learning Link site for this text to find answer guidance to the questions and exercises in this chapter.*

 *Take your learning further by viewing videos relevant to this chapter on the Oxford Learning Link site.*

## Notes

1. Gil (2009).
2. Clark and Fujimoto (1990), call these, respectively, external and internal product integrity in new product development.
3. Barnes and Wearne (1993).
4. Collectively, these are sometimes called QuEnSH criteria.
5. From an engineering perspective, the product breakdown structure (PBS) is also important—see Turner (2014)—but this, by definition, does not include intermediate (temporary) outputs such as the scaffolding in Figure 7.2, which are required to deliver the final output.
6. Galbraith (1995: 1).
7. Kates and Galbraith (2007); others have more recently come to the same conclusion—see Miterev et al. (2017).
8. See Söderlund and Tell (2009) for the evolution of organization design in a P-form corporation, Kwak et al. (2015) in a Professional Service Firm, and Sun and Zhang (2011) for an owner organization.
9. The is a particular problem on projects with large amounts of site-specific execution where teams—often called 'gangs'—are paid on different bases by their respective employing PBFs; see Lumley (1980).
10. Puranam (2018).
11. Carter and DeChurch (2014); Pryke et al. (2018).

12. Winch (2010: 6).

13. Archer (1995).

14. *Comi and Whyte (2018).

15. Bechky (2006).

16. Edmondson and Harvey (2017).

17. Feldman and Pentland (2003); Becker and Knudsen (2005).

18. Carlile (2002).

19. Cummings and Pletcher (2011).

20. Strauss (1988).

21. Archer (2000).

22. Brown and Eisenhardt (1997).

23. Serrador and Pinto (2015).

24. Boehm and Turner (2004) is the standard reference.

25. Dikert et al. (2016); Hobbs and Petit (2017).

26. *Bianchi et al. (2020).

27. Hobbs and Petit (2017). This phase is sometimes called 'agile zero'.

28. Hodgson and Briand (2013).

29. Kutsch et al. (2016).

30. Schoemaker and Day (2009).

31. *Williams et al. (2012); Haji-Kazemi et al. (2013).

32. Klein (2017).

33. Peters and Waterman (1982).

34. Fleming (2004: 166).

35. This well-known phrase, initially developed by the Quaker Movement in the 1950s, is popular with project managers on our executive education programmes.

36. Edmondson (2019).

37. Brown et al. (2017).

38. Williams (2002); Lyneis and Ford (2007).

39. Brooks (1995: 25).

40. Taylor and Ford (2006).

 **Case 7**   Stage One: 'Where your extraordinary is their ordinary'

Stage One is a UK-based creative services organization with 25 years of experience in staging creative events worldwide. It was founded in the 1980s by its two original members, an electrical engineer and a scenery maker, who realized the power of making beautiful things which could move and be memorable to people. This organizational identity as 'makers' continues today. Stage One specializes in bringing to life an artistically created design concept. It delivers highly innovative and creative projects under tight schedule constraints and ambitious requirements anywhere in the world. The projects range from art installations, ceremonies (e.g. London 2012 Olympics, 48th UAE National

Day, Special Olympics World Summer Games 2019, Sochi 2014 Winter Olympics), cultural pavilions (The Serpentine Gallery), and corporate events, to sets for theatre, TV, and film productions. For instance, The Hive for the Milan Expo of 2015 consisted of 32 spiralling hexagonal cells to create an immersive 'bee's-eye view' of the world. It arrived at Stage One as a rough sketch for delivery in a few months requiring 169,300 unique parts, all manufactured in their factory for delivery to Milan.

The company started with modest projects in theatres and visitor centres, and staging events for corporates. Essentially, they brought theatre into corporate presentations and performances. Stage One's breakthrough came in 2004, when it was commissioned to deliver the technical elements of the opening ceremony of the Athens Olympics. Since then, the company has been involved in every winter and summer Olympic Games except Tokyo. Their most recent engagement was the opening and closing ceremonies for the 2018 Winter Olympics in Pyeong chang. Stage One currently employs around 100 staff across a wide range of roles such as project manager, engineer, artist, cost analyst, and site manager. These are deployed in teams, such as computer-aided design (CAD), production, machining, technical, automation, and installation crew.

Managing projects is a core capability of the organization. They are typically introduced to project owners such as national Olympic organizing committees by creative agencies that come to them with ideas and concepts captured in sketches or drawings—some more developed than others—that have never been built before. This means high levels of uncertainty and threats to successful delivery. Uncertainty is a key component of what Stage One does; they recognize it and have learnt to deal with it. They consider their ability to cope with it their principal value-added service to owners. Their approach from concept development to delivery is integrative and collaborative. Stage One team with the architects, engineers, and the owner to ensure that the requirements are met. To do this effectively, their project delivery teams need to translate the design concept into knowledge and bring together all the different know-how efficiently to be able to deliver the project vision to a fixed deadline. Their projects are not like other construction projects, where the final deadline can be moved; the opening of the spectacular is fixed—'the show must go on'. Organizing by projects allows the delivery teams to coordinate, innovate, proactively manage threats, and to solve problems in real time.

Designing the delivery organization is fundamental. Having a shared definition of the project mission is one of the most important aspects, and that is where a project begins. The project-shaping process enables the design intent to be shared and considered with all the heads of departments. Here drawings, timelines, constraints, team composition, and so on are presented and the whole project is shaped, and the project delivery plan starts to take form. The process can be in two stages: first, a conceptual briefing, where the concept is shared and discussed for the team to consider and think about the intent more carefully; and a second briefing, where the team considers how to achieve the design intent. Having a shared understanding of the project mission and communicating it to external stakeholders is vital. For example, bringing out people's emotions allows the team to get the buy-in that is key to delivery. Having the owner engaged is also important. This can be done by inviting them to visit the workshops, which allows them to see how the work is progressing, providing them with a sense of ownership and reassurance. Sometimes owners can struggle to visualize the end product, especially in the early stages, so 'it does require a leap of faith' from the owner. As the project progresses, all can begin to see 'the emergence of the butterfly coming out from the chrysalis'. The reality is that the brief can truly only be fully appreciated once the installation is fully mounted.

The team composition is also carefully considered. Stage One attracts people who are creative and natural problem-solvers, who take pride in the work they do as it arrives on the world stage—be it a cube that rotates in the sea, a piece of art work for a gallery, or a TV production set. Therefore, the competencies—technical, artistic—that a project requires are considered in assembling a project delivery team. The type of project, creative agency, and project manager are all carefully chosen. For example, some project managers have a very good artistic eye, or know what language to use to express themselves to particular creative agencies, such artists or show producers. As the Stage One Projects Director put it:

> Our project managers are hands on—they don't sit behind a desk. They have to be passionate and committed to delivery and they have to be flexible and able to solve problems on the fly . . . There are times when you are really pushed to the limit, but you get a dopamine hit when you solve a really complex problem—it's addictive.

Narrative is important when leading a project. The appropriate narrative can help break down hierarchical barriers and sets the tone for working together as a team, for example saying, 'I work with this team rather than this team works for me.' This is considered a foundation of Stage One's delivery identity, where a 'sense of togetherness' can be created, and where empowering people, enabling different views to be shared, and enabling diverse team members to make inputs are all important. The delivery of the weird, wonderful, or wacky can be fraught with challenges, one of which is working to very short time scales. Sometimes projects have to be delivered in two or three weeks, from concept, design, and manufacturing to delivery on site. What allows Stage One delivery teams to pull it off is 'a show must go on attitude'. Everyone works as a team and there is a clear understanding that the job has to happen and that the end date is fixed. Teams work together with the correct attitude to ensure that what has been promised is delivered. This mindset, in turn, influences the structure of the project. The view is that a much more organic working structure is needed, given the levels of innovation required, and that what is important is the ability to adapt and for the project mission to define the structure of the project delivery team rather than creating a 'clumsy' structure which does not reflect the reality of how the work gets done.

Stage One project managers engage with the usual project management processes of organizing, coordinating, resourcing, scheduling, budgeting, and managing tasks, threats, and stakeholder expectations. It employs the standard tools and techniques presented in Chapter 11, such as Gantt charts, resource planning, costing spreadsheets linked to in-house information, and resource management systems. Their proprietary project information system logs data on all previous projects, providing the core of project planning. Project managers are pragmatic in its use, depending on the type of project. Each project manager manages the project in their own way, depending on their strengths, knowledge, and understanding of the project. The benefit of the standard toolsets is that they can provide the team with a sense of control, but the team is always driven by the opening or launch date. The plans reflect an intent—'what we hope will happen over the next period'—but sometimes what they hope will happen is not necessarily the case. Therefore, they recognize the need to be flexible, pragmatic, and innovative, especially when the opening date is close. They are more end-driven, with a 'battlefield mentality', but still in a controlled way. Tasks are broken down, cascaded to the team, and reported back in real time. 'We free ourselves from the shackles of project management tools and get on and do it ... we abandon tools because we do not have time to have a 90-minute meeting to decide and plan what we are going to do'—the show must go on.

*Sources*: https://www.stageone.co.uk (accessed 22 March 2021); Saunders (2019); interviews with Tim Leigh, Managing Director (19 November 2020) and Dan Kelly, Project Manager (22 January 2021).

### Discussion questions

1. Why do you think project management is a core capability for the company?

2. How do they apply teaming principles to project delivery?

3. What similarities and differences do you see in relation to their approach to managing projects compared to other project-based sectors?

# Part C

## The Three Interfaces of Strategic Project Organizing

Figure C  'Anguish' (Cole's manhood)
Source: National Gallery of Art.

In Figure C, our project manager is riding the project life cycle—the flow is accelerating and the project threatens to be dashed on the rocks of adversity. 'Anguish' is the predominant tone, and the way ahead no longer seems clear to the project manager. The guardian angel is still there, but is obscured by menacing clouds. Whatever will go wrong next?

In Part B we looked at each of the three domains as organizational forms; in Part C we turn to the dynamic relationships between them. We cover the three interfaces of strategic project organizing (SPO) in turn, with a chapter dedicated to each. These interfaces are between the three types of organization that make up the project coalition and each poses a design problem for the project leader, which can be one source of anguish.

In these chapters, we:

- characterize projects by owner strategy implementation;
- develop a holistic framework for designing the governance interface, stressing both formal and informal aspects;
- distinguish between project, programme, and portfolio management;
- identify the different perspectives across the commercial interface held by owner organizations and project-based firms;
- develop a framework for designing the contracting strategy of the owner;
- develop a matching framework for the project strategy of the project-based firm, stressing the importance of capture management;
- indicate the dark side of managing across the commercial interface because of the threat of corruption;
- analyse the balance between the needs of the project and the needs of the resource pools which 'hold' human resources;
- cover the geographic and international aspects of human resources;
- explore technology readiness and the implications of new digital technologies for SPO.

To support learning, we provide cases of how the Venice Biennale governs its festival projects (Case 8), and how the rapid development of COVID-19 vaccines was transformed by redesigning the commercial interface (Case 9). In the final case in this section, we explore how projects to upgrade the thermal performance of housing to meet the challenge of climate change are threatened by the lack of human resources (Case 10). The three interfaces complete our analysis of the organizational level of SPO, and in Part D, we turn to the individual level, professional competencies and career development.

# The governance interface

## 8.1 Introduction: ensuring the delivery organization delivers

Chapters 5–7 explored the three domains of project organizing. We now move on to explore the three interfaces between these domains and the factors which affect their design. We first look at the governance interface between the owner organization and the temporary delivery organization. In essence, the governance interface is about how the owner ensures that what they get at the end of the project as output is as close as feasible to what they expected when they shaped the project mission. For this reason, the owner's governance capability forms one of the five business cases presented in Table 5.1. We will start by discussing what we mean by strategy and its implementation, before moving on to distinguish between 'projects' and 'programmes'. We then explore the formal aspects of structures and processes for governing the interface, before discussing more informal aspects. As we shall see in our case of the Venice Biennale, governance structures and processes need to be aligned with the owner's purpose and identity.

## 8.2 Projects as strategy implementation

As we argued in Chapter 5, projects are about how owner organizations implement their strategies[1] and it is worth reflecting on what we mean by 'strategy'. The word implies proactive engagement that directs action; traditionally, it has been associated with the notion of a plan, but in a world of uncertainty plans rarely survive intact for very long once they are deployed.[2] This is because events take their course, throwing up opportunities and threats which reshape the project through the life cycle, as illustrated in Figure 8.1. Project missions as statements of strategic intent are not always fully realized because:

- they are formulated under high levels of uncertainty regarding the social and economic conditions in which the output will be transformed into outcomes;
- assumptions made as the basis for shaping the project mission prove to be untenable as new information becomes available through the project life cycle;

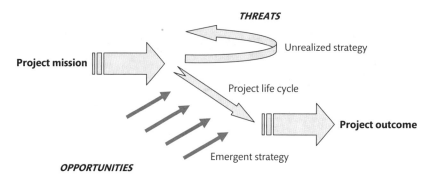

Figure 8.1 The project mission through the life cycle.

*Sources*: developed from Mintzberg (1987: figure 1) and Winch (2010: figure II.1).

- new opportunities present themselves to which the output can be adapted to achieve different outcomes;
- stakeholders change their minds.

It follows from this analysis that the key criterion for project success is not that the original project mission is fully achieved, but that the outcome fully matches the owner's needs *at the time of achievement*. Why, then, bother to define a project mission if it is going to change anyway? There are three very good reasons:

- the process of shaping the project mission as the stakeholders articulate their understandings tests both projecting and the supporting value proposition for consistency and viability, as discussed in section 5.5;
- it enables the crafting of a coherent project-shaping narrative, as discussed in section 4.4;
- the shaping narrative allows the communication of strategic intent to diverse project stakeholders—both those whose active participation is required to deliver the outputs and outcomes and those who have the power to disrupt delivery;
- the defined mission enables the development of the project scope, as discussed in section 7.2, without which the project cannot move forwards through the life cycle, and the crafting of the project DNA, discussed in section 4.5.

## 8.3 Projects and programmes

Some authors argue that project management and programme management are different disciplines.[3] In this view, projects deliver outputs such as a new school and programmes deliver the strategic outcomes such as more effective learning for children. In other words, programmes concern themselves with the value added by the output, while projects do not; an advantage of this definition is that it emphasizes the realization of the benefits. However, it poses the curious challenge of trying to find a project where the project output provides no benefits. Under the conventional definition, all projects must be programmes because all are aimed at providing benefits for those that invest in them; it is a distinction without a difference. A deeper reason for rejecting this distinction is that it obscures the different responsibilities of the project managers working for the owner organization and the delivery organization shown in Table 12.1. Moving from outputs to outcomes inevitably implies changes in the operational capabilities of the owner organization to deliver for its customers—this was the whole point of the investment in the first place. Only the owner organization can change its ways of working embodied in the structures, processes, and resources that make up operational capability. The danger is that conflating responsibility for outcomes with programme management can tempt owners to think that their suppliers can achieve the necessary changes for them—they cannot! Projects that successfully—as defined by the project delivery triangle in Figure 7.1—deliver outputs but not outcomes are 'successful failures'.[4]

In strategic project organizing (SPO), we propose that the difference between projects and programmes is that the latter consist of packages within the work breakdown structure (WBS) that require different project management approaches. We can identify two main types of programme, as illustrated in Figure 8.2. **Modular programmes** do not have sequential dependencies but share important work packages. For instance, a retailer might roll out a new store format, with the overall 'look and feel' of the store design being common, and programme-level purchase of major components such as display cabinets and carpets. However, site-specific

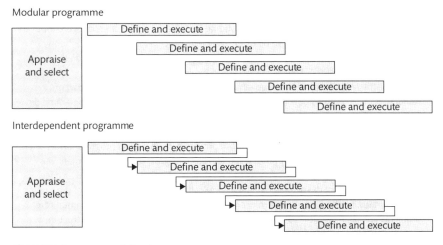

Modular programme

Interdependent programme

**Figure 8.2** Programmes defined.

*Source*: developed from Winch (2010: figure 15.2).

work on particular stores is managed as a portfolio of discrete projects and those working on the execution of the local project may not even be aware of the larger programme context. Projects may also be sequenced within the programme to smooth overall cash flow and enable learning from project to project regarding the technologies deployed and they provide an excellent basis for investment in standardized technologies and collaborative supply chains.

The second type of programme is the **interdependent programme** which consists of a set of discrete projects which for various reasons need to be managed separately but *also* have sequential dependencies. These reasons could be geographical dispersion of the supply of the various elements of the final asset, very different competencies required for each project element such as the construction, research and development (R&D), and information systems elements of the BT project in Vignette 7.1. For instance, the UK West Coast Main Line upgrade programme consisted of multiple blockades over 1,031 route kilometres between 2000 and 2008, each of which had to be managed as a separate project to very tight schedule constraints and also as a programme implementing a common technology cumulatively building to a high-speed line by 2009. Within a programme, individual projects may deliver intermediate outcomes.[5]

---

### Vignette 8.1    Governance on the Type 45 destroyer programme

The Type 45 destroyer is the Royal Navy's new air defence platform, supplied by a joint venture between BAE Systems and Vosper Thorneycroft called BVT (the two supplier firms have since merged). It featured in the Bond film *No Time to Die*. The programme of 12 ships was originally launched in 1998, but by the time the ships were coming into service after 2010 it had been cut to six less capable ships due to rapidly escalating budgets following a contract renegotiation in 2007. The outturn budget was £1 bn per ship. In operation in the high temperatures of the Middle East, the Type 45s suffered severe motive power reliability issues and had to be extensively refitted. One reason for this unhappy story was poor design and implementation of the governance interface between the owner—the UK Ministry of Defence (MoD)—and the Type 45 programme.

Overall, the MoD lacked effective governance of the Type 45 programme. As part of standard human relations policies, the MoD's lead personnel assigned to the programme did not stay at their jobs long enough to develop a complete understanding of developments. The MoD's project team lacked 'suitably qualified staff and relied on consultants'. As a consequence, the 'department relied on BVT to provide data on project progress, costs and risks. BVT continued to be optimistic about project progress and the Department was therefore not well placed to challenge BVT's assumptions.' The MoD did not have a 'single high-level overview' of the whole project that would allow in-time assessments of the project's status. Further, the owner project management team was unable to communicate problems up the chain within the MoD, suggesting an impervious bureaucratic structure or a senior management overwhelmed by operational requirements.

*Sources*: Lombardi and Rudd (2013); NAO (2009); Wikipedia (accessed 22 February 2021).

## 8.4  Defining the governance interface

Owners have important responsibilities towards the delivery organization through-out the life cycle, indeed the US courts have found the owner liable in some failed projects for not fulfilling their 'legal responsibility to participate actively in the pro-ject's management'[6] and as Vignette 8.1 and Case 5 show, weak governance by the owner leads to major challenges for project outputs and outcomes. These issues of project governance have been of growing concern of late in both the public and pri-vate sectors. Concerns for corporate governance led to the passing of the Sarbanes-Oxley Act in 2002 and subsequent issuance of internal control requirements in the United States, and the incorporation of the 1999 Turnbull Guidance on internal con-trol into the Combined Code which regulates audit practice in the United Kingdom. Thus corporations quoted on the world's two largest stock exchanges—London and New York—are obliged to meet new and demanding requirements for project assur-ance which require their corporate boards to have much more knowledge of what is happening on the projects in which they are investing on a real-time basis. Simi-larly, new public management,[7] which emphasizes performance and outcomes, has placed new obligations on the senior management of public-sector organizations.

Project governance has therefore been an expanding area of research and prac-tice over recent years, but there is little agreement on the definition of 'governance' in this context, and many of the contributions are at a high level of abstraction[8] which syncretize different literatures,[9] making it difficult to understand how gov-erning actually gets done. Here we attempt to clarify the debate by defining the focus of our concern on the governance interface shown in Figure 2.1 and treat-ing it as a design challenge for project leaders with formal and informal aspects.[10] The principal aim of the owner in managing the governance interface is to ensure that the value proposition (and hence the project mission) is sustained through the project life cycle as a reference point for decision-making.[11] In order to govern ef-fectively, the owner organization needs to design a set of structures and processes as defined in section 7.3 that are mutually reinforcing,[12] to meet the challenges of the particular project that both empower the delivery organization and ensure that it is delivering what is expected.[13] These structures and processes are both formal and informal, and supported by appropriate routines.[14] Figure 8.3 shows how these elements complement each other on a major digital transformation project. These elements are portfolio management, stage gates, project sponsors, project boards, project assurance, and project management offices. We discuss these seriatim.

---

### Exercise 8.1

Review Vignette 8.1. What do you think were the weaknesses of the MoD with respect to project governance?

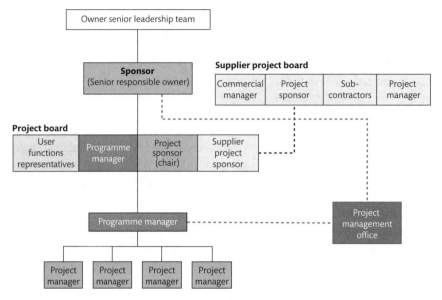

**Figure 8.3** Governance structure for a digital transformation project.

*Source:* developed from an original figure by Cliff Mitchell.

### 8.4.1 **Portfolio management**

Project portfolios are the sum of the individual projects that an organization holds. This is the investment project portfolio for the owner and the order portfolio for a project-based firm (PBF)[15]—project portfolios and their management are, therefore, inherently strategic for the organization.[16] These portfolios embody both the planned strategy of the organization and the potential for adjustment of the portfolio as new opportunities arise and some projects become unviable—Figure 8.1 applies at the portfolio level, too. The projects in the portfolio do not have any dependencies between them but, crucially, they *do* share resources.[17] These resources are both financial and human; material resources are not usually an issue, except for assets such as heavy lift equipment. Portfolio management techniques tend to work best where individual projects are a relatively small proportion of the total portfolio, as shown in Figure 8.4. This is usually the case for new product development (NPD) projects, but less often the case for infrastructure and transformation projects. Many organizations therefore take a mixed approach.[18] For instance, in a 'bet the company' project such as the Tesla Model 3,[19] where the investment budget is a significant proportion of the market capitalization of the investor, portfolio management would simply get in the way of direct governance by the senior leadership team. For upgrades to existing models, on the other hand, a portfolio management approach is entirely appropriate. Similarly, an infrastructure owner such as Highways England has a set of regional renewals and upgrades portfolios, while managing its major programmes outside that portfolio.

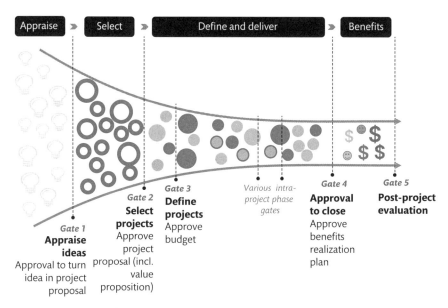

Figure 8.4 Project portfolio management.

*Source*: developed from Wheelwright and Clark (1992: exhibit 5.6).

From a financial perspective, the underlying principle of portfolio management is well established.[20] From an SPO perspective, this can be reformulated, as individual projects might fail to achieve either outputs or outcomes, but so long as other projects in the portfolio do achieve beneficial returns in compensation, then the viability of the organization as a whole is not threatened.[21] In order to select projects for the portfolio, owners usually rank-order the value proposition, as defined in Chapter 5, and select those that offer the greater expected benefits. However, this emphasis upon the economic case is often overridden by arguments from the strategic case—indeed, such projects are often called 'strategic'—and this competition between projects within the portfolio is an important source of strategic misrepresentation and 'framing contests'[22] as projects compete for financial resources. Where a significant proportion of benefits are non-financial, then framing contests are likely to be even more fraught. For an owner, it goes without saying that it should be able to finance all the projects that it takes forward to implementation from its portfolio; unfortunately, this is not always the case, as Vignette 8.2 illustrates. For suppliers, the overall shape of their project portfolio is an important consideration in the bid/no bid decision discussed in section 9.3, and their version of the 'strategic project' is the 'must win' bid.

The other principal resource that is shared across the portfolio is people—that is, the supply of the competencies required to make up the teams in the delivery organization. We will discuss this particular aspect of portfolio management for

Vignette **8.2**    A failure in portfolio management

The refurbishment programme for further education colleges that focus on the education of 16–18-year-olds and adult learners in the United Kingdom started in 2001 as part of the broader government strategy for the renewal of the United Kingdom's ageing educational infrastructure. The agency responsible, the Learning and Skills Council, enthusiastically promoted the programme and encouraged colleges to bid for the funds available. By March 2008, projects valued at £4.2 bn had been approved, which included £1.7 bn of grant funding from the Council, but the great success of the programme and its growing momentum meant that things were now getting out of control. The Council approved a further £2.3 bn of grant funding in the period of April to December 2008. Its total forward commitments were now significantly in excess of its authorized budget, yet it continued to approve all projects that passed the appropriate approval thresholds rather than developing criteria for the prioritization of projects within its budget.

The project approval process was a two-stage one, moving through 'approved in principle' to 'approved in detail' and so colleges incurred significant costs in obtaining approvals. Promotion costs by colleges in obtaining matched funding and consultants' fees meant that getting to detailed approval stage could cost over 3 per cent of total project costs. Once the scale of the problem became clear in 2009, most projects were cancelled, thereby dashing the hopes of colleges for the redevelopment of their infrastructure and hitting the scheduled workload of PBFs that had geared up once projects received detailed approval. As a direct result of this waste of millions of pounds on cancelled projects, the chief executive officer (CEO) of the Learning and Skills Council resigned and the agency was abolished in 2010.

*Source*: UK Parliament Public Accounts Committee 48th Report, 2008–2009 Session.

PBFs further in section 10.2 because it is a central element in the resource interface. Here, we focus on one particular resource from the owner perspective—project managers. We have already argued in section 5.7 that owner capability is essential for the effective transformation of the project mission into project outcomes, and that capability needs to have both the appropriate mix of competencies *and* the capacity to manage the size of the portfolio. This is a strategic issue because firms grow endogenously, principally through investment projects to expand capacity, enter new markets, and launch new products. It follows that the capacity of the firm's project management capability is the principal constraint on its endogenous growth.[23] If the owner does not have the managerial capacity to manage its overall portfolio, then it needs to reduce the size of that portfolio because it is very difficult to increase that capacity in the short term—hiring temporary additional resources is associated with poor project performance.[24]

---

### Exercise 8.2

How does portfolio management complement project and programme management?

8.4.2 **Stage gates**

Stage gates in the project life cycle were first developed for NPD projects[25] but have since become best practice for infrastructure projects for government owners[26] and private-sector owners where they are often branded as corporate life-cycle models such as the 'BP Way'. The basic premise of a stage-gate model of the SPO Life-Cycle Model is that the project can be divided into a number of notionally sequential stages. Moving from one *stage* to another then requires that parties external to the project team review progress on delivery at planned milestones or gates. It therefore addresses the 'who, when, what' questions of *who* should make decisions on the progress of project *when* in the life cycle, on the basis of *what* progress information[27] and is the principal element of process in formal project governance.

In Figure 8.4, we present an extended version of the generic project life cycle introduced in Figure 2.7. We have extended it to include both an initial phase during project shaping, when the investment opportunity is identified, and the benefits realization phase, where the output from the project is transformed into outcomes by the owner organization. Opportunity identification is an inherently diffuse process and the responsibility of the senior leadership team of the owner as potential investor. Many opportunities will be identified, and many of these will be authorized for further shaping work on the value proposition during the Appraise stage, but many fewer will move to the Select stage for full development of the scope and the project delivery plan (PDP). Once a project starts moving through the Define stage, it is unlikely to be stopped due to the perceived sunk costs of investment, even if these are typically only around 5 per cent of total costs, and the personal commitments of the project team to the project as it gains momentum. This means that rigour in the management of the early stage gates is crucial.

Stage gates are essentially control points where the owner senior leadership team can take a balanced, objective view of whether the preceding stage has completed successfully and whether the project is ready to proceed with the next stage in sequence. The principal question to be asked at each gate is shown in Figure 8.5, and the answers can take different forms:

- soft—any required rework is undertaken within next stage; the project moves forward and the previous stage closes;
- hard—rework has to be completed within the previous stage; the project moves forward only if all tasks are completed, not if some are outstanding;
- fuzzy—rework within the previous stage; the compliant part moves forward, the non-complying part is reworked in the previous stage, and the previous stage remains open.

Best practice project governance considers the key hard gates are at the end of the Select stage (is the scope complete, and is there a project delivery plan?) and at the end of the Define stage (are we ready for the Execute stage, and therefore to commit the remaining ~95 per cent of the investment?).[28]

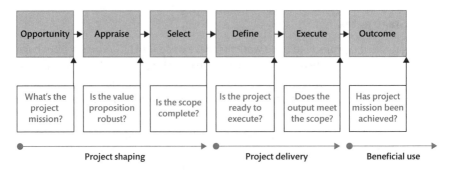

Figure 8.5 The extended project life cycle.

*Source*: authors.

### 8.4.3 **The project sponsor**

The *project sponsor* works at the interface between the owner's project management team and the senior leadership team of the owner organization that initiated the project, and is defined as the individual who is accountable for the delivery of the outputs and the realization of the business case.[29] She, therefore, needs to be of sufficient seniority to be credible to the leadership team and know the owner organization intimately in order to be able to resolve cross-functional issues.[30] Effective project sponsors have a significant impact on project performance,[31] particularly on transformation projects because of the challenges of benefits realization. The project sponsor is clearly distinguished from (a) the **project leader** (director or manager) who has delegated responsibility for delivering the project outputs, and (b) the **project champion** discussed in section 4.9, who may have no formal role in the project organization.

The project sponsor typically chairs the project board (if there is one), and more generally provides 'cover' for the owner project team. Where the owner organization uses portfolio management, the portfolio director typically acts as project sponsor. PBFs may also nominate project sponsors, where they are typically also the managing director or portfolio director of the business unit concerned—see Case 6. Project sponsor in practice is a somewhat diffuse and under-developed role in many owner organizations, with little role-specific training available.[32] There is a significant chance that the appointed project sponsor will see the role as just another thing to do and not provide the level of support that the project requires—the 'absent sponsor' is a widespread issue.

### 8.4.4 **The project board**

The **project board**[33] as shown in Figure 8.3 has administrative oversight over the project or programme; a portfolio board is similarly placed with respect to project portfolios, acting as a forum for coordination and internal stakeholder management.

It is typically chaired by the project sponsor[34] and its members are usually appointed from three different stakeholder groups—the owner; the user groups within the owner organization; and tier-one suppliers, as defined in section 6.3. It may also include the programme manager to represent the owner project team. The supplier representatives are usually the project sponsors from the PBFs. Clearly, project boards can only work effectively if the project coalition is governed through a collaborative commercial relationship, as discussed in section 9.5. An important dimension is whether the project board is advisory or accountable—if the board includes suppliers, it can only be advisory. The litmus test of authority is whether the board has the right to terminate a project, or whether that is reserved to the owner strategic leadership team.

### 8.4.5 Project assurance: the three lines of defence

Project assurance[35] is the formal organizational procedure by which the senior management of the owner organization is assured that the project is on track to achieve the project mission. The concept is borrowed from the financial services sector.[36] Reporting by the owner project team through the project management office

---

Vignette **8.3**    Three lines of defence for the London Olympics

The 2012 Olympic and Paralympic Games were awarded to London in 2005, giving it seven years to transform a derelict and polluted East London site into an Olympic Park. The UK government set up the Olympic Delivery Authority (ODA) as project owner, which then appointed a joint venture of three construction PBFs as a delivery partner, dubbed CLM, to provide it with the capability to be a complex project owner. CLM took a programme management approach and engaged with suppliers on a collaborative basis. The ODA's stakeholder network was extraordinarily complex and the megaproject could not have had a higher profile nationally and internationally. One element in ensuring that little went wrong was the development of the 'three lines of defence' approach to project assurance.

The first line of defence was management controls by the programme team within CLM who were responsible for the management and control of delivery by the suppliers. The second line was compliance by the dedicated programme assurance function (PAF) within the ODA charged to 'coordinate, facilitate, challenge and oversee the effectiveness and integrity of the first line'. The PAF reported directly to the CEO of the ODA. Assurance on commercial and technical matters also reported to the PAF. The third line was internal audit by the ODA's Audit Committee, which reported to its senior leadership team charged to 'review and assure the effectiveness of the control framework'. It hired Ernst & Young to carry out this function. Externally, the ODA reported to the UK Government Department for Culture, Media and Sport, and was subject to audit by the UK Parliament's National Audit Office.

*Sources*: Hone et al. (2011); webarchive.nationalarchives.gov.uk/20130403014237/http://learninglegacy. independent.gov.uk/publications/programme-assurance-on-the-olympic-delivery-authority-co.php (accessed 23 February 2021).

(PMO) in its controller role to the project sponsor, who then reports to the owner senior leadership team independently of the project director, is the essence of project assurance. At its most sophisticated (as shown in Vignette 8.3), assurance is structured as the 'three lines of defence': effective project controls by the PMO; internal assurance functions independent of the PMO; and internal audit. There is a considerable variety of arrangements for project assurance, with mixed success, while the impact of formal assurance procedures has been limited on government projects.[37]

### 8.4.6 **The project management office**

The PMO is the function within the organization that is responsible for project management capability. Both suppliers and owners will have a PMO with similar responsibilities, but those of the owner PMO are typically larger, reflecting the broader responsibilities of the owner for the projects it initiates. In particular, suppliers' PMOs are focused on their particular contribution to the project, rather than the project as a whole. The delivery organization can also have its own PMO, particularly on larger projects, but the responsibilities will largely be confined to the planning responsibilities discussed in Chapter 11 and to assurance. So here we focus on the owner PMOs, which can be very diverse, depending on the types of projects the owner organization typically promotes[38] and their level in the owner organization, with those at corporate level having a more strategic role and those at business unit level a more delivery-focused role.[39]

We can identify four distinct roles for the owner's PMO: coordinator, controller, supporter,[40] and developer. As **coordinator**, one role of the PMO is to ensure that the required resources are allocated to the project. These are essentially human resources with the appropriate project management professional competencies, whether these be technical competencies associated with project execution planning such as scheduling, or social competencies associated with managing stakeholders or teams. Having the right people in the right place at the right time is essential for effective governance of projects.[41] A second role is to ensure that the resource requirements of the different projects initiated from the investment portfolio are 'smoothed' to ensure that there are no unsustainable peaks and troughs in resource requirements—we will return to this topic in section 10.2. Where suppliers are expected to draw on limited pools of scarce resources such as craft operatives, this obligation is broader than project management competencies—see Vignette 10.1.

As **controller**, the PMO has responsibility for designing the governance structure and processes for the project. A first responsibility is to manage the stage-gate process, and, in particular, to organize the gate reviews. These typically involve senior management, but may also include elements of peer reviews. A second responsibility is to ensure that the information loop discussed in Figure 11.3 both is properly implemented and continues to function effectively through the project life cycle. This includes assurance functions reporting to project sponsors in particular. In this role, the owner PMO will collaborate closely with the PMO within the delivery organization. A third responsibility is portfolio management itself through ensuring both that rigorous project selection processes are in place and that they are followed and that gaming the system is minimized. The final controlling responsibility is to step in if the project is going seriously awry, and even to stop the project if it cannot be feasibly recovered. This will usually require senior management support, and is often very difficult to do.[42]

As supporter, the PMO has two roles. First, it can support the delivery of projects by coaching project managers and providing advice to the project team, either through 'peer assist' or by more formal internal consultancy. It would also normally be responsible for supporting the implementation of the relevant software tools discussed in section 10.8 and Case 11 by providing training and encouraging experimentation. Second, the PMO can greatly help the 'bottom up' development of owner capability by facilitating the working of 'communities of practice' which connect project managers from different parts of the organization to share expertise and enable continuous improvement.

Finally, as developer, the PMO has three of its most important roles. First, it is tasked with developing project management processes and structures for the organization, and in particular, the routines that support teaming such as a standardized WBS, templates for reporting, and meeting schedules. Second, it is tasked with developing the professional competencies of the project managers. While hiring will likely be the responsibility of the HR function, the PMO should play a major role in writing job descriptions and interviewing applicants. This job description should be based on a detailed competency framework that covers all the project management competencies, including those associated with the commercial interface. Training in project management technical competencies executive education to develop social competencies are both important—we will return to this issue in Part D. The third role of the PMO is in promoting innovation on the project,[43] particularly around the 'windows of opportunity' discussed in section 4.7.

Where owners have a sustained portfolio of investment projects, then there is a strong case for significant investment in a full-service, in-house PMO. Provision through external consultants is inherently weaker because capability development through learning by doing is largely captured by the consultant organization and incentives can never be fully aligned between an owner organization and its suppliers. However, owners with intermittent investment projects are in a more difficult position because the PMO rapidly becomes an overhead with limited benefits in the gaps between projects. Many organizations retain in-house capability for smaller projects, while using consultants for their more intermittent major investment programmes. For instance, a city will typically manage a project portfolio for road or housing maintenance internally, but cities (hopefully) only ever build one opera house and so will hire specialist consultants to undertake most of the owner role. Similarly, many organizations will have their own IT function, but when it comes to a major change initiative such as digital transformation, external consultants will be commissioned to, in effect, manage the owner to manage the governance interface.

## 8.5 Governing informally: crucial conversations

Project delivery is a dynamic process and leaders need to continually engage while riding the project life cycle. Wise Dr Skeptic, as project leader, is continually engaging in five crucial conversations:[44]

#1: Are we planning around facts? There is considerable pressure on projects to agree to budgets and deadlines which are not achievable, but which make the value proposition stand up. The job of the owner's project leader is to stand up to this kind of strategic misrepresentation by ensuring that the best available evidence is used to develop the economic case.

#2: Is the project sponsor providing support? Active and appropriate engagement by project sponsors is a crucial part of governing the interface but sponsors can often become absent once the project is launched and only return to complain at the end of the project.

#3: Are we faithful to the process? Owner organizations have mandated governance processes, yet these are often more honoured in the breach and 'selexecute' is the norm where governance procedures are overridden by a desire to 'get the job done' and gates are 'crashed'.

#4: Are we honestly assessing our progress? It is easy to downplay the importance of the unknowns identified in the elicitation of possible threats to the project and focus on the known knowns because there are routines readily available to address them, as discussed in section 11.7. Never forget that a p90[45] for a project budget or schedule is not a real number but an aggregate of judgements and suppositions given a specious precision by analysis.

#5: Are team members pulling their weight? Suppliers have different motivations from owners in project delivery, yet they are contracted through the commercial interface to deliver resources to the delivery organization, as discussed in section 9.3. Difficult conversations may be required to ensure that this is done consummately rather than perfunctorily, and further attention given to incentive design in the SPO Star Model presented in Figure 7.3.

---

### Exercise 8.3

**Why do you think effective project governance has both formal and informal aspects?**

---

## 8.6 Summary

This chapter has explored the governance interface between the owner organization and the project delivery organization. Governing this interface is essential because the owner and its stakeholders need to be assured that the investment project is on track for delivery. The inherently uncertain nature of projects means that this is not simply a matter of making the correct decision at the start and checking back at the end of delivery; rather, it is a process of both consummate design of the structures and process of governing, and 'crucial conversations' within and beyond the owner project team. We now turn to the commercial interface.

## 8.7 Further reading

Barshop, P. 2016. *Capital Projects*. Hoboken, NJ: Wiley.
  Provides detailed analysis of most aspects of formal governance.

Loch, C., Mähring, M., and Sommer, S. 2017. 'Supervising projects you don't (fully) understand: lessons for effective project governance by steering committees'. *California Management Review*, 59(2): 45–67.
  The challenges for project boards of supervising complex projects.

Grenny, J., Maxfield, D., and Shimberg, A. 2007. 'How project leaders can overcome the crisis of silence'. *MIT Sloan Management Review*, 48(4): 46–52.
  Classic statement of informal project governance.

## 8.8 Summary review questions

1. What is the difference between managing projects and managing programmes?
2. What is the difference between managing projects and managing project portfolios?
3. What are the three lines of defence in project assurance?
4. What is the difference between formally and informally managing the governance interface?
5. What are the four roles of the PMO?

 *Visit the Oxford Learning Link site for this text to find answer guidance to the questions and exercises in this chapter.*

 *Take your learning further by viewing videos relevant to this chapter on the Oxford Learning Link site.*

# Notes

1. Morris and Jamieson (2005); Loch and Kavadias (2011).
2. Mintzberg (1994).
3. Pellegrinelli (2011); Axelos (2020).
4. Doherty et al. (2012).
5. Patanakul and Pinto (2017).
6. Cited in Morris (1994: 252).
7. Hood and Dixon (2015).
8. *ul Musawir et al. (2020).
9. Ahola et al. (2014).
10. Simard et al. (2018).
11. Einhorn et al. (2019).
12. Riis et al. (2019).
13. Sergeeva (2019).
14. Brunet (2019).
15. Turner and Müller (2017).
16. Kopmann et al. (2017).
17. Archer and Ghasemzadeh (1999).
18. Patanakul and Pinto (2017).
19. Bloomberg, 13 July 2018.
20. Markowitz (1952).
21. From our own experience, a rule of thumb for PBFs is that one in six projects will fail to make a profit.
22. Kaplan (2008).
23. Penrose (1995).
24. Merrow (2011).
25. Cooper (1993).
26. Volden and Samset (2017).
27. Winch (2010).
28. Barshop (2016).
29. *Zwikael et al. (2019). This contribution refers to the sponsor as 'owner', following the definition in Axelos (2020), of the senior responsible owner. However, 'sponsor' is the more widely used term—see Sankaran et al. (2017).
30. Helm and Remington (2005).
31. Barshop (2016); Kloppenborg and Tesch (2015).
32. Breese et al. (2020).
33. We take this term from Axelos (2017), which provides a clear definition; various kinds of steering committees are used in project governance with diffuse responsibilities—see Lechler and Cohen (2009); Loch et al. (2017); McGrath and Whitty (2019).
34. Zwikael et al. (2019).
35. NAO (2010).
36. Davies and Zhivitskaya (2018).

37. Young et al. (2012).

38. Aubry and Brunet (2016).

39. Müller et al. (2013).

40. *Unger et al. (2012).

41. Merrow (2011).

42. Royer (2003); Staw and Ross (1989).

43. Sergeeva and Ali (2020).

44. Grenny et al. (2007).

45. A p90 is the predicted value which gives a 90 per cent probability of the final project outturn budget falling under, usually calculated by Monte Carlo analysis.

 **Case 8**   The Venice Biennale

Prepared by Viktoriya Pisotska, LUISS University Rome.

## The Venice Biennale

The Venice Biennale (La Biennale di Venezia: http://www.labiennale.org, accessed 18 August 2021) is one of the oldest and most prestigious cultural institutions in the world. It was founded in 1895 as the first Exhibition of Contemporary Art, becoming immediately a huge success, attracting over 180,000 visitors, despite difficult logistics. It welcomed artists such as Klimt (1899), Renoir, Picasso (1910), Matisse, Cezanne, Van Gogh (1920), Dali (1948), Kandinskij (1948), Mirò (1948), and Pollock (1950). The distinctive culture of the Venice Biennale resided in its artistic research, far from commercial and business intentions of other exhibitions existing at that time.

## The Biennale: From Autonomous Board to Foundation

From the beginning, the aim was to make the Venice Biennale a permanent organization with its range of exhibitions taking place on a recurrent basis and it has undergone a long evolution of corporate governance over the past 125 years. In the 1930s, the Venice Biennale was transformed into an Autonomous Board passing from the control of the Municipality of Venice to the Italian Government, and in the 1970s a Governing Council was established with multiple stakeholders represented.

However, there was a growing need for autonomy and independence for the Venice Biennale. In 1998, the new statute was approved and it is now a public institution governed by private law which allows it to operate according to entrepreneurial principles. The former President of the Venice Biennale, Paolo Baratta, stressed that being a public institution implies the need 'to provide something more than what the market offers, the avoidance of pursuing ends which are non-artistic, economic or politically propagandistic'.

## The Contemporary Biennale

In 2004, the statute was revised to give the Venice Biennale even more autonomy and entrepreneurial orientation. It was renamed the Biennale Foundation—'Fondazione della Biennale di Venezia'. New management and governance systems were implemented.

Article 7 of the Statute specified the bodies of the Foundation: the President, the Board of Directors, and the Board of Auditors, and the Board of Directors changed from 19 to five members. The President was given a clear mandate to guide the institution more effectively and efficiently.

The Venice Biennale has a multilevel corporate governance, led by the Board of Directors representing regional stakeholders. It is chaired by the President and defines the strategic objectives of the organization and how they are to be executed. The Director General is accountable to the Board for the execution of the Foundation's strategic objectives.

Today, the Venice Biennale is active in six cultural sectors of Arts (1895), Architecture (1980), Cinema (1932), Dance (1999), Music (1930), and Theatre (1934). Cultural sectors are inherent and inseparable parts of the Venice Biennale, determining its existence and identity. One of the main objectives of the Venice Biennale is to pursue innovation and rationalization of its Sectoral Festivals through the accountability of top management.

Each cultural sector is led by an Artistic Director, who may be appointed for more than one mandate, thereby developing a trusting relationship with the Biennale management team. This is especially relevant for the Cinema Sector in order to develop cinema programming:

> The Directors of the Sectors are chosen from personalities, including foreign ones, with particular expertise in the related disciplines, and take care of the preparation and carrying out the activities of the Sector within its competence, in the context of programmes approved by the Board of Directors and their resources attributed by the Board itself. They remain in office for a maximum period of four years and in any case for a period not exceeding the term of office of the Board of Directors that appointed them.
>
> Statute of the Biennale

## The Venice Film Festival 2019

One of the most important exhibitions in the Biennale's annual calendar is the Venice International Film Festival, which is often compared to the Cannes Film Festival and the Berlinale Film Festival in Europe for the level of prestige, audience numbers, and public attention it attracts. The Festival is recognized by the International Federation of Film Producers Association (FIAPF). Each annual film festival is delivered through a temporary organization under the auspices of the Foundation. The Artistic Director is entirely responsible for artistic choices of the Film Festival, enjoying the full artistic autonomy and relying on the support of the organizational structure of the Biennale for logistics and finance. Regarding the selection of submitted films, the Artistic Director is assisted by his or her staff of experts and a group of correspondents and international consultants, each responsible for different geographical areas. The Director General reported that 'assistants of the Artistic Director (e.g. selectors) have collaboration contacts related to the development of artistic projects'. Selectors and others are appointed on temporary contacts because the specific people profiles required imply temporary engagement. However, temporary contracts do not preclude repeated employment over the years. Indeed, highly specialized and professional people (e.g. some selectors) can be recruited the following year, thanks to their reputation and continuing relationships with the

Biennale. This aspect is typical of many film festivals, including the Cannes, Berlinale, and Rotterdam Film Festivals. These highly specialized people also work on a temporary basis for different film festivals during the year.

There are six sections of the Venice Film Festival: (1) Official Selection; (2) Out of Competition; (3) Orizzonti; (4) Venice Classics; (5) Sconfini; and (6) Venice Virtual Reality. In addition, there is a film market—the Venice Production Bridge—and independent sections of the Festival. The Festival organization is built around the values of art, spirit of research and experimentation, close interaction between artists and audience, reputation, hospitality, internationalism, and autonomy. The Director General affirmed:

> Promoting research in contemporary arts at international level in Venice—that is our DNA! For that you need to be open to the world. For example, we put Netflix films in competition. So what? Are they movies? Yes! Do people watch them? Yes! If people don't watch them in theatres, it's not our problem, as our artistic director Alberto Barbera usually reminds us. We believe we should not be traditionalists, conservatives. It is not part of our DNA.

## The Governance Interface

In order to be faithful to its corporate mission and identity, the Venice Biennale has to rely on a solid organizational structure able to establish a dialogue with Artistic Directors. The Deputy Director stressed:

> Experimenting is in our DNA. That's why we must have structures with people ready to talk to artistic directors to understand how to do things. For instance, implementing a VR (i.e., virtual reality) section wasn't simple. Our technicians and our Director [referring to the Director General] understood what was needed and figured out the best way to set things up.

He stresses the fundamental principle of the Biennale—its double autonomy consisting in the autonomy of artistic choices, delegated to Artistic Directors, and autonomy of its management from any political and governmental influences. The Artistic Director dealing with artistic decisions does not intervene in the organizational matters of the Biennale and vice versa. The Director General stressed that 'our Artistic Directors must be enabled to make choices that are not determined by economic interests'. Strategic objectives can be then achieved through 'a dialogue between the President of the Biennale, Board of Directors and the Artistic Director—this is the highest verification' (Deputy Director).

The Venice Exhibition Sectors operate under the umbrella of the Biennale Foundation, which has developed a distinctive way to manage the interface between the Foundation and the annual film festival. The Venice Biennale does not have a PMO. The Director General stressed that:

> There is not one who does not reason in terms of PMO. That is our *modus operandi*. Every year we know very well that we go to war. There is a time to prepare the battle, to enter the battle and to come back home after the battle. This is absolutely transversal, there are no excuses.

The Venice Biennale has central functions transversal to all cultural sectors. However, projects of each cultural sector are different, therefore requiring specialized staff with sectoral experience. Artistic Directors, being fully responsible for artistic choices of their sectors for an assigned period of time, constitute key figures influencing project governance. The coordination between different sectors is done by the Board of Directors, supported by the Director General. The Deputy Director sums up the culture thus: 'being elastic constitutes an organizational strength of the Venice Biennale'.

## Discussion questions

1. How does the Biennale Foundation govern its annual festivals as projects?

2. How does the organizational identity of the Venice Biennale influence its governance of its annual festivals?

3. What lessons are there for the governance interface in strategic project organizing more generally?

# 9  The commercial interface

## 9.1 Introduction: collaborating to deliver the project mission

The commercial relations between the owner and its suppliers are some of the most contentious in strategic project organizing (SPO), and considerable effort is required to ensure that they remain collaborative rather than purely transactional. The fundamental problem is that the interests of the owner and the supplier project-based firms (PBFs) are different, yet at the same time, those interests need to be aligned in order for project delivery to be possible. Typically, the owner, as an investor, wants suppliers to charge the lowest feasible prices for the services they supply. Paying 'too much' for the project means that future funding streams from realizing the benefits created by the project are reduced for the owner. At the same time, the PBFs have an interest in charging the highest prices the market will bear in order to improve their profits. Even where owner and supplier are different parts of the same organization, tensions remain if they independently are responsible for profits. While these issues are part of the field of commercial management,[1] we argue that they are also central to SPO. In this chapter, we look at the commercial interface from the perspective of the owner and its contracting strategy, and then from the perspective of the supplier and its project strategy. From the owner perspective, the commercial interface is a design problem that addresses the commercial case in Table 5.1. We then turn to demonstrate how the interactions between these two strategies can move relationships from a transactional basis to a collaborative one within the delivery domain, for the mutual benefit of all parties. We show the importance of the design of the commercial interface for COVID-19 vaccine development in Case 9.

## 9.2 The owner perspective: contracting strategy

As the owner organization moves through the project life cycle, it needs to enter into commercial relations with the suppliers of the various services required for the successful delivery of the output. Some of these suppliers will act as specialist advisors during the Appraise and Select stages but the principal engagement with suppliers is during project delivery, particularly the Execute stage as shown in Vignette 9.1. Agreements may also be made with suppliers to support the outputs delivered by the project during benefits realization, as shown in Figure 6.4. The owner needs to address three main challenges in its contracting strategy. The first is how to partition the tasks defined in the work breakdown structure (WBS) (see Figure 7.2) into coherent packages that can be delivered by PBFs with different capabilities—the **packaging challenge**. The second is how to choose and motivate suppliers to deliver each package—the **procurement challenge**. The differentiation of the scope into delivery packages generates a third problem, that of ensuring that the packages are coordinated so that package performance is not at the cost of the project performance—the **oversight challenge**.

There are two basic approaches to owner contracting strategy:

- **single prime supplier** where the owner contracts with a sole first-tier supplier that is responsible for delivering the entire scope of the project as specified at the end of the Select stage;

- **multiple prime supplier** where the owner contracts directly with first-tier suppliers of different packages within the WBS in a project chain, as shown in Figure 6.3, where the owner retains responsibility for oversight and coordination between packages.

Evidence from benchmarking is that the second option performs better for owners,[2] and we focus on it for this chapter. However, where the output defined in the project scope is relatively simple, and the owner organization is relatively immature in terms of capability, the single prime approach is perfectly viable as a 'turnkey' project.

To help understand these three challenges in a multiple prime supplier approach, we propose the use of **contracting maps**.[3] These are two-dimensional graphical representations of the contracting strategy for a particular project. The two dimensions of the contracting map are the WBS on the x axis (i.e. *which* tasks have to be done) and the stage of the project life cycle on the y axis (i.e. *when* tasks have to be done). The cells in the matrix thereby generated are clustered in accordance with the resolution of the packaging challenge into work packages let to different suppliers. These packages are usually coloured and textured to show which supplier does what and the type of contract selected for each package. A generic contracting map is presented in Figure 9.1. This shows the cells in the matrix formed by the WBS and the project life cycle. Each cluster of cells produces a package, as defined in section 7.2, within which the interfaces between the tasks are invisible to the owner; the interfaces between each package remain visible to the owner. Thus, the clustering of tasks into packages strongly influences the owner's 'line of visibility' into the project[4] and specifies the focus of attention for the owner's project management team on the owner-visible interfaces between packages. Each package can then be let to a supplier on the most appropriate contractual terms for that package to manage the owner-invisible

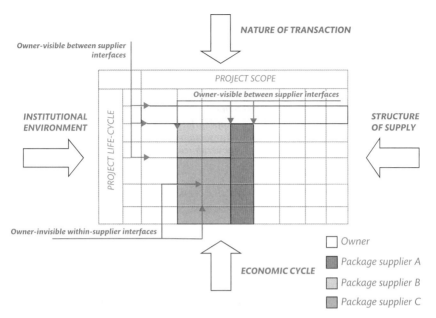

Figure 9.1  Generic owner contracting map.

*Source*: authors.

interfaces between their subcontractors. Figure 9.1 shows the retention of project management services (usually the first row in the map) in-house, although owners can and do choose to outsource this service to specialist project management services companies as well.

### 9.2.1 The packaging problem

The basic principle for packaging is long established, proposing that 'organizations seek to place reciprocally interdependent positions tangent to one another, in a common group which is (a) local and (b) conditionally autonomous'.[5] Positions that require only sequential coordination can be coordinated by standardization, rather than mutual interaction.[6] In contracting strategy terms, this translates into packaging together work elements that require relatively intensive levels of coordination and thereby letting the supplier manage them hierarchically within the package. There is a number of different perspectives which are relevant here, all of which address different aspects of contracting strategy design, which we capture in Figure 9.1 as the **four forces** of contracting strategy.

The first force focuses on the **nature of the transaction**, and our theoretical reference point is transaction cost economics,[7] which analyses the preferred relationship between supplier and owner for a given package. The contingencies along which the nature of the transaction varies are usually characterized as

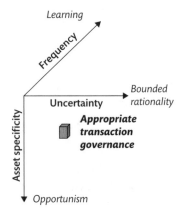

**Figure 9.2** Framework for the *nature of the transaction* force.

*Source*: Winch (2001: figure 1).

uncertainty, asset specificity, and frequency, as shown in Figure 9.2. We discussed the concept of uncertainty in Chapter 2. **Asset specificity** refers to the condition where a particular resource has limited availability for whatever reason. Prior to a contract being formed, this usually means that the PBF holding that resource can charge the owner a higher price for its supply. After contract formation, asset specificity typically refers to the position of that resource on the critical path of the schedule generating the 'hold-up' problem.[8] **Frequency** refers to the number of transactions between the owner and a supplier; it is, by definition, very low for the single project. The essence of the design challenge for the owner here is the interaction between uncertainty and asset specificity. If it were not for uncertainty, the owner and its chosen supplier could come to a complete agreement on how to deliver the project together, given the perceived level of asset specificity. However, on complex projects emergence is inevitable and commercial arrangements will need to be renegotiated during delivery. Under these conditions, the PBF is able to be *opportunistic*—should it choose to be—and exploit its bargaining power by posing the hold-up problem for the owner.

The second force focuses on the **structure of the supply** shown in Figure 9.3. The questions for the owner here revolve around how critical the task package is for project delivery and the technological complexity (see Figure 2.6) of the task package. Where there are many suppliers and the task package is both non-critical and at the simpler end of the spectrum, then reliance on competition to obtain the best offer on a transactional basis is appropriate. Where a failure of the supply of resources for a package might cause a **bottleneck**, this generates the risk of hold-up and then a more proactive managerial approach would be appropriate, while relying on transactional contracting. As technological complexity rises, a shift to a more relational commercial relationship needs to be leveraged to ensure that what is supplied is exactly what is required, and changes in requirements

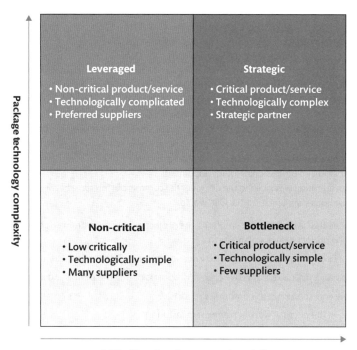

Figure 9.3 Framework for the structure of supply.

*Source*: developed from Kraljic (1983: exhibit 1).

are handled smoothly. Very often, owners move to a preferred supplier commercial arrangement with leveraged packages. Where a package technology is both truly complex and critical, then a strategic approach is preferred, which needs to be highly collaborative and may go so far as a joint venture or even acquisition of the supplier by a higher-tier supplier or the owner if transaction frequency is high enough.

The third force is the point in the economic cycle. Capitalist economies are inherently cyclical, and those cycles are reflected in the dynamics of supply sectors, where the amplitude of the cycle at the macroeconomic level is amplified by the accelerator effect[9] within project-based sectors. For contracting strategy, the implication of the economic cycle is that the strategy for contracts agreed near the peak of the cycle will be very different from those agreed nearer the trough. First-tier suppliers tend to be most profitable during the early phases of a recession when contracts agreed during boom times are being executed. The academic discipline that addresses issues around economic cycles is econometrics, but its record in spotting turning points in the cycle, which is the information that is most useful in shaping contracting strategy, is rather poor.

## Vignette 9.1   Bron‖Broen

The Bridge is a 12 km road and rail fixed link across the Øresund between Copenhagen and Malmö, consisting of a cable-stayed high bridge and a tunnel. It opened in 2000, ahead of schedule and on budget at €1.99 bn. The Danish and Swedish governments created an owner, Øresunds Konsortiet (ØSK), which on completion became operator as Øresundsbron Konsortiet. Delivery was packaged into seven design-and-construct contracts with support to ØSK from specialist consultants. ØSK managed the interfaces between the packages, but during the final stages proposed an integrated programme, where the contractors worked across contractual interfaces. Each contract had a dispute resolution board consisting of three experienced professionals jointly appointed.

Careful attention was given to the design of the commercial interface between the owner and the various supplier consortia. ØSK would:

- approve the basic design assumptions, the project quality programme documentation, and the project delivery planning;
- visit, observe, discuss, witness, review quality records, and carry out random sampling;
- review and, if required, approve change proposals during the Define and Execute stages;
- review and approve non-conformity reports;
- approve the physical work at payment milestones.

ØSK would not:
- get involved in day-to-day supervision, inspection, and approval of construction;
- inspect setting out;
- inspect construction joints, rebar placement, formwork, and the like;
- inspect every radiograph of welds;
- watch every batch of concrete being poured;
- be present all day, every day at each construction site;
- produce quality records.

Through this commercial interface design, ØSK had oversight of the project delivery organization, but did not exercise detailed control, which was delegated to the contractors who were responsible for their own quality control. ØSK did a small number of random checks using engineering advisors ASO and ØLC, but trusted the contractors to deliver consummately.

*Sources*: Drouin and Turner (2022); Wikipedia (accessed 25 February 2021).

There remains a number of issues that can be considered as the fourth, **institutional** force. Projecting always takes place in a particular institutional context,[10] which is typically defined at the national level by the national business system[11] in which PBFs are structured into project-based sectors as discussed in Chapter 6, each with its own sectoral business system.[12] One framework for analysing the institutional force is the PESTLE (political, economic, socio-cultural, technological, legal, and environmental) framework.[13] There are also important differences in national business cultures between countries, which will need to be taken into account if owners are investing in a foreign country or suppliers are based abroad, which are discussed further in section 10.4. Entry into many markets in developing countries often requires international firms to joint venture with national firms. Frequently, these national firms have different—some might say less sophisticated—approaches to the procurement problem and prefer fixed price when the international firm would prefer more sophisticated procurement arrangements. These tendencies are often reinforced by international agencies, such as the World Bank, which favour fixed-price contracting because of its greater inherent transparency and reduced potential for corruption, despite the play of the other forces.

### 9.2.2 **The procurement problem**

Contracts are central to the commercial relationships between organizations, yet in management they are rarely studied systematically.[14] The fundamental factor underlying contract design is the level of uncertainty regarding the subsequent phases of the project at the time the contract is drawn up. If the level of information available at contract design means that a simple spot contract[15] is not viable, then a choice of three basic types of complex contract is available: reimbursable, fixed price, and incentive contracts,[16] as shown in Figure 9.4.

Reimbursable contracts are those where goods and services are provided at an agreed rate as a function of an agreed parameter. Reimbursable contracts are

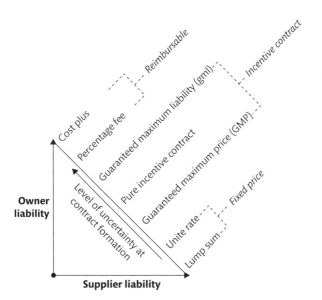

**Figure 9.4** Owner and supplier liability for change under different contract types.

*Source*: developed from Winch (2010: figure 6.5).

used where it is possible to identify broadly the type of resources required, but not in enough detail to specify closely. Such contracts are typically used in high-uncertainty situations, such as in the earlier phases of the project life cycle. **Fixed-price contracts** are those where the price is fixed for the supply of an agreed amount of work. They can either be a true lump sum, where the contract price is fixed, or be a schedule of rates (bill of quantities), where the precise quantity of work to be done is not known in advance. Fixed-price contracts are used in situations where a large amount of information is available, and so the contract is relatively complete at the time of agreement. Such contracts frequently contain provisions for minor adjustments to the price to take account of inflation and the management of change. **Incentive contracts** mix features of both reimbursable and fixed-price contracts. There is a wide variety of such contracts, but what unites them is the attempt to provide positive incentives within the contract to motivate collaborative relationships through 'gainsharing' between the parties.

These different options offer different risk profiles in terms of allocation of responsibility for the costs of changes in the scope of the project, illustrated in Figure 9.4. The full reimbursable contract effectively writes an open cheque to the supplier, and so detailed assurance as discussed in section 8.4.5 is typically in place to justify invoices and minimize opportunism—time-sheet management becomes a major task. However, such contracts tend to be relatively low value and are used under conditions of high uncertainty during the Appraise and Select stages. In effect, the owner is investing in a process of uncertainty reduction so that contracts let during the Define and Select stages for much higher values can transfer greater liability to the supplier for possible threat events. Fixed-price contracts tend to offer more protection for the owner because they are much less open to opportunistic behaviour on the part of the supplier, so long as the scope does not change. Fixed-price contracts transfer most liability to the supplier, although even here the supplier is usually protected against changes generated from sources beyond its control. Where the fixed price is based on unit rates, such as a bill of quantities, the uncertainties in the precise amount of work to be done are shifted to the owner, which opens up a margin for opportunism in the pricing of the unit rates. Incentive contracts allocate liability more equally between the parties, with a guaranteed maximum price (GMP) favouring the owner and a guaranteed maximum loss (GML) the supplier.

One of the main challenges with both reimbursable and fixed-price contracts is that they create perverse incentives for the supplier. Under reimbursable contracts, it is in the interests of the supplier to generate work to be done. There is certainly no direct incentive to minimize the project budget, subject to the constraint that the owner will cancel the project if the price rises to the point where the value proposition becomes negative. Similarly, those tendering for a fixed-price contract have an interest in maximizing the contract value, subject to the constraint that they are competing with others for the contract. For this reason, different owners pay different prices for technically similar facilities in accordance with suppliers' perceptions of what the market will bear.[17] Incentive contracts are an attempt to remove these perverse incentives by creating efficient contracts which balance the liabilities for change against the incentive gains that result.

### 9.2.3 The oversight problem

Responsibilities for the commercial interface tend to be split between the owner project team and the owner commercial team, yet the project team remains responsible for the delivery of the outputs from the project. The first task in project oversight is for the project team to establish the commercial arrangements required to enable that delivery. Most project-based sectors have standard forms of contract that structure the commercial interface,[18] which are usually difficult to change for a single project. What can be changed are the appendices (schedules) to the standard form. For instance, if the owner project team requires that suppliers perform root cause analysis of errors in delivery, this needs to be in the contract schedules; similarly, if the team requires the ability to visit factories manufacturing subsystems to verify conformance to specification or progress against schedule, then this also needs to be in the contract schedules.[19]

During project delivery, addressing the oversight problem requires continued engagement by the owner project team. It is important to have accurate information on project progress against schedule and budget, discussed in Chapter 11. The design challenge here is that the project management office (PMO) in its controller function, discussed in section 8.4.6, needs to ensure that the information loop is both functioning as the full responsibility of the owner PMO, and not left to the supplier to provide progress information. 'Management by wandering around'[20] is a crucial part of the project leader's role, particularly on those projects involving execution on site. Getting to know the team leaders from the various PBFs deployed on site, and giving them the confidence to 'speak truth to power' is a vital way of getting early warning signs of problems with progress, as discussed in section 7.6. Similarly, materials stockpiled instead of being fixed—sites are usually tight for space and operate a just-in-time logistics system—is a sign that something is going awry with the schedule. Even if the progress reporting from the supplier is timely and accurate, it will still be lagged information compared to spotting these early warning signs. The project leader's mantra here is 'trust but verify'.[21]

---

### Exercise 9.1

Review Vignette 9.1. Which factors do you think shaped the design of the commercial interface on the Øresundsbron?

## 9.3  The supplier perspective: project strategy

We now turn to look at the commercial interface from the point of view of the supplier, and in particular the PBF's project strategy,[22] which we define as the process of a supplier capturing an order from an owner and then delivering that output successfully—see Case 6. While for the owner the project is about strategy implementation, for the PBF the project—or rather the project portfolio—is the strategy. The argument also applies to a sub-supplier winning an order from a tier-one prime. The project life cycle from the point of view of a supplier is shown in Figure 9.5, with a sequence of four generic phases:

- **Develop business** is about business development through understanding the market and identifying those owners that are likely to be initiating projects— ideally during project shaping and achieving 'customer intimacy'.[23] It answers the question, 'What are the opportunities for us?'

- **Bid** is the process of moving from invitation to tender negotiating a successful contract. It answers the questions, 'What is our offer to the owner?' and 'Does the project fit our portfolio?'

- **Deliver** is the process of delivering the output specified in the owner's scope. It answers the question, 'Have we delivered the outputs to the owner to the agreed schedule, budget, and quality level?'

- **Support** is about ensuring the availability of the output through life to enable the owner to achieve the outcomes desired by the project mission.

Project capture needs to be closely aligned with an understanding of the owner's project-shaping process and the identification of the owner's 'hot buttons' for the project. For instance, the public sector is typically most concerned with the budget for the project, while private-sector investors may be more concerned with schedule in order to have 'job 1' or 'first oil' as soon as possible in order to start

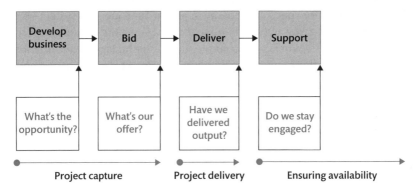

**Figure 9.5**  PBF project life cycle.

*Source*: authors.

the benefits stream flowing. Both are aspects of the quality of realization defined in Figure 7.1. Other owners may be most concerned with quality of specification or quality of conception. For instance, the military are typically most interested in 'battlefield capability' (quality of specification), which tends to produce tensions with defence ministries that tend to emphasize budget (quality of realization). Quality of conception tends to win out for opera houses and the like, and can seriously conflict with quality of realization, as the case of the Elbphilharmonie shows.[24] From this understanding, a capture strategy can be developed which plays to the competitive strengths of the supplier. If a viable capture strategy cannot be developed, it implies a no-bid decision. Without a clear capture strategy, bidding is likely to be an expensive waste of time. Central to the implementation of the capture strategy is the assignment of a capture team to deliver the final bid; indeed, project capture is arguably a specialist form of SPO, where the life cycle is days and weeks rather than months and years. The supplier will also need to establish appropriate arrangements for the governance of the capture process. These will typically involve senior management review and sign-off at gates, as shown in Case 6, and also peer review to ensure that all aspects of the owners' mission requirements are included and threats to consummate delivery are identified.

The bid/no bid decision at the end of the Develop business phase and the ready-to-submit decision at the end of the Bid phase are key stage gates, and are usually the responsibility of the supplier's senior management rather than the capture team itself. The decision to bid does not have to result in a bid submission if the bid development process uncovers surprises, but it usually does because the decision to bid is a significant investment in its own right. For this reason, best practice is to 'left shift' the bid process by investing more resources in the Develop business phase so that the quality of decision-making at the bid/no bid stage is improved.[25] From the supplier's point of view, it only enters the owner's project life cycle once it has successfully completed the pre-contract-signing negotiation with the owner prior to delivery.

The capture strategy is the key output from the Develop business phase, while the two outputs from the bid phase are (or should be) the technical **solution design** and the project delivery plan. A major element in the pre-selection of possible suppliers is usually their technological capabilities, as illustrated in Figure 9.3, so the solution design is key to order winning in project capture. For instance, are suppliers' technologies capable of operating at the leading edge of technology? Do they have a reputation for exciting designs? Are their systems totally reliable? Suppliers also need to be able to integrate these technologies into usable products and this is often where the complicated becomes complex in systems integration. Unless the supplier firm has confidence that it can deliver on its technological promises, it is better not to bid. The PBF's project delivery plan identifies how the solution design can be delivered to meet the owner's scope consisting of the schedule, budget, and delivery risk register, and is aligned to the owner's project delivery plan during contract negotiation. The evidence is that projects perform better when owners and suppliers negotiate over well-developed project delivery plans.[26]

## 9.4  Designing the commercial relationship: crafting collaboration

Section 9.2.3 drew on the standard economic and legal approach to the commercial interface that is often described as *transactional*, and reflects the differing interests of the two parties. However, the success of the project relies on these differing interests to be aligned and the inherent uncertainty of SPO means that collaborative relations are vital if the project is to be successful. The commercial interface, therefore, also needs to be *relational* in order to incentivize collaborative behaviours and a cooperative culture on the project, as shown in Vignette 9.2. In a very important sense, the transactional and relational aspects of the commercial interface are complements.[27] Few owners would want to spend large amounts of money without a legally enforceable agreement with their suppliers, but at the same time, a purely transactional approach will get in the way of consummate performance in the delivery domain. For this reason, initiatives known variously as 'partnering', 'alliancing', and 'collaborative working' have been important features of project organizing around the world for the past 20 years.[28]

Figure 9.6 shows the project stages for the supplier and the owner together and indicates how they can relate collaboratively. The dashed lines enclose the **transactional relationship** where the owner's invitation to tender is based on price competition against a specification produced at the end of the Define stage, or perhaps at some point during the Define stage. The dotted lines enclose more **collaborative relations**, where the supplier is brought in earlier in the project life cycle to advise on the viability of the options being evaluated during the Select stage. This may involve a two-stage supplier selection process, with the first stage on a reimbursable basis and the second stage on an incentive contract. These collaborative relations can also extend through to providing support for the achievement of outcomes by

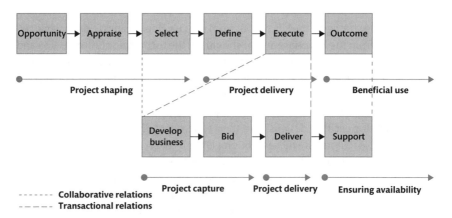

**Figure 9.6**  From transactional to collaborative relations across the commercial interface.

*Source*: authors.

## Vignette 9.2   @one Alliance

Anglian Water is the water utility for the east of England which, over the past 30 years, has developed a sophisticated approach to alliancing for the maintenance and upgrading of its water and sewage facilities. For capital projects, it formed the @one Alliance in 2005 with suppliers of engineering and construction services and water treatment technologies. It has since reduced capital costs by 30 per cent and embodied carbon by 50 per cent. In the period to 2030, it plans to deliver over 800 projects, with a target capital value of £1.2 bn. The alliance is structured into 'clusters' akin to the packages in Figure 9.1, in which suppliers work with Anglian on particular elements of scope such as tanks and pumps, or pipework and valves. Alliance members carry out 80 per cent of the work themselves, with around 20 per cent subcontracted to lower-tier suppliers.

The principal aim of the alliance is to incentivize 'outperformance' against the budget baseline for the project established by Anglian on the criteria of capital cost, whole life cost, carbon, and schedule. Alliance partners receive their direct costs, but can only generate a return for themselves by delivering outturns which are less than the baseline. These surpluses are placed in a common Alliance pool, from which overruns on the baseline are deducted. The amounts in the pool are periodically shared between the Alliance members.

One example of how it works is the Cambridge Water Recycling Centre project—a £22 m investment which was delivered in 10 months at £9 m below the baseline budget, with a high level of innovation in materials, construction techniques, and asset management technologies. This was achieved by paying very close attention to the design of the interfaces in the contracting map.

*Sources*: http://www.onealliance.co.uk (accessed 24 February 2021); Mills et al. (2020); ICG (2017).

ensuring the continued availability for the owner of the outputs through activities such as maintenance, as shown in Vignette 9.2.

The development of collaborative relations greatly facilitates innovation. These can be organizational innovations such as integrated project teams,[29] in which the owner and tier-one supplier project teams are co-located and work by allocating the most appropriate people to teams, notwithstanding who their original employer is. They can also be technical innovations because they extend the 'window of opportunity' defined in section 4.7 for innovation, as shown in Figure 9.6, from just the Execute stage to the Select and Define stages of the owner's project life cycle.

Further opportunities for partnering come from linking the owner's portfolio strategy discussed in section 8.4.1 with its contracting strategy. In Figure 9.2, we identified the way in which higher transaction frequency can generate learning across the parties about each other's capabilities. This potential connects the commercial interface to the governance interface because portfolio management can be used to generate multiple transactions with the same suppliers through framework agreements, where suppliers are contracted to supply services to a number of different projects over a fixed period—say five years on a partnering basis. Raising transaction frequency in this way enables owners and suppliers to learn more about each other's routines, minimize search and selection costs, and make relationship-specific investments that can lead to reduced production costs. Perhaps most importantly, it enables the generation of trust between the parties.[30] From the supplier perspective, the investment in project capture is much reduced in framework agreements, and a more stable horizon for workload facilitates investment in developing human resources. However, seizing the opportunity of framework agreements requires strong owner portfolio management and well-developed commercial capabilities. As BAA's Construction Director for the Heathrow Terminal 5 project put it, 'partnering is tough; it requires a huge investment in time, training and coaching'.[31]

---

### Exercise 9.2

Review Vignette 9.2. How does the @One Alliance design the commercial interface to address incentives?

---

## 9.5 Corruption

An important issue in the commercial interface is probity, that is to say, ensuring that negotiating the commercial interface is done in an open and honest manner. However, the large size of the contracts available has tempted many suppliers to move beyond such high standards and to offer inducements to owners to favour their services.[32] Such corruption is, broadly, of two kinds:

- personalized—where one or more public officials extract bribes from suppliers in return for favouritism in the award of contracts. It can usually be controlled, even if not eliminated, through the maintenance of effective assurance audit procedures as discussed in section 8.4.5;

- institutionalized—where work is shared out between suppliers and in return those suppliers make donations to political parties. This is inherently corrosive and can only be resolved through reform of political institutions, as shown in Vignette 9.3.

Personalized corruption is widespread, particularly in developing countries, where it can become so pervasive that the effective management of projects becomes impossible. Transparency International[33] rank-orders perceived levels of corruption of public officials in most countries. The data on perceived corruption do not measure levels of institutionalized corruption, yet this is also a major challenge in the commercial interface.[34] These 'stakeholders of the shadows'[35] are a major hindrance to effective delivery of projects and hence the development of economy and society.

---

### Exercise 9.3

What do you think the longer-term threats to probity in the commercial interface might be as a result of collaborative working?

---

## Vignette **9.3**    Institutionalized corruption on the Ile de France

Between 1989 and 1995, the procurement of contractors for the construction, refurbishment, and maintenance of schools in the Ile de France—the region that includes Paris—was institutionally corrupt. At least nine French construction firms—including the local subsidiaries of some of the world's largest construction corporations—were implicated, including what are now Bouygues and Vinci. Contracts to a total of ~€2.5 bn were shared out between these firms, which were then obliged to pay a sum equalling 2 per cent of the contract value to a fund. From this fund, the three main political parties shared pay-outs—1.2 per cent to the ruling coalition of the Rassemblement pour la République (RPR) and the Republican Party, and 0.8 per cent to the opposition Socialist Party. Unsurprisingly, it was the Green Party which exposed the scandal in 1996. Payments were made both directly in cash and through the creation of fictional employees, and the process was coordinated by the office of the Mayor of Paris. At the time, Jacques Chirac was both Mayor of Paris and President of the RPR.

The trial finally started in 2005 and some 43 people were convicted following much comment about the 'empty chair' at the hearings due to the absence of Jacques Chirac—then President of France and hence immune to prosecution or being asked to testify. Appeal hearings in 11 cases confirmed the convictions, including prison sentences, in early 2007, and the construction contractors were fined a total of €47 m later that year for their role in the scandal. Jacques Chirac was finally indicted for this and other corruption offences in November 2007, after he had left office, and received a two-year suspended sentence in 2011.

*Sources*: Le Monde 25 July 2001; 23 March 2005; 7 July 2005; 11 May 2007; 21 November 2007. Wikipédia (accessed 7 August 2008; 1 March 2021).

## 9.6  Summary

In this chapter, we have explored the commercial interface from the point of view of both the owner's contracting strategy and the supplier's project strategy. We have also shown how these can be aligned to gain the mutual benefits of collaborative working and trust. We now turn to the final interface in the three domains approach—the resource interface.

## 9.7  Further reading

Kraljic, P. 1983. 'Purchasing must become supply management'. *Harvard Business Review*, 61(5): 109–117.
    Classic statement of the owner's supply chain strategy.

Gil, N. 2009. 'Developing cooperative project client–supplier relationships: how much to expect from relational contracts?'. *California Management Review*, 51(2): 144–169.
    Analyses the innovative commercial agreement for the Heathrow Terminal 5 megaproject.

Cova, B. Ghauri, P., and Salle, R. 2002. *Project Marketing; Beyond Competitive Bidding*. Hoboken, NJ: Wiley.
    A valuable guide to project capture for PBFs.

## 9.8 Summary review questions

1. What are the three challenges the owner needs to address in its contracting strategy?
2. How do the four forces shape the owner's contracting strategy?
3. What are the different types of contracts available to the owner?
4. Why is the supplier's project life cycle different from that of the owner?
5. What is probity and why is it important?

 *Visit the Oxford Learning Link site for this text to find answer guidance to the questions and exercises in this chapter.*

 *Take your learning further by viewing videos relevant to this chapter on the Oxford Learning Link site.*

## Notes

1. Lowe (2013).
2. Independent Project Analysis.
3. Contracting maps are widely use in the oil and gas sector to visually capture the owner contracting strategy. The four forces approach, which gives analytic power to the maps, was developed at AMBS in collaboration with BP.
4. Winch et al. (1998).
5. Thompson (1967: 58).
6. Mintzberg (1979).
7. Williamson (1985); Rubin (1990).
8. Chang and Ive (2007); *Masten et al. (1991).
9. Ive and Gruneberg (2000).
10. Morris and Geraldi (2011); Söderlund and Sydow (2019).
11. Whitley (2007).
12. Winch (2000); Sergeeva and Winch (2020).
13. Pitkethly (2003).
14. Roehrich et al. (2020).
15. A 'spot' contract is like buying an item on a market stall; the goods are available for inspection, and the price can be negotiated face-to-face and paid at the moment of transaction.
16. See Sadeh et al. (2000) for defence acquisition and Jørgensen et al. (2017) for digital projects.
17. Fine (1975).
18. Stinchcombe (1985).
19. Both of these were issues on BP projects.
20. Peters and Waterman (1982).

21. According to BP project leaders.

22. Artto et al. (2008); Patanakul and Shenhar (2012).

23. Cova et al. (2002).

24. Fiedler and Schuster (2015).

25. We learned this from BAE Systems.

26. Merrow et al. (2009).

27. *Poppo and Zenger (2002).

28. See Jeffries and Rowlinson (2016) for a review.

29. Roehrich et al. (2020); Winch and Maytorena-Sanchez (2020).

30. Gil et al. (2011).

31. Andrew Wolstenholme, presentation Construction Innovation Conference, Ottawa, June 2001.

32. *Locatelli et al. (2017).

33. http://www.transparency.org (accessed 19 August 2021).

34. See Bologna and Del Nord (2000) for Italy; Reeves (2002) for Japan; Dorée (2004) for the Netherlands.

35. Winch (2017).

 **Case 9**   Operation Warp Speed

The COVID-19 pandemic killed millions and devastated economies around the world. Social lockdowns saved lives, but are unsustainable for anything above the shortest time period. Obtaining 'herd immunity' naturally was deemed too deadly by all governments and so the only alternative was to develop a vaccine. The typical time taken to develop a vaccine is measured in years rather than months, so how has it been achieved at 'warp speed'—or more precisely, in 326 days from the Chinese publication of the genetic sequence on 11 January 2020 to the UK licensure of the Pfizer/BioNTech vaccine on 2 December? The key is that project owners (in the form of governments responsible for national health-care systems) removed the liabilities for development project failure from suppliers (in the form of pharmaceutical companies large and small) by both pre-purchasing vaccines and funding research and development projects directly.

In vaccine development, 'the greatest hurdle is translating basic science advances into real vaccines that can be produced in adherence to stringent regulatory requirements on a sufficient scale to have a meaningful public health impact'. This typically costs millions and takes years. Generically, the life cycle for pharmaceutical development projects is like that shown in Figure 8.4. However, a candidate drug may fail at any gate for reasons beyond the control of the project team because, simply put, it does not work. Vaccine development projects face even greater difficulties because: (a) safety concerns are enhanced because they are injected into otherwise healthy people; (b) they need to be manufactured at a scale of billions of doses; and (c) the virus may naturally exhaust itself before the vaccine is ready, which happened with earlier coronavirus epidemics. The external threats facing vaccine development projects are existential.

In response to these threats, vaccine development projects move cautiously through tightly managed stage gates, as shown in the upper half of Figure 9.7. Following a pre-clinical phase, including animal testing, Phase 1 typically involves 25–30 volunteers and

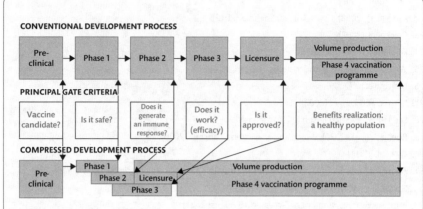

**Figure 9.7** Schedule acceleration in vaccine development.

*Source*: authors.

principally assesses the safety of the vaccine candidate. Phase 2 follows with hundreds of volunteers, including a control group, to assess whether the candidate stimulates an immune response. Phase 3 involves thousands of volunteers across multiple countries, half of whom are in a control group who receive a placebo, to see whether the candidate actually works in practice. Phase 3 is a significant investment in its own right, which needs to be supported by an initial investment in manufacturing facilities. The length of Phase 3 is indeterminate because it relies upon volunteers becoming infected 'naturally' to test the efficacy of the candidate. Suppliers from countries such as China, which successfully suppressed the virus through lockdowns, were obliged to test their vaccines candidates in other countries which had been less successful. Phases 2 and 3 are 'blind' in that the investigators and participants do not know who has received the placebo. Once the data are in from phase 3 trials, they can be submitted to national regulatory authorities for licensure. Scale-up and licencing for volume manufacturing follows. Phase 4 is monitoring the effectiveness of vaccination programmes. Here, countries such as Israel were able to secure early supplies of vaccines (Pfizer/BioNTec) by agreeing to share fully the data collected by their health-care systems during this phase.

Each of these phases is subject to oversight by external independent monitors to ensure rigour in the evaluation methods. This opened up the opportunity for 'rolling' regulatory approval. Normally, national regulators wait until phases 1–3 are complete before starting their evaluation prior to licensure. The rolling approach involves the regulator in engaging with the data as it is being released by the trial phase, and this, too, has compressed the development process. The output of the development process is a safe vaccine with a known efficacy at preventing infection (e.g. Sputnik V developed by Gamaleya Institute has 91.6 per cent efficacy). Phase 4 data are currently showing that all approved candidates are almost 100 per cent effective at preventing hospitalization and death.

This schedule can often take years because gate reviews need all the data from the preceding phase. Schedule compression in vaccine development essentially involves taking decisions at gates on incomplete information, thereby generating the threat of wasted investment if the candidate fails during later phases. Innovations in scientific research had already compressed the pre-clinical phase (for instance, the Oxford/AstraZeneca candidate

Table 9.1  Operation warp speed support to vaccine suppliers as of 1 March 2021 (spend in USD)

| Company | Vaccine type | Contract value | Specification | Outcome |
|---|---|---|---|---|
| Pfizer/BioNTech | mRNA | $5,970 m | 300 m doses | Approved |
| Moderna | mRNA | $4,940 m | 300 m doses | Approved |
| | | $945 m | Development | |
| AstraZeneca/ Oxford University | Viral vector | $1,200 m | 300 m doses | Phase 3 |
| Johnson & Johnson/Janssen | Viral vector | $1,000 m | 100 m doses | Approved |
| | | $456 m | Development | |
| Novavax | Protein | $1,600 m | 100 m doses | Phase 3 |
| Sanofi/GSK | Protein | $2,040 m | 100 m doses | Phase 2 |
| | | $30.8 m | Development | |
| Merck/IAVI | Viral vector | $38 m | Development | Discontinued |

was designed over a weekend from the Chinese sequenced genetic data) but the trial phases are not so easily compressed. Instead, they must be overlapped as shown in the lower half of Figure 9.7. This overlapping—as in all project delivery—is a major threat to the investor in the project. Schedule compression was only possible thanks to innovative design of the commercial interface, in which owners removed all significant liabilities from suppliers through direct subsidies to suppliers to support projects in the development phases, and pre-purchase of vaccines to support early investment in volume manufacturing facilities and the stockage of vaccines prior to licensure. For instance, India's Serum Institute—the world's largest vaccine manufacturer—has contracts with AstraZeneca and Novavax.

Operation Warp Speed was the US $18 bn public–private partnership launched in May 2020 principally to develop vaccines. It provided finance as shown in Table 9.1. Other Western countries also provided support to these same suppliers, as did not-for-profit organizations such as the Coalition for Epidemic Preparedness Innovations (CEPI). Russian (Gamaleya and Vektor) suppliers were fully supported by their government. Chinese (Sinopharm, Sinovac, and CanSino) suppliers were fully supported by their Ministry of Science and Technology. Neither relied on pre-purchase programmes in the same way as Western suppliers, but both are now marketing their vaccines internationally and setting up manufacturing overseas (e.g. Gamaleya in Italy; Sinopharm in the United Arab Emirates).

As implied in Table 9.1, owners took a portfolio approach to the projects they financed. Western governments typically pre-purchased around five different vaccines because they could not know: (a) which would survive clinical trials; (b) when they would be approved; (c) how well they would work; or (d) how well manufacturing facilities would scale up. As of 1 December 2020, six Western countries (counting the EU as one) had ordered four or more doses per capita for a two-dose regime. The remarkable success of the various development projects (only Sanofi/GSK from Table 9.1 hit major challenges during phase

2) means that many Western health-care systems had a potential surplus of vaccines and so started to make commitments to donating surplus vaccines to COVAX, the international alliance committed to distributing vaccines to developing countries. For instance, by mid-February 2021, the United Kingdom had ordered a portfolio of over 400 m doses of vaccine from seven different suppliers, with the largest orders going to suppliers which committed to establish manufacturing facilities in the United Kingdom (AstraZeneca, Valneva, CureVac, and Novavax), each with a different vaccine technology.

One remarkable unintended consequence of this massive public subsidy to vaccine suppliers is a complete reconfiguration of the structure of supply (see Table 9.1) for vaccines. Prior to 2020, the four main players were GSK, Merck, Sanofi, and Pfizer; currently only Pfizer has a viable product. These incumbents are 'amazingly large businesses with apparently high barriers to entry. It's very, very expensive to build one of these vaccine facilities.' Merck has dropped out completely; GSK and Sanofi are partnering with biotech companies comparable to BioNTech but are off the pace. AstraZeneca was not a player in the vaccines market until it won the right to develop Oxford's vaccine thanks to its commitment to provide at cost to developing countries; it is now the largest global supplier of COVID vaccines.

Following licensure, manufacturing facilities are ramped up and vaccines doses delivered to health-care systems so that benefits realization can begin and the project output of a safe and effective vaccine is transformed into the project outcome of pandemic suppression. For all health-care systems, this was a major programme in its own right.

We are grateful to Sujuan Zhang, Xiamen University and Dongping Cao, Tongji University for their help in developing this case study.

*Sources*: Buckland (2005); *Financial Times*, 11 December 2020, 16 December 2020, 10 February 2021; 12 February 2021; 16 February 2021; 24 March 2021; http://www.who.int; http://www.cepi.net (accessed 26 February 2021); Lurie et al. (2020); Logunov et al. (2021).

## Discussion Questions

1. Why did some Western governments responsible for health-care systems around the world choose to redesign the commercial interface with suppliers for COVID-19 vaccines?

2. How successful do you think they have been in doing this?

3. Think about the vaccination programme in your country. How successful has it been in (a) securing adequate supplies; and (b) delivering the supplied vaccines into people's arms?

# 10 The resource interface

## 10.1 Introduction: resourcing the delivery domain

The delivery domain needs resources in order to deliver projects. The financial resources required come from the owner domain, but the human and techno-logical resources required are the responsibility of the supplier domain, in which the project-based firms (PBFs) form resource bases that develop and deploy the required resources. The most important resources on the project are human—projects are done by people! Technology resources are not usually a constraint in project organizing because the Select stage of the project life cycle in Figure 2.7 is about choosing technologies that are, in principle, available. These are then integrated into the output during the Define stage. However, the project mission may call for technologies that are still in development and so require innovation, as discussed in section 4.7.

The first part of the chapter focuses on human resources. We address the issues of mobilizing those resources from the supplier domain onto the project in the delivery domain, and introduce the concepts of responsibility chart, matrix organ-ization, and tools for managing resources. We then turn to the importance of par-ticular cities that maintain project ecologies in resourcing delivery organizations. Many projects are now inherently international because suppliers can be drawn from many different countries, and so we will discuss the inter-cultural challenges this poses. What people bring to projects is knowledge, so we will then turn to knowledge integration on projects. Finally, we look at technology readiness and an increasingly important resource in project organizing—digital technology. Our case study on whole house retrofits discusses the challenge of delivering projects where resources are highly constrained.

## 10.2 Mobilizing resources on the project

In the strategic project organizing (SPO) Star Model presented in Figure 7.3, we identified the importance of designing the project delivery organization. Resources are allocated to the project structure resulting from this design by the PBFs from

Table 10.1  A RACI diagram

| Fast Project | | WHAT (WBS) | | |
| | | Task 1:<br>Engineering | Task 2:<br>Manufacture | Task 3:<br>Assembly |
| --- | --- | --- | --- | --- |
| WHO (team project managers) | Julie | A | C | C |
| | Fred | R | I | I |
| | Marie | C | A | I |
| | Asaf | I | R | C |
| | Chenlu | C | C | A |
| | Kurt | I | R | I |

their resource bases. A valuable tool for doing this is the RACI chart shown in Table 10.1.[1] This relates the project organization to the work breakdown structure (WBS) shown in Figure 7.2 consisting of:

- a y axis of the array of the resource bases mobilized on the project;
- an x axis of the tasks to be executed on the project derived from the WBS;
- a system of symbols to identify different types of involvement in executing a specified task.

One symbol system is RACI, where **R** stands for who is responsible for executing the task, **A** stands for who is accountable for assuring the task is executed properly, **C** stands for who needs to be consulted about task execution, and **I** stands for who needs to be informed that it has started, finished, or both. The point where the two dimensions intersect defines a task to be executed by a nominated resource base team with someone named as **R**esponsible for that execution as team leader. The difference between **R**esponsible and **A**ccountable is subtle, but important. The **R**esponsible person actually organizes execution of the task and leads the task execution team, while the **A**ccountable person appoints the **R**-person, and ensures that the **R**-person delivers. In sensitive areas such as health and safety, it is said that 'Responsible is what you get sacked for; **A**ccountable is what you go to jail for'.[2] Due to the temporary nature of the delivery organization, organization design needs to be explicitly tackled early in the life cycle as part of the project delivery plan (PDP), rather than being allowed to evolve naturally. While the precise nature of responsibilities will change through the life cycle, the principles of allocating resources are valid during both shaping and delivery.

The RACI process generates the relationship between the WBS and the project organization structure shown in Figure 10.1, which is known as a project matrix organization.[3] On the y axis are the resource bases, which may be from different PBFs or from the same firm, depending on the contracting strategy discussed in section 9.2. Along the x axis is the high-level WBS, in this case broken down by each element of output (building type)

## Vignette 10.1    Overcommitting on human resources

The period over Christmas and New Year is a relatively quiet one for rail travel in the United Kingdom and so is often used for 'blockades' of sections of track so that they can be closed to rail traffic and upgrade work can be carried out more effectively. Over the 2007/2008 holiday, three upgrade projects in different parts of the country significantly overran and caused considerable disruption to the planned reinstatement of rail services after the New Year holiday. This caused significant loss of revenue for the train operators and considerable inconvenience and distress for passengers returning to their daily commute.

The principal problem was common—lack of availability of catenary (overhead power cable) workers and supervisors. Although this shortage of competent human resources had been identified as a threat to project delivery by the infrastructure owner and operator, Network Rail, it relied on its suppliers to recruit and deploy the required human resources to the upgrade projects as required. There was no overall coordination at the portfolio level of this key human resource between what were otherwise completely separate projects in different parts of the country delivered by different suppliers. While the project-level planning of the principal blockade was deemed exemplary by the regulator, the Office of Rail Regulation, that planning did not extend to the portfolio level of key human resources shared with other projects. As a result of this debacle, Network Rail proposed bringing in-house such key human resources as catenary workers on the basis that the owner is the only party capable of planning the allocation of scarce human resources across the portfolio of projects.

*Source*: Office of Rail Regulation (2008).

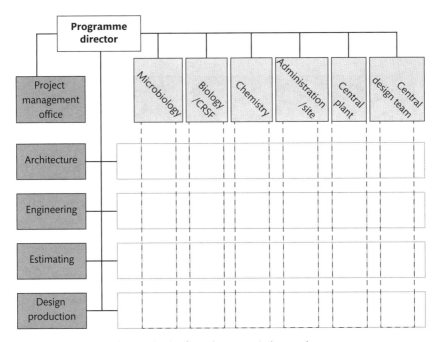

Figure 10.1  Project matrix organization for a pharmaceutical research campus.

*Source*: developed from Winch (2010: figure 15.10).

which forms the project mission. The one exception is the central design team which is responsible for design elements that are common to each building, as well as the over-all landscaping of the campus. Note also that the delivery project management office (PMO) reports directly to the programme director, while the managers for each resource base will also report to line managers within their respective PBFs. The project manager for each output in the programme reports to the programme director.

Within the project matrix, the balance between the responsibility of the project managers compared to the resource base managers varies across different projects,[4] shown in Figure 10. 2. Where resource base managers have complete responsibility, the project manager has little more than a liaison role, so this can be considered to be a **functional project organization**. Where the project manager has clear respon-sibilities for overall coordination, monitors progress, and brokers competition for resources, but is, in the end, reliant on the resource base managers to make appro-priate allocations of resources to the project, this can be considered a **lightweight project organization**. Where the converse is true, and the project manager has the stronger hand, overriding resource allocations made by resource base managers, then this is **heavyweight project organization**. Finally, where the project manager has complete autonomy, including the possibility of hiring staff directly, then this is an **autonomous project organization**, which is common on megaprojects. Au-tonomous project organizations can have a slightly covert aura; the famous 'skunk works' of Lockheed were autonomous project organizations.[5] The test of which form of project matrix is being implemented is who holds the project budget—the resource base manager or the project manager.[6] Above this level, the project spon-sor remains accountable, as discussed in section 8.4.3.

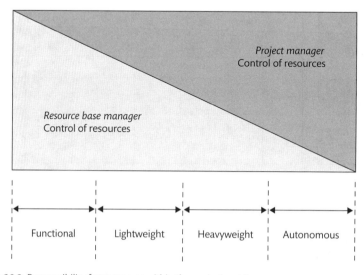

**Figure 10.2** Responsibility for resources within the project matrix.

*Source*: developed from Winch (2010: figure 15.1).

Table 10.2  Responsibilities of the project manager and the resource base manager

| Project manager | Resource base manager |
| --- | --- |
| What is the task to be done? | How will the task be done? |
| When will the task be done? | Where will the task be done? |
| Why will the task be done? | Who will do the task? |
| What is the budget for the task? | What are the resources required for the task? |
| Integration of task output into final output | Quality of task output |

*Source*: developed from Winch (2010: table 15.1).

As the project organization matures, the distinctive roles of the resource base and project managers become more clearly articulated, as summarized in Table 10.2. As is implicit in Figure 10.2, it is never possible to fully distinguish these roles—some tension, and even conflict, is inevitable, but not necessarily dysfunctional.[7] Rather than this tension being solely negative, it can be a source of creativity in problem-solving. What is dysfunctional is poor conflict resolution due to suppressing or ignoring the tensions.

The allocation of human resources to project delivery organizations generates considerable tensions as project managers and resource base managers compete for resources. Project managers focus on delivering 'their' project, while resource base managers have to allocate resources across the portfolio of projects held by the PBF. This can generate significant problems of overload and work–life balance,[8] and if scarce human resources are not managed at portfolio level, as in Vignette 10.1, schedules can slip. As a coping mechanism, project managers tend to focus on fire-fighting in project execution rather than balancing resources effectively. In principle, the agile working methods described in section 7.5 should ease resource allocation tensions because they eliminate the problem of schedule overrun and hence the retention of resources by a particular project when they are needed on another project. However, they face challenges in being implemented on larger projects governed through stage gates.[9] Further resourcing challenges for PBFs include taking people off project delivery teams to form capture teams to ensure a future stream of work for the PBF,[10] and the retention of people on projects nearing their completion when exciting new projects beckon, as shown in Vignette 10.2.

## 10.3 Project ecologies

So far we have been discussing human resources from the point of view of the PBFs that employ the members of resource bases. However, many of the resources required for projects are supplied much more flexibly through project ecologies.[11] Project ecologies are regions—typically major cities—where the human resources required for the delivery of projects congregate. These human resources provide a

## Vignette 10.2    Creating commitment at Rocky Flats

The decommissioning and closure of the Rocky Flats nuclear weapons manufacturing facility in Colorado was always going to be difficult. The facility had 800 buildings and other installations, some with high levels of radioactive pollution, and relationships with local stakeholders and regulators were very poor. Relationships with trades unions were also poor and the accident rate higher than that of the construction industry generally. Yet the principal contractor, Kaiser-Hill, achieved one of the most rapid and effective nuclear clean-ups ever by 2005.

Kaiser-Hill negotiated a contract with the US Department of Energy with a very high incentive for early completion. Kaiser-Hill then needed to incentivize the workforce. It faced two different problems in doing this—workers might shirk to spin out their employment longer or they might quit for longer-term opportunities while their competencies were still needed. The solution was an incentive scheme that paid well for early completion against targets, but not all bonuses were paid immediately. The balance—called 'scrip'—was put into an incentive pool on a diminishing curve. In the early years, up to 80 per cent of the bonus went into the pool; in later years, it dropped to 45 per cent. If the maximum bonus in the overall contract were earned, scrip would be worth $1.00 per share, diminishing as earnings against the target schedule diminished. Workers who were laid off retained their scrip in the bonus pool; workers who quit lost their rights to the scrip they had earned. This arrangement also discouraged workers whose tasks were completed early in the schedule and then laid off from completing their targets in a way that jeopardized the performance of later tasks in the schedule. The levels of bonus earned in this way were described as 'lifestyle changing'.

*Source*: Cameron and Lavine (2006).

'pool' which can be drawn on by suppliers on a more or less casual basis to enable them to resource their projects. One of the most obvious examples of a project ecology is the film industry of southern California. Project ecologies are, however, much more common than this, being found in software development (e.g. Silicon Valley), advertising[12] (where London is a global centre), and various other project-based sectors. It is also noticeable that large engineering Professional Service Firms (PSF)—see section 6.5—cluster together in a few global cities, such as London for civil engineering[13] and Houston for oil and gas.

The principal advantage that project ecologies offer is flexibility in the supply of competent human resources. From the point of view of the professional engineer, architect, or other specialist, the wide range of job opportunities available in one travel-to-work area offers the potential for rapid career advancement and alternative opportunities if the present project does not go ahead. For PBFs, the deep pool of skills makes it relatively easy to mobilize if successfully capturing a project requires a rapid increase in capacity. However, the downside is that the project ecology tends to be better at exploiting existing competencies than in developing new ones. Professionals need to fund their own competency development in terms of both time and cost, and learning-by-doing remains with the individual rather than being captured by the employing organization. Innovation can thereby be stifled.

> ### Exercise 10.1
>
> What do you think are the benefits and disbenefits of working in a project ecology rather than being permanently employed by a PBF?

## 10.4 Resourcing internationally

The second globalization since 1950 has generated both massive demand for the outputs from projects and created a global market for the services of PBFs.[14] Project coalitions can consist of PBFs from many countries, and so project delivery becomes a multinational endeavour. Vibrant project ecologies also attract immigrants and so delivery teams are often multilingual.[15] In combination, these create a heady mix.[16] Broadly, there are two cross-cultural aspects that affect project organizing: the expectations of how leaders behave and interactions within project teams.

Leadership behaviours are culturally endorsed[17] and therefore affect the way followers perceive leaders. While there are many cultural differences in preferred leadership styles, there are also some important universals across all dimensions of the Project Leadership Model (PLM) presented in Figure 3.1. The positive ones are being trustworthy and honest; having foresight and planning; and being positive, encouraging, and communicative. The universally negative aspects include being a loner, a-social; non-cooperative and irritable; and dictatorial. Turning to examples of differences, 'charismatic' leaders (inspirational and decisive) are more culturally endorsed in Anglo- and north European cultures than in Middle Eastern cultures, while 'self-protective' (status-conscious and face-saving) leaders are more culturally endorsed in Asian and Middle Eastern cultures, and less so in Anglo- and north European cultures. Of particular interest for SPO is the construct 'uncertainty avoidance' because of the importance of sense-making in the PLM. Uncertainty avoidance captures the extent to which orderliness, clarity of expectations, and formalized processes are preferred. In high uncertainty avoidance countries, 'self-protective' and 'team-orientated' leadership is preferred, even at the cost of innovation, while in low uncertainty avoidance countries, 'participative' leadership is preferred—again, the differences are clustered around northern European and North American countries, on the one hand, and middle Eastern and Asian countries, on the other. These differences create mental schema[18] which affect sense-making and relating in particular.

Cross-cultural issues affect the teaming dynamics captured in Figure 7.4. Differing levels of familiarity with routines such as scheduling tools used as boundary objects within cross-cultural teams can lead to cultural groups perceiving the imposition of other cultural values.[19] Preferences for direct spoken communication rather than contextually nuanced communication can lead to misunderstandings.[20] One coping mechanism is to focus on the technical issues across a shared professional identity, rather than the differences highlighted by cultural identity, and to use out-of-office social events to develop cross-cultural understandings.[21] For both leaders and teams, identification with the project mission, as well as the team task, is crucial. As one leader on the Channel Fixed Link put it:

> l'achèvement du Projet tient du miracle compte tenu des différences culturelles linguistiques, morales, et sociales. La réussite résulte probablement dans l'adhésion d'une majorité à un objectif commun.[22]

## 10.5  Knowledge as a resource

So far we have talked about human resources in general terms, but what do those resources bring to the delivery organization? Fundamentally, it is *knowledge*— knowing how to do the tasks competently that the delivery organization needs to do. However, it is worth clarifying the difference between 'information' and 'knowledge' because there are no clear definitions of these two terms that are widely accepted. For the information-processing approach taken in SPO, there is an important difference between the two concepts analogous to the economist's distinction between stocks and flows.[23] **Knowledge** is a stock of information held by a resource base that has the potential to be mobilized on the project to deliver the project mission. It can be *tacit*, in that it is not fully expressed and is closely related to the personal competencies of an individual and only meaningful in specific contexts, or it can be *explicit* in that it is fully communicable between any two or more individuals. Knowledge can be traded internationally in the form of intellectual property, or it can be held in secret as proprietary knowledge to gain competitive advantage. Whatever the form in which it is held, knowledge is a resource which only creates value once it is mobilized to deliver the project mission. To extend our river analogy from section 7.3, knowledge is a reservoir that is used to supply the river in order to maintain water flow levels, or to provide a head for greater pressure. **Information** is knowledge in use—the river in flow—mobilized to deliver the project mission. A book in the library is knowledge—only when mobilized by a reader does it become usable information.

There are two main approaches to knowledge mobilization depending on the level of codification of the available knowledge—the 'codification' and 'personalization' strategies.[24] Where PBFs aim to craft their solutions to specific owner needs, then the personalization strategy is more appropriate, with an emphasis on hiring highly competent people, developing them through intensive coaching, and developing communities of reflective practitioners.[25] Where the aim is to deliver standardized solutions to owners, then less competent people are hired and there is a greater reliance on IT-based knowledge management systems, and less individual attention to personnel development. Those PBFs that operate when dynamic uncertainty is high and mobilize on high-complexity projects favour the personalization strategy, while those that tend to operate later in the project life cycle and to mobilize on lower-complexity projects favour the codification strategy.

While utilizing knowledge as a resource is essential in SPO, and many organizations have established strategies for its acquisition and deployment, these often remain ineffective for a number of reasons:

- *Time*: in many PBFs, delivering the current project and capturing the next is the overwhelming priority. The time required to take a day for the post-project meeting, to add to the intranet database, or to make presentations at professional conferences is all time that is not directly fee-earning.

- *Incentives*: the aim of organizational knowledge strategies is to turn individual learning into organizational learning. This means that incentives are required to encourage people to share their expertise. Where employment relationships are collegial, organizational culture can play an important role in generating incentives; where employment is casualized through project ecologies, there are positive disincentives to share personal learning organizationally.

- *Centralization*: there are important trade-offs between the centralization of knowledge capture within the organization so that diffusion is maximized, and its decentralization so that more intensive team learning is favoured. In many centralized, IT-based systems, senior managers become arbiters of what is appropriate knowledge, and knowledge management becomes seen as a specialist function. The ultimate parody of the centralized knowledge manager is Jorge the blind librarian in Umberto Eco's novel *The Name of The Rose*, who would rather commit murder and burn down the library than allow ordinary monks access to the knowledge it contained which he could not himself access.

---

### Exercise 10.2

Think about the different sets of knowledge that were required on a recent project you were involved in. How were those knowledge bases integrated?

---

## 10.6 Knowledge integration and learning

We have argued that the knowledge required for delivering the project mission is held either explicitly or tacitly by resource bases. From the owner's point of view, these resource bases are typically a diverse set of PBFs; from the PBF point of view, knowledge required to deliver on their commitments to the delivery organization is often held by other PBFs. This generates the problem of knowledge integration, or the combination of disparate types of knowledge into the information that the delivery organization needs to achieve the project mission. This is one reason why the trusting and collaborative commercial relationships discussed in section 9.5 are so important, particularly when they allow co-location of project teams.[26]

Knowledge is created through learning, both from experience and experimentation. However, as we have indicated, learning from experience on projects can be challenging for both supplier and owner organizations.[27] The nub of the problem is that much of the learning takes place within the delivery domain, yet the project delivery organization is, by definition, temporary. At the end of the project it is dissolved and the learning by the individuals who worked on the project is dispersed as those individuals move on to new jobs, particularly if their employment was casual rather than permanent with the PBF. Capturing this learning is a process of organizational learning from the delivery experience and is a vital element of the project life cycle. There are three main ways of capturing learning from projects by PBFs so as to renew their resource bases and to develop their capacity to realize projects more effectively in the future:

- conducting post-project reviews shortly after project close.[28] Key participants are brought together to debrief and identify main learning points from their experiences on the project;

- using intranets such as Yammer within the resource bases to capture and diffuse learning points;

- establishing centres of excellence in the capabilities required by owners to integrate learning.[29]

Organizational learning is a process of creating, retaining, and transferring knowledge within an organization. Teaming, as discussed in sections 3.6 and 7.4, is the key to organizational learning. The way in which individuals interpret, make sense, and communicate is vital to the PBF as a learning organization, and connecting and sharing is an important part of this process. Verbal, written, and symbolic stories, as discussed in section 4.6, facilitate the processes of communicating and sharing knowledge that generates learning. Organizations, both permanent and temporary, learn through the ways people speak, communicate, interpret, and share in the context of teaming. Project leaders play an important role in crafting these stories,[30] as well as sharing the ones they learn from their teams. They also share stories with different stakeholders, and hence storytelling is an important part of learning and knowledge integration in SPO.

## 10.7 Technology readiness

PSFs also supply the material resources that the delivery project requires to achieve the desired outputs. These can range from commodity items such as steel pipe through to proprietary knowledge embodied in specialist technologies. The supply of commodity items is not normally an issue, although the supply of a specialist steel, for instance, may be expected to be short. Such threats should be identified during the Select stage and may be treated as 'long lead' items and purchased in advance by the owner on behalf of the PBF appointed later in the life cycle. Proprietary technology poses much greater challenges, and some projects deploy very advanced technologies to deliver on the project mission. The technology readiness level (TRL) index shown in Figure 10.3, originally developed by NASA, has now been adopted for technology-based projects in a number of sectors.[31] The aim is to provide an objective assessment of the amount of further development work required before the technology can be incorporated into the planned output by the delivery organization with the confidence that it will work as expected. The assessment of the additional tasks required can then be included in the WBS, and hence in the PDP discussed in section 7.2.

In complex projects, one of the principal sources of uncertainty is emergence, as discussed in section 2.4. In an important sense, therefore, the TRL is a complexity index, and the point of inflection between a complex and a complicated technology as defined in section 2.4 is somewhere between levels 8 and 9 in Figure 10.3. Even if the technology is comfortably at level 9, if it is deployed in combination

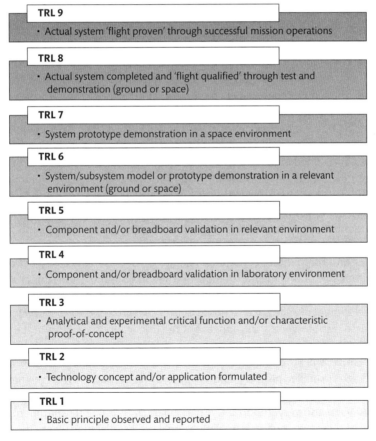

**TRL 9**
- Actual system 'flight proven' through successful mission operations

**TRL 8**
- Actual system completed and 'flight qualified' through test and demonstration (ground or space)

**TRL 7**
- System prototype demonstration in a space environment

**TRL 6**
- System/subsystem model or prototype demonstration in a relevant environment (ground or space)

**TRL 5**
- Component and/or breadboard validation in relevant environment

**TRL 4**
- Component and/or breadboard validation in laboratory environment

**TRL 3**
- Analytical and experimental critical function and/or characteristic proof-of-concept

**TRL 2**
- Technology concept and/or application formulated

**TRL 1**
- Basic principle observed and reported

Figure 10.3  NASA technology readiness levels.

*Source*: NASA.

with technologies different from the 'proven' situation, or deployed in a differ-ent operating environment, there is still the threat of emergence. Developing a full understanding of the TRL of the technologies that are incorporated into the output being delivered by the project at both the subsystem and whole system levels is a vital part of project shaping, especially during the Select stage. Any score below 9 requires additional provision in the budget and schedule and entry on the threat register discussed in section 11.7 because it will inevitably require ad-ditional resources during the Define stage.

## 10.8  Digital technology as a resource

As discussed in section 1.2, the technologies that are driving the third and fourth Industrial Revolutions are changing our world and thereby having a profound ef-fect on SPO. Broadly, there are two types of effect. The first is that project missions are changing. The third Industrial Revolution brought a new type of project—the digital transformation programme—as owner organizations sought to take up op-portunities for both operational efficiencies and new products and services for customers. The fourth Industrial Revolution is generating even more profound changes because even where physical outputs remain largely made from concrete and steel, the requirement to incorporate digital technologies into those systems is growing, creating both cyber-physical systems and digital twins, as shown in Vignette 10.3. These technological advances will likely merge the previously dis-tinctive categories of projects of infrastructure projects and digital transforma-tion projects defined in section 1.1—arguably this has already happened for many types of new product development (NPD) projects. However, this new type of projecting will pose new challenges for project teams[32] and it is not clear that the current generation of project leaders who take an analytic decomposition ap-proach symbolized by the WBS in Figure 7.2 have the complementary integrative skills that these new cyber-systems require.[33]

The second profound effect of technologies on SPO is the way project organ-izing will change during the fourth Industrial Revolution, and it is on this challenge that we will concentrate here. An early example of responding to this challenge is the development of agile approaches to delivery which reduce project cycles so as to increase responsiveness to change, but the implications are likely to be much wider. The third Industrial Revolution has already provided sophisticated informa-tion systems.[34] MS Project[35] is ubiquitous as a tool for scheduling, budgeting, and resourcing on smaller projects, and Primavera[36] is common on larger projects. The technical basis of many projects means that varieties of computer-aided de-sign (CAD) are also very important. A particularly interesting development is the merging of these two tools in four-dimensional project planning where the three-dimensional digital model of the output is connected to the schedule (through the WBS) to allow visualization, simulation, and optimization of the delivery schedule through time.

Vignette **10.3**     Rebuilding Notre Dame digitally

On the night of 15 April 2019, flames swept through the iconic cathedral of Notre Dame de Paris, destroying the timber and lead structures of the roof and spire. President Macron has ordered that the cathedral be restored in time for the opening of the Paris Olympics in 2024. This is—literally—a monumental project mission. There are many resource constraints in delivering on this mission, most notably the supply of carpenters, plumbers, and stonemasons skilled in the techniques of mediæval building. However, digital resources are playing a vital role in supporting the delivery of the project mission.

During 2010, a laser survey created a three-dimensional digital twin of the cathedral composed of over 1 billion data points with an accuracy greater than 5 mm, which was used to understand the architectural history of the structure. This survey had been complemented over the years by further lasergrammetry and photogrammetry. Within hours of the fire starting, a 'commando operation' was launched by Art Graphique et Patrimoine, a Parisian digital architecture atelier which had worked on the original laser survey, to capture digitally the condition of the structure using drones to measure those areas which were unsafe to access. These data were then used to update the existing digital twin as a starting point for the design and planning of the restoration project.

The digital twin can be updated in real time by data on progress on site execution and can be accessed remotely by multiple parties across the world, which has been very important during COVID-19-related lockdowns. AI tools are used to analyse the images in the twin to identify elements of the structure which survived the fire well enough to be reincorporated in the new elements.

*Sources*: Sandron and Tallon (2020); *Financial Times*, 16 February 2021; http://www.artgp.fr (accessed 24 March 2021).


Social media are increasingly important for improving communications on projects; digital technologies are vehicles for collaboration and collective actions. Social media and digital communication are used widely by project organizations to broadcast their ideas and reach wider audiences. These technologies can help organizations to introduce novel ideas into their market and make their ideas understandable and easily adoptable. Digital platforms are increasingly changing the ways owners, PBFs, and project-based sectors operate. Digital technologies and platforms can be viewed as the vehicle of collective actions of organizations that want to share and drive innovations. Examples include mobilizing other organizations within the project-based sector to cooperate through lobbying efforts and creating industry associations. Such collective actions have the potential to transform organizational structures, reshape demands, and even redefine shared best-practice routines operating in the project sector. Digital technologies and platforms also enable more loosely coupled forms of cross-sector collaboration or emerge at the intersections of sectors.[37] Here, project ecologies integrate with ecosystem innovation[38] to create dynamic innovation environments for project organizing. The classic example is Silicon Valley, which is the location for many of the projects that have created the technologies for the fourth Industrial Revolution, but London forms an innovation ecosystem for the application of platform technologies to the management of infrastructure megaprojects.[39]

Table 10.3  Digital affordances for SPO

| Affordance | Description | Implications |
|---|---|---|
| Shareable | Digital information can be shared, copied, edited, and moved without loss of integrity | Reduced transaction costs across the commercial interface; efficiencies in data handling for all members of the project coalition; owner receives a digital model of the output to support benefits realization |
| Accessible | Remote and immediate access to information by multiple parties wherever they are located, whether using cloud computing or dedicated servers | PBF location becomes less relevant; project coalitions form distributed information networks; resilience during pandemics; potential to include Internet of Things in information networks; social media platforms used for stakeholder and team member engagement |
| Searchable | Digital information can be aggregated, linked, and searched | Aggregation of data into progress reporting dashboards; potential for big data and machine learning applications; faster feedback on implementation of decisions |
| Updateable | Data acquisition becomes nearly real time | Facilitates smoother flow of the project information loop (Figure 11.3); provides a direct window onto the status of project delivery; reduction of uncertainty due to greater timeliness of reporting |

*Source*: developed from Whyte (2019: Table 1).

The implications of this new wave of digital innovation for project organizing are summarized in Table 10.3, which identifies four distinctive affordances[40] that digital technologies offer SPO, and some implications for project delivery. However, the shareability of digital information can also become a trap if it is not appropriately governed. Assurance of the integrity of the data held within digital systems becomes an even greater challenge as they enable faster delivery of projects—the GIGO mantra of 'garbage in; garbage out' still holds in the fourth Industrial Revolution. One issue that has not yet been addressed is how the digital systems interface across the three domains in Figure 2.1:

- Digital information is largely created within engineering information systems held by the supplier PBFs and needs to be passed to similar systems used by other PBFs. Seamless integration here is not assured because of different system vendors and protocols used by PBFs.

- This digital information also needs to interface with the project management information systems used to manage the information flows within the delivery domain, yet these are usually supplied by vendors separate from the ones supplying engineering information systems.

- As permanent organizations, owners and PBFs also have enterprise management systems, which are again supplied by different vendors and are rarely project-orientated in their architecture.

An important difference between third-generation and fourth-generations systems is that the latter are actively addressing these interface issues, but much progress is still to be made.

> **Exercise 10.3**
>
> Think about the digital tools available for managing projects. In what ways could they be improved? How can all the benefits of the latest web technologies be utilized on projects?

## 10.9 Summary

In this chapter, we have focused on how the human resources that embody the knowledge required by the project delivery organization to achieve the project mission are deployed in the project matrix, and the importance of technology readiness and digital technologies. These resources need to be organized so that the competencies of the individuals in the resource bases can be mobilized by PBFs into the capabilities to deliver the project. In an important sense, technologies also embody human knowledge and their readiness needs to be carefully assessed and managed to ensure that emergence does not disrupt the schedule and escalate the budget, while digital technologies are changing team dynamics on projects profoundly. This chapter completes the presentation of the three interfaces of strategic project organizing. We now move from the organizational to the individual level of analysis and analyse the professional competencies required for managing and leading in SPO.

## 10.10 Further reading

Hansen, M. T., Nohria, N., and Tierney, T. 1999. 'What's your strategy for managing knowledge?'. *Harvard Business Review*, 77(2): 106–116.
A classic on knowledge management.

Whyte, J. 2019. 'How digital information transforms project delivery models'. *Project Management Journal*, 50(2): 177–194.
Insightful analysis of the digital transformation on infrastructure projects.

Sandron, D. and Tallon, A. 2020. *Notre Dame Cathedral: Nine Centuries of History.* University Park, PA: Pennsylvania State University Press.
A hymn to a digital twin.

## 10.11  Summary review questions

1. What are the responsibilities of a project manager and a resource base manager?
2. What are project ecologies and why are they important for resourcing the delivery domain?
3. Which are the universally accepted positive and negative leadership behaviours?
4. What are the two different approaches to knowledge mobilization?
5. What effects are the technologies driving the fourth Industrial Revolution having on SPO?

 *Visit the Oxford Learning Link site for this text to find answer guidance to the questions and exercises in this chapter.*

 *Take your learning further by viewing videos relevant to this chapter on the Oxford Learning Link site.*

## Notes

1. This may also be called a linear responsibility chart—see Cleland and King (1983b), and the y axis is also known as the organizational breakdown structure (OBS)—see Turner (2014).
2. This definition is used within BP.
3. Galbraith (1977).
4. Wheelwright and Clark (1992).
5. Stalk and Hout (1990).
6. Winch (1994).
7. Thamhain and Wilemon (1975)
8. *Delisle (2020); Zika-Viktorsson et al. (2006).
9. Bianchi et al. (2020); Dikert et al. (2016).
10. Bayer and Gann (2006).
11. Grabher and Ibert (2011).
12. Grabher (2002).
13. Rimmer (1988).
14. While the first globalization (1870–1914) was driven in important ways by projecting (see Linder, 1994), the globalization of PBFs appears to be a phenomenon of the second globalization since 1950—see Scott et al. (2011).
15. Chevrier (2003).
16. *Smits et al. (2015).
17. House et al. (2004). Hofstede's 2001 framework suffers from methodological flaws, and does not predict behaviours on projects—see Winch et al. (1997).
18. Fellows and Liu (2016).
19. Barrett and Oborn (2010).

20. Ochieng and Price (2010).

21. Chevrier (2003).

22. The achievement of the project was a miracle taking into account the cultural, linguistic, ethical, and social differences. The success probably resulted from the commitment of the majority to a common objective. Cited in Winch et al. (2000: 679).

23. Winch (2010).

24. Hansen et al. (1999).

25. Schön (1983).

26. Bektaş et al. (2015).

27. Brady and Davies (2004); McClory et al. (2017).

28. Gulliver (1987); Williams (2008).

29. Jagersma (2020).

30. Sergeeva and Roehrich (2018).

31. Mankins (2009).

32. Marnewick and Marnewick (2019).

33. Winch and Msulwa (2019c).

34. Winch (2010: ch. 14) provides a detailed discussion of third-generation digital systems for project organizing.

35. https://www.microsoft.com/en-gb/microsoft-365/project/project-management-software (accessed 23 August 2021).

36. http://www.oracle.com/uk/applications/primavera/products/project-management.html (accessed 19 August 2021).

37. Gawer and Cusumano (2014); Randhawa et al. (2017).

38. Thomas et al. (2014).

39. Whyte (2019).

40. *Volkoff and Strong (2013); Fayard and Weeks (2014).

 **Case 10**    Achieving net zero: retrofitting UK housing

The Paris Agreement on Climate Change of 2015 committed 196 signatories to 'holding the increase in the global average temperature to well below 2°C above pre-industrial levels and pursuing efforts to limit the temperature increase to 1.5°C above pre-industrial levels'. As a signatory, the UK Parliament made a legally binding commitment in 2019 to achieve national carbon neutrality by 2050. Central to this ambition is upgrading the thermal performance of the existing housing stock and decarbonizing the remaining energy inputs.

Across the United Kingdom, housing accounts for over 25 per cent of all energy use and 15 per cent of greenhouse gas emissions. The principal reason is the reliance on a fossil fuel—natural gas—for heating and hot water. More or less all of the 27.5 m existing houses will still be in use in 2050, and so they will need extensive renovation in order to make their contribution to the 2050 target. The United Kingdom has the oldest housing stock in Europe (and probably the world), with 77 per cent of properties constructed before 1980, when building regulations started to take energy efficiency seriously. Virtually all UK housing has been subject to incremental upgrades from an energy point of view since 1980, such as loft insulation, double glazing, cavity wall insulation, and condensing boilers. As a result, the energy performance of the UK housing stock improved by 38 per cent between 1996 and 2017, as did its condition more generally. However, this is far from achieving the level of upgrade required to achieve ambitious carbon neutrality targets and a massive programme of 'whole-house retrofits' is called for at an estimated cost of up to £250 bn by 2050. How is this to be achieved?

There is a clear deadline for the programme, and there is a clear criterion for programme success because the energy efficiency of a house can be measured by the Standard Assessment Procedure (SAP) rating. Good data already exist on the performance of the housing stock, so progress can easily be measured. When applying the SPO Three Domains Model, we can quickly identify some challenges in delivering on this worthy mission. The first is on the owner side. Housing tenure in the United Kingdom is divided into three groups—owner-occupiers (63.1 per cent); private landlords (19.1 per cent); and social landlords (17.7 per cent). The vast majority of private landlords are small private landlords who own one or a few houses and see their houses as a way of saving for their pensions. This means that well over 80 per cent of house owners are private individuals who have little or no interest in tackling global warming by investing in their properties; rather, they are interested in home improvements to kitchens and bathrooms and the comfort of themselves or their tenants. The 2050 target is a policy-driven approach rather than an owner-led approach, and as we have emphasized throughout this book, owners must be capable of projecting their own mission for the upgrade project and governing it so that they achieve both their desired outputs in the shape of a functioning house and desired outcomes in the shape of an attractive and comfortable home. Most owners lack confidence in their ability to do this effectively and so are very reluctant to engage in major energy retrofits.

House owners need three kinds of resources for their retrofit projects—knowledge, technologies, and competencies. They need knowledge of the implications of household energy use for global warming and good ideas for doing something about it that they can understand and afford; they need cost-effective retrofit technologies that are easy to use; and they need competent contractors who can specify and install the most appropriate technologies for their particular house and lifestyle. The supplier domain is the principal source of all three of these resources—suppliers to house owners for their retrofit projects are 'middle actors' in energy policy terms between the policy makers at national level on the one hand and the home owners who need to initiate retrofits on the other. The group of suppliers and installers of energy upgrades measures that serves the bulk of the market for owner-occupiers and private landlords consists mainly of microenterprises. In 2019, 92 per cent of British construction firms employed seven people or fewer, and 13 per cent of these were sole traders. These microenterprises are supported by networks of manufacturers of retrofit technologies and specialist merchants who distribute them to installers.

In terms of knowledge, general awareness of the net-zero grand challenge is growing, but knowledge of what can be done about it cost-effectively by house owners is less widespread. House owners remain focused on comfort and amenity and only consider energy retrofits as part of broader renovation schemes, particularly due to the inevitable disruption they entail. Retrofit technologies that are minimally invasive and do not change the house's façade significantly are strongly preferred. Technologies for whole-house retrofit are being developed, such as Energiesprong, but these are best adapted to the sort of standardized house types and lower occupier discretion over the process more associated with social housing than privately owned housing. They also make massive changes to the façade of the house. Additionally, private landlords face the problem of split incentives in which the energy-saving benefits accrue to the tenant, while the investment costs accrue to the owner. Technologies to introduce green hydrogen generated from renewable electricity are being developed, but are not yet commercially viable, and they would still require a massive campaign for boiler replacement. Heat pumps are effective, but their present operating temperatures require extensive reconfiguration of most heating systems, although higher temperature systems are presently under development.

One of the challenges of whole-house retrofits is the craft-based division of labour around traditional competencies, which does not conceptualize houses as systems. While the relatively loose fit of traditional housing construction methods meant that this was not a major issue, both the novelty of many retrofit technologies and the tighter requirements for the house as a system to address issues such as thermal bridging, airtightness, and ventilation mean that this needs to change. Getting this wrong can cause massive problems, as the case of an area scheme for 390 terraced houses in Preston built around 1900 shows. The vocational and educational training systems that the microenterprises that renovate privately owned houses rely upon to execute projects have yet to address this issue. Instead, training packages are provided focused on particular retrofit technologies without consideration of how they will work in the context of the house system as a whole. Similar jurisdictional separations can be found on the design side, with architects and heating engineers focusing on their own areas of expertise rather than on designing the house as a whole system.

Recent analysis has identified new sets of competencies around:

- retrofit installers, mainly at craft level;
- retrofit designers, mainly at technician level;
- retrofit coordinators—specialist project managers.

The additional numbers of human resources required are massive. In the peak year of 2028, an additional 29 k graduates, 44 k technicians, and 100 k craft workers will be required over the 2019 baseline for the UK housing retrofit programme.

These people will need to be deployed onto projects by competent suppliers. Home owners are wary of the quality of service they receive from the microenterprises that offer to install energy retrofit technologies. For this reason, the UK government has established accreditation schemes for installers and only firms holding these accreditations are eligible for payments under government schemes to encourage house owners to upgrade. This in itself is posing a major challenge on the supply side. The accreditation schemes are seen as bureaucratic and slow by the microenterprises and the short-term nature of government schemes gives weak incentives to supplier firms to invest in gaining the accreditations. For this reason, the current UK retrofit incentive scheme for house owners—the Green Homes Grant—has had a very disappointing take-up because it is simply too difficult for owners and suppliers to use.

*Sources*: https://unfccc.int (accessed 18 March 2021); https://www.energiesprong.uk (accessed 22 March 2021); https://passivehouseplus.ie/news/health/disastrous-preston-retrofit-scheme-remains-unresolved (accessed 22 March 2021); Bonfield (2016); CCC (2019); Eunomia (2021); Parag and Janda (2014); Piddington et al. (2020); Wilson et al. (2018).

## Discussion questions

1. What do you think the particular competencies of a 'retrofit coordinator' as a specialist project manager might be?

2. How might suppliers be encouraged to be more capable at delivering energy retrofit projects?

3. How is your country addressing the challenge of retrofitting housing stock to achieve the Paris agreement commitments?

# Part D

# Being a Project Professional: Managing and Leading in SPO

**Figure D** 'Achievement' (Cole's old age)

*Source*: National Gallery of Art.

In Figure D, our project manager has achieved the project outcome and is now in calmer waters again. The project is rather battered around the edges, but is still afloat and value has been added with the guardian angels returning to view. In 'Achievement', the project manager is certainly older, and hopefully a lot wiser, at the end of the project life cycle.

We now turn in Part D to focus on the individual rather than the organization and her professional career development from project manager to project leader. Across two chapters, we first explore the technical competencies required for managing and leading projects in strategic project organizing (SPO), and then explore the social competencies required to develop from being a project manager to becoming a project leader.

In these chapters, we:

- distinguish between managing and leading;
- stress the importance of project technical competencies for the successful delivery of project outputs;
- review the key tools for scheduling, budgeting, and managing conformance to requirements;
- review the key tools for managing threats to successful project delivery;
- identify the differences between owner and supplier project managers;
- discuss the importance of ethics and diversity in leading projects;
- discuss leadership development in SPO;
- finish with an illustration of leading authentically in SPO.

To complete our exploration of SPO, we look towards the future with case studies on the new exciting developments in technical competencies around project data analytics in Case 11, and the UK Association for Project Management's Projecting the Future thought-leadership exercise in Case 12.

# 11 Being a project manager in SPO

## 11.1 Introduction: technical competencies for delivering project outputs

We have completed exploring the three interfaces of strategic project organizing (SPO) and now turn to the professional competencies that project managers and leaders need for SPO, focusing here on the technical competencies. These make up the core of the various professional bodies of knowledge and are therefore what individual project managers are certified against in professional qualification, although there is growing awareness of the importance of the social competencies for career development as well, which we address in Chapter 12. From the point of view of leading projects, it is the social competencies which are important, but it is also important to understand what team members are doing as they manage the project through the Define and Execute stages to deliver the output. Irrespective of which project-organizing domain you are involved in, there are therefore a number of core skills a project leader should be aware of during the governance (owner's responsibility) or resourcing (supplier's responsibility) of the project.

One of the most important debates over the past 50 years in organization has been the difference between managers and leaders.[1] It is generally agreed that there is a difference, with managers being more task-orientated, focused on activities such as planning, and leaders being more relationship-orientated, focused on activities such as the dimensions of the SPO Project Leadership Model (PLM). Although this difference is largely one of emphasis, it is helpful for structuring our argument as we focus on individuals and their career development in SPO. The focus of this chapter, therefore, is on the technical competencies that are the basis of task-orientation of project managers as professionals during project delivery. These technical competencies, particularly as mandated by professional associations and corporate project management offices (PMOs) discussed in section 8.4.6, are the principal source of the routines used in project teaming, as discussed in section 7.4. We first position the contribution of these technical competencies to SPO as the processes of preserving the value created during project shaping. We then turn to the synergy of planning and control, with the information loop at its heart, before examining in more detail scheduling, budgeting, managing conformance to requirements, and managing threats to the successful delivery of project outputs. Case 11 presents some of the exciting enhancements to technical competencies associated with **project data analytics**, drawing on the fourth Industrial Revolution technologies discussed in section 1.2.

## 11.2 Project delivery as value preservation

As outlined in sections 2.8 and 7.2, the project life cycle can usefully be divided into two distinct phases—project shaping and project delivery.[2] Project shaping is the source of value generation on projects, as discussed in section 5.5; it follows, therefore, that project delivery is fundamentally about preserving the value generated during project shaping. The project owner is accountable for project shaping and 'owns' the project value proposition, while delivery is the responsibility of the project delivery organization, resourced by the selected supplier organizations as required. Therefore, while the technical competencies discussed in this chapter will largely be deployed within the delivery domain, they need to be understood by project leaders working in the owner and supplier domains to ensure effective design and management of the governance and resource interfaces. This perspective is illustrated in Figure 11.1. It shows how project value is embodied in the project delivery plan (PDP) at the end of the Select stage, which is typically the last stage gate before full commitment is made by the owner organization to the value proposition, and full financial resources are committed to the project.[3] Based on the PDP, planning continues through the Define stage at a greater levels of detail as the work breakdown structure (WBS) is developed, budgets are finalized, and the schedule refined. Procurement of suppliers is typically most intense during the Define stage, although the tier-one contractors will likely be procured during the Select stage, along with suppliers of key specialist technologies and long-lead components. The principal outputs from the Define stage are the resource-loaded **project execution plan** (PEP), a complete specification for the output, and the principal members of the project coalition.

Figure 11.1 is clear that the delivery phase is about managing threats to delivery; all opportunities for the project should have been embodied in the value proposition and associated PDP. This argument is counter to the mainstream in project organizing,[4] but it is important nonetheless. In essence, change is a threat to the resilience of the project and threatens unintended consequences, as discussed in section 7.7. Of course, change will occur during the development of the scope and associated WBS, but it needs to be carefully managed. This is the responsibility of configuration management and strict **management of change** processes.[5] Once the PEP has been agreed by the owner and the tier-one suppliers, the project moves into the Execute stage, where the *management of* **no** *change* becomes the priority, even if this is rarely fully achieved. This means that the palliation of actual threat events,

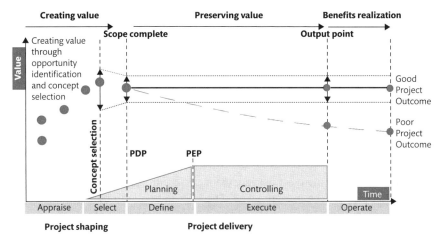

Figure 11.1  The project delivery challenge: preserving value.

*Source*: authors.

as shown in Figure 11.11, should be the only source of change. As can be seen from Figure 11.1, the project delivery challenge is to preserve the value embodied in the PDP when delivering the project output, and project delivery success can be defined as preserving the maximum value. The output is then handed over to the owner, who is accountable for achieving the outcomes projected in the project mission, but the owner can do little to replace value lost during delivery and so outcomes are inevitably challenged if delivery is not successful.

> **Exercise 11.1**
>
> Why is the owner making voluntary changes during the Execute stage usually a bad idea?

## 11.3 Planning and controlling

Planning is fundamental to SPO. Essentially, the process of planning answers the question, 'How are we going to deliver the output specified in the PDP?' This delivery process is one of the main challenges for the project manager. For over 70 years, planning has focused on scheduling and budgeting supported by a range of planning tools.[6] Professional bodies stress its importance and it is considered one of the main factors for project success. However, although planning is important, it is not in itself a predictor of project success; planning is not enough[7] and too much planning can be counterproductive.[8]

The PEP provides the delivery team with the information needed to execute the project in terms of what needs to be done (scope captured in the WBS), how it will get done (sequencing activities), how long it will take (scheduling), who will do it (resources), how much it will cost (budget), and how the project is progressing against plan (monitor). Planning is a social, iterative process, and plans can be subject to change. Therefore, plans need to reflect identified threats and incorporate approaches for monitoring and controlling so the plan can be adapted to the context of the project and to threat events during the Execute stage. The way this information all comes together is captured in Figure 11.2.

The main task of the project delivery team is to control against the PEP using the information loop shown in Figure 11.3. The information loop during the Execute stage starts with the PEP as a whole and then breaks it into units of months, weeks, and days, as appropriate. Establishing the appropriate cadence for the information loop is one of the principal tasks of designing the project delivery organization, as discussed in section 7.3. The approach usually adopted is the 'rolling wave',[9] where longer-term plans are set in broad terms, while nearer-term plans are set more precisely, as shown in Figure 11.4. This is because more information is typically available for what is to be done next month than for what is to be done next year. As uncertainty is progressively reduced through the project life cycle, as shown in Figure 2.4, planning at a greater level of detail becomes possible and information loops become more tightly wound.

We then *measure performance* by comparing current performance against the PEP. This comparison results in one of three options for action:

- *continue with the plan* unchanged if performance aligns with the PEP;
- take *corrective action* if the plan and performance do not align;
- *revise the PEP* if the original plan is no longer achievable due to new information becoming available.

These information loops vary at different stages of the life cycle. For example, changing the scope is a widely adopted corrective action during the Select stage, but is foolhardy during the Execute stage, as discussed in section 11.2. This does not mean that it does not happen, but there are usually serious consequences for project success. Some information loops have very long timespans—the longest being as long as the life cycle of the project itself, as shown in Figure 11.2. The shortest, such as managing an agile sprint, is measured in days rather than weeks. Many of the loops are nested inside each other, with daily cycles at the lowest level of management, weekly cycles higher up in the hierarchy, and quarterly cycles for the most senior participants in the project. The process is a synergy of planning and control, and the central project management problem throughout the project life cycle is to establish and maintain appropriate information loops for each task on the project. If things

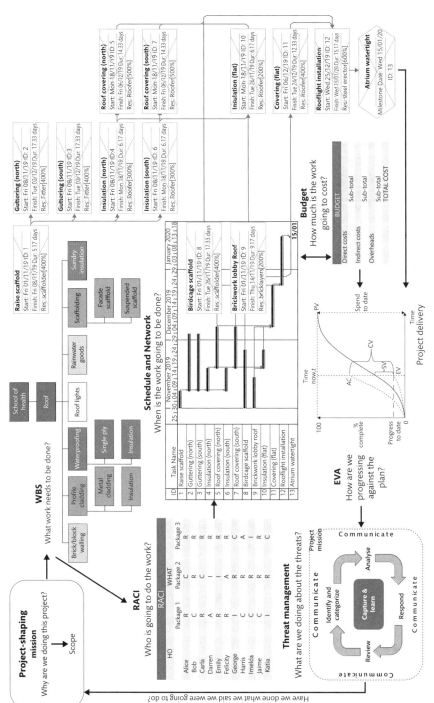

Figure 11.2 Planning and controlling an integrated SPO model.

*Source:* authors.

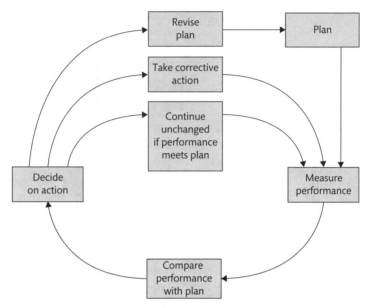

**Figure 11.3** Generic information loop.

*Source*: developed from Winch (2010: figure IV.I).

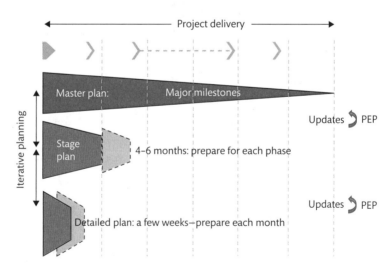

**Figure 11.4** Rolling wave planning.

*Source*: developed from an original figure by Cliff Mitchell.

are going wrong on the project, then the failure of an information loop is often at the heart of the problem:

- new information becomes available and corrective action has not been taken;
- tasks are over budget or behind schedule, but opportunistic behaviour hides this fact;
- measurement is not taking place, so nobody knows the level of performance against objectives;
- the PEP is so poorly defined that it is unclear whether it has been delivered or not.

Project managers recognize planning and controlling as a social process. Project organizing is a collaborative endeavour and requires project managers to deploy their social competencies to develop and maintain relationships, to explore the project situation, to communicate and negotiate with stakeholders, and to develop and adapt the plan accordingly.[10]

## 11.4 Scheduling

All projects are designed and planned to have an end date, therefore having a realistic schedule is important for ensuring the delivery of the project outputs at the desired future date. Scheduling alongside budgeting and conformance management are fundamental for managing project execution.[11] The schedule provides a timeline of the sequences by which tasks within the WBS will be executed. The schedule therefore answers the question, 'When will the work be done?' Developing the project schedule is an iterative process. The most commonly used technique for developing the project schedule is the critical path method (CPM).[12] In essence, the schedule sequences all the tasks in the WBS through time, taking into account their dependencies where a dependency means that a particular task has to be completed before another task can commence.[13] This creates a temporal network of tasks interlinked (or not) by their dependencies with various possible paths through it. Figure 11.5 shows the School of Health planned critical path network.

Next, each task duration is estimated based on historical data or past experience. Estimates can be deterministic, or probabilistic if the data on task durations show variance. To determine the total project duration, we move along the sequence of tasks and add up the duration of each task on each path. The path with the longest sequence of tasks from project start to finish is the critical path indicated by the bold path in Figure 11.5. The tasks on the critical path are critical in terms of schedule only; that is, if any of the tasks on the critical path are delayed,

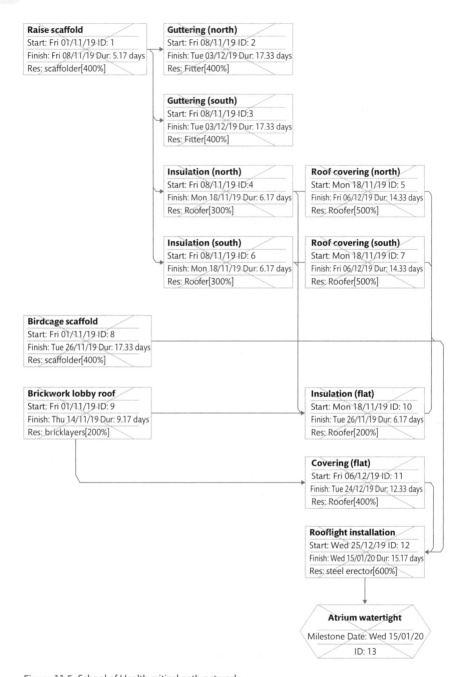

Figure 11.5  School of Health critical path network.

*Sources*: activity on the node network; prepared in MS Project 2016.

all subsequent tasks on the critical path will also be delayed and the project will therefore take longer to complete. 'Criticality' does not imply importance for the final output functionality.

In addition to determining the project duration and critical path, it is also important to calculate the earliest and latest time each task off the critical path can start and finish. We do this in two steps: first, we carry out a forward pass where earliest start and finish times for each task are calculated. Second, we carry out a backward pass, where the latest start and finish times for each task are calculated starting from the project end date. Project networks are straightforward to draw and analyse for small-scale projects. However, for larger-scale projects, software packages—see the discussion in section 10.8—facilitate the process of creating, amending, and changing the network.

By analysing the sequence of tasks and their duration, we can determine when each task should be undertaken, where the dependencies between tasks are, how much float (spare time) is available, and the minimum time needed to complete the project. However, an important constraint on the scheduling of tasks is the availability of the resources required to execute the task. These constraints can be around material items (heavy lift equipment is a common problem here), but they are typically around human resources. Vignette 10.1 illustrates what can happen if attention is not paid to this issue, and much of the development of scheduling techniques in recent years has been around the handling of human resource constraints.[14] This insight is behind the development of the critical chain scheduling techniques.[15] The questions that need to be addressed are: 'What resources are required for each task for the project to be completed in the planned time?' and 'How long will the project take if the resources are constrained?' Each task within the network is 'loaded' with the required resources and aggregated to determine the project resource load, which may then be 'smoothed' to ease resource constraints. On projects where task execution creates the workspaces for subsequent tasks such as in shipbuilding and construction, critical space analysis[16] may also be important.

Critical path networks are quite difficult to read for a project of any size, and are more useful for schedule analysis than reporting, and so they are often summarized graphically in Gantt charts, as shown in Figure 11.6. On simpler projects, Gantt charts alone can be used for scheduling, and in either case they can act as boundary objects between teams, as discussed in section 7.4. Although these scheduling routines are widely used, it is important to recognize some of their limitations: first, the possibility of opportunistic behaviour in estimating task duration; second, the use of deterministic estimates in an uncertain world; third, the schedule becoming disconnected from the realities of day-to-day managing; and fourth, inherent over-optimism in estimating task durations, as explained in Vignette 11.1.

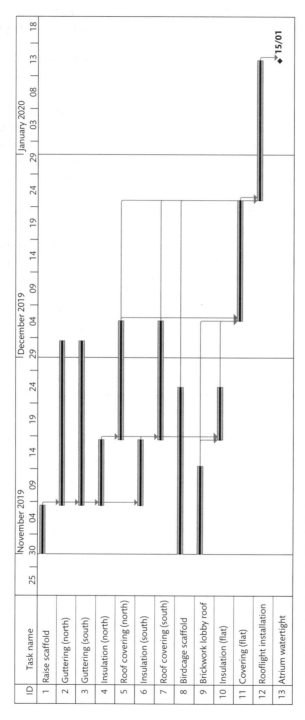

**Figure 11.6** School of Health roof Gantt chart.

*Source:* prepared in MS Project 2016.

## Vignette 11.1   The planning fallacy

Research has shown that when individuals are asked to estimate the duration to complete a future task they tend to be over-optimistic in their estimates and underestimate the time, which could lead to undesirable consequences such as failure to complete the task. This occurs even when individuals have had plenty of experience in undertaking a similar task. The reason for this is that when asked to estimate task durations, individuals tend to focus on the immediate task rather than thinking about all their experiences of the time it took to complete a similar task. Wishful thinking also comes into play, as individuals think tasks can be completed easily and quickly because that is a more pleasing imagined future. When individuals were asked about their past performance they tended to blame overruns on external influences. But when things went well they claimed that it was due to their abilities. Studies have looked at debiasing task duration estimates. For example, the segmentation effect may be one way in which allocated time durations to tasks can be increased, resulting in less evidence of planning fallacy bias. Task segmentation consists of adding the time allocation for a project's subtasks rather than providing an estimate for an entire single task. However, this is cognitively demanding and does not reflect everyday decision-making.

*Sources*: Buehler et al. (2010); Forsyth and Burt (2008).

## 11.5 **Budgeting**

Managing the budget during delivery is also a key competence required by project managers. It begins with a process of estimating the cost of the resources required for the execution of all the tasks in the WBS to produce a budget baseline for the project. The project budget should capture the realistic costs of the project, taking into consideration the outcome of risk assessments and response strategies. The budget answers the question, 'How much will it cost?' and is used to manage the costs throughout the Execute stage.

Budget estimation is an iterative process carried out at different stages of the project life cycle with increasing levels of accuracy. The estimates are improved and accuracy levels increase as new and relevant information is received and processed at the end of each stage of the life cycle, as shown in Figure 11.7, but with a consistent bias towards underestimation of budgets. Although estimating approaches vary across industries, we can broadly identify four methods for estimating costs:[17]

1. ballpark, usually used early in the life cycle when there is very limited information or time to prepare with an accuracy range of ~90 percentage points;[18]

2. the PDP, where estimates are established from preliminary engineering work with an accuracy range of ~75 percentage points;

3. comparative, where cost estimates are developed by comparing to past similar projects to provide an *outside view*[19] with the aim of reducing the variance in 1 and 2;

4. the PEP, which provides estimates based on the work during the Define stage, with an accuracy range of ~38 percentage points;

By definition, outturn costs are equal to the actual expenditure.

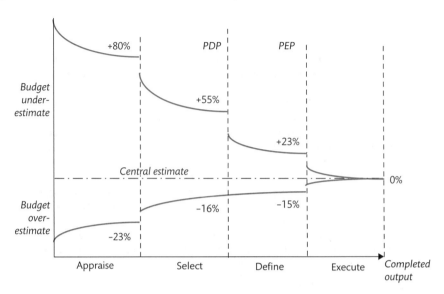

Figure 11.7 Accuracy of estimates through the project life cycle.

*Sources*: developed from Winch (2010: figure 10.1) and Barshop (2016: table 8.1). Data are from Independent Project Analysis for 102 engineering projects and show the p90 (overestimate) and p10 (underestimate) range around the central estimate.

Estimating and budgeting go hand in hand. Creating a project budget involves allocating costs to the WBS based on the estimated resources required to deliver the project. To monitor the expended costs, the budget baseline is used to compare the actual use of resources against those budgeted, but this is not an effective measurement as expended cost can denote more or less progress. During execution, information is gathered in terms of how much has been spent to date and how much is left to be spent. However, it is also important to measure actual performance—which is known as **earned value**, defined as the proportion of tasks completed at a specific point in time in the life cycle.

Earned value analysis (EVA) was developed in the 1960s by the US Department of Defense (DoD) for measuring performance on complex projects.[20] This technique is now used in other project-based sectors as a way to measure performance against budget and schedule. EVA allows the project manager to know which tasks have been completed as a result of the expenditure to date. For example, a project team might have spent a significant amount of time on a task but not achieved anything, or they could have spent limited time on a task and successfully completed it. EVA measures project progress by relating budget and schedule. EVA takes into consideration three measures and questions a project manager asks.

1. Earned value (EV): budgeted cost of work completed at a specific point in the schedule. How much work have we actually completed?

2. Actual cost (AC): actual spend to date. How much did we spend to complete the work?

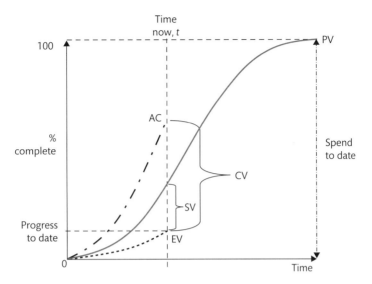

Figure 11.8  Earned value chart.

Note: actual cost (AC) should be read against the right-hand axis.

*Source*: Winch (2010: figure 10.7).

3. Planned value (PV): what ought to have been spent at a specific point in the schedule according to the budget. How much work did we plan to complete?

These are captured in an EVA chart, as shown in Figure 11.8, where we look at the cost variance (CV) where CV = EV – AC and schedule variance (SV) where SV = EV – PV to see if the project shows a cost overrun or underperformance. If cost variance is negative, this indicates a cost overrun; if schedule variance is negative, it indicates that the project is behind schedule. An important aspect to the effective use of EVA is the measurement methods and criteria used to estimate progress on a task. The most appropriate measures should be selected based on the type of project and, therefore, the nature of tasks within the WBS.

---

### Exercise 11.2

Why do you think that the accuracy of budget estimates improves through the project life cycle?

---

## 11.6 Managing conformance to requirements

As shown in Figure 7.1, the management of conformance to requirements is equally as important as managing budget and schedule. The underlying principles derive from significant developments in quality management over the past 25 years such as advances in product and service quality, quality as an integral part of strategic planning, and quality leadership.[21] Quality is defined in the international standard ISO 9000 as 'the degree to which a set of inherent characteristics fulfilled requirements'. In this section, we focus on QUENSH: QUality of conformance to the requirements specified by the owner in the PDP, including meeting the ENvironmental, Safety, and Health regulations and standards.

The PDP captures the requirements for the project, which are an output of the project-shaping phase, where the owner identifies and specifies those requirements supported by advisors. The principal effort during the Define stage is to work out how those requirements will be met during the Execute stage to an acceptable budget and schedule, as embodied in the PEP. From an owner perspective, the challenge is to minimize the potential quality gaps[22] at each stage of the life cycle, as shown in Figure 11.9. The details of how conformance is achieved will vary across project types, but irrespective of project type, conformance requirements should be specified in the PDP and defined tightly in the PEP. This is a proactive approach to reduce the threat of non-conformance issues emerging during the Execute stage, as discussed in section 11.7.

Managing conformance is an iterative process that needs to be tailored to each project. This tailoring integrates the PBF's QUENSH processes with those of the owner to design a project-specific set of QUENSH processes and the PEP needs to reflect this. The PBF's QUENSH processes are designed for consistency across its portfolio of projects rather than across the project coalition on a particular project. Managing conformance is a continuous process of iterating through the information loop shown in Figure 11.3, monitoring, recording, and reporting on the results

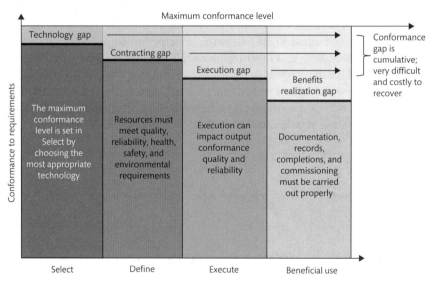

**Figure 11.9** Quality gaps at SPO life-cycle stages.

*Source*: authors.

of the quality management activities that evaluate quality. The results are compared with the relevant standards and corrective action taken if non-conformance is identified, as discussed in section 11.3. Activities involved in controlling quality include testing, review, inspection, verification, and validation. Controlling ensures that the project outputs meet the specified requirements.

## 11.7  Managing threats

Managing threats to the achievement of outputs and outcomes is the essence of SPO. Whereas opportunities for creating value are identified during project shaping, preserving value through the management of threats is the core of project delivery, as shown in Figure 11.1. Managing threats is a systematic process of identification, analysis, response, review, and communication of threats carried out continuously throughout the project life cycle. Various standards, guides, and publications decompose the threat management process into several stages,[23] which can be summarized in four basic subprocesses as shown in Figure 11.10: identification and categorization of threats; analysis of threats; response to the threats; and review of the threats, which are all iteratively looped within the context of the project mission.

The threat identification process is the most important, for if threats are not properly identified they cannot be analysed and subsequently managed.[24] The key point of this process is to identify possible future threat events and their consequences. The identification of threats should be carried out in a structured and systematic manner and one should be careful not to let this process become habitual. The identification process is a creative one, for it is about how we perceive and think about the future. One must aim to capture the unusual, not previously experienced

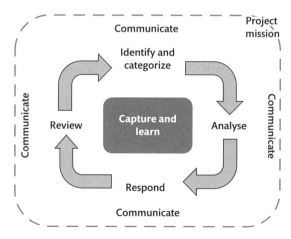

Figure 11.10  Threat management process.

*Source*: modified from Maytorena-Sanchez (2013: figure 4.3).

events, and move beyond the known knowns defined in Figure 2.5 by deploying the sense-making and relating dimensions of the SPO PLM defined in Figure 3.1. Threats are identified by relating, drawing on knowledge and available historical data. Techniques such as brainstorming and interviews are commonly used to identify threats and these are subsequently captured in a threat register, which becomes the basis for knowledge integration and learning, as discussed in section 10.6, remembering that capturing is not the same as learning. Attention needs to be paid to the design and facilitation of threat identification workshops, as approaching these through an inquiring (exploratory and questioning) approach has been shown to be more effective.[25] An effective approach to identification is to conduct a project pre-mortem and go through a prospective hindsight process[26] (see Vignette 11.2), which we have used successfully in executive education.

Once threats have been identified, we can then progress to the process of analysis, for which multiple techniques are well developed.[27] When undertaking these analyses, it is important to understand first what the quality of the information used in the analysis is, as shown in the 'confidence' dimension in Figure 2.5. Attempts to use quantitative techniques designed for objective probabilities to analyse subjective probabilities is to fall victim to the ludic fallacy,[28] and to confuse a summary assessment of the threats facing project delivery such as P80[29] with a real number. In addition, we need to recognize the role cognitive biases play in the process of estimating subjective probabilities, as they can affect the way in which individuals, teams, and organizations choose to manage threats. For example,

---

### Vignette 11.2    Conducting a pre-mortem

We have discovered with our executive education delegates that conducting a project pre-mortem is an effective way to identify threats. First, we ask individual team members to think of the current project they are involved in. Second, we ask them to imagine that the project has failed! Third, we ask them to write down all the possible reasons for the failure of the project. Finally, we conduct a facilitated discussion to explore further all the possible reasons and their interdependencies for the imagined failure of the project, to enable a holistic and systemic view of the project threats.

This process is called **prospective hindsight**—imagining a future event with certainty. Studies have shown that prospective hindsight can improve the ability of identification of reasons for a possible future outcome by 30 per cent. In addition, it encourages future perfect thinking and talking to promote action; it can also help with over-optimism, overconfidence, and spotting early warning signs (see Chapter 7).

Prospective hindsight works because asking individuals to think of a single outcome (success or failure) and multiple reasons is cognitively easier than asking individuals to imagine multiple outcomes as well as multiple reasons for those multiple outcomes. The latter approach is what we tend to experience in threat identification workshops when we pose the starting question, 'What could go wrong?'

*Source*: Klein (2007).

failure to recognize a threat or ignoring it, and underestimation of probabilities or impact of a threat, have consequences on how we respond and manage the threat. Vignette 11.3 provides a brief overview of heuristics and biases relevant for threat assessment.

Response covers a wide variety of managerial interventions that can be made to reduce either the possibility (proactive mitigation) or impact (reactive palliation) of an identified possible future event, as shown in Figure 11.11. It is important to distinguish between mitigation and palliation, and these two should be captured separately in the threat register. Proactive mitigations are aimed at reducing the possibility of the identified threat event occurring. Proactively, contractual arrangements can be used by owners to transfer responsibility for identified events to suppliers, as discussed in section 9.2.2; changes to requirements can be made to mitigate the possibility of an event occurring, as discussed in section 11.2, or the decision to cancel the project can be taken, which is the ultimate mitigation! Reactive palliations are aimed at reducing the impact of the threat event, should it occur, such as emergency response teams. Contingency allowances in the budget are another form of palliation. Threat mitigation can generate the possibility of secondary

## Vignette 11.3    Cognitive biases

Research has shown that individuals use mental short cuts or strategies known as heuristics, to quickly form judgements and make decisions. While these intuitive strategies do not require great cognitive resources, they can lead to errors in judgement and biases in perceptions of probabilities of events. Here, we present some that are relevant for the process of estimating probabilities of threat events.

The availability heuristic is the systematic tendency we have of judging the probability of occurrence of an event by how easily the event is brought to mind; these will tend be unusual or rare events rather than thinking about the whole distribution of events.

The representativeness heuristic is the tendency we have of judging the probability of the occurrence of an event by the degree to which it is similar to a representative case.

Anchoring is the systematic tendency to judge the probability of an event occurring by relying on a single piece of information as a starting point, referred to as an 'anchor', and then adjusting based on this reference point.

Optimism bias is the systematic tendency to overestimate the probability of positive things happening to us and underestimate the probability of negative things happening to us.

The illusion of control is the systematic tendency to believe that we can control future events.

This body of research has implications for estimation processes of time, costs, and threats. The general recommendation is to be aware of the role of heuristics in decision-making and judgement and the inherent nature of biases. Stopping the momentum of intuitive thinking by probing with questions to move towards a more analytical mode of thinking can help, to an extent.

*Source*: Kahneman et al. (1982).

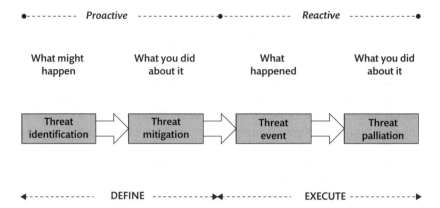

Figure 11.11  Threat mitigation and palliation.

*Source*: developed from Winch (2010: figure 13.1).

threat events. For example, transferring the responsibility for responding to a threat event to a supplier—see Figure 9.4—could mean that its impact causes that supplier to fail, whereupon the threat returns to the owner. In addition, knowledge about the plans for reactive palliation can increase the possibility of an event happening—this is known as **threat homeostasis**.[30]

The review process through the information loop typically receives much less attention, but is no less important in effectively managing threats. Here, someone is designated as responsible for each possible event identified within the threat register. Their job is to monitor the status of the threat and raise the alarm if any of the assumptions made during the analysis or response processes become invalid. This is usually done via formal reporting procedures, but these have to be complemented by informal processes, such as relating to stakeholders, managing by walking around, and interpreting early warning signs, as discussed in section 7.6.

A neglected aspect of managing threats is effective communication. This is vital for:[31]

- understanding both the benefits of good threat management and the consequences of poor threat management;
- understanding the limitations of quantitative analysis;
- recognition of changes in the threat status;
- identification of new threats—previously unk-unks;
- ensuring that threat ownership details are unambiguous in contracts and agreements;
- capturing, sharing, and developing on lessons learnt.

The challenges of threat communication should not be underestimated. There are at least three key aspects to consider during the threat communication process:[32]

- the social amplification of threats[33]—when communicating threats, we must consider the way in which individual and social processes can transform how threat information is received and interpreted;
- individual values and their influence on how the receivers of the threat communication will behave;[34]
- the purpose (why?), processes (how?), and effectiveness in communicating threats.[35]

---

### Exercise 11.3

Why is managing threats to delivery so important in SPO?

---

## 11.8 Summary

In this chapter, we focused on the technical competencies that project managers deploy in managing project delivery. We began by arguing that the principal role of the project manager during project delivery is to preserve the value embodied in the owner's value proposition. We then showed how the WBS forms the foundation for creating the schedule and budget. The schedule adds a time dimension to the WBS and is visually represented in networks and Gantt charts. The budget estimates the costs of the resources required for the tasks identified in the WBS. We identified a range of estimating methods and highlighted some of the challenges of estimating accurately. We emphasized the importance of measuring the progress of task execution with the use of EVA. We looked at managing quality in terms of the process of ensuring conformance to requirements specified in the PDP and further defined in the PEP; this also included meeting environmental, safety, and health standards.

Given the uncertainty at the heart of SPO, managing threats is its essence. We provided a perspective on managing threats which emphasizes identification, analysis, response, and review as a cyclical process through the life cycle, and the differences in response between proactive mitigation and reactive palliation. Throughout, we emphasized the value of the information loop as a framework for planning and controlling during project execution. Project leaders should remember that project management technical competencies are at best thought of as sense-making tools that help both leaders and managers to direct their attention, and to offer different perspectives to improve understanding of the challenges of SPO. The design of the project delivery organization can enable or hinder information flows. Therefore, careful thought and consideration as to designing processes, how they are implemented, and when to implement them is needed, as discussed in section 7.3—this is an essential part of creating in the SPO PLM shown in Figure 3.1. The process of defining and managing project delivery is a social one, so we now turn to the social competencies of SPO and emphasize project leading rather than project managing. This is where the enabling (sense-making and relating), action (projecting and creating) dimensions of the SPO PLM come together to deliver the outputs and outcomes to the owner.

## 11.9  Further reading

Goldratt, E. M. 1997. *Critical Chain*. Great Barrington, MA: North River Press.
    A fluent critique of mainstream approaches to managing projects, and an introduction to the concept of critical chain.

Chapman, C. and Ward, S. 2011. *How to Manage Project Opportunity and Risk*. Chichester: John Wiley & Sons.
    A sophisticated presentation of the mainstream approach to managing risk and opportunity.

Meredith, J. and Shafer, S. M. 2021. *Project Management in Practice*, 7th edn. Hoboken, NJ: John Wiley & Sons.
    A standard text covering the key technical competencies of project management.

## 11.10  Summary review questions

1. Why do we view project delivery as a process of preserving value?
2. What is the difference between the PDP and the PEP?
3. What is rolling wave planning?
4. Why are planning and control synergistic?
5. What is a critical path?

 *Visit the Oxford Learning Link site for this text to find answer guidance to the questions and exercises in this chapter.*

 *Take your learning further by viewing videos relevant to this chapter on the Oxford Learning Link site.*

## Notes

1. Kniffin et al. (2020); Zaleznik (1977).
2. Many of the ideas in this section came from discussions with BP.
3. This is often called 'financial authorization'.
4. See, for instance, Chapman and Ward (2011).
5. Morris (2013); Turner (2014).

6. Kerzner (2017).

7. Dvir and Lechler (2004).

8. Zwikael and Gilchrist (2021).

9. Morris (2013); Kerzner (2017).

10. Winch and Kelsey (2005).

11. Pinto (2020).

12. Meredith and Shafer (2021).

13. For instance, a beam cannot be placed before the columns have been erected.

14. Herroelen (2005).

15. For instance, ProChain (https://www.prochain.com, accessed 23 August 2021) implements resource loading in an MS Project schedule using Goldratt's (1997) critical chain principles.

16. Winch and North (2006).

17. See Lock (2010) and Pinto (2020).

18. That is to say, the variance can be +/–45 per cent, which is typically biased (as measured by outturn cost) towards an underestimate.

19. Lovallo and Kahneman (2003).

20. Fleming and Koppelman (2016).

21. Kerzner (2017).

22. Winch et al. (1998).

23. Chapman and Ward (2011).

24. Maytorena-Sanchez et al. (2007).

25. Maytorena-Sanchez et al. (2007).

26. Klein (2007).

27. Chapman and Ward (2011).

28. Taleb (2007).

29. A P80 is an 80 per cent (subjective) probability of achieving a given target.

30. Adams (1995).

31. Maytorena-Sanchez (2013).

32. Maule (2008).

33. Kasperson et al. (2003).

34. French et al. (2004).

35. Covello et al. (1986).

 **Case 11   Data analytics in projects**

There is increasing interest in the use of data analytics in managing projects. Within the context of the planning–controlling cycle, project managers are increasingly looking towards the use of data analytics to enhance their practice in scheduling, resourcing, budgeting, and threat management. The power of the analytic techniques, in combination with the richness of project data, can help managers to measure and analyse the performance of a project to enhance decision-making.

During the project planning and control cycles, large quantities of data are collected, usually only used once, and then archived. These are known as data plumes, which collectively contain a vast amount of potentially useful data on project performance, and their analysis can yield useful insights that could be used to improve performance on future projects by helping to predict project outcomes in a timely manner.

Data analytics uses project data from past and current projects to support decision-making during project delivery. Data analytics can be descriptive or predictive. Use of descriptive analytics is a common practice in many organizations, where they combine specialist software—usually off the shelf—and processes to collect, store, and analyse big data from a range of sources and convert it into useful information. Some project portfolio management (PPM) software providers are enabling fully digital PMOs. For example, within a project organization, dashboards present past and present data to highlight insights into the current status of the project stage, providing real-time metrics to support decision-making. Benchmarking is another example of descriptive analytics across organizations.

The use of predictive analytics is less common in and across project organizations. It focuses on how to enable more informed estimates about future projects for developing the PDP and PEP. Big data are analysed to identify potential challenges and make recommendations, which can be adapted to the project stage and the specific type of project. The predictive solutions tend to be bespoke to the specific project challenges of the organization. Machine learning provides a wide range of predictive insights through the use of algorithms, mathematics, and statistics to find patterns in large amounts of data (words, images, numbers, videos, emails, status reports, etc.). The patterns in project characteristics can be on threats, quality, schedule, cost, safety, resources and teams, benefits and outcomes, change, and commercial aspects. The patterns provide a better understanding to the project team of the project status and can provide probabilistically based recommendations of options for action.

Currently, data analytics is being used across a range of project-based sectors helping owners, project-based firms, and project delivery teams. What follows next are some examples of data analytics implementation.

Data analytics has been used for predicting schedule variance. nPlan is a company which specializes in algorithm-led threat analysis and assurance. It collects datasets of tens of thousands of projects and uses them to create models that forecast the outcome of future projects. For example, on a major liquified natural gas (LNG) project, it correctly forecast a 15-month delay. With Network Rail, it is using machine learning to improve the way major rail projects are delivered. nPlan's recent test of its threat analysis and assurance solution on the Great Western Main Line showed that a £30 m cost saving could be achieved through the identification and mitigation of threats that the project team had not previously identified.

Highways England is using data analytics across different stages of its projects to help the delivery of the projects. For example, it takes the lessons learnt from one project by using advanced data analytics to identify insights and inform decision-making to apply to three other projects in relation to safety, customer experience, and delivery. Highways England believes that project delivery in the future will be driven by advanced data analytics. It provides timely information to help decision-making and offers the opportunities to implement long-term solutions to projects. It is developing the competencies of its project teams to align with this new delivery approach.

Oil and gas companies are embracing digitalization to transform the industry. Companies can use the technology for drilling operations diagnoses, predictive maintenance, pipeline asset management, and threat detection, among other things. For example, BP realized that information people used to make decisions were either in people's heads, on spreadsheets, or on different systems, which sometimes could not be accessed and where not everyone trusted the information in them. Therefore, BP began a process of digitalization, which meant bringing all the relevant data together in a manner that would be helpful, insightful, accessible, and trustworthy to people to use during their decision-making processes. The outlook is that this will help to reduce operating costs, improve safety, and reduce emissions. This transformation required a change in technology, but also in mindset, skillsets, and the ways people think of and interact with data.

In the construction sector, organizations are developing technologies to: help monitor construction sites to improve safety; reduce the amount of embodied carbon in building and infrastructure projects and therefore help to achieve net zero targets; develop a digital compliance ecosystem to help support firms navigate the regulatory landscape; develop new ways to provide geotechnical surveys; help spot early warning signs in schedules and budgets and enable mitigating actions; help with resourcing the projects across the project portfolio; and predict the likelihood of a contractor capturing a new construction project.

With all these potential opportunities also come some challenges, which organizations looking to embrace business analytics need to recognize and address.

- Align the problem and the data. Remember to start with the question or problem you are trying to solve, then start collecting the data.
- Ensure good data quality. Collect data that are meaningful and data that will inform your decision-making.
- Define and agree data quality and standards.
- Have simple guidelines for data collection to ensure consistency.
- Ensure you collect sufficient data volume.
- Too many different digital systems being used in the organization creates data silos. Data need to be connected.
- There is a need to go beyond organizational boundaries and work across organizations to create accessible datasets.
- Share data and solutions across organizations, rather than working in silos.
- Develop skills to reach across project managers, data scientists, and data analysts.
- Ensure high-level buy-in.
- Develop a strategy to support the implementation.

Although it is important to embrace new advances in technology, let us not forget the role of the project professionals in all of these developments. If software programmes can help with the repetitive tasks and technical aspects of managing projects, use it. There are already plenty of project management software applications available that can help. The opportunities for project professionals then are about where they can add value. Developing social competencies as communicators, influencers, motivators, negotiators, and facilitators is still required.

*Sources*: APM (2020); Paver (2018); PDATF (2020); https://www.networkrailmediacentre.co.uk/news/network-rail-using-innovative-technology-to-transform-project-planning-and-delivery (accessed 30 May 2021); https://www.pmi.org.uk/events/webinar-library-current/1472-october-2020-machine-learning-will-transform-how-we-deliver-projects-by-dr-james-smith (accessed 27 May 2021); https://www.energyvoice.com/promoted/316963/its-time-to-wrangle-the-data-across-the-energy-industry-says-oil-and-gas-veteran-articleisfree (accessed 29 May 2021); https://www.cio.com/article/3612317/the-data-driven-project-manager-using-analytics-to-improve-outcomes.html (accessed 28 May 2021); https://www.projectdataanalytics.co.uk (accessed 27 May 2021); https://www.accenture.com/gb-en/services/industry-x-0/capital-projects (accessed 30 May 2021).

## Discussion questions

1. How do you see the role of the controller function within the PMO (see section 8.4.6) changing with the advent of project data analytics?

2. What do you think are the challenges and enablers to using data analytics effectively in projects?

3. Review Table 10.2—what are the principal affordances of project data analytics?

# 12 Being a project leader in SPO

## 12.1 Introduction: the social competencies for delivering project outcomes

'If you want to attract the brightest and the best to become project managers, you've got to make it clear that we're the enablers who are shaping the future of the world.'[1] Perhaps the greatest challenge for career development in strategic project organizing (SPO) is transforming the profession from a phalanx of process guardians to a galaxy of projectors who, indeed, change the world. After all, project managers largely enter the profession for its entrepreneurial spirit and the ability to get things done.[2] Yet we need to move beyond the narrative of heroic 'master builders' striding the globe[3]—projecting is now a team sport played in a complex stakeholder environment.

Teaming is the smallest unit of future-making and the emphasis throughout this book has been on *organizing*, because projects beyond the smallest are delivered by teams of teams, as discussed in section 7.4; yet teams consist of people, and so in this chapter we turn to focus more on the lived experience of managing projects within and across the three domains and the social competencies required for becoming a project leader. In particular, we chart the career of project leaders from their initial professional roles in managing projects; ensuring diversity and inclusion; through to becoming a project leader, its ethical aspects, and the career paths to that aspiration. We also identify the particular stresses that come with leading projects, and the associated issues of well-being. We finish on authenticity in leading SPO. Our case study presents a stimulating exercise in debating what projecting the future means for career opportunities.

## 12.2 The professional project manager

Much has changed over the past 30 years with respect to both training and aspirations. One notable feature is the rise of specific project management professional associations. Foremost is the Project Management Institute (PMI)[4] based in the United States, complemented by the International Project Management Association

(IPMA),[5] of which the United Kingdom's Association for Project Management (APM)[6] is the largest constituent member. Membership of such organizations is correlated with career advancement and job satisfaction for project managers.[7] At the core of the professional association offer is a body of knowledge against which the competencies of individual project managers can be certified, such as PMI's Project Management Professional. This certification is usually done by a multiple-choice questionnaire plus a work experience log, although higher-level certifications, such as the new Chartered Project Professional qualification from the APM, usually include an interview. Training in attaining the certification is usually provided by independent training providers, who are accredited by the professional institution.

However, important challenges remain in the professionalization of project managers and associated career development.[8] For instance, although there are an estimated 2.13 m people employed in project management roles in the United Kingdom,[9] only around 1.5 per cent of these are members of either the APM or PMI UK,[10] and fewer than these totals will hold formal project management qualifications. Project professional associations are far from the occupational closure achieved by professions such as engineering in many jurisdictions.[11] A first issue is that in many of the more traditional project-based sectors defined in section 6.2, such as construction and defence acquisition, there are long-established professional bodies which also claim to cover areas of project organizing. Indeed, the Institution of Civil Engineers, founded in 1818, is the oldest professional institution in the world[12] and has long had an interest in project organizing as part of engineering practice. In such sectors, professional associations of project managers can be seen as secondary to the more established professions and therefore not the primary professional self-identity. Project professional qualifications facilitate specialization within a career in engineering or construction rather than a distinctive career path. However, perceptions are changing,[13] and being a project manager is becoming an increasingly attractive option for career development validated by appropriate professional qualifications with the prospect of becoming a project leader.

A second issue is that of professional self-identity or employer self-identity for the aspiring project manager as cosmopolitans or locals.[14] A cosmopolitan is someone whose primary self-identity is with their profession ('I am a project manager'); a local is someone whose primary self-identity is with their employer ('I work for BAE Systems'). The professions evolved in the latter part of the nineteenth century in response to perceived need for the provision of knowledge services that were not driven by the market.[15] The solution was the licensing of accredited professionals, such as engineers, by the state to act monopolistically in the provision of those services. However, this solution poses challenges for professionals who are employed by large enterprises or the state to deliver their strategic investment initiatives. This is the situation of project managers who face balancing between the cosmopolitanism of self-identity with the profession and the localism of self-identity with their employer. **Cosmopolitan project managers** are attracted by the opportunities for a 'boundaryless career'[16] in which they switch employers with ease—or

## Vignette 12.1   UK Government project delivery profession

In the United Kingdom, almost all central government policy is delivered through projects and programmes managed by a thriving community of around 14,000 project delivery professionals. The hub for the profession is the Infrastructure and Projects Authority, where it is overseen by a Head of Profession. Its members are employed across all government departments. The profession is structured around a Project Delivery Capability Framework (PDCF) designed to support the competency development of all project delivery professionals in government and containing three main elements:

- Career Pathways, which set out the 19 Job Roles within the profession;
- technical and behavioural competencies aligned to these roles;
- structured development opportunities.

The Job Roles are in three groups: Leadership (e.g. Programme Director); Project Delivery Specialist (e.g. Project Planner), and Business Analysis and Change Specialist (e.g. Benefits Manager). Civil Service grade of appointment to each of these Roles is usually a function of project complexity.

The Project Delivery Competencies required for each Job Role are grouped into 19 Technical Competencies aligned to the APM Competence Framework and 10 Behavioural/Leadership Competencies aligned to the UK Civil Service Success Profiles. Each member of the profession is expected to access the training required to meet these competencies through their Personal Development Plan on the 70:20:10 model—70 per cent learning on the job, 20 per cent learning by sharing with peers, and 10 per cent formal training and education. Members are expected to do a minimum of five days' training each year.

Competence development starts with formal accreditation by the APM or the Axelos suite. It then progresses to Academies within specific ministries, before moving up to the generic leadership programmes across the Profession—the Project Leadership Programme (Cranfield University) and the Major Projects Leadership Academy (Oxford University) for those delivering the most complex programmes.

*Source*: https://www.gov.uk/government/organisations/civil-service-project-delivery-profession/about (accessed 26 October 2020).

indeed national boundaries in the case of megaproject leaders—taking on greater challenges as their experience grows. **Local project managers** work their way up organizational hierarchies to positions of leading, a path that is becoming easier to follow in many organizations, as shown in Vignette 12.1. The choices made will, to a large extent, be the outcome of whether the aspiring project leader prefers to work in one of the two permanent domains of SPO with infrequent moves from employer to employer, or to work within the delivery domain, moving from project to project within a project ecology, as discussed in section 10.3—often on a self-employed basis. For some, this is a lifestyle choice,[17] with benefits of a greater sense of well-being than employed professionals.[18]

A third issue is that it is not at all clear which SPO-specific competencies beyond the technical ones discussed in Chapter 11 should be developed in project managers.[19] While the bodies of knowledge have attempted to address this, there is much debate about how far they should extend beyond the 'core' technical competencies.[20] While many 'soft skills' are advocated, these tend to be generic managerial skills rather than specific to project organizing. Perhaps as a result, employers see possession of project management certification as relatively unimportant for project managers.[21]

---

### Exercise 12.1

As you think about your career development as a project manager, do you prefer a local career, identifying with an employer, or a cosmopolitan career, identifying as a person who does projects? Why do you make this choice?

---

## 12.3 Professional roles in SPO

Roles are the outcome of the design processes summarized in the SPO Star Model presented in Figure 7.3, which allow individuals to align with the organization of which they are a member—be it the owner, supplier, or delivery organization. There is little standardization of these roles in project organizing,[22] and we are not brave enough here to offer such a nomenclature. However, we think it appropriate to offer some insights into project organizing role descriptions which derive specifically from the three domains approach and to indicate the differences in career paths that they offer aspiring project managers. A first insight is that there are important differences between being a project manager in the owner domain and the supplier domain, even though these two will be working collaboratively within the delivery domain, as shown in Table 12.1. This is principally because of the relatively restricted engagement by suppliers in the owner's project life cycle shown in Figure 9.6—the greater the range of collaboration through the project life cycle, the greater the extent of the supplier project manager's role.

A second insight is clarification of the role of the sponsor, discussed in section 8.4.3. This role has been characterized as the 'champion' or 'promotor' of the project, or in some formal project management methodologies as the Senior Responsible Owner[23] (SRO). In SPO, the sponsor sits inside the owner organization with accountability for the project delivery organization, and the 'owner' is an organization, not an individual. Champions and promotors play their roles at the very front end in shaping the strategic case for the project and the associated project narrative—see section 4.9— but tend to be less involved as the project moves through the life cycle. An important aspect of the sponsor's competencies is their knowledge and authority within the broader organization, so it is unlikely that they will have only a project organizing background and this is not necessary.[24] Within an owner organization, the sponsor is typically a delegated member of the corporate executive team, while within a project-based firm (PBF) such as BAE Systems, it is usually the chief executive officer (CEO) of the business unit.

Table 12.1 The owner and supplier project manager roles

| Owner project manager | Supplier project manager (first tier) |
|---|---|
| Managing the strategic context to ensure that the value proposition remains valid | Managing delivery to the commercial contract and making proposals for improvement in delivery performance |
| Managing the owner organization to ensure it interacts appropriately with the supplier organizations and the owner's project sponsor | Managing the supply chain (see Figure 6.3) organizations to ensure they interact appropriately with the owner organization |
| Keeping the sponsor briefed on progress, that the project remains visible, and that there are no surprises | Reporting regularly on progress, possible threats, and threat events to the owner |
| Ensuring that the outputs are transformed into outcomes | Delivering the outputs of the project as specified in the project execution plans |
| Driving the value proposition through the delivery process, including all approvals | Driving the delivery process |
| Managing the commercial interface with first-tier suppliers collaboratively | Managing the commercial interface with the owner collaboratively |
| Managing the governance interface in line with industry best practice | Providing the required inputs into the owner's assurance processes |
| Ensuring that the delivery organization is supplied with the right information at the right time | Requesting information from the owner on behalf of sub-suppliers, as required |

*Source*: developed from Godbold (2016: 63).

The project (or programme) director typically reports to the sponsor. Some organizations, such as BP, often break down this role into appraisal general manager responsible for shaping, and programme general manager responsible for delivery. In others, responsibilities are split between the programme manager responsible for delivery and the business change manager responsible for benefits realization, with the SRO ensuring coordination between the two.[25] These roles may be—and preferably are[26]—filled by employees of the owner organization, but some owners which rarely launch investment projects may rely on external advisors as part of the owner project team.

## 12.4 Diversity in project organizing

Diversity is central to SPO as a problem-solving discipline; the more diverse the background and experience of project team members, the greater the opportunity for innovative solutions to emerge. Cognitive diversity[27] (differences in perspective or information-processing styles) rather than gender, age, or ethnic diversity in teams is the key factor in explaining team performance in new, uncertain, and complex situations. However, during project delivery, cognitive diversity needs to be tempered by a shared commitment to the project mission.[28] Fundamentally, cognitive diversity reduces the potential for groupthink[29] within the project leadership team and psychological safety is central to releasing the potential of that cognitive diversity during the project shaping of both the project mission and the value proposition, as discussed in Chapter 5, and also during project delivery in assessing early warning signs, as discussed in Chapter 7. Psychological safety is an organizational phenomenon, not an individual one, and so is greatly enhanced by perceived gender and ethnic equality in the positions held across organizational levels, including the project's senior leadership team.[30] The importance of experience in judging, tempered by the importance of looking at challenges afresh in areas such as threat identification,[31] points, too, to the importance of a balance of age within the project delivery teams. Diversity and inclusion are therefore vital enablers of effective teaming at all levels of the project organization.

Diversity and inclusion are key enablers of organizational performance[32] because employee diversity improves decision-making, problem-solving, creativity, innovation, and flexibility.[33] The notion of inclusion and diversity in the workplace has received much attention over the years and is now being considered more holistically rather than through a single lens of gender, age, culture, or ethnicity.[34] Research shows that for women, becoming a leader requires much more than being in a leadership role, developing new competencies, or adapting one's approach. It requires a self-identity shift, which may be hindered by the organization's policies and practices.[35] Men and women are similar in attributes such as confidence, risk appetite, and negotiation skills; therefore, the key aspect that organizations should address is the conditions which lead to higher retention and promotion rates for women.[36]

Greater age is considered a competitive disadvantage in many corporations.[37] Older age is associated with being perceived as less capable, adaptable, and flexible when compared to younger employees. However, age is associated with wisdom and successful start-ups, for example.[38] Knowledge and expertise increase with age and these are considered the main predictors for job performance. Older employees will contribute more if they are intellectually engaged, and if they are allowed to contribute their expertise.[39] Indeed, age is obviously an important determinant of experience and hence judging in the SPO Project Leadership Model (PLM) in section 3.3.3 and the intuition required to interpret the early warning signs discussed in section 7.6.

## 12.5  Ethics in strategic project organizing

the honest projector is he who, having by fair and plain principles of sense, honesty, and ingenuity brought any contrivance to a suitable perfection, makes out what he pretends to, picks nobody's pocket, puts his project in execution, and contents himself with the real produce as the profit of his invention.[40]

For project professionals, ethics are an important consideration,[41] but what do we mean by 'ethics'? One perspective[42] argues that these revolve around three sets of issues:

- **relationship issues**—both interpersonal issues within the project team and inter-organizational issues within and across the interfaces between the three domains;
- **optimization issues** arising from trade-offs within the project mission and scope;
- **transparency issues** around the extent to which information is shared with stakeholders.

Relationship issues in SPO are crucial. Standards of behaviour in interpersonal relationships should be high to ensure psychological safety free from bullying behaviour to enable creative future-making and spotting early warning signs, as discussed in sections 7.4 and 7.6. In the pressurized world of managing projects, this can appear at times difficult to achieve, but there is no alternative if projects are to be successfully delivered for owners. Standards of behaviour across the commercial interface within the tiers of the supply and project chains as shown in Figure 9.6 also need to be high in order to develop the kind of collaborative working discussed in section 9.5.

Optimization issues are a continual challenge for decision-makers on projects. The appropriate balance between costs and benefits is always hard won, with multiple decisions around trade-offs to be made. This is the case during both project shaping and the Define phase, where negotiating the trade-off triangles shown in Figure 7.1 can be punishing. Where making these trade-offs becomes an ethical issue is around the Quality of Conformance to the requirements specified by the owner in the PDP, including meeting the Environmental, Safety, and Health regulations and standards (QUENSH) areas discussed in section 11.6. These are quality of conformance issues— no asset should endanger the environment in which it is delivered and operates or the health of those who deliver or use it, but when budget and schedule pressures mount, this is easily forgotten. The ethical project leader remembers this imperative.

Transparency issues are less clear cut. Issues around the commercial sensitivity of contracts with both stakeholders and suppliers can limit the amount of information that can be shared. A particular ethical issue that has been identified during project shaping is the ethics around the development of the value proposition[43] discussed in section 5.6, and the 'cooking of the books' to make investment projects appear more attractive than they are. A second is corruption across the commercial interface discussed in section 9.8, particularly where the owner is a state agency.[44]

---

## Exercise 12.2

How do you think the ethical standards of project leaders can be improved?

## 12.6 Becoming a project leader

How does a project manager become a project leader? Vignette 12.2 tells one personal story. This is an important question, as effective project managers, in any of the three domains, have the potential to become project leaders. Leading projects is inherently fractal,[45] with project leaders at all levels from delivery team leaders to programme directors leading a cast of thousands. The difference between project managers and project leaders is that the latter move beyond the technical competencies and develop consummate social skills—leading projects is an inherently social process[46] that requires projecting the project mission, judging the best way to achieve it, and inspiring the delivery teams. We introduced the SPO PLM in Figure 3.1, which identifies important dimensions of leading on projects and the need to complement the incomplete leader with other senior leadership team members, who are more competent on certain dimensions than others. Leading complex projects requires team building and collaboration. Judging is an important dimension that project leaders learn throughout their careers—understanding yourself and other people's emotions, respecting and supporting each other. Throughout the project life cycle, there may be difficulties in personal relationships, arguments in work-related situations, and the like. But usually these get resolved through time in a continuous process of interpersonal negotiation and building professional and personal relationships. The successful completion of a project makes a project leader proud of her achievements.

In many organizations, project managers are promoted to roles where social competencies as leaders are more important based on their performance in managing their last project. Such an approach can invoke the 'Peter Principle', in which managers

Vignette **12.2**    Nora'in MD Salleh

Nora'in is a project leader working for a major South East Asian national oil company (NOC). NOCs are typically mandated by their owning governments to develop and operate the national oil and gas resources, sometimes in joint venture with international oil companies, which can provide technology and finance. They are typically functionally organized and so project leaders operate in a lightweight matrix, as defined in Figure 10.3. This demands particular skills for relating to the functional heads who control the human resources required for the project.

Nora'in started her career managing portfolios of minor asset upgrade projects, where working closely with both the relevant engineering functions and operational teams was key to success. She then moved on to work for the national regulator for the sector. This gave her the opportunity to observe how a variety of companies managed their projects and thereby extend her learning on project delivery. Returning to the NOC, she applied her skills to leading projects in a lightweight matrix, where the project leader has no authority to fall back upon and has to work by communicating widely with integrity to develop the trust essential for willing 'followership'.

She summarizes her leadership style:

> first, in order for you to be considered a good leader you must be able to make a decision and stand by it. Second, as a leader, if you are not calm and stable enough but rather skittish and jumpy, you will discourage people from coming to you and explaining and sharing their issues with you. The third one is walk the talk. Because in projects it's really important for you to be in the shoes of your team and your contractors and only then will you be able to form good cooperation among the team.

*Source*: Merrow and Nandurdikar (2018).

are promoted to their level of incompetence.[47] This happens because project managers need to develop their social competencies through collaborating, learning, and maintaining momentum in project delivery[48] as they take on more challenging senior positions and move towards becoming project leaders. High performance at one level does not necessarily predict higher performance at a more senior level—an inability to delegate and a reliance on micromanagement are characteristic of many junior high performers. Avoiding invoking the Peter Principle implies that *potential* leaders need to be identified and then nurtured. The psychometric evidence is that between one-third and one-half of leadership potential is innate. That is to say, it is developed prior to people entering the workforce as a result of genetics, family background, and education.[49] These areas include cognitive skills,[50] emotional intelligence, and the big five underpinning psychological traits discussed in section 3.3.2. This leaves between one-half and two-thirds of leadership potential to be developed through the career as a project manager transitioning to becoming a project leader.

One crucial element of career development is getting the right kind of experience. Employers should consider carefully the development paths of their more promising project managers, preparing them for more senior roles by giving them smaller projects to manage to gain experience of leading teaming.[51] However, if this success is achieved by micromanagement rather than delegation, it is a good indicator of lack of leadership potential. An intriguing development opportunity is secondment to 'non-operated ventures' as part of a joint venture, where a partner owner is responsible for beneficial use. The opportunity to see how other owners manage their projects without having responsibility for delivery appears to be a good predictor for successfully leading major projects.[52] The second is participating in appropriate leadership development programmes. While MSc and MBA qualifications can be an important contribution to career development, they typically do not facilitate the identification and development of leadership potential. Many organizations offer generic leadership development programmes, but for the specific challenges of leading complex projects, many owners and project-based firms are now offering bespoke development programmes in leading complex projects.[53] Vignette 12.3 presents such a programme.

Vignette **12.3**    Leading complex projects, programmes, and portfolios (LCP3)

LCP3 was commissioned by BAE Systems plc from Alliance Manchester Business School (AMBS) and launched in 2016. It is a global programme with two residential workshops delivered in the United Kingdom, the United Arab Emirates, Australia, and the United States. It is delivered over a 16-month cycle to cohorts of ~30 mid-career delegates in a blended learning format combining two residential weeks with online action learning sets. Assessment is through reflective practice papers, which connect the classroom to the workplace, and delegates earn credits towards a University of Manchester Postgraduate Certificate.

LCP3 focuses upon six project leadership competences:

1.  Understand yourself as a leader, and the impact of your behaviour on others in a project team environment focused on results.

2.  Manage complexity, risk, and uncertainty in complex projects, programmes, and portfolios.

3.  Engage stakeholders for mutually beneficial collaborative relationships outside the project team.

4.  Drive business growth through winning new and follow-on business through collaborative working with new and existing customers.

5.  Achieve effective design and development of project/programme/portfolio execution strategies.

6.  Achieve effective leadership of project/programme/portfolio execution.

Pressure for change within BAE Systems generated by LCP3 delegates led the company to create the two-day Sponsoring CP3 for board-level delegates, including the group chief executive officer. Most recently, a four-day Integrating CP3 was launched online in 2020 to fill the gap between the acquisition of professional project management certifications and becoming a project leader.

Tom Arseneault, President and Chief Executive Officer of BAE Systems Inc., commented that:

> The LCP3 programme allows us to address changing business trends: more demanding customers, increasingly complex and risky projects and greater competition for the recruitment and retention of talent. LCP3 will ensure our Project Managers are equipped to tackle current and future challenges and lead change throughout the organization.

*Source*: authors.

## 12.7  The person in the middle

One important implication of the project matrix discussed in section 10.2 is that the project manager or leader is the person 'in between' two reporting lines to structure—the functional report responsible for resources and the marketing report responsible for ensuring that the customer's needs are met.[54] This 'tween position is well captured in Figure 10.1, which shows the programme director at the interface between the individual projects making up the programme and the functional managers providing the resources to those projects in a project delivery organization. In each cell of Figure 10.1, the project managers leading the delivery of work packages will be facing the same matrix. In a complex stakeholder environment, the tensions have three dimensions, as is shown in Figure 12.1, which illustrates the challenges of being a programme director in the owner domain. The programme director is positioned between the various external project stakeholders; the internal stakeholders; and the various coalitions across the projects which make up the programme, most of whose members will work for supplier organizations rather than the owner organization. In essence, the role of the owner programme director is to act as the owner's agent[55] at the interface between the owner's value proposition and the delivery resources managed by the suppliers' project managers. In this respect, the owner programme director performs a role in complex projects that neither the owner's functional managers, nor the suppliers' project managers can achieve—the overall coordination of the project so that it delivers the project mission.

The pressures inherent in being in the middle can take their toll on project leaders. Project managers typically report higher levels of stress on a number of dimensions than people working in other sectors and the kinds of stress-related behaviours that suppress psychological safety are more prevalent in project managers.[56] Burnout as

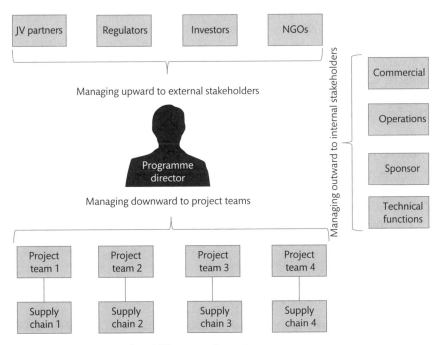

Figure 12.1  The person in the middle on complex projects,

*Source*: developed from Merrow and Nandurdikar (2018: figure 3.1).

a psychological syndrome resulting from sustained stress is defined as 'overwhelming exhaustion; feelings of cynicism and detachment from the job; and a sense of ineffectiveness and lack of accomplishment'.[57] Managers on complex projects were found to be susceptible to burnout, typically experienced by women as exhaustion and by men as cynicism, which could be mitigated by higher levels of job control and co-worker support and is seen most commonly in mid-career project managers.[58]

---

### Exercise 12.3

Think about those situations when you have felt stressed at work. Which stressors made the situation worse? How were they palliated?

---

## 12.8 Conflict in the project matrix

As might be expected, conflict is inherent between these different roles;[59] the challenge for the project leader is to manage that conflict so that it becomes a source of creativity rather than a sink of energy. Conflict within project delivery organizations is mainly, but not entirely, around schedules, priorities for the use of resources, and the allocation of human resources to the project. Thus, the matrix presented in Figure 12.1 is in continual tension. One response to conflict is to try to smooth it over with a rhetoric—rather than reality—of teaming because conflict is seen as dysfunctional and its occurrence as a sign of failure. More seasoned observers see conflict as something to be acknowledged and managed so that its positive aspects are realized for the benefit of all. There are various ways of managing conflict within the project organization:

- articulate a clear and coherent project mission—much of the research on conflict has shown that it is more likely to occur where there is not a clear point around which to rally;[60]
- argue about facts, not opinions—in a context where technical people predominate, respect is more likely to be given to positions backed by data. It is the responsibility of the project manager to ensure that appropriate data are collected, collated, and deployed in dispute resolution;
- use third-party experts to break deadlocks;
- use decision-making tools that allow both the expression of difference and the identification of commonality.

Projecting is crucial here, as is shown by our quotation from the Channel Fixed Link project leader in section 10.4.

## 12.9  Leading projects authentically

Project leaders are expected to construct a clear and firm sense of self to encourage everybody in the organization to buy into and sustain a coherent projecting narrative; at the same time, self-identities are multiple, fluid, and dynamic and often expressed through stories of everyday life experiences. Experience is constituted through individual stories about 'self', others, and what has happened and is happening to them. People enact meanings on the basis of their memories, present experiences, and expectations from available social, public, and cultural narratives.[61] Self-identity concerns the meanings that individuals reflexively attach to themselves, others, and situations within which they find themselves, which are developed through processes of social interaction.[62] The ways project leaders see themselves in relation to followers and the broader context is an important part of leading authentically. There is an ongoing process of building self-identity in the context of social interactions and broader contexts within which project leaders operate.

As Mark Thurston, the CEO of HS2 Ltd, put it:

> I see myself as authentic; I don't pretend to be something I'm not. Of course I adapt, there's a style that you adapt for different circumstances, but in every circumstance, I'm authentic, I can't pretend. So if I engage with the Secretary of State or an Apprentice, or yesterday with the Chief Executive of a City Council, I'll be authentic. I'm not pretending, I'm not masquerading, I'm not doing it for effect, and although my style might be different for a different set of circumstances, still it's authentic leadership.[63]

The first dimension of leading authentically[64] is self-awareness, which includes personal values, emotions, self-identity, informal roles, and goals. The second is understanding others' emotions, behaviours, and actions, which form part of emotional intelligence, discussed in section 3.3.2. The third is unbiased collection and interpretation of self-related information, authentic behaviour, and relational transparency, which means that the leader displays high levels of openness, self-disclosure, and trust in close relationships—in summary, wise judging, as discussed in section 3.3.3. Leading authentically assumes that the leader's personal history (family influences, early challenges, educational and work experiences) and key trigger events (including crises, as well as positive trigger events, such as a promotion or stretch assignment) serve as antecedents and opportunities for learning.

## 12.10  Summary

In this chapter, we reviewed what it takes to become a project leader, particularly on larger and more complex projects. It is not a profession for everyone, demanding stamina and high levels of authenticity. The clear message from the data is that successful project leaders focus on the strategic and relational rather than the technical on their projects, and the more complex the project the more important that is. Managing the technical competencies discussed in Chapter 11 should be delegated to others. We also saw that cognitive diversity is central to effective project teaming but can hinder delivery unless strongly aligned by the leader to the project mission. Psychological safety is vital for the expression of cognitive diversity, yet this safety will be compromised in organizations that are not perceived to be equitable with respect to gender, ethnicity, disability, and age. Diversity and inclusion are therefore vital enablers of effective teaming at all levels of the organization. Above all, the project leaders need to be authentic.

Twenty-first-century projecting for the fourth Industrial Revolution is a team sport played in a complex stakeholder environment experiencing rapid technological change. Leading projects requires the ability to cope with uncertainty and complexity through sense-making and relating to stakeholders, and from these materials projecting the narrative that will mobilize the resources to deliver the project and creating how to do that delivery. Bringing all this together through wise judging is how projects change the world. In this final chapter, we have shown how ambitious young project managers can develop their careers as authentic leaders and projectors in changing our world.

## 12.11  Further reading

Laufer, A., Hoffman, E. J., Russell, J. S., and Cameron, W. S. 2015. 'What successful project managers do'. *MIT Sloan Management Review*, 56(3): 42–51.
A mature reflection on project managing as a social process.

Corritore, M., Goldberg, A., and Srivastava, S. B. 2020. 'The new analytics of culture'. *Harvard Business Review*, 98(1): 76–83.
A refreshing look at cultural and cognitive diversity in software development teams.

Gardner, W. L., Avolio, B. J., Luthans, F., May, D. R., and Walumbwa, F. 2005. '"Can you see the real me?" A self-based model of authentic leader and follower development'. *The Leadership Quarterly*, 16(3): 343–372.
Develops the concept of leading authentically.

## 12.12  Summary review questions

1. What are some of the challenges in the professionalization of project managers?
2. What are the main differences between being a project manager in the owner and supplier domains?
3. Why are diversity and inclusion important in project organizing?
4. Why is the programme director role in the owner domain stressful?
5. What are the three dimensions of leading authentically?

*Visit the Oxford Learning Link site for this text to find answer guidance to the questions and exercises in this chapter.*

 *Take your learning further by viewing videos relevant to this chapter on the Oxford Learning Link site.*

## Notes

1. Waller (2020: 35).
2. *Havermans et al. (2019).
3. Middlemas (1963).
4. http://www.pmi.org (accessed 20 August 2021).
5. http://www.ipma.world (accessed 20 August 2021).
6. http://www.apm.org.uk (accessed 20 August 2021).
7. Blomquist et al. (2018); McKevitt et al. (2017).
8. Akkermans et al. (2020).
9. APM (2019).
10. Project Management Institute UK Membership 3000 (http://www.pmi.org.uk, accessed 7 October 2020); APM membership 28000 (APM, 2019).
11. Abbott (1988).
12. Watson (1988).
13. Hodgson et al. (2011).
14. Hodgson and Muzio (2011); Hodgson and Paton (2016).
15. Perkin (1989); Larson (1977).
16. *DeFillippi and Arthur (1994).
17. Evans et al. (2004).
18. Cheung et al. (2020).
19. Nijhuis et al. (2018).
20. Morris (2013).
21. APM (2019: figure 2).
22. Zwikael and Meredith (2018).
23. Axelos (2020).
24. Barshop (2016).
25. Axelos (2020).
26. Outsourcing such responsibilities is associated with poor project performance—see Merrow (2011).
27. Syed (2019).
28. Corritore et al. (2020).
29. Janis (1972).
30. Edmondson (2019).
31. Maytorena-Sanchez et al. (2007).
32. McKinsey (2020).

33. Burrell (2016).
34. Folayan (2020).
35. *Ibarra et al. (2013).
36. Tinsley and Ely (2018).
37. Deloitte (2020).
38. Azoulay et al. (2018).
39. Bersin and Chamorro-Premuzic (2019).
40. Defoe (1697: 21).
41. Jonasson and Ingason (2013).
42. Kvalnes (2017).
43. Flyvbjerg (2011).
44. Locatelli et al. (2017).
45. Bowen et al. (1994a).
46. Laufer et al. (2015).
47. Peter and Hull (1969).
48. Laufer et al. (2015).
49. Silzer and Borman (2017).
50. Schmidt and Hunter (1998).
51. Bowen et al. (1994a).
52. Merrow and Nandurdikar (2018).
53. Internationally, the earliest one of which we are aware is NASA's Academy of Program/Project & Systems Engineering Leadership, founded in 1998—see Hoffman and Boyle (2017).
54. Gaddis (1959).
55. Turner and Müller (2004).
56. Cheung et al. (2020).
57. Maslach et al. (2009: 90).
58. Pinto et al. (2014); Yang et al. (2017).
59. Thamhain and Wilemon (1975).
60. Sherif (1958).
61. Cunliffe and Coupland (2012).
62. Alvesson et al. (2008); Brown (2015).
63. Cited in Sergeeva and Davies (2021: 56).
64. Gardner et al. (2005).

 **Case 12**    Projecting the future

> We always overestimate the change that will occur in the next two years and underestimate the change that will occur in the next ten.

Bill Gates' words cited from his 1994 book, *The Road Ahead*, serve as the epigraph for the United Kingdom's Association for Project Management (APM) *Projecting the Future* initiative launched in June 2019 to debate the challenges and opportunities for the profession. It built on the 2017 *Future of Project Management* exercise conducted by Arup and University College London for the APM. The premise was that:

> We are in the early days of the fourth industrial revolution, driven by artificial intelligence, big data and robots. Climate change and sustainability demand that we radically rethink how our economy works, while the revolution in human longevity is ripping up long-standing norms about how we live and work. The project profession, meanwhile, is starting to outgrow its roots as a niche technical discipline to become—well, what exactly?

Projects are about how change happens, so the project profession will be at the centre in shaping the future. But precisely what role will it play? In the context of a profoundly changed world, how do we truly thrive? If technology is ushering in the age of 'industry 4.0', how do we build 'project management 4.0'? Answering those questions needs an outward-looking and far-reaching discussion about the future. *Projecting the Future* aimed to kick-start that process.

Over the following year, the APM undertook a 'big conversation' across the profession using a variety of channels guided by an industry team chaired by Tim Banfield of the Nichols Group. The stimulus for this conversation was a set of six short—but well-written and erudite—challenge papers as follows:

1. 'The fourth Industrial Revolution: data, automation, and artificial intelligence' addressed the promise of a digital future and the associated digital transformation projects, and the opportunities it offers the profession around big data and the development of project data analytics.

2. 'Climate change, clean growth and sustainability' identified the challenges of our changing environment and the opportunities for projects to address those challenges with infrastructure projects such as renewable energy generation and flood defences.

3. 'Aging and demographics: the 100-year life' discussed the opportunities offered by growing longevity and the implications for society and economy, and also identified a wide range of new medical product development projects.

4. 'The future of mobility and transport' laid out the exciting world of autonomous vehicles and the multiple new product development projects to achieve that vision supported by infrastructure projects to achieve the electrification of existing transportation modes.

5. 'Smart cities, urbanization and connectivity' assessed the implication of the growing importance of cities in our economy and society, and how cities can become truly smart through new product development projects for intelligent sensors and mobile devices and the infrastructure projects that allow them all to connect up.

6. 'The future of work and skills' explored the implications of digital transformation projects for working lives—both the development of platform systems and the gig economy and the transformation of office work in a world of artificial intelligence (AI). It also assessed the place of project managers in this transformed world of work.

These six challenge papers were broad in scope and thought-provoking in the questions they asked. Broadly, they sketched out a positive future for project managers, while emphasizing the importance of the social competencies, rather than the traditional technical ones, for project managers. Paper 6 cited a PricewaterhouseCoopers white paper which argued:

> it is technical project management skills which could most usefully, and most easily, be automated or augmented by technology. When it comes to decision making, tech can help with data and modelling—but it cannot replace the elements of human judgement that are ultimately needed. Neither can AI take emotional [n]or social dynamics into account, which means it cannot replace the management, leadership and interpersonal skills needed around important decisions.

The responses to these challenge papers captured through social media, meetings, and surveys, as well as a corporate partner forum in early 2020, formed a wide-ranging conversation, which drew out the following insights as the basis for recommendations for the profession:

- Project management casts itself as the 'adaptive profession' at the heart of creating and delivering change in organizations and society. This requires adaptation to shifting conditions through continual learning, while developing competencies from project data analytics to teaming and stakeholder engagement.
- Meeting these global challenges requires a resilient 'pipeline' of entrants to the profession, both from those leaving education and from those entering the profession in mid-career, such as armed forces personnel. They will be attracted by an 'emphasis less on the processes of project management and more on the transformational, inspirational, benefits of projects'.
- The profession must be strengthened by supporting learning through life, with project managers taking responsibility for their careers.
- The profession must win a 'seat at the top table' in corporate board rooms, perhaps in the role of chief project officer, who would take a strategic view of projects, as well as a delivery view. Executive development for senior project managers as project and programme directors needs to be developed.
- Collaborating with complementary organizations will be essential to improve the delivery of projects.
- It is necessary to promote the APM itself to broaden its influence and the contribution of the profession 'as an agent of change working across the economy and society'.
- An evidence base needs to be developed of what works on projects despite their non-repetitive nature.
- Sustainability must be embedded in the heart of what the profession does.

From these insights, the process generated a set of actions for the next 5–10 years for project professionals wishing to develop their careers:

- Generate an 'adaptive mindset' because in a volatile, uncertain, complex, and ambiguous (VUCA) world, change is inevitable and so project managers need to be ready to proactively shape change through learning and resilience.

- Invest in continuing professional development with an emphasis upon two particular areas:
  - technical skills associated with project data analytics;
  - leading and teaming skills deployed internally and externally to the project.
- Step up to lead and prepare for a seat at the top table.

Project professionals who aspire to lead projects need to have curiosity, be prepared to think imaginatively, and develop 'out of the box' thinking. Building on their unique core expertise and technical skills, project professionals should develop a broader perspective on project and organisational aims, and how they can be achieved. Shape strategy not just delivery.

Actions for the employers of project professionals—whether in owner or supplier organizations—wishing to develop their project capabilities include the following:

- Bring expertise in project organizing to the C-suite. This can be either through the role of a chief projects officer, or by wider development of awareness across the C-suite so 'that project expertise is part of deciding what to do—not just how it can be done'.
- Recognize the contribution of project professionals to strategy development and delivery and ensure that their expertise is embedded in decision-making.
- Work with the APM to implement and further develop the organizational principles underpinning successful project delivery.
- Commit to developing a diverse talent pipeline for project managers by supporting initiatives to bring younger people into the profession.
- Support the further development of competencies within the profession through CPD and mentoring.
- Improve the communication of project benefits and outcomes, showing how they address environmental and societal challenges.

Actions for policy-makers include the following:

- Support educational initiatives to support the development of a diverse pipeline into the profession.
- Support retraining initiatives to bring a wider cohort of experienced people into the profession.
- Develop the capability of government as the largest owner of projects in most economies. This includes both the actions as a major employer of project professionals and actions ensuring that its suppliers develop their own project organizing capability.

*Projecting the Future* started with the assertion: 'The future could look daunting, but for the project profession, it shouldn't—because projects are the way that successful change happens.' It concludes by saying that *Projecting the Future* 'is the launchpad for the next phase of the project profession's development. The ideas here point the way forward for the profession to become more adaptive to our changing world. It falls to us all, together, to make it a reality.'

*Sources*: http://www.apm.org.uk/projecting-the-future/ (accessed 13 October 2020). Interview, Tim Banfield, Nichols Group, 10 November 2020.

## Discussion questions

1. What do you think the distinctive role of project professionals is for shaping our shared future?

2. Do project professionals deserve a seat at the top table, or are they members of an essentially delivery profession?

3. Can membership of an organization such as the Association for Project Management or the Project Management Institute help you to advance your career as a project professional?

# Bibliography

Abbott, A. 1988. *the System of Professions: An Essay on the Expert Division of Labour*. Chicago, IL: University of Chicago Press.

Acha, V., Davies, A., Hobday, M., and Salter, A. 2004. 'Exploring the capital goods economy: complex product systems in the UK'. *Industrial and Corporate Change*, 13(3): 505–529.

Ackermann, F., Howick, S., Quigley, J., Walls, L., and Houghton, T. 2014. 'Systemic risk elicitation: using causal maps to engage stakeholders and build a comprehensive view of risks'. *European Journal of Operational Research*, 238(1): 290–299.

Adams, J. 1995. *Risk*. London: UCL Press.

Ahola, T., Ruuska, I., Artto, K., and Kujala, J. 2014. 'What is project governance and what are its origins?'. *International Journal of Project Management*, 32(8): 1321–1332.

Akkermans, J., Keegan, A., Huemann, M., and Ringhofer, C. 2020. 'Crafting project managers' careers: integrating the fields of careers and project management'. *Project Management Journal*, 51(2): 135–153.

Alvesson, M., Lee Ashcraft, K., and Thomas, R. 2008. 'Identity matters: reflections on the construction of identity scholarship in organization studies'. *Organization*, 15(1): 5–28.

Ancona, D., Malone, T. W., Orlikowski, W. J., and Senge, P. M. 2007. 'In praise of the incomplete leader'. *Harvard Business Review*, 85(2): 108–118.

Andrews, M. 2004. 'Opening to the original contributions: counter-narratives and the power to oppose'. In M. Bamberg, and M. Andrews (eds), *Considering Counter-Narratives: Narrating, Resisting, Making Sense*: 1–6. Philadelphia, PA: John Benjamins.

Ansoff, H. I. 1968. *Corporate Strategy*. Harmondsworth: Penguin.

APM. 2019. *The Golden Thread: A Study of the Contribution of Project Management and Projects to the UK's Economy and Society*. Princes Risborough: Association for Project Management.

APM. 2020. *Project Data Analytics: The State of the Art and Science*. Princes Risborough: Association for Project Management.

Archer, M. S. 1995. *Realist Social Theory: The Morphogenetic Approach*. Cambridge: Cambridge University Press.

Archer, M. S. 2000. *Being Human: The Problem of Agency*. Cambridge: Cambridge University Press.

Archer, N. P. and Ghasemzadeh, F. 1999. 'An integrated framework for project portfolio selection'. *International Journal of Project Management*, 17(4): 207–216.

Aristotle. 1974. *Categories and De Interpretatione*. Oxford: Clarendon.

Aritua, B., Male, S., and Bower, D. 2009. 'Defining the intelligent public sector construction client'. *Proceedings of the Institution of Civil Engineers-Management, Procurement and Law*, 162(2): 75–82.

Artto, K., Martinsuo, M., Dietrich, P., and Kujala, J. 2008. 'Project strategy: strategy types and their contents in innovation projects'. *International Journal of Managing Projects in Business*. 1(1): 49–70.

Ashforth, B. E. 2019. *Role Transitions in Organizational Life: An Identity-Based Perspective*. London: Routledge.

Aubry, M. and Brunet, M. 2016. 'Organizational design in public administration: categorization of project management offices'. *Project Management Journal*, 47(5): 107–129.

Austin, J. L. 1962. *How to Do Things with Words*. Cambridge, MA: Harvard University Press.

Axelos. 2017. *Managing Successful Projects with PRINCE2* (6th edn). London: Axelos.

Axelos. 2020. *Managing Successful Programmes* (5th edn). London: Axelos.

Azoulay, P., Jones, B., Kim, J. D., and Miranda, J. 2018. 'The Average Age of a Successful Startup Founder Is 45'. *Harvard Business Review On-Line*, https://hbr.org/2018/07/research-the-average-age-of-a-successful-startup-founder-is-45.

Bakker, R. M. 2010. 'Taking stock of temporary organizational forms: a systematic review and research agenda'. *International Journal of Management Reviews*, 12(4): 466–486.

Bakker, R. M., DeFillippi, R. J., Schwab, A., and Sydow, J. 2016. 'Temporary organizing: promises, processes, problems'. *Organization Studies*, 37(12): 1703–1719.

Ball, J. 2013. *The Other Side of Eden*. Kernow: FootSteps Press.

Barnard, C. I. 1968. *The Functions of the Executive* (30th anniversary edn). Boston, MA: Harvard University Press.

Barnes, N. M. L. and Wearne, S. H. 1993. 'The future for major project management'. *International Journal of Project Management*, 11(3): 135–142.

Barney, J. B. 2001. 'Resource-based theories of competitive advantage: a ten-year retrospective on the resource-based view'. *Journal of Management*, 27(6): 643–650.

Barrett, M. and Oborn, E. 2010. 'Boundary object use in cross-cultural software development teams'. *Human Relations*, 63(8): 1199–1221.

Barshop, P. 2016. *Capital Projects: What Every Executive Needs to Know to Avoid Costly Mistakes and Make Major Investments Pay Off*. Hoboken, NJ: Wiley.

Baumeister, R. F. and Newman, L. S. 1994. 'How stories make sense of personal experiences: motives that shape autobiographical narratives'. *Personality and Social Psychology Bulletin*, 20(6): 676–690.

Bayer, S. and Gann, D. 2006. 'Balancing work: bidding strategies and workload dynamics in a project-based professional service organisation'. *System Dynamics Review*, 22(3): 185–211.

Bechky, B. A. 2006. 'Gaffers, gofers, and grips: role-based coordination in temporary organizations'. *Organization Science*, 17(1): 3–21.

Becker, M. C. and Knudsen, T. 2005. 'The role of routines in reducing pervasive uncertainty'. *Journal of Business Research*, 58(6): 746–757.

Bektaş, E., Lauche, K., and Wamelink, H. 2015. 'Knowledge sharing in megaprojects: a case study of a co-location approach'. In A. Van Marrewijk (ed.), *Inside Megaprojects: Understanding Cultural Practices in Megaprojects*: 137–174. Copenhagen: CBS Press.

Bersin, J. and Chamorro-Premuzic, T. 2019. 'The case for hiring older workers'. *Harvard Business Review On-Line*, https://hbr.org/2019/09/the-case-for-hiring-older-workers.

Bettin, P. J. and Kennedy Jr, J. K. 1990. 'Leadership experience and leader performance: some empirical support at last'. *The Leadership Quarterly*, 1(4): 219–228.

Bianchi, M., Marzi, G., and Guerini, M. 2020. 'Agile, Stage-Gate and their combination: exploring how they relate to performance in software development'. *Journal of Business Research*, 110: 538–553.

Blomquist, T., Farashah, A. D., and Thomas, J. 2018. 'Feeling good, being good and looking good: motivations for, and benefits from, project management certification'. *International Journal of Project Management*, 36(3): 498–511.

Boehm, B. and Turner, R. 2004. *Balancing Agility and Discipline: A Guide for the Perplexed*. Boston, MA: Addison-Wesley.

Boje, D. 2008. *Storytelling Organizations*. London: Sage.

Bologna, R. and Del Nord, R. 2000. 'Effects of the law reforming public works contracts on the Italian building process'. *Building Research & Information*, 28(2): 109–118.

Bonfield, P. 2016. *Each Home Counts: An Independent Review of Consumer Advice, Protection, Standards and Enforcement for Energy Efficiency and Renewable Energy*. London: Department for Business, Energy, and Industrial Strategy; Department for Communities and Local Government.

Bowen, H. K., Clark, K. B., Holloway, C. A., and Wheelwright, S. C. 1994a. *The Perpetual Enterprise Machine: Seven Keys to Corporate Renewal through Successful Product and Process Development*. New York: Oxford University Press.

Bowen, H. K., Clark, K. B., Holloway, C. A., and Wheelwright, S. C. 1994b. 'Make projects the school for leaders'. *Harvard Business Review*, 72: 131–140.

Bowker, G. 2020. 'How to build and emergency hospital in two weeks'. *Health Estate Journal*, June: 18–22.

Boyd, D. and Chinyio, E. 2006. *Understanding the Construction Client*. Oxford: Blackwell.

BP. 2009. *BP 100*. London: BP plc.

Brady, T. and Davies, A. 2004. 'Building project capabilities: from exploratory to exploitative learning'. *Organization Studies*, 25(9): 1601–1621.

Breese, R., Couch, O., and Turner, D. 2020. 'The project sponsor role and benefits realisation: more than "just doing the day job"'. *International Journal of Project Management*, 38(1): 17–26.

Brockhoff, K. 2020. 'Virtual global project management in eighteenth-century astronomy'. *Journal of Management History*, 26(4): 535–555.

Brooks, F. P. 1995. *The Mythical Man-Month: Essays on Software Engineering* (20th anniversary edn). Reading, MA: Addison-Wesley.

Brown, A. D. 2015. 'Identities and identity work in organizations'. *International Journal of Management Reviews*, 17(1): 20–40.

Brown, K. A., Ettenson, R., and Hyer, N. L. 2011. 'Why every project needs a brand (and how to create one)'. *MIT Sloan Management Review*, 52(4): 61–68.

Brown, K. A., Hyer, N. L., and Ettenson, R. 2013. 'The question every project team should answer'. *MIT Sloan Management Review*, 55(1): 49–57.

Brown, K. A., Hyer, N. L., and Ettenson, R. 2017. 'Protect your project from escalating doubts'. *MIT Sloan Management Review*, 58(3): 79.

Brown, S. L. and Eisenhardt, K. M. 1997. 'The art of continuous change: linking complexity theory and time-paced evolution in relentlessly shifting organizations'. *Administrative Science Quarterly*, 42(1): 1–34.

Browning, T. R. and Ramasesh, R. V. 2015. 'Reducing unwelcome surprises in project management'. *MIT Sloan Management Review*, 56(3): 53–62.

Brunet, M. 2019. 'Governance-as-practice for major public infrastructure projects: a case of multilevel project governing'. *International Journal of Project Management*, 37(2): 283–297.

Bryman, A., Bresnen, M., Beardsworth, A. D., Ford, J., and Keil, E. T. 1987. 'The concept of the temporary system: the case of the construction project'. *Research in the Sociology of Organizations*, 5: 253–283.

Buckland, B. C. 2005. 'The process development challenge for a new vaccine'. *Nature Medicine*, 11(4): S16–S19.

Buehler, R., Griffin, D., and Peetz, J. 2010. 'The planning fallacy: cognitive, motivational, and social origins'. *Advances in Experimental Social Psychology*, 43: 1–62.

Burke, C. M. and Morley, M. J. 2016. 'On temporary organizations: a review, synthesis and research agenda'. *Human Relations*, 69(6): 1235–1258.

Burrell, L. 2016. 'We just can't handle diversity'. *Harvard Business Review*, 94(7/8): 71–74.

Cameron, K. and Lavine, M. 2006. *Making the Impossible Possible. Leading Extraordinary Performance: the Rocky Flats Story*. San Francisco, CA: Berrett-Koehler.

Carlile, P. R. 2002. 'A pragmatic view of knowledge and boundaries: boundary objects in new product development'. *Organization Science*, 13(4): 442–455.

Carter, D. R. and DeChurch, L. A. 2014. 'Leadership in multiteam systems: a network perspective'. In D. V. Day (ed.), *The Oxford Handbook of Leadership and Organizations*: 482–504. Oxford: Oxford University Press.

CCC. 2019. *UK Housing: Fit for the Future?* London: Committee on Climate Change.

CDBB. 2020. *Flourishing Systems: Re-Envisioning Infrastructure as a Platform for Human Flourishing*. Cambridge: Centre for Digital Built Britain.

Cha, J., Newman, M., and Winch, G. M. 2018. 'Revisiting the project management knowledge framework'. *International Journal of Managing Projects in Business*, 11(4): 1026–1043.

Chang, C.-Y. and Ive, G. 2007. 'The hold-up problem in the management of construction projects: a case study of the Channel Tunnel'. *International Journal of Project Management*, 25(4): 394–404.

Chapman, C. and Ward, S. 2011. *How to Manage Project Opportunity and Risk* (3rd edn). Chichester: Wiley.

Cheung, C. M., Cattell, K. S., Bowen, P. A., and Davis, J. C. 2020. *The Wellbeing of Project Professionals*. Princes Risborough: Association for Project Management.

Chevrier, S. 2003. 'Cross-cultural management in multinational project groups'. *Journal of World Business*, 38(2): 141–149.

Clark, K. B. and Fujimoto, T. 1991. *Product Development Performance: Strategy,*

*Organization, and Management in the World Auto Industry*. Boston, MA: Harvard Business School Press.

Clegg, S. R., Pitsis, T. S., Rura-Polley, T., and Marosszeky, M. 2002. 'Governmentality matters: designing an alliance culture of inter-organizational collaboration for managing projects'. *Organization Studies*, 23(3): 317–337.

Clegg, S. R., Skyttermoen, T., and Vaagaasar, A. L. 2020. *Project Management: A Value Creation Approach*. London: Sage.

Cleland, D. I. and King, W. R. 1968. *Systems Analysis and Project Management*. New York, NY: McGraw-Hill.

Cleland, D. I. and King, W. R. 1983a. *Project Management Handbook*. New York, NY: Van Nostrand Reinhold.

Cleland, D. I. and King, W. R. 1983b. 'Linear responsibility charts in project management'. In D. I. Cleland and W. R. King (eds), *Project Management Handbook*: 364–382. New York, NY: Van Nostrand Reinhold.

Climatekos. 2020. *The Great Green Wall Implementation Status and Way Ahead to 2030*. Bonn: United Nations Convention to Combat Desertification.

Comi, A. and Whyte, J. 2018. 'Future making and visual artefacts: an ethnographic study of a design project'. *Organization Studies*, 39(8): 1055–1083.

Conan Doyle, A. 1892. 'Silver Blaze'. *The Strand Magazine*, 4.

Cooper, R. G. 1993. *Winning at New Products: Accelerating the Process from Idea to Launch* (2nd edn). Reading, MA: Addison-Wesley.

Corritore, M., Goldberg, A., and Srivastava, S. B. 2020. 'The new analytics of culture'. *Harvard Business Review*, 98(1): 76–83.

Cousin, V. 1998. 'Research information. Innovation awards: a case study'. *Building Research and Information*, 26(5): 302–310.

Cova, B., Ghauri, P. N., and Salle, R. 2002. *Project Marketing: Beyond Competitive Bidding*. Chichester: Wiley.

Covello, V. T., Von Winterfeldt, D., and Slovic, P. 1986. 'Risk communication: a review of the literature'. *Risk Abstracts*, 3: 171–182.

Coyle, R. G. 2003. 'Scenario thinking and strategic modelling'. In D. O. Faulkner and A. Campbell (eds), *The Oxford Handbook of Strategy*: 308–349. Oxford: Oxford University Press.

Cummings, J. and Pletcher, C. 2011. 'Why project networks beat project teams'. *MIT Sloan Management Review*, 52(3): 75–80.

Cunliffe, A. and Coupland, C. 2012. 'From hero to villain to hero: making experience sensible through embodied narrative sensemaking'. *Human Relations*, 65(1): 63–88.

Cusumano, M. A. and Nobeoka, K. 1998. *Thinking beyond Lean: How Multi-Project Management Is Transforming Product Development at Toyota and Other Companies*. New York: Free Press.

Damanpour, F., Walker, R. M., and Avellaneda, C. N. 2009. 'Combinative effects of innovation types and organizational performance: a longitudinal study of service organizations'. *Journal of Management Studies*, 46(4): 650–675.

Davies, A. 2014. 'Innovation and project management'. In M. Dodgson, D. M. Gann, and N. Phillips (eds), *The Oxford Handbook of Innovation Management*: 625–647. Oxford: Oxford University Press.

Davies, A. and Brady, T. 2016. 'Explicating the dynamics of project capabilities'. *International Journal of Project Management*, 34(2): 314–327.

Davies, A. and Hobday, M. 2005. *The Business of Projects: Managing Innovation in Complex Products and Systems*. Cambridge: Cambridge University Press.

Davies, A., Gann, D., and Douglas, T. 2009. 'Innovation in megaprojects: systems integration at London Heathrow Terminal 5'. *California Management Review*, 51(2): 101–125.

Davies, A., MacAulay, S., DeBarro, T., and Thurston, M. 2014. 'Making innovation happen in a megaproject: London's crossrail suburban railway system'. *Project Management Journal*, 45(6): 25–37.

Davies, A., Dodgson, M., Gann, D., and MacAulay, S. 2017. 'Five rules for managing large, complex projects'. *MIT Sloan Management Review*, 59(1): 73–78.

Davies, H. and Zhivitskaya, M. 2018. 'Three lines of defence: a robust organising framework, or just lines in the sand?'. *Global Policy*, 9: 34–42.

Dawkins, R. 1976. *The Selfish Gene*. Oxford: Oxford University Press.

De Meyer, A. C. L., Loch, C. H., and Pich, M. T. 2002. 'Managing project uncertainty: from variation to chaos'. *MIT Sloan Management Review*, 43(2): 60–67.

DeFillippi, R. J. and Arthur, M. B. 1994. 'The boundaryless career: a competency-based perspective'. *Journal of Organizational Behavior*, 15(4): 307–324.

DeFillippi, R. J. and Sydow, J. 2016. 'Project networks: governance choices and paradoxical tensions'. *Project Management Journal*, 47(5): 6–17.

Defoe, D. 1697. *An Essay on Projects*. London: Cockerill.

Delisle, J. 2020. 'Working time in multi-project settings: how project workers manage work overload'. *International Journal of Project Management*, 38(7): 419–428.

Deloitte. 2020. *The Social Enterprise at Work: Paradox as a Path Forward*. Deloitte Insights.

Denning, S. 2005. *The Leader's Guide to Storytelling: Mastering the Art and Discipline of Business Narrative*. Hoboken, NJ: Wiley.

Denton, S. 2016. *The Profiteers: Bechtel and the Men Who Built the World*. New York, NY: Simon & Schuster.

Department for Transport (DfT). 2017. *Transport Infrastructure Efficiency Strategy*. London: Department for Transport.

Dikert, K., Paasivaara, M., and Lassenius, C. 2016. 'Challenges and success factors for large-scale agile transformations: a systematic literature review'. *Journal of Systems and Software*, 119: 87–108.

Doherty, N. F., Ashurst, C., and Peppard, J. 2012. 'Factors affecting the successful realisation of benefits from systems development projects: findings from three case studies'. *Journal of Information Technology*, 27(1): 1–16.

Dorée, A. G. 2004. 'Collusion in the Dutch construction industry: an industrial organization perspective'. *Building Research & Information*, 32(2): 146–156.

Dragoni, L., Oh, I. S., Vankatwyk, P., and Tesluk, P. E. 2011. 'Developing executive leaders: the relative contribution of cognitive ability, personality, and the accumulation of work experience in predicting strategic thinking competency'. *Personnel Psychology*, 64(4): 829–864.

Driscoll, C. and Starik, M. 2004. 'The primordial stakeholder: advancing the conceptual consideration of stakeholder status for the natural environment'. *Journal of Business Ethics*, 49(1): 55–73.

Drouin, N. and Turner, J. R. 2022. *The Elgar Advanced Introduction to Megaprojects*. Cheltenham: Edward Elgar.

Drouin, N., Sankaran, S., van Marrewijk, A., and Müller, R. 2021. *Megaproject Leaders: Reflections on Personal Life Stories*. Cheltenham: Edward Elgar.

Dvir, D. and Lechler, T. 2004. 'Plans are nothing, changing plans is everything: the impact of changes on project success'. *Research Policy*, 33(1): 1–15.

Edmondson, A. C. 2012a. *Teaming: How Organizations Learn, Innovate and Compete in the Knowledge Economy*. San Francisco, CA: Jossey-Bass.

Edmondson, A. C. 2012b. 'Teamwork on the fly'. *Harvard Business Review*, 90(2): 72–80.

Edmondson, A. C. 2019. *The Fearless Organization: Creating Psychological Safety in the Workplace for Learning, Innovation, and Growth*. Hoboken, NJ: Wiley.

Edmondson, A. C. and Harvey, J.-F. 2017. *Extreme Teaming: Lessons in Complex, Cross-Sector Leadership*. Bingley: Emerald.

Eggers, W. D. and O'Leary, J. 2009. *If We Can Put a Man on the Moon . . . Getting Big Things Done in Government*. Boston, MA: Harvard Business Press.

Einhorn, F., Marnewick, C., and Meredith, J. 2019. 'Achieving strategic benefits from business IT projects: the critical importance of using the business case across the entire project lifetime'. *International Journal of Project Management*, 37(8): 989–1002.

Elder-Vass, D. 2010. *The Causal Power of Social Structures: Emergence, Structure and Agency*. Cambridge: Cambridge University Press.

Emirbayer, M. and Mische, A. 1998. 'What is agency?'. *American Journal of Sociology*, 103(4): 962–1023.

Engelen, J. 2012. 'The Large Hadron Collider project: organizational and financial matters (of physics at the terascale)'. *Philosophical Transactions of the Royal Society A: Mathematical, Physical and Engineering Sciences*, 370(1961): 978–985.

Engwall, M. and Westling, G. 2004. 'Peripety in an R&D drama: capturing a turnaround in project dynamics'. *Organization Studies*, 25(9): 1557–1578.

Ethiraj, S. K., Kale, P., Krishnan, M. S., and Singh, J. V. 2005. 'Where do capabilities come from and how do they matter? A study in the software services industry'. *Strategic Management Journal*, 26(1): 25–45.

Eunomia. 2021. *Building Skills for Net Zero*. Peterborough: Construction Industry Training Board.

Evans, J. A., Kunda, G., and Barley, S. R. 2004. 'Beach time, bridge time, and billable hours: the temporal structure of technical contracting'. *Administrative Science Quarterly*, 49(1): 1–38.

Fayard, A.-L. and Weeks, J. 2014. 'Affordances for practice'. *Information and Organization*, 24(4): 236–249.

Feldman, M. S. and Pentland, B. T. 2003. 'Reconceptualizing organizational routines as a source of flexibility and change'. *Administrative Science Quarterly*, 48(1): 94–118.

Fellows, R. and Liu, A. 2016. 'Sensemaking in the cross-cultural contexts of projects'. *International Journal of Project Management*, 34(2): 246–257.

Fiedler, J. and Schuster, S. 2015. *Public Infrastructure Project Planning in Germany: The Case of the Elb Philharmonic in Hamburg*. Berlin: Hertie School of Governance.

Fiedler, J. and Wendle, A. 2015. *Public Infrastructure Project Planning in Germany: The Case of the BER Airport in Berlin-Brandenburg*. Berlin: Hertie School of Governance.

Fine, B. 1975. 'Tendering strategy'. In D. A. Turin (ed.), *Aspects of the Economics of Construction*: 202–221. London: Godwin.

Fleming, I. 2004. *Goldfinger*. London: Penguin Classics.

Fleming, Q. W. and Koppelman, J. M. 2016. *Earned Value Project Management* (4th edn). Newtown Square, PA: PMI.

Flyvbjerg, B. 2011. 'Over budget, over time, over and over again: managing major projects'. In P. W. G. Morris, J. K. Pinto, and J. Söderlund (eds), *The Oxford Handbook of Project Management*: 321–344. Oxford: Oxford University Press.

Flyvbjerg, B. 2016. 'The fallacy of beneficial ignorance: a test of Hirschman's hiding hand'. *World Development*, 84: 176–189.

Flyvbjerg, B. (ed.). 2017. *The Oxford Handbook of Megaproject Management*. Oxford: Oxford University Press.

Flyvbjerg, B., Bruzelius, N., and Rothengatter, W. 2003. *Megaprojects and Risk: An Anatomy of Ambition*. Cambridge: Cambridge University Press.

Flyvbjerg, B., Garbuio, M., and Lovallo, D. 2009. 'Delusion and deception in large infrastructure projects: two models for explaining and preventing executive disaster'. *California Management Review*, 51(2): 170–194.

Folayan, N. 2020. 'We need to look closer to home for a fairer society'. *Project*, Autumn: 16–17.

Fontevecchia, A. 2011. 'Exxon Mobil: a profit-making machine despite falling production'. *Forbes Magazine*, http://www.forbes.com (accessed 17 August 2021).

Forsyth, D. K. and Burt, C. D. B. 2008. 'Allocating time to future tasks: the effect of task segmentation on planning fallacy bias'. *Memory & Cognition*, 36(4): 791–798.

Forsyth, S. and Gavin, C. 2017. 'Developing "third wave" project leaders'. *Project*, Autumn: 54–55.

French, D. P., Sutton, S. R., Marteau, T. M., and Kinmonth, A. L. 2004. 'The impact of personal and social comparison information about health risk'. *British Journal of Health Psychology*, 9(2): 187–200.

Gabriel, Y. 2000. *Storytelling in Organizations: Facts, Fictions, and Fantasies*. Oxford: Oxford University Press.

Gaddis, P. O. 1959. 'The project manager'. *Harvard Business Review*, 37(3): 89–97.

Galbraith, J. R. 1977. *Organization Design*. Reading, MA: Addison-Wesley.

Galbraith, J. R. 1995. *Designing Organizations: An Executive Briefing on Strategy, Structure and Process*. San Francisco, CA: Jossey-Bass.

Galford, R. and Drapeau, A. S. 2003. 'The enemies of trust'. *Harvard Business Review*, 81(2): 88–95.

Gandhi, M. and Rutherford, G. W. 2020. 'Facial masking for Covid-19—potential for "variolation" as we await a vaccine'. *New England Journal of Medicine*, 383(18): e101.

Gann, D. M. and Salter, A. J. 2000. 'Innovation in project-based, service-enhanced firms: the construction of complex products and systems'. *Research Policy*, 29(7–8): 955–972.

Gardner, W. L., Avolio, B. J., Luthans, F., May, D. R., and Walumbwa, F. 2005. '"Can you see the real me?" A self-based model of authentic leader and follower development'. *The Leadership Quarterly*, 16(3): 343–372.

Gawer, A. and Cusumano, M. A. 2014. 'Industry platforms and ecosystem innovation'. *Journal of Product Innovation Management*, 31(3): 417–433.

Geraldi, J., Maylor, H., and Williams, T. 2011. 'Now, let's make it really complex (complicated): a systematic review of the complexities of projects'. *International Journal of Operations & Production Management*, 31(9): 966–990.

Gerstner, C. R. and Day, D. V. 1997. 'Meta-analytic review of leader–member exchange theory: correlates and construct issues'. *Journal of Applied Psychology*, 82(6): 827.

Giard, V. and Midler, C. 1993. *Pilotages de Projet et Entreprises: Diversités et convergences*. Paris: Economica.

Gil, N. 2009. 'Developing cooperative project client–supplier relationships: how much to expect from relational contracts?', *California Management Review*, 51(2): 144–169.

Gil, N. A., Pinto, J. K., and Smyth, H. 2011. 'Trust in relational contracting and as a critical organizational attribute'. In P. W. G. Morris, J. K. Pinto, and J. Söderlund (eds), *The Oxford Handbook of Project Management*: 438–462. Oxford: Oxford University Press.

Godbold, A. 2016. 'A tale of two disciplines'. *Project*, Spring: 62–63.

Goldberg, L. R. 1990. 'An alternative "description of personality": the big-five factor structure'. *Journal of Personality and Social Psychology*, 59(6): 1216.

Goldratt, E. M. 1997. *Critical Chain: A Business Novel*. Great Barrington MA: North River Press.

Goleman, D. 1998. 'What makes a leader?'. *Harvard Business Review*, 76(6): 93–102.

Goleman, D. 2000. 'Leadership that gets results'. *Harvard Business Review*, 78(2): 4–17.

Goodpasture, J. C. 2004. *Quantitative Methods in Project Management*. Boca Raton, FL: J. Ross Publishing.

Grabher, G. 2002. 'The project ecology of advertising: tasks, talents and teams'. *Regional Studies*, 36(3): 245–262.

Grabher, G. and Ibert, O. 2011. 'Project ecologies: a contextual view on temporary organizations'. In P. W. G. Morris, J. K. Pinto, and J. Söderlund (eds), *The Oxford Handbook of Project Management*: 175–200. Oxford: Oxford University Press.

Greenhalgh, T., Schmid, M. B., Czypionka, T., Bassler, D., and Gruer, L. 2020. 'Face masks for the public during the Covid-19 crisis'. *British Medical Journal*, 369.

Grenny, J., Maxfield, D., and Shimberg, A. 2007. 'How project leaders can overcome the crisis of silence'. *MIT Sloan Management Review*, 48(4): 46–52.

Gulino, M. L., Sergeeva, N., and Winch, G. 2020. 'Owner capabilities in social infrastructure projects: towards an expansion of the dynamic capabilities' framework'. *International Journal of Managing Projects in Business*, 13(6): 1263–1282.

Gulliver, F. R. 1987. 'Post-project appraisals pay'. *Harvard Business Review*, 65(2): 128–132.

Haji-Kazemi, S., Andersen, B., and Krane, H. P. 2013. 'A review on possible approaches for detecting early warning signs in projects'. *Project Management Journal*, 44(5): 55–69.

Hall, P. 1982. *Great Planning Disasters*. Berkeley, CA: University of California Press.

Hansen, M. T., Nohria, N., and Tierney, T. 1999. 'What's your strategy for managing knowledge?'. *The Knowledge Management Yearbook 2000–2001*, 77(2): 106–116.

Havermans, L. A., Van der Heijden, B. I., Savelsbergh, C., and Storm, P. 2019. 'Rolling into the profession: exploring the motivation and experience of becoming a project manager'. *Project Management Journal*, 50(3): 346–360.

Helfat, C. E. and Winter, S. G. 2011. 'Untangling dynamic and operational capabilities: strategy for the (N) ever-changing world'. *Strategic Management Journal*, 32(11): 1243–1250.

Helfat, C. E., Finkelstein, S., Mitchell, W., Peteraf, M. A., Singh, H., Teece, D. J., and Wineter, S. G. 2007. *Dynamic Capabilities: Understanding Strategic Change in Organizations*. Oxford: Blackwell.

Helm, J. and Remington, K. 2005. 'Effective project sponsorship an evaluation of the role of the executive sponsor in complex infrastructure projects by senior project managers'. *Project Management Journal*, 36(3): 51–61.

Henderson, N. 1987. *Channels and Tunnels: Reflections on Britain and Abroad*. London: Weidenfeld and Nicolson.

Henning, C. H. C. A. and Wald, A. 2019. 'Toward a wiser projectification: macroeconomic effects of firm-level project work'. *International Journal of Project Management*, 37(6): 807–819.

Herroelen, W. 2005. 'Project scheduling—theory and practice'. *Production and Operations Management*, 14(4): 413–432.

Herzberg, F. 1968. 'One more time: how do you motivate employees?' *Harvard Business Review*, 46(1): 53–62.

Hirschman, A., O. 1967. *Development Projects Observed*. Washington, DC: The Brookings Institution.

HMT. 2020. *The Green Book: Central Government Guidance on Appraisal and Evaluation*. London: HM Treasury.

Hobbs, B. and Petit, Y. 2017. 'Agile methods on large projects in large organizations'. *Project Management Journal*, 48(3): 3–19.

Hobday, M. 2000. 'The project-based organisation: an ideal form for managing complex products and systems?'. *Research Policy*, 29(7–8): 871–893.

Hodgson, D. and Briand, L. 2013. 'Controlling the uncontrollable: "agile" teams and illusions of autonomy in creative work'. *Work, Employment and Society*, 27(2): 308–325.

Hodgson, D. and Cicmil, S. 2006. *Making Projects Critical*. Basingstoke: Palgrave.

Hodgson, D. and Muzio, D. 2011. 'Prospects for professionalism in project management'. In P. W. G. Morris, J. K. Pinto, and J. Söderlund (eds), *The Oxford Handbook of Project Management*: 107–132. Oxford: Oxford University Press.

Hodgson, D., Paton, S., and Cicmil, S. 2011. 'Great expectations and hard times: the paradoxical experience of the engineer as project manager'. *International Journal of Project Management*, 29(4): 374–382.

Hodgson, D. E. and Paton, S. 2016. 'Understanding the professional project manager:

cosmopolitans, locals and identity work'. *International Journal of Project Management*, 34(2): 352–364.

Hoffman, E. and Boyle, J. 2017.' REAL knowledge at NASA: a knowledge services model for the modern project environment'. In S. Sankaran, R. Müller, and N. Drouin (eds), *Cambridge Handbook of Organizational Project Management*: 215–235. Cambridge: Cambridge University Press.

Hofstede, G. 2001. *Culture's Consequences: Comparing Values, Behaviors, Institutions, and Organizations across Nations* (2nd edn). Thousand Oaks, CA: SAGE.

Hone, D., Higgins, D., Galloway, I., and Kintrea, K. 2011. 'Delivering London 2012: organisation and programme.' *Proceedings of the Institution of Civil Engineers: Civil Engineering*, 164: 5–12.

Hood, C. and Dixon, R. 2015. *A Government that Worked Better and Cost Less?: Evaluating Three Decades of Reform and Change in UK Central Government*. Oxford: Oxford University Press.

House, R. J. and Aditya, R. N. 1997. 'The social scientific study of leadership: quo vadis?'. *Journal of Management*, 23(3): 409–473.

House, R. J., Hanges, P. J., Javidan, M., Dorfman, P. W., and Gupta, V. 2004. *Culture, Leadership, and Organizations: The GLOBE Study of 62 Societies*. Thousand Oaks, CA: Sage.

Huemann, M., Keegan, A., and Turner, J. R. 2007. 'Human resource management in the project-oriented company: a review'. *International Journal of Project Management*, 25(3): 315–323.

Hughes, M. 2013. 'The Victorian London sanitation projects and the sanitation of projects'. *International Journal of Project Management*, 31(5): 682–691.

Ibarra, H. and Lineback, K. 2005. 'What's your story?'. *Harvard Business Review*, 83(1): 64–71.

Ibarra, H., Ely, R., and Kolb, D. 2013. 'Women rising: the unseen barriers'. *Harvard Business Review*, 91(9): 60–66.

ICG. 2017. *From Transactions to Enterprises: A New Approach to Delivering High Performing Infrastructure*. London: Institution of Civil Engineers.

Ika, L. A., Love, P. E. D., and Pinto, J. K. 2020. 'Moving beyond the planning fallacy: the emergence of a new principle of project behavior'. *IEEE Transactions on Engineering Management*.

Ive, G. and Gruneberg, S. L. 2000. *The Economics of the Modern Construction Sector*. Basingstoke: Macmillan.

Jagersma, P. K. 2020. *On Becoming Extraordinary: Decoding Accenture and Other Star Professional Service Firms*. Amsterdam: Inspiration Press.

Janda, K. B. and Parag, Y. 2013. 'A middle-out approach for improving energy performance in buildings'. *Building Research & Information*, 41(1): 39–50.

Janis, I. L. 1972. *Victims of Groupthink: A Psychological Study of Foreign-Policy Decisions and Fiascoes*. Boston, MA: Houghton Mifflin.

Jefferson, T., Del Mar, C. B., Dooley, L., Ferroni, E., Al-Ansary, L. A., Bawazeer, G. A. et al. 2011. 'Physical interventions to interrupt or reduce the spread of respiratory viruses'. *Cochrane Database of Systematic Reviews*, 7.

Jeffries, M. and Rowlinson, S. 2016. *New Forms of Procurement: PPP and Relational Contracting in the 21st Century*. Abingdon: Routledge.

Jensen, M. and Meckling, W. 1976. 'Theory of the firm: management behavior, agency costs and capital structure'. *Journal of Financial Economics*, 3(4): 305–360.

Jenssen, J. I. and Jørgensen, G. 2004. 'How do corporate champions promote innovations?'. *International Journal of Innovation Management*, 8(01): 63–86.

Johnson, S. B. 1997. 'Three approaches to big technology: operations research, systems engineering, and project management'. *Technology and Culture*, 38(4): 891–919.

Johnson, S. B. 2013. 'Technical and institutional factors in the emergence of project management'. *International Journal of Project Management*, 31(5): 670–681.

Jonasson, H. I. and Ingason, H. T. 2013. *Project Ethics*. Farnham: Gower.

Judge, T. A., Bono, J. E., Ilies, R., and Gerhardt, M. W. 2002. 'Personality and leadership: a qualitative and quantitative review'. *Journal of Applied Psychology*, 87(4): 765.

Judge, T. A., Colbert, A. E., and Ilies, R. 2004. 'Intelligence and leadership: a quantitative review and test of theoretical propositions'. *Journal of Applied Psychology*, 89(3): 542.

Jørgensen, M., Mohagheghi, P., and Grimstad, S. 2017. 'Direct and indirect connections between type of contract and software project outcome'. *International Journal of Project Management*, 35(8): 1573–1586.

Kahneman, D., Slovic, P., and Tversky, A. 1982. *Judgment under Uncertainty: Heuristics and Biases*. Cambridge: Cambridge University Press.

Kaplan, S. 2008. 'Framing contests: strategy making under uncertainty'. *Organization Science*, 19(5): 729–752.

Kaplan, S. and Orlikowski, W. 2014. 'Beyond forecasting: creating new strategic narratives'. *MIT Sloan Management Review*, 56(1): 23–28.

Kasperson, J. X., Kasperson, R. E., Pidgeon, N., and Slovic, P. 2003. 'The social amplification of risk: assessing fifteen years of research and theory'. In N. Pidgeon, R. E. Kasperson, and P. Slovic (eds), *The Social Amplification of Risk*: 13–46. Cambridge: Cambridge University Press.

Kates, A. and Galbraith, J. R. 2007. *Designing Your Organization: Using the Star Model to Solve 5 Critical Design Challenges*. San Francisco, CA: Jossey-Bass.

Katzenbach, J. R. and Smith, D. K. 1993. 'The discipline of teams'. *Harvard Business Review*, 70(2): 111–120.

Kay, J. and King, M. 2020. *Radical Uncertainty: Decision-Making for an Unknowable Future*. London: Bridge Street Press.

Keller, A. 1966. 'The age of projectors'. *History Today*, 16(7): 467–474.

Kerzner, H. 2017. *Project Management: A Systems Approach to Planning, Scheduling, and Controlling* (12th edn). Hoboken, NJ: John Wiley & Sons.

Keynes, J. M. 1921. *A Treatise on Probability*. London: Macmillan.

Keynes, J. M. 1937. 'The general theory of employment'. *The Quarterly Journal of Economics*, 51(2): 209–223.

Keynes, J. M. 1961. *The General Theory of Employment, Interest and Money*. London: Macmillan.

Kilduff, M., Chiaburu, D. S., and Menges, J. I. 2010. 'Strategic use of emotional intelligence in organizational settings: exploring the dark side'. *Research in Organizational Behavior*, 30: 129–152.

King, A. and Crewe, I. 2013. *The Blunders of Our Governments*. London: Oneworld.

King, P. 1999. 'Introduction'. In E. Shackleton (ed.), *South*: 7–18. London: Pimlico.

Klein, B. and Meckling, W. 1958. 'Application of operations research to development decisions'. *Operations Research*, 6(3): 352–363.

Klein, G. 2007. 'Performing a project premortem'. *Harvard Business Review*, 85(9): 18–19.

Klein, G. 2017. *Sources of Power: How People Make Decisions* (20th anniversary edn). Cambridge, MA: MIT Press.

Kloppenborg, T. J. and Tesch, D. 2015. 'How executive sponsors influence project success'. *MIT Sloan Management Review*, 56(3): 27.

Kniffin, K. M., Detert, J. R., and Leroy, H. L. 2020. 'On leading and managing: synonyms or separate (and unequal)?'. *Academy of Management Discoveries*, 6(4): 544–571.

Knight, F. H. 1921. *Risk, Uncertainty and Profit*. New York: Houghton Mifflin.

Kopmann, J., Kock, A., Killen, C. P., and Gemünden, H. G. 2017. 'The role of project portfolio management in fostering both deliberate and emergent strategy'. *International Journal of Project Management*, 35(4): 557–570.

KPMG. 2019. *Independent Review of Crossrail: Governance*. London: KPMG.

Kraljic, P. 1983. 'Purchasing must become supply management'. *Harvard Business Review*, 61(5): 109–117.

Kreiner, K. 2020. 'Conflicting notions of a project: the battle between Albert O. Hirschman and Bent Flyvbjerg'. *Project Management Journal*, 51(4): 400–410.

Kujala, S., Artto, K., Aaltonen, P., and Turkulainen, V. 2010. 'Business models in project-based firms–towards a typology of solution-specific business models'. *International Journal of Project Management*, 28(2): 96–106.

Kutsch, E., Hall, M., and Turner, N. 2016. *Project Resilience: The Art of Noticing, Interpreting,* *Preparing, Containing and Recovering*. Abingdon: Routledge.

Kvalnes, Ø. 2017. 'Ethics in projects'. In S. Sankaran, R. Müller, and N. Drouin (eds), *Cambridge Handbook of Organizational Project Management*: 285–294. Cambridge: Cambridge University Press.

Kwak, Y. H., Sadatsafavi, H., Walewski, J., and Williams, N. L. 2015. 'Evolution of project based organization: a case study'. *International Journal of Project Management*, 33(8): 1652–1664.

Larson, L. and DeChurch, L. A. 2020. 'Leading teams in the digital age: four perspectives on technology and what they mean for leading teams'. *The Leadership Quarterly*, 31(1): 101377.

Larson, M. S. 1977. *The Rise of Professionalism: A Sociological Analysis*. Berkeley, CA: University of California Press.

Laufer, A., Hoffman, E. J., Russell, J.-S., and Cameron, W. S. 2015. 'What successful project managers do'. *MIT Sloan Management Review*, 56(3): 42–51.

Lechler, T. G. and Cohen, M. 2009. 'Exploring the role of steering committees in realizing value from project management'. *Project Management Journal*, 40(1): 42–54.

Lee, J., Bagheri, B., and Kao, H.-A. 2015. 'A cyber-physical systems architecture for industry 4.0-based manufacturing systems'. *Manufacturing Letters*, 3: 18–23.

Lenfle, S. and Loch, C. 2010. 'Lost roots: how project management came to emphasize control over flexibility and novelty'. *California Management Review*, 53(1): 32–55.

Ligthart, R., Oerlemans, L., and Noorderhaven, N. 2016. 'In the shadows of time: a case study of flexibility behaviors in an interorganizational project'. *Organization Studies*, 37(12): 1721–1743.

Linder, M. 1994. *Projecting Capitalism: A History of the Internationalization of the Construction Industry*. Westport, CT: Greenwood Press.

Locatelli, G., Mariani, G., Sainati, T., and Greco, M. 2017. 'Corruption in public projects and megaprojects: there is an elephant in the room!'. *International Journal of Project Management*, 35(3): 252–268.

Loch, C. and Kavadias, S. 2011. 'Implementing strategy through projects'. In P. W. G. Morris, J. K. Pinto, and J. Söderlund (eds), *The Oxford Handbook of Project Management*: 224–251. Oxford: Oxford University Press.

Loch, C., Mähring, M., and Sommer, S. 2017. 'Supervising projects you don't (fully) understand: lessons for effective project governance by steering committees'. *California Management Review*, 59(2): 45–67.

Lock, D. 2013. *Project Management* (10th edn). Farnham: Gower.

Logunov, D. Y., Dolzhikova, I. V., Zubkova, O. V., Tukhvatullin, A. I., Shcheblyakov, D. V., Dzharullaeva, A. S., Grousova, D. M., Erokhova, A. S., Kovyrshina, A. V., and Botikov, A. G. 2020. 'Safety and immunogenicity of an rAd26 and rAd5 vector-based heterologous prime-boost COVID-19 vaccine in two formulations: two open, non-randomised phase 1/2 studies from Russia'. *The Lancet*, 396(10255): 887–897.

Lombardi, B. and Rudd, D. 2013. 'The Type 45 Daring-class destroyer: how project management problems led to fewer ships'. *Naval War College Review*, 66(3): 99–116.

Lord, R. G. and Hall, R. J. 2005. 'Identity, deep structure and the development of leadership skill'. *The Leadership Quarterly*, 16(4): 591–615.

Lovallo, D. and Kahneman, D. 2003. 'Delusions of success'. *Harvard Business Review*, 81(7): 56–63.

Lowe, D. 2013. *Commercial Management: Theory and Practice*. Oxford: Wiley-Blackwell.

Lownds, S. 1998. *Fast Track to Change on the Heathrow Express*. London: Institute of Personnel and Development.

Lumley, R. 1980. 'Industrial relations on a large industrial construction site: the influence of security of employment'. *Journal of Management Studies*, 17(1): 68–81.

Lundin, R. A. and Söderholm, A. 1995. 'A theory of the temporary organization'. *Scandinavian Journal of Management*, 11(4): 437–455.

Lundin, R. A., Arvidsson, N., Brady, T., Ekstedt, E., Midler, C., and Sydow, J. 2015. *Managing and Working in Project Society: Institutional Challenges of Temporary Organizations*. Cambridge: Cambridge University Press.

Lurie, N., Saville, M., Hatchett, R., and Halton, J. 2020. 'Developing Covid-19 vaccines at pandemic speed'. *New England Journal of Medicine*, 382(21): 1969–1973.

Lyneis, J. M. and Ford, D. N. 2007. 'System dynamics applied to project management: a survey, assessment, and directions for future research'. *System Dynamics Review: The Journal of the System Dynamics Society*, 23(2–3): 157–189.

Maister, D. H. 1982. 'Balancing the professional service firm'. *Sloan Management Review*, 24(1): 15–29.

Maister, D. H. 1993. *Managing the Professional Service firm*. New York, NY: Free Press.

Mankins, J. C. 2009. 'Technology readiness assessments: a retrospective'. *Acta Astronautica*, 65(9–10): 1216–1223.

Manning, S. and Sydow, J. 2011. 'Projects, paths, and practices: sustaining and leveraging project-based relationships'. *Industrial and Corporate Change*, 20(5): 1369–1402.

March, J. G. 1994. *Primer on Decision Making: How Decisions Happen*. New York, NY: Free Press.

Markowitz, H. 1952. 'Portfolio selection'. *Journal of Finance*, 7(1): 77–91.

Marnewick, C. and Marnewick, A. L. 2019. 'The demands of industry 4.0 on project teams'. *IEEE Transactions on Engineering Management*, 67(3): 941–949.

Martin, R., Thomas, G., Legood, A., and Dello Russo, S. 2018. 'Leader–member exchange (LMX) differentiation and work outcomes: conceptual clarification and critical review'. *Journal of Organizational Behavior*, 39(2): 151–168.

Maslach, C., Leiter, M. P., and Schaufeli, W. 2009. 'Measuring burnout'. In S. Cartwright and C. L. Cooper (eds), *Organizational Well-Being*: 86–108. Oxford: Oxford University Press.

Massa, L., Tucci, C. L., and Afuah, A. 2017. 'A critical assessment of business model research'. *Academy of Management Annals*, 11(1): 73–104.

Masten, S. E., Meehan Jr, J. W., and Snyder, E. A. 1991. 'The costs of organization'. *Journal of Law Economics and Organization*, 7: 1–25.

Maule, J. 2008. 'Risk communication in organizations'. In G. P. Hodgkinson and W. H. Starbuck (eds), *The Oxford Handbook of Organizational Decision Making*: 517–533. Oxford: Oxford University Press.

Mayer, C. P. 2018. *Prosperity: Better Business Makes the Greater Good*. Oxford: Oxford University Press.

Mayer, J. D., Roberts, R. D., and Barsade, S. G. 2008. 'Human abilities: emotional intelligence'. *Annual Review of Psychology*, 59: 507–536.

Maytorena-Sanchez, E. 2013. 'Perspectives on managing risk and uncertainty'. In D. Lowe (ed.), *Commercial Management: Theory and Practice*: 108–131. Oxford: Wiley-Blackwell.

Maytorena-Sanchez, E., Winch, G. M., Freeman, J., and Kiely, T. 2007. 'The influence of experience and information search styles on project risk identification performance'. *IEEE Transactions on Engineering Management*, 54(2): 315–326.

Mazzucato, M. 2021. *Mission Economy: A Moonshot Guide to Changing Capitalism*. London: Allen Lane.

McCartney, L. 1988. *Friends in High Places: The Bechtel Story*. New York, NY: Simon & Schuster.

McClory, S., Read, M., and Labib, A. 2017. 'Conceptualising the lessons-learned process in project management: towards a triple-loop learning framework'. *International Journal of Project Management*, 35(7): 1322–1335.

McGrath, S. K. and Whitty, S. J. 2019. 'Do steering committees really steer?'. *International Journal of Managing Projects in Business*, 12(3): 785–807.

McKevitt, D., Carbery, R., and Lyons, A. 2017. 'A profession but not a career? Work identity and career satisfaction in project management'. *International Journal of Project Management*, 35(8): 1673–1682.

McKinsey. 2017. *Reinventing Construction: A Route to Higher Productivity*. McKinsey Global Institute.

McKinsey. 2020. *Diversity Wins: How Inclusion Matters*. McKinsey & Co.

Meredith, J. R. and Shafer, S., M. 2021. *Project Management in Practice* (7th edn). Hoboken, NJ: Wiley.

Meredith, J. R., Mantel, S. J., and Shafer, S. M. 2017. *Project Management: A Strategic Managerial Approach* (10th edn). Hoboken, NJ: Wiley.

Merrow, E. W. 2011. *Industrial Megaprojects: Concepts, Strategies, and Practices for Success*. Hoboken, NJ: Wiley.

Merrow, E. W. and Nandurdikar, N. 2018. *Leading Complex Projects: A Data-Driven Approach to Mastering the Human Side of Project Management*. Hoboken, NJ: Wiley.

Merrow, E. W., Sonnhalter, K. A., Somanchi, R., and Griffith, A. F. 2009. *Productivity in the UK Engineering Construction Industry*. London: Department for Business, Innovation and Skills.

Middlemas, R. K. 1963. *The Master Builders*. London: Hutchinson.

Midler, C. 1995. '"Projectification" of the firm: the Renault case'. *Scandinavian Journal of Management*, 11(4): 363–375.

Miller, R. and Lessard, D. R. 2000. *The Strategic Management of Large Engineering Projects: Shaping Institutions, Risks, and Governance*. Cambridge, MA: MIT Press.

Miller, R., Hobday, M., Leroux-Demers, T., and Olleros, X. 1995. 'Innovation in complex systems industries: the case of flight simulation'. *Industrial and Corporate Change*, 4(2): 363–400.

Mills, G., Evans, D., and Candish, C. 2020. 'Anglian Water @one Alliance: a new approach to supply chain management'. In S. Pryke (ed.), *Successful Construction Supply Chain Management: Concepts and Cases* (2nd edn): 237–250. Oxford: Wiley Blackwell.

Mintzberg, H. 1979. *The Structuring of Organizations: A Synthesis of the Research*. Englewood Cliffs, NJ: Prentice-Hall.

Mintzberg, H. 1987. 'The strategy concept I: five Ps for strategy'. *California Management Review*, 30(1): 11–24.

Mintzberg, H. 1994. *The Rise and Fall of Strategic Planning*. New York, NY: Prentice Hall.

Miterev, M., Mancini, M., and Turner, R. 2017. 'Towards a design for the project-based organization'. *International Journal of Project Management*, 35(3): 479–491.

Momeni, K. and Martinsuo, M. 2019. 'Integrating services into solution offerings in the sales work of project-based firms'. *International Journal of Project Management*, 37(8): 956–967.

Morrell, D. 1987. *Indictment: Power and Politics in the Construction Industry*. London: Faber.

Morrell, M. and Capparell, S. 2001. *Shackleton's Way: Leadership Lessons from the Great Antarctic Explorer*. London: Nicholas Brealey.

Morris, P. W. G. 1994. *The Management of Projects*. London: Thomas Telford.

Morris, P. W. G. 2012. 'Cleland and King: project management and the systems approach'. *International Journal of Managing Projects in Business*, 5(4): 634–642.

Morris, P. W. G. 2013. *Reconstructing Project Management*. Chichester: Wiley-Blackwell.

Morris, P. W. G. and Geraldi, J. 2011. 'Managing the institutional context for projects'. *Project Management Journal*, 42(6): 20–32.

Morris, P. W. G. and Jamieson, A. 2005. 'Moving from corporate strategy to project strategy'. *Project Management Journal*, 36(4): 5–18.

Morris, P. W. G. and Pinto, J. K. 2004. *The Wiley Guide to Managing Projects*. Hoboken, NJ: Wiley.

Morris, P. W. G., Pinto, J. K., and Söderlund, J. 2011. *The Oxford Handbook of Project Management*. Oxford: Oxford University Press.

Morrison, R. 2012. *The Principles of Project Finance*. Farnham: Gower.

Mullins, J. W. 2007. 'Discovering "Unk-Unks"'. *MIT Sloan Management Review*, 48(4): 17.

Murray, P. 2004. *The Saga of the Sydney Opera House: The Dramatic Story of the Design and Construction of the Icon of Modern Australia*. London: Spon.

Müller, M. 2015. '(Im-) Mobile policies: why sustainability went wrong in the 2014 Olympics in Sochi'. *European Urban and Regional Studies*, 22(2): 191–209.

Müller, R. and Turner, J. R. 2010. *Project-Oriented Leadership*. Farnham: Gower.

Müller, R., Glückler, J., and Aubry, M. 2013. 'A relational typology of project management offices'. *Project Management Journal*, 44(1): 59–76.

Nakhla, M. and Soler, L.-G. 1996. 'Pilotage de Projet et Contrats Internes'. *Revue Française de Gestion* 110: 17–29.

NAO. 2009. *Providing Anti-Air Warfare Capability: The Type 45 Destroyer*. London: National Audit Office.

NAO. 2010. *Assurance for High Risk Projects*. London: National Audit Office.

NAO. 2019. *Completing Crossrail*. London: National Audit Office.

Nijhuis, S., Vrijhoef, R., and Kessels, J. 2018. 'Tackling project management competence research'. *Project Management Journal*, 49(3): 62–81.

Ninan, J. and Sergeeva, N. 2021. 'Labyrinth of labels: narrative constructions of promoters and protesters in megaprojects'. *International Journal of Project Management*, 39(5): 496–506.

Ochieng, E. G. and Price, A. D. F. 2010. 'Managing cross-cultural communication in multicultural construction project teams: the case of Kenya and UK'. *International Journal of Project Management*, 28(5): 449–460.

O'Connell, D., Hickerson, K., and Pillutla, A. 2011. 'Organizational visioning: an integrative review'. *Group & Organization Management*, 36(1): 103–125.

ODA. 2007. *Equality and Diversity Strategy*. London: Olympic Delivery Authority.

Office of Rail Regulation. 2008. *Report of ORR's Investigation into Engineering Overruns*. London: Office of Rail Regulation.

Olander, S. and Landin, A. 2008. 'A comparative study of factors affecting the external stakeholder management process'. *Construction management and economics*, 26(6): 553–561.

Parag, Y. and Janda, K. B. 2014. 'More than filler: middle actors and socio-technical change in the energy system from the "middle-out"'. *Energy Research & Social Science*, 3: 102–112.

Patanakul, P. and Pinto, J., K. 2017. 'Program management'. In S. Sankaran, R. Müller, and N. Drouin (eds), *Cambridge Handbook of Organizational Project Management*: 106–118. Cambridge: Cambridge University Press.

Patanakul, P. and Shenhar, A. J. 2012. 'What project strategy really is: the fundamental building block in strategic project management'. *Project Management Journal*, 43(1): 4–20.

Paver, M. 2018. 'Will data science change project management forever? A future vision'. *PM World Journal*, VII (IX): 1–6.

PDATF 2020. *Transforming Project Performance with Data: Unlocking the Power of Data to Deliver Project Success*. London: Project Data Analytics Task Force.

Peck, M. J. and Scherer, F. M. 1962. *The Weapons Acquisition Process; An Economic Analysis.* Boston, MA: Harvard University.

Peeples, L. 2020. 'What the data say about wearing face masks'. *Nature*, 586: 186–189.

Pellegrinelli, S. 2011. 'What's in a name: Project or programme?'. *International Journal of Project Management*, 29(2): 232–240.

Penrose, E. T. 1995. *The Theory of the Growth of the Firm.* Oxford: Oxford University Press.

Pentland, A. S. 2012. 'The new science of building great teams'. *Harvard Business Review*, 90(4): 60–69.

Perkin, H. 1989. *The Rise of Professional Society: England since 1880.* London: Routledge.

Persky, J. 2001. 'Cost–benefit analysis and the classical creed'. *Journal of Economic Perspectives*, 15(4): 199–208.

Peter, L. J. and Hull, R. 1969. *The Peter Principle.* London: Souvenir Press.

Peters, T. J. and Waterman, R. H. J. 1982. *In Search of Excellence: Lessons from America's Best-Run Companies.* New York, NY: Harper & Row.

Piddington, J., Nicol, S., Garrett, H., and Custard, M. 2020. *The Housing Stock of the United Kingdom.* Watford: BRE Trust.

Pinney, B. W. 2001. *Projects, Management and Protean Times: Engineering Enterprise in the United States 1870–1960.* Boston, MA: Massachusetts Institute of Technology.

Pinto, J. K. 1998. *The Project Management Institute: Project Management Handbook.* San Francisco, CA: Jossey-Bass Publishers.

Pinto, J. K. 2020. *Project Management: Achieving Competitive Advantage* (5th edn). London: Pearson.

Pinto, J. K., Dawood, S., and Pinto, M. B. 2014. 'Project management and burnout: implications of the demand–control–support model on project-based work'. *International Journal of Project Management*, 32(4): 578–589.

Pisano, G. P. 1997. *The Development Factory: Unlocking the Potential of Process Innovation.* Boston, MA: Harvard Business School Press.

Pisotska, V. 2022. *The Management of Tensions and Paradoxes in Creative Industries.* Rome: LUISS Guido Carli University.

Pitkethly, R. 2003. 'Analysing the environment'. In D. O. Faulkner and A. Campbell (eds), *The Oxford Handbook of Strategy*: 231–266. Oxford: Oxford University Press.

Pollack, J. and Matous, P. 2019. 'Testing the impact of targeted team building on project team communication using social network analysis'. *International Journal of Project Management*, 37(3): 473–484.

Poppo, L. and Zenger, T. 2002. 'Do formal contracts and relational governance function as substitutes or complements?'. *Strategic Management Journal*, 23(8): 707–725.

Prencipe, A., Davies, A., and Hobday, M. 2003. *The Business of Systems Integration.* Oxford: Oxford University Press.

Pryke, S. 2012. *Social Network Analysis in Construction.* Chichester: Wiley-Blackwell.

Pryke, S., Badi, S., Almadhoob, H., Soundararaj, B., and Addyman, S. 2018. 'Self-organizing networks in complex infrastructure projects'. *Project Management Journal*, 49(2): 18–41.

Puranam, P. 2018. *The Microstructure of Organizations* (1st edn). Oxford: Oxford University Press.

Ramasesh, R. V. and Browning, T. R. 2014. 'A conceptual framework for tackling knowable unknown unknowns in project management'. *Journal of Operations Management*, 32(4): 190–204.

Ramirez, R. 1999. 'Value co-production: intellectual origins and implications for practice and research'. *Strategic Management Journal*, 20(1): 49–65.

Randhawa, K., Josserand, E., Schweitzer, J., and Logue, D. 2017. 'Knowledge collaboration between organizations and online communities: the role of open innovation intermediaries'. *Journal of Knowledge Management*, 21(6): 1293–1318.

Reeves, K. 2002. 'Construction business systems in Japan: general contractors and subcontractors'. *Building Research & Information*, 30(6): 413–424.

Reisner, M. P. 1986. *Cadillac Desert: The American West and Its Disappearing Water.* New York, NY: Viking.

Ren, X. 2008. 'Architecture as branding: mega project developments in Beijing'. *Built Environment*, 34(4): 517–531.

Riis, E., Hellström, M. M., and Wikström, K. 2019. 'Governance of projects: generating value by linking projects with their permanent organisation'. *International Journal of Project Management*, 37(5): 652–667.

Rimmer, P. J. 1988. 'The internationalization of engineering consultancies: problems of breaking into the club'. *Environment and Planning A*, 20(6): 761–788.

Roehrich, J. K., Davies, A., Frederiksen, L., and Sergeeva, N. 2019. 'Management innovation in complex products and systems: the case of integrated project teams'. *Industrial Marketing Management*, 79: 84–93.

Roehrich, J. K., Selviaridis, K., Kalra, J., Van der Valk, W., and Fang, F. 2020. 'Inter-organizational governance: a review, conceptualisation and extension'. *Production Planning & Control*, 31(6): 453–469.

Royer, I. 2003. 'Why bad projects are so hard to kill'. *Harvard Business Review*, 81(2): 48–57.

Rubin, P. H. 1990. *Managing Business Transactions: Controlling the Cost of Coordinating, Communicating, and Decision Making*. New York NY: Free Press.

Sabbagh, K. 2000. *Power into Art*. London: Allen Lane.

Sadeh, A., Dvir, D., and Shenhar, A. 2000. 'The role of contract type in the success of R&D defense projects under increasing uncertainty'. *Project Management Journal*, 31(3): 14–22.

Sandron, D. and Tallon, A. 2020. *Notre Dame Cathedral: Nine Centuries of History*. University Park, PA: Pennsylvania State University Press.

Sankaran, S., Müller, R., and Drouin, N. (eds). 2017. *Cambridge Handbook of Organizational Project Management*. Cambridge: Cambridge University Press.

Saunders, A. 2019. 'The show must go on'. *Project*, Winter: 46–51.

Savage, L. J. 1954. *The Foundations of Statistics*. New York, NY: Wiley.

Sawyer, J. E. 1952. 'Entrepreneurial error and economic growth'. *Explorations in Economic History*, 4(4): 199.

Schein, E. H. 1992. *Organizational Culture and Leadership* (2nd edn). San Francisco,CA: Jossey-Bass.

Schmidt, F. L. and Hunter, J. E. 1998. 'The validity and utility of selection methods in personnel psychology: practical and theoretical implications of 85 years of research findings'. *Psychological Bulletin*, 124(2): 262.

Schoemaker, P. J. H. and Day, G. S. 2009. 'How to make sense of weak signals'. *MIT Sloan Management Review*, 50(2): 81–89.

Schutz, A. 1967. *The Phenomenology of the Social World*. Evanston, IL: Northwestern University Press.

Schwab, K. 2018. *Shaping the Future of the Fourth Industrial Revolution: A Guide to Building a Better World*. London: Portfolio Penguin.

Schön, D. A. 1983. *The Reflective Practitioner: How Professionals Think in Action*. New York, NY: Basic Books.

Scott, W. R., Levitt, R. E., and Orr, R. J. 2011. *Global Projects: Institutional and Political Challenges*. Cambridge: Cambridge University Press.

Sen, A. K. 1977. 'Rational fools: a critique of the behavioral foundations of economic theory'. *Philosophy & Public Affairs*, 6(4): 317–344.

Senge, P. 1990. *The Fifth Discipline: The Art and Practice of the Learning Organization*. New York: Doubleday.

Sergeeva, N. 2019. 'Towards a more flexible approach to governance to allow innovation: the case of UK infrastructure'. *International Journal of Managing Projects in Business*, 13(1): 1–19.

Sergeeva, N. and Ali, S. 2020. 'The role of the Project Management Office (PMO) in stimulating innovation in projects initiated by owner and operator organizations'. *Project Management Journal*, 51(4): 440–451.

Sergeeva, N. and Davies, A. 2021. 'Storytelling from the authentic leader of High Speed 2 (HS2) Ltd. Infrastructure megaproject in the United Kingdom'. In N. Drouin, S. Sankaran, A. van Marrewijk, and R. Müller (eds), *Life Stories of Megaproject Leaders: Insights from Personal Perspectives*: 47–61. Cheltenham: Edward Elgar.

Sergeeva, N. and Green, S. D. 2019. 'Managerial identity work in action: performative narratives and anecdotal stories of innovation'. *Construction Management and Economics*, 37(5): 636–651.

Sergeeva, N. and Roehrich, J. K. 2018. 'Temporary multi-organizations: constructing identities to realize performance improvements'. *Industrial Marketing Management*, 75: 184–192.

Sergeeva, N. and Winch, G. M. 2020. 'Narrative interactions: how project-based firms respond to government narratives of innovation'. *International Journal of Project Management*, 38(6): 379–387.

Sergeeva, N. and Winch, G. M. 2021. 'Project narratives that potentially perform and change the future'. *Project Management Journal*, 52(3): 264–277.

Serrador, P. and Pinto, J. K. 2015. 'Does Agile work?–a quantitative analysis of Agile project success'. *International Journal of Project Management*, 33(5): 1040–1051.

Shackleton, E. 1999. *South: The Story of Shackleton's Last Expedition 1914–17*. London: Pimlico.

Shenhar, A. J. and Dvir, D. 2007. *Reinventing Project Management: The Diamond Approach to Successful Growth and Innovation*. Boston, MA: Harvard Business School Press.

Sherif, M. 1958. 'Superordinate goals in the reduction of intergroup conflict'. *American Journal of Sociology*, 63(4): 349–356.

Silzer, R. F. and Borman, W. C. 2017. 'The potential for leadership'. In D. G. Collings, K. Mellahi, and W. F. Cascio (eds), *The Oxford Handbook of Talent Management*: 87–114. Oxford: Oxford University Press.

Simard, M., Aubry, M., and Laberge, D. 2018. 'The utopia of order versus chaos: a conceptual framework for governance, organizational design and governmentality in projects'. *International Journal of Project Management*, 36(3): 460–473.

Simon, H. A. 1955. 'A behavioral model of rational choice'. *The Quarterly Journal of Economics*, 69(1): 99–118.

Simon, H. A. 1962. 'The architecture of complexity'. *Proceedings of the American Philosophical Society*, 106(6): 467–482.

Simon, H. A. 1996. *The Sciences of the Artificial* (3rd edn). Cambridge, MA: MIT Press.

Smit, T. 2000. *The Lost Gardens of Heligan* (Rev. edn). London: Gollancz.

Smit, T. 2001. *Eden*. London: Bantam.

Smith, A. 1776. *An Inquiry into the Nature and Causes of the Wealth of Nations*. London: Strahan & Cadell.

Smits, K., Van Marrewijk, A., and Veenswijk, M. 2015. 'The collabyrinth of cross-cultural collaboration in the Panama Canal megaproject'. In A. Van Marrewijk (ed.), *Inside Megaprojects: Understanding Cultural Practices in Project Management*: 103–136. Copenhagen: CBS Press.

Snowden, D. J. and Boone, M. E. 2007. 'A leader's framework for decision making'. *Harvard Business Review*, 85(11): 68–76.

Söderlund, J. and Sydow, J. 2019. 'Projects and institutions: towards understanding their mutual constitution and dynamics'. *International Journal of Project Management*, 37(2): 259–268.

Söderlund, J. and Tell, F. 2009. 'The P-form organization and the dynamics of project competence: project epochs in Asea/ABB, 1950–2000'. *International Journal of Project Management*, 27(2): 101–112.

Stalk, G. and Hout, T. M. 1990. *Competing against Time: How Time-Based Competition Is Reshaping Global Markets*. New York: The Free Press.

Staw, B. M. and Ross, J. 1989. 'Understanding behavior in escalation situations'. *Science*, 246(4927): 216–220.

Stephens, S. 2003. 'The unwitting wisdom of Rumsfeld's unknowns'. *Financial Times*, 12 December 2003.

Stewart, G. L. 2006. 'A meta-analytic review of relationships between team design features and team performance'. *Journal of Management*, 32(1): 29–55.

Stewart, R. and Barsoux, J.-L. 1994. *The Diversity of Management: Twelve Managers Talking*. Basingstoke: Macmillan.

Stinchcombe, A. L. 1985. 'Contracts as hierarchical documents'. In A. L. Stinchcombe and C. A. Heimer (eds), *Organization Theory and Project Management: Administering Uncertainty in Norwegian Offshore Oil*: 121–171. Oslo: Oslo University Press.

Strauss, A. 1988. 'The articulation of project work: an organizational process'. *Sociological Quarterly*, 29(2): 163–178.

Stride, P. 2019. *The Thames Tideway Tunnel: Preventing Another Great Stink*. Stroud: The History Press.

Sudjic, D. 2001. *Blade of Light: The Story of London's Millennium Bridge*. London: Penguin.

Sun, J. and Zhang, P. 2011. 'Owner organization design for mega industrial construction projects'. *International Journal of Project Management*, 29(7): 828–833.

Svejvig, P. and Andersen, P. 2015. 'Rethinking project management: a structured literature review with a critical look at the brave new world'. *International Journal of Project Management*, 33(2): 278–290.

Sydow, J. and Staber, U. 2002. 'The institutional embeddedness of project networks: the case of content production in German television'. *Regional Studies*, 36(3): 215–227.

Syed, M. 2019. *Rebel Ideas: The Power of Diverse Thinking*. London: John Murray.

Taleb, N. N. 2007. *The Black Swan: The Impact of the Highly Improbable*. New York, NY: Random House.

Tao, F., Qi, Q., Wang, L., and Nee, A. Y. C. 2019. 'Digital twins and cyber–physical systems toward smart manufacturing and industry 4.0: correlation and comparison'. *Engineering*, 5(4): 653–661.

Taylor, A. R. 2012. 'The square kilometre array'. *Proceedings of the International Astronomical Union*, 8(S291): 337–341.

Taylor, T. and Ford, D. N. 2006. 'Tipping point failure and robustness in single development projects'. *System Dynamics Review: The Journal of the System Dynamics Society*, 22(1): 51–71.

Thamhain, H. J. and Wilemon, D. L. 1975. 'Conflict management in project life cycles'. *Sloan Management Review*, 16(3): 31–50.

Thomas, L. D. W., Autio, E., and Gann, D. M. 2014. 'Architectural leverage: putting platforms in context'. *Academy of Management Perspectives*, 28(2): 198–219.

Thompson, J. D. 1967. *Organizations in Action: Social Science Bases of Administrative Theory*. New York, NY: McGraw-Hill.

Thurm, D. 2005. 'Master of the house: why a company should take control of its building projects'. *Harvard Business Review*, 83(10): 120–129.

Tidd, J. and Bessant, J. 2021. *Managing Innovation: Integrating Technological, Market and Organizational Change* (7th edn). Chichester: Wiley.

Tikkanen, H., Kujala, J., and Artto, K. 2007. 'The marketing strategy of a project-based firm: the Four Portfolios framework'. *Industrial Marketing Management*, 36(2): 194–205.

Tinsley, C. H. and Ely, R. J. 2018. 'What most people get wrong about men and women: research shows the sexes aren't so different'. *Harvard Business Review*, 96(3): 114–121.

Tomory, L. 2011.' Building the first gas network, 1812–1820'. *Technology and Culture*, 52(1): 75–102.

Tomory, L. 2015. 'London's water supply before 1800 and the roots of the networked city'. *Technology and Culture*, 56(2): 704–737.

Tuckman, B. W. 1965. 'Developmental sequence in small groups'. *Psychological Bulletin*, 63(6): 384–399.

Turner, J. R. 1993. *The Handbook of Project-Based Management: Improving the Processes for Achieving Strategic Objectives*. Maidenhead: McGraw-Hill.

Turner, J. R. 2014. *The Handbook of Project-Based Management: Leading Strategic Change in Organizations* (4th edn). London: McGraw-Hill.

Turner, J. R. and Keegan, A. 2001. 'Mechanisms of governance in the project-based organization: roles of the broker and steward'. *European Management Journal*, 19(3): 254–267.

Turner, J. R. and Müller, R. 2004. 'Communication and co-operation on projects between the project owner as principal and the project manager as agent'. *European Management Journal*, 22(3): 327–336.

Turner, J. R. and Müller, R. 2017. 'The governance of organizational project management'. In S. Sankaran, R. Muller, and N. Drouin (eds), *The Cambridge Handbook of Organizational Project Management*: 75–91. Cambridge: Cambridge University Press.

ul Musawir, A., Abd-Karim, S. B., and Mohd-Danuri, M. S. 2020. 'Project governance and its role in enabling organizational strategy implementation: a systematic literature review'. *International Journal of Project Management*, 38(1): 1–16.

UNEP. 2020. *2020 Global Status Report for Buildings and Construction: Towards a Zero-Emission, Efficient and Resilient Buildings and Construction Sector*. Nairobi: United Nations Environment Programme.

Unger, B. N., Gemünden, H. G., and Aubry, M. 2012. 'The three roles of a project portfolio management office: their impact on portfolio management execution and success'. *International Journal of Project Management*, 30(5): 608–620.

Vaara, E. and Tienari, J. 2011. 'On the narrative construction of multinational corporations: an antenarrative analysis of legitimation and resistance in a cross-border merger'. *Organization Science*, 22(2): 370–390.

Vaara, E., Sonenshein, S., and Boje, D. 2016. 'Narratives as sources of stability and change in organizations: approaches and directions for future research'. *The Academy of Management Annals*, 10(1): 495–560.

Van de Ven, A. H. and Lifschitz, A. 2013. 'Rational and reasonable microfoundations of markets and institutions'. *Academy of Management Perspectives*, 27(2): 156–172.

Van Marrewijk, A. 2017. 'The multivocality of symbols: a longitudinal study of the symbolic dimensions of the high-speed train megaproject (1995–2015)'. *Project Management Journal*, 48(6): 47–59.

Vaughan, D. 1996. *The Challenger Launch Decision: Risky Technology, Culture, and Deviance at NASA*. Chicago, IL: The University of Chicago Press.

Veenswijk, M., Van Marrewijk, A., and Boersma, K. 2010. 'Developing new knowledge in collaborative relationships in megaproject alliances: organising reflection in the Dutch construction sector'. *International Journal of Knowledge Management Studies*, 4(2): 216–232.

Volden, G. H. 2019. 'Assessing public projects' value for money: an empirical study of the usefulness of cost-benefit analyses in decision-making'. *International Journal of Project Management*, 37(4): 549–564.

Volden, G. H. and Samset, K. 2017. 'Governance of major public investment projects: principles and practices in six countries'. *Project Management Journal*, 48(3): 90–108.

Volkoff, O. and Strong, D. M. 2013. 'Critical realism and affordances: theorizing IT-associated organizational change processes'. *MIS Quarterly*, 37(3): 819–834.

Waller, D. 2020. 'The big interview: Sir Tim Smit'. *Project*, Spring: 32–35.

Walton, M. 1997. *Car: A Drama of the American Workplace*. New York NY: W. W. Norton.

Watson, G. 1988. *The Civils: The Story of the Institution of Civil Engineers*. London: Thomas Telford.

Wearne, S. and White-Hunt, K. 2014. *Managing the Urgent and Unexpected: Twelve Project Cases and a Commentary*. Farnham: Gower.

Weaver, W. 1948. 'Science and complexity'. *American Scientist*, 36: 536–544.

Weick, K. E. 1995. *Sensemaking in Organizations*. Thousand Oaks, CA: Sage.

Wheelwright, S. C. and Clark, K. B. 1992. *Revolutionizing Product Development: Quantum Leaps in Speed, Efficiency, and Quality*. New York: Free Press.

Whitley, R. 2006. 'Project-based firms: new organizational form or variations on a theme?'. *Industrial and Corporate Change*, 15(1): 77–99.

Whitley, R. 2007. *Business Systems and Organizational Capabilities: the Institutional Structuring of Competitive Competencies*. Oxford: Oxford University Press.

Whittington, R., Pettigrew, A., Peck, S., Fenton, E., and Conyon, M. 1999. 'Change and complementarities in the new competitive landscape: a European panel study, 1992–1996'. *Organization Science*, 10(5): 583–600.

Whyte, J. 2019. 'How digital information transforms project delivery models'. *Project Management Journal*, 50(2): 177–194.

Wikström, K., Hellström, M., Artto, K., Kujala, J., and Kujala, S. 2009. 'Services in project-based firms–four types of business logic'. *International Journal of Project Management*, 27(2): 113–122.

Williams, T. 2008. 'How do organizations learn lessons from projects—and do they?'. *IEEE Transactions on Engineering Management*, 55(2): 248–266.

Williams, T., Klakegg, O. J., Walker, D. H. T., Andersen, B., and Magnussen, O. M. 2012. 'Identifying and acting on early warning signs in complex projects'. *Project Management Journal*, 43(2): 37–53.

Williams, T. M. 2002. *Modelling Complex Projects*. Chichester: Wiley.

Williamson, O. E. 1985. *The Economic Institutions of Capitalism*. New York, NY: Free Press.

Wilson, C., Pettifor, H., and Chryssochoidis, G. 2018. 'Quantitative modelling of why and how homeowners decide to renovate energy efficiently'. *Applied Energy*, 212: 1333–1344.

Winch, G. M. 1994. *Managing Production: Engineering Change and Stability*. Oxford: Oxford University Press.

Winch, G. M. 1998. 'Zephyrs of creative destruction: understanding the management of innovation in construction'. *Building Research & Information*, 26(5): 268–279.

Winch, G. M. 2000. 'Institutional reform in British construction: partnering and private finance'. *Building Research & Information*, 28(2): 141–155.

Winch, G. M. 2001. 'Governing the project process: a conceptual framework'. *Construction Management and Economics*, 19(8): 799–808.

Winch, G. M. 2003. 'How innovative is construction? Comparing aggregated data on construction innovation and other sectors—a case of apples and pears'. *Construction Management and Economics*, 21(6): 651–654.

Winch, G. M. 2004. 'Managing project stakeholders'. In P. W. G. Morris and J. K. Pinto (eds), *The Wiley Guide to Managing Projects*: 321–339. Hoboken, NJ: Wiley.

Winch, G. M. 2005. 'Managing complex connective processes: innovation broking'. In A. Manseau and R. Shields (eds), *Building Tomorrow: Innovation in Construction and Engineering*: 81–100. Aldershot: Ashgate.

Winch, G. M. 2010. *Managing Construction Projects: An Information Processing Approach* (2nd edn). Oxford: Wiley-Blackwell.

Winch, G. M. 2013. 'Escalation in major projects: lessons from the Channel Fixed Link'. *International Journal of Project Management*, 31(5): 724–734.

Winch, G. M. 2014. 'Three domains of project organising'. *International Journal of Project Management*, 32(5): 721–731.

Winch, G. M. 2015. 'Project organizing as a problem in information'. *Construction Management and Economics*, 33(2): 106–116.

Winch, G. M. 2017. 'Megaproject stakeholder management'. In B. Flyvbjerg (ed.), *The Oxford Handbook of Megaproject Management*: 339–361. Oxford: Oxford University Press.

Winch, G. M. and Cha, J. 2020. 'Owner challenges on major projects: the case of UK government'. *International Journal of Project Management*, 38(3): 177–187.

Winch, G. M. and Kelsey, J. 2005. 'What do construction project planners do?'. *International Journal of Project Management*, 23(2): 141–149.

Winch, G. M. and Leiringer, R. 2016. 'Owner project capabilities for infrastructure development: a review and development of the "strong owner" concept'. *International Journal of Project Management*, 34(2): 271–281.

Winch, G. M. and Maytorena-Sanchez, E. 2011. 'Managing risk and uncertainty on projects: a cognitive approach'. In P. W. G. Morris, J. K. Pinto and J. Söderlund (eds), *The Oxford Handbook of Project Management*: 345–364. Oxford: Oxford University Press.

Winch, G. M. and Maytorena-Sanchez, E. 2020. 'Institutional projects and contradictory logics: responding to complexity in institutional field change'. *International Journal of Project Management*, 38(6): 368–378.

Winch, G. M. and Msulwa, R. S. 2019a. 'Building the Northern Powerhouse: cost–benefit analysis and regional development', Manchester: Infrastructure@Manchester, https://www.alliancembs.manchester.ac.uk/news/infrastructure-investment-opportunity-to-get-northern-powerhouse-back-on-track/.

Winch, G. M. and Msulwa, R. S. 2019b. 'Building the Northern Powerhouse: the role of infrastructure owners and operators', Manchester: Infrastructure@Manchester, https://www.alliancembs.manchester.ac.uk/news/infrastructure-investment-opportunity-to-get-northern-powerhouse-back-on-track/.

Winch, G. M. and Msulwa, R. S. 2019c. 'Building the Northern Powerhouse: infrastructure delivery models', Manchester: Infrastructure@Manchester, https://www.alliancembs.manchester.ac.uk/news/infrastructure-investment-opportunity-to-get-northern-powerhouse-back-on-track/.

Winch, G. M. and North, S. 2006. 'Critical space analysis'. *Journal of Construction Engineering and Management*, 132(5): 473–481.

Winch, G. M. and Schmidt, S. E. 2016. 'Public–private partnerships: a review of the UK Private Finance Initiative'. In M. Jeffries and S. Rowlinson (eds), *New Forms of Procurement: PPP and Relational Contracting in the 21st Century*: 35–50. London: Routledge.

Winch, G. M. and Schneider, E. 1993. 'Managing the knowledge-based organization: the case of architectural practice'. *Journal of Management Studies*, 30(6): 923–937.

Winch, G. M., Millar, C., and Clifton, N. 1997. 'Culture and organization: the case of Transmanche-Link'. *British Journal of Management*, 8(3): 237–249.

Winch, G. M. Usmani, A., and Edkins, A. 1998. 'Towards total project quality: a gap analysis approach'. *Construction Management & Economics*, 16(2): 193–207.

Winch, G. M., Clifton, N., and Millar, C. 2000. 'Organization and management in an Anglo-French consortium: the case of Transmanche-Link'. *Journal of Management Studies*, 37(5): 663–685.

Winter, M., Smith, C., Morris, P., and Cicmil, S. 2006. 'Directions for future research in project management: the main findings of a UK government-funded research network'. *International Journal of Project Management*, 24(8): 638–649.

Yang, F., Li, X., Zhu, Y., Li, Y., and Wu, C. 2017. 'Job burnout of construction project managers in China: a cross-sectional analysis'. *International Journal of Project Management*, 35(7): 1272–1287.

Young, R., Young, M., Jordan, E., and O'Connor, P. 2012. 'Is strategy being implemented through projects? Contrary evidence from a leader in new public management'. *International Journal of Project Management*, 30(8): 887–900.

Zaccaro, S. J. 2014. 'Leadership memes: from ancient history and literature to twenty-first century theory and research'. In D. V. Day (ed.), *The Oxford Handbook of Leadership and Organizations*: 13–39. Oxford: Oxford University Press.

Zaleznik, A. 1977. 'Managers and leaders: are they different?'. *Harvard Business Review*, 55(3): 55–78.

Zietsma, C., Groenewegen, P., Logue, D. M., and Hinings, C. R. 2017. 'Field or fields? Building the scaffolding for cumulation of research on institutional fields. *Academy of Management Annals*, 11(1): 391.

Zika-Viktorsson, A., Sundström, P., and Engwall, M. 2006. 'Project overload: an exploratory study of work and management in multi-project settings'. *International Journal of Project Management*, 24(5): 385–394.

Zwikael, O. and Gilchrist, A. 2022. 'Planning to fail: when is project planning counterproductive?'. *IEEE Transactions on Engineering Management*.

Zwikael, O. and Meredith, J. R. 2018. 'Who's who in the project zoo? The ten core project roles'. *International Journal of Operations & Production Management*, 38(2): 474–492.

Zwikael, O., Meredith, J. R., and Smyrk, J. 2019. 'The responsibilities of the project owner in benefits realization'. *International Journal of Operations & Production Management*, 39(4): 503–524.

# Glossary

**Adoptive innovation**  Where a technology already used and proven by other organizations externally is adopted by a member—or usually collaborating members—of the project coalition to meet the owner's requirements.

**Agile project delivery**  Project delivery through time-boxed iterative cycles in which scope is flexed rather than schedule or budget.

**Ambiguity**  The condition where the required information is potentially available but cannot be adequately processed by the decision-maker.

**Anchoring**  The systematic tendency to judge the probability of an event occurring by relying on a single piece of information as a starting point, referred to as an 'anchor', and then adjusting based on this reference point.

**Appraise**  The first of four phases in the SPO Project Life-Cycle Model, which addresses the question of whether there is a viable project for investment to produce the desired returns as captured in the project's value proposition.

**Asset specificity**  The condition where a particular resource has limited availability.

**Autonomous project organization**  A project where the project manager has complete autonomy, including hiring staff directly.

**Autonomous vehicles**  Vehicles that combine sensors such as radar, lidar, and sonar, with positioning technologies such as the global positioning system (GPS), odometry, and inertial measurement managed by advanced control systems to identify appropriate navigation paths and avoid obstacles.

**Availability heuristic**  The systematic tendency to judge the probability of occurrence of an event by how easily the event is brought to mind, which tends to be a highly salient event rather than thinking about the whole distribution of events.

**Backward pass**  The latest start and finish times for each task on a path are calculated, starting from the project end date.

**Bid**  The second phase of the SPO supplier project life cycle, the process of moving from invitation to tender to negotiating a successful contract.

**Bottleneck**  Potential constraint in supply of resources for a package within a project.

**Bridging window**  Part of the innovation framework of a project, used during project shaping, when innovative ideas are generated, and learning and practice from other projects are used.

**Budget**  Provides a cost model of the project broken down by task to calculate how much the work breakdown structure will cost to deliver.

**Capture management**  The management of the first two phases of the supplier's project life cycle (Develop opportunity and Bid).

**Close-out**  The closing down of the project after delivering the output specified in the scope.

**Collaborative relationship**  Where the supplier is brought into the project life cycle earlier to advise on the viability of the options being evaluated during the Select stage.

**Commercial case**  The element of the project mission that identifies that suppliers can deliver against the project mission on a basis acceptable to the owner.

**Commercial interface**  The interface between the owner organization and its suppliers; its effective management ensures that the owner and the supplier organizations are aligned in their incentives for the successful delivery of outputs.

**Competencies**  One of the key parameters of the project organization Star Model, which is the skills required of the team members deployed on the project. Both technical and social competencies are essential in effective project organizing.

**Complex**  The condition where the interrelationships between the elements of the system are not fully known to the decision-maker and therefore are emergent, thereby generating uncertainty.

**Complexity**  The large number of interdependencies generated between the elements of a project, such as people in social systems, components in technical systems, and sophisticated combinations of the two in socio-technological systems.

**Complicated** The condition characterized by cause-and-effect relationships that require intense analysis, but are, in principle, knowable. For instance, chess is a complicated game, not a complex one, because it is entirely rule-bound.

**Contracting map** A two-dimensional graphical representation of the contracting strategy for a particular project.

**Contracting strategy** The owner's chosen strategy for managing the commercial interface on the project.

**Contractor** A project-based firm which provides more widely available commodity inputs to the delivery domain, as well as systems integration in the first tier.

**Controller** One role of the project management office, which is responsible for designing the governance structure and processes for the project, ensuring that the stage-gate process is managed and that the information loop is properly implemented and continues to function effectively through the project life cycle.

**Coordinator** One role of the project management office, which is to ensure that the required resources, and the appropriate professional competences, are allocated to the project.

**Cosmopolitan project manager** A project manager whose primary occupational identity is with their profession, usually attracted by the opportunities for a 'boundaryless career', where they can switch employers with ease.

**Creating** One of the five dimensions of the Project Leadership Model, involving innovating and designing the project delivery organization and its interfaces.

**Critical chain** The longest sequence of resource-loaded tasks in the project schedule with no slack.

**Critical path** The longest sequence of tasks in a project schedule with no slack.

**Critical space** Task execution spaces that are physically constrained which need to be sequenced so that workers do not disrupt or endanger each other.

**Cyber-physical systems** Systems where physical and computational elements are deeply intertwined to create self-managing systems for various purposes.

**Data plume** Large quantities of project data generated by the information loop but often collected and used only once, then archived.

**Define** The third stage of the SPO Project Life-Cycle Model, which covers the detailed specification of the scope of the project to ensure that all the elements are in place to support effective delivery.

**Deliver** The third phase of a supplier's project life cycle, the process of delivering the output specified in the owner's scope.

**Deliverables** Clusters of tasks, or major components of the output, delivered by the supplier to the owner on a project.

**Delivery** The third and fourth stages of the owner project life cycle (Define and Execute).

**Delivery domain** Consists of the temporary organizations that draw on the financial resources from the owner domain and the human and material resources from the supplier domain to deliver the outputs to the owner.

**Delivery identity narrative** Articulated during the project delivery phase by the owner project team and shared with the project-based firms in the supplier domain, this forms a narrative about the project identity to mobilize effort in one direction.

**Descriptive analytics** Using a combination of specialist software and processes to collect, store, and analyse big data from a range of sources and convert it into useful information.

**Designing** A facet of creating in the PLM which crafts the organization design for project delivery, including the governance and commercial interfaces.

**Develop business** The first phase of a supplier project life cycle, concerning business development through understanding the market and identifying those owners that are likely to be initiating projects.

**Developer** One role of the project management office, involving developing project management processes and structures, and in particular, the routines that support teaming, such as a standardized work breakdown structure, templates for reporting, and meeting schedules.

**Digital twins** Provide parallel models to enable simulation of the behaviour of a physical system under various conditions, including stress scenarios.

**Dynamic capabilities** The abilities of an organization to explore new opportunities and thereby grow and change, creating new operational capabilities.

**Earned value** The actual proportion of planned value that has been completed at a specified point in project delivery.

**Economic case** The element of the five business cases that identifies which options should be selected for the project in cost–benefit terms.

**Economic cycle** The cycle of capitalist economies, reflected in the dynamics of supply sectors, where the amplitude of the cycle at the macroeconomic level is amplified by the accelerator effect within project-based sectors.

**Emergence** The potential within the project system for unpredictable change.

**Engaging window** Part of the framework of innovation of a project, when tendering and contractual processes are used by the owner to encourage suppliers to develop innovative ideas.

**Environmental impact** The impact of the project output and outcomes on the natural environment.

**Exchanging window** Part of the framework of innovation of a project, when innovative ideas can be combined with those of other projects in the innovation ecosystem during post-project review.

**Execute** The fourth stage of the Project Life-Cycle Model, which delivers the specified output of the project, but is highly dependent upon the successful management of the prior three stages.

**Financial case** The element of the five business cases that identifies whether the investment can be financed and whether the funding streams to repay that finance are affordable by the owner organization.

**Five business cases** The five elements of the project mission.

**Fixed-price contract** A contract where the price is fixed for the supply of an agreed amount of output.

**Float** Spare time in a project schedule between tasks that are off the critical path.

**Forward pass** Earliest start and finish times for each task on a path are calculated.

**Four forces of contracting strategy** These are the nature of the transaction, the structure of supply, the point in the economic cycle, and the institutional force.

**Framework agreement** Suppliers are contracted to supply services to a number of different projects over a fixed period on a partnering basis.

**Frequency** The number of transactions between the owner and the supplier.

**Functional project organization** A project where resource base managers have complete responsibility and the project manager has little more than a liaison role.

**Future-making** The contribution of teaming to future-perfect thinking through the project life cycle.

**Future perfect thinking** The process by which we organize future-orientated action (as opposed to present-orientated behaviour) by projections visions of desired future states in which an action always has the nature of a project.

**Governance case** The element of the five business cases which assesses how the owner organization is going deliver the project in terms of its project capabilities to design and implement the governance interface and realize the benefits afforded by the project output.

**Governance interface** The interface between the owner organization and the temporary organization charged with delivering the outputs to ensure that the delivery organization remains in line with the project mission.

**Heavyweight project organization** A project where the project manager has overall control, overriding resource allocations made by resource base managers.

**Identity** One of the key parameters in the project organization Star Model, which is the alignment with the project delivery identity narrative in both shaping and delivery.

**Illusion of control** The systematic tendency to believe that we can control future events.

**Image-shaping narrative** Narrative about project image and expected value articulated at the project-shaping phase of the life cycle, with the purpose of projecting the desired future to external stakeholders.

**Incentive contracts** Contracts that contain a mixture of the features of both reimbursable and fixed-price contracts.

**Incentives** One of the key parameters of the project organization Star Model, which involves the ways in which teams and their members are rewarded for their contribution to the project.

**Incomplete leader**  The notion that a successful leader does not have to excel at all dimensions of the Project Leadership Model but can build a team that covers all those dimensions.

**Incremental innovation**  The application of a technology previously used by a member of the project coalition to the project in hand. Typically, a supplier organization will supply its technology to meet the requirements of the owner's value proposition.

**Industry 4.0**  Takes factory automation and the associated supply chains to new levels to achieve responsive 'mass customization' in manufacturing and localized production through 3-D printing.

**Information**  Flows like a river as the essence of process in organizing, mobilizing knowledge to deliver outputs and outcomes bounded by the project organization structure.

**Information loop**  The flow of information that allows the control of the project through the project life cycle against the original mission and scope.

**Infrastructure projects**  Projects that enable other things to happen, particularly the provision of goods and services: examples include fibre broadband networks, urban transit systems, and satellite systems for geo-positioning.

**Innovating**  A facet of creating, central to strategic project organizing, which enhances delivery against the project mission.

**Innovation champion**  Employed by project owners or suppliers to spend time working across the owner organization to identify and bring forward new ideas, engage people, and think about doing things differently. Their role is context dependent.

**In-service support**  Support provided by the supplier to the owner during the transition from output to outcome in realizing the project mission.

**Institutional force**  One of the forces of contracting strategy, defined at national level by the national business system, in which project-based firms are structured into project-based sectors, each with its own sectoral business system.

**Interdependent programme**  Consists of a set of discrete projects which, for various reasons, need to be managed separately but also have sequential dependencies.

**Iterative process**  The process of generating the project scope from the project mission, defining both the technical specifications for the output and the project delivery plan for its realization.

**Judging**  One of the five dimensions of the Project Leadership Model, a decision-making competency drawing on psychology, framing, and experience.

**Knowledge**  A stock of information, either tacit or explicit, held by the resource base that has the potential to be mobilized on the project to deliver the project mission.

**Known knowns**  Often called 'risk', where we can make inferences from historical data using appropriate probabilistic techniques, assuming that there will be no change in the validity of that data in the future.

**Known unknowns**  Where a possible future threat or opportunity even can be identified but there are no reliable data available from which to make quantitative inferences.

**Leading**  The binder of common interest to common purpose in the three domains model captured in the Project Leadership Model developed from the incomplete leader concept.

**Learning organization**  An organization that creates, retains, and transfers knowledge within its own boundaries through connecting, sharing, and storytelling.

**Leverage**  The ratio between the number of salaried staff and the number of principals in a Professional Service Firm (PSF) in what is typically a triangular organization structure of principals, associates, who oversee the work, and junior professionals, who actually do the work.

**Leveraging window**  Part of the framework of innovation of a project, when all the parties involved are mobilized during project delivery to develop innovative ideas, new technologies, and improvements.

**Lightweight project organization**  A project where the project manager has clear responsibilities for overall coordination, monitors progress, and brokers competition for resources, but is reliant on the resource base managers to make appropriate allocations of resources to the project.

**Local project manager**  A project manager whose primary occupational identity is with their employer who works their way up an organizational hierarchy to a position of leading projects.

**Management of change**  The controlled management of changes to scope during the Define stage of the owners' project life cycle.

**Margin**  The ratio of profits to fee income (profits as a percentage of sales) in a Professional Service Firm.

**Market diversification** The entry of a supplier organization into new markets, often through following internationally mobile owners.

**Mission complexity** The complexities in terms of stakeholder management, technical requirements, iconic status, with regard to fulfilling the project mission.

**Mitigation** The plan for reducing the possibility of a threat event occurring on the project.

**Mobile telephony** Linking personal hand-held devices through global 5G networks, which can also be used to track $CO_2$ emissions, detect traffic accidents, provide situational awareness to first responders, and monitor cardiac patients.

**Modular programme** A programme that does not have sequential dependencies but shares important work packages with the other projects within the programme.

**Multiple prime supplier** Owner contracting strategy where the owner contracts directly with first-tier suppliers of different packages within the work breakdown structure in a project chain.

**Narrative** The means by which stakeholders are convinced, resources are mobilized, and project teams are enthused within a project.

**Nature of the transaction** One of the four forces of the contracting strategy of a project.

**New product development (NPD) projects** Projects that create new goods and services in response to market opportunities: examples include anti-viral vaccines, ever-smarter phones, and TV blockbuster series.

**Novelty** The level of innovation required on the project to provide the specified outputs on a scale of incremental, through adoptive, to radical.

**Operational capability** The ability of the organization to operate resources efficiently and effectively, enabling it to match its resources with the needs of its customers. For owners, these are not project-based; for suppliers, they are project-based.

**Opportunity** A possible future event that could improve the ability of a project to achieve the project mission.

**Optimism bias** The systematic tendency to overestimate the probability of positive things happening to us and underestimate the probability of negative things happening to us.

**Optimization issues** These arise from trade-offs within the project mission and scope.

**Organization** A legal entity in the public, private, or third sectors.

**Organizational complexity** Scaled using a three-part scale from simple through complicated to complex, largely independent of the technological complexity dimension. High organizational complexity can be generated by relationships internal to the three domains, such as an unwieldy owner joint venture or myriad layers of subcontracted suppliers.

**Outcome** The end result of a project, which may be in the form of social, economic, or environmental benefits such as increased revenue streams from customers, improved services for the public, or reduced costs, or a combination of all three.

**Output** The final product of a project delivered by the supplier domain, which could be as varied as a bridge, a 'blockbuster' TV series, or a new information system which provides the basis for achieving project outcomes.

**Oversight challenge** The problem of ensuring that the packages of a project are coordinated so that package performance is not at the cost of the project performance.

**Owner domain** Includes investor and operator organizations that shape project missions to realize benefits by moving from project outputs to project outcomes.

**Owner project capability** The dynamic capability of project owners to move successfully from shaping the project mission to achieving project outcomes.

**Owner** The organizational entity responsible for shaping the project mission, raising the finance for the investment in the project, ensuring that the temporary organization delivers the outputs specified in the project mission, and moving these outputs into beneficial use.

**Owner value proposition** The cost–benefit relationship between the economic case for the project and the finance case as part of the project mission.

**Pace** The timing of a project, which may be at a natural pace, time-paced because the output needs to be ready for beneficial use by a certain date, earlier than would be defined by natural pace, or emergency, where external events demand action as quickly as possible, such as disaster recovery projects.

**Packages** Clusters of tasks involved in the delivery of a project which are let to a single supplier.

**Packaging challenge**  How to partition the tasks of the project in the work breakdown structure into coherent packages that can be delivered by PBFs with different capabilities.

**Palliation**  The plan for reducing the impact on the project of a threat event once it has occurred.

**Politician**  A meme of leadership which emphasizes those who can mobilize large groups, particularly through their oratory and example. Traits associated with this meme include charisma, oratory, and diplomacy.

**Post-project evaluation narratives**  Narratives about realized outputs and outcomes to articulate the value created for society from the project once it is completed.

**Predictive analytics**  Focus on how to enable more informed estimates about future projects for developing project delivery plans and project execution plans.

**Preferred supplier.**  A supplier who is favoured by the owner to provide a particular set of services.

**Problem-solver**  A meme of leadership in which the leader is the one who generates wise solutions to difficult problems that others cannot solve. Traits associated with this meme include wisdom, integrity, and tenacity.

**Processes**  One of the key parameters of the project organization Star Model, which is the design of the way information flows between the various teams deployed on the projects.

**Procurement challenge**  How to choose and motivate suppliers to deliver each package within the project.

**Product development**  See **New product development (NDP) projects**.

**Productivity**  The relationship between planned worker hours to deliver the scope and the actual worker hours used typically measured by earned value. Note that this is a distinctive project organizing definition, and not the same as economic productivity, which is the ratio of worker hours to unit of output.

**Professional competencies**  The technical and social competencies required for managing and leading projects.

**Project**  A temporary endeavour undertaken to create a unique product, service, or result.

**Project assurance**  The formal organizational procedure by which the senior management of the owner organization is assured that the project is on track to achieve the project mission.

**Project-based sector**  An industrial sector in which multiple-interface networks of suppliers that form a complex project network in order to deliver outputs for the owner.

**Project board**  The committee which oversees the project on behalf of the owner.

**Project capability**  The most important dynamic capability for the endogenous growth of owner organizations and thereby achieve change in operational capabilities.

**Project capture**  The process by which suppliers win work on projects from owners.

**Project chain**  A chain of suppliers with contractually equal status at the first tier, with sub-suppliers under each first-tier supplier with a contractually hierarchical status coordinated by the tier above.

**Project champion**  A person who advocates why the project should be done—either from within the owner organization or from an associated position.

**Project data analytics**  The use of big data and machine learning as part of the controller function of the PMO.

**Project delivery capabilities**  One of the operational capabilities of a project-based firm that ensures that it meets its obligations to the owner as part of the project coalition for delivery, and also its obligations to its shareholders as a profitable business.

**Project delivery plan (PDP)**  Provides the overall strategy for the delivery phase of the project.

**Project ecologies**  Regions—typically major cities—where the human resources required for the delivery of projects congregate, providing a 'pool' which can be drawn upon by suppliers on a casual basis to enable them to resource their projects.

**Project execution plan (PEP)**  The detailed plan for the execution stage of the project.

**Project identity narrative**  Conveyed internally to the project team and the supply chain, this is what the project managers tell the team in order to achieve shared understanding and vision; it gives the sense of what the delivery organization's purpose is.

**Project image narrative**  The image projected to external stakeholders such as investors, campaigners, and policymakers to stimulate stakeholders to commit themselves to the project.

**Project leader**  Director or manager of the project who has delegated responsibility for delivering the project outputs.

**Project leadership model (PLM)**  The functional leadership model for strategic project organizing based on the incomplete leader model.

**Project mission**  The strategic reason why the project is being undertaken.

**Project networks**  The dynamic networks of firms in the supplier domain, based on past, present, and potentially future relationships, which owners will typically evaluate in the process of selecting their suppliers.

**Project scope**  Defines in progressive detail what is actually to be delivered to achieve the project mission by the delivery organization, as defined in the work breakdown structure, and is accountable for the delivery of the outputs and the realization of the business case.

**Project shaping**  See **Shaping**. The first phase of the owner project life cycle, including the Appraise and Select stages in which the project mission is developed iteratively.

**Project sponsor**  The accountable person who works at the interface between the owner's project management team and the senior leadership team of the owner organization that initiated the project.

**Project strategy**  The supplier's delivery strategy for the project.

**Projectification**  The development of economy and society so that more and more activity is carried out through projects.

**Projecting**  One of the five dimensions of the Project Leadership Model, carried out through narrating and storytelling.

**Prospective hindsight**  The process of imagining a future event in a project as certain.

**Psychological safety**  The organizational culture which gives members confidence to express concerns about progress on the project.

**Quality of conception**  The extent to which the output being created subjectively delights the final customers of the owner in line with the requirements of the value proposition.

**Quality of conformance**  See **QUENSH**.

**Quality of realization**  Assesses the extent to which a viable project delivery plan has been developed to deliver the project mission in alignment with the value proposition.

**Quality of specification**  The technical fitness for purpose of the final output of the project.

**Quality preference**  Whether the owner wishes to emphasize quality of conception or quality of specification within a project, which typically affects the selection of supplier Professional Service Firms.

**QUENSH**  The quality of conformance criteria by which the delivery of the project output is assessed.

**Radical innovation**  An output new to the world which offers the potential of radically new outcomes.

**Railtrack effect**  The effect of running down in-house project management capabilities during a recession, as did the UK rail infrastructure operating company Railtrack during the 1990s.

**Reference narrative**  A project narrative that communicates the strategy of a project, embodies the projects image and identity, and is central to how the project leaders project under high levels of uncertainty, typically in the earlier phases of a project life cycle.

**Reimbursable contract**  A contract where goods and services are provided at an agreed rate as a function of an agreed parameter, used when it is possible to identify the types of resources required, but not in enough detail to specify closely.

**Relating**  One of the five dimensions of the Project Leadership Model, involving relating with both the internal project team and external stakeholders.

**Relational capabilities**  One of the operational capabilities of a supplier organization which allows it to manage across the commercial interface with the owner.

**Relationship issues**  Interpersonal issues within the project team and inter-organizational issues within and across the interfaces between the three domains.

**Relationship portfolio**  The set of inter-firm relationships, both across the commercial interface with all the owners with which agreements take place, and with all the other project-based firms with which there are agreements in place for current delivery projects.

**Representativeness heuristic**  The tendency to judge the probability of the occurrence of an event by the degree to which it is similar to a representative case.

**Resource base**  Members of the supplier domain responsible for providing the human and technological resources that actually deliver the output of a project.

**Resource interface** The interface between the temporary organization and the supplier organizations to ensure that the suppliers are providing the right human and material resources at the right time to meet the requirements of delivery.

**Resources** For a firm these mainly consist of the competencies of the professionals it employs.

**Routines** The standards, best practices, and mandated internal processes of a firm mobilized for generating appropriate solutions to the owner's problem and the delivery of those solutions in the form of task execution for the owner.

**Schedule** A sequential array through time of all the tasks in the work breakdown structure of a project, identifying when tasks should be executed.

**Schedule pressure** The amount of work remaining to be done on a project in the time remaining.

**Scope** One of the key parameters in the SPO project organization Star Model; see **Project scope**.

**Select** The second phase in the Life-Cycle Model, which addresses the question of how the project is going to be delivered in terms of the selection of the elements of the socio-technical system that forms the output of the project.

**Sense-making** One of the five dimensions of the Project Leadership Model, involving coping with uncertainty and complexity answering the question what is going on here.

**Shaping** See **Project shaping**.

**Simple** The condition characterized by clear cause-and-effect relationships with predictable patterns of activity and analytically linear interdependencies.

**Single prime supplier** Part of the owner contracting strategy where the owner contracts with a sole first-tier supplier that is responsible for delivering the entire scope of the project, as specified at the end of the Select stage.

**Smart cities** systems of systems where high monitoring allows responses to be rapidly made to stress points in the system, and digital twins enable managing assets through their life cycles and analysing the complex trade-offs required between sectors to achieve net-zero targets.

**Smart grids** Grids for energy distribution, which provide resilience through self-healing properties, allow the connection of localized generation units such as rooftop solar panels, remote metering of usage, and the management of peak charging loads generated by electric vehicles.

**Social competencies** The social skills needed by project leaders to achieve successful strategic project organizing.

**Solution design** One of the outputs of the Develop business phase of the supplier project life cycle, which is key to order winning.

**Specialist technology supplier** A project-based firm whose technological capabilities are crucial to the creation of complex systems, often with a significant investment in research and development and manufacturing facilities.

**Sprint** A short, defined phase of delivery in agile project delivery.

**Strategic case** The reason why the project is being proposed.

**Strategic change** An investment initiated with deliberate intent to achieve change an organization.

**Strategic misrepresentation** Where the decision-makers within the owner domain are systematically biased towards overestimation of the benefits of a project and underestimation of the costs.

**Structure** One of the key parameters in the SPO Star Model, which is the design of the set of reporting relationships within the project delivery organization across the multiple teams from the different project-based firms deployed within the project coalition.

**Structure of the supply** One of the four forces of contracting strategy, revolving around how critical the task package is for project delivery and its technological complexity.

**Supplier domain** Populated by a diverse range of different types of project-based firm (PBF), which share a common business model in which they supply the resources required by owners to deliver the outputs.

**Supply chain** Chain of sub-suppliers under each first-tier supplier with a contractually hierarchical status coordinated by the tier above.

**Support** The fourth phase of a supplier project life cycle, about ensuring the availability of the output through life to enable the owner to achieve the outcomes desired by the project mission.

**Supporter**  A role of the project management office, involving coaching project managers and providing advice to the project team, either through 'peer assistance' or by more formal internal consultancy and training.

**Systems paradigm**  The foundations of project organizing laid down by Cleland and King in 1968, including mutually reinforcing relationships between strategic planning and project implementation, projects as organizational systems addressing complex challenges, projects as purposive and future-orientated, the importance of stakeholders in strategic planning, projects as temporary matrix organizations, the project life cycle, and project planning and control and supporting tools and techniques.

**Teacher**  A meme of leadership traditionally associated with religious leaders, but now widely associated with the contemporary styles of leadership recommended in many management texts. Traits associated with this meme include humility, authenticity, and empathy.

**Teaming**  The basic organizational building block of strategic project organizing through which teams deliver against tasks using appropriate routines.

**Technical competencies**  These include the competencies needed by project professionals to participate in SPO, for instance, scheduling and budgeting, and managing threats to delivery, quality, safety, and environmental issues during delivery.

**Technological complexity**  A three-part scale ranging from simple through complicated to complex, used to characterize the technical complexity of a project.

**Threat**  A possible future event that could reduce the ability of a project to achieve the project mission. Also known as a 'risk'.

**Threat homeostasis**  Knowledge about the plans for reactive palliation, which can increase the possibility of an event happening.

**Threat register**  A register of all the potential threats (known knowns; known unknowns) to the delivery of the scope on schedule and budget in a project, analysed both quantitatively and qualitatively.

**Three domains model**  The structuring model for strategic project organizing showing the two permanent and one temporary domains of project organizing and their interfaces.

**Timeboxing**  The allocation of resources to a project for a specified period of time.

**Transactional relationship**  Where the owner's invitation to a supplier to tender is based on price competition against a specification produced at the end of the Define stage, or perhaps at some point during the Define stage.

**Transformation projects**  Projects that create new organizational forms in response to opportunities derived principally from information systems: examples include online retailing systems, collaborative working environments such as MS Teams, and the transformation of public services such as benefits payment systems.

**Transparency issues**  The extent to which information is shared with stakeholders and regulatory authorities.

**Uncertainty**  The fundamental challenge of strategic project organizing, being the lack of information required to make a decision in a specific point in time.

**Unknown knowns**  When threats or opportunities have been identified by someone but have not yet been disclosed to the decision-maker.

**Unknown unknowns**  When threats or opportunities have not been identified; in other words, the decision-maker is in a state of ignorance.

**Value proposition**  The relationship between the finance and economic cases in value-for-money terms.

**Warrior**  This meme of leadership is a model of 'leader as hero' and is widespread in the more sensational management literature. Traits associated with this meme are courage, honour, and cunning.

**Waterfall process**  The overall linear framework for project delivery provided by the project delivery plan.

# Index

Note: Tables and figures are indicated by an italic *t* and *f* following the page number.